
Latin American Cyberculture and Cyberliterature

Edited by Claire Taylor
and Thea Pitman

LIVERPOOL UNIVERSITY PRESS

Edited by Claire Taylor and Thea Pitman

Liverpool University Press

First published 2007 by
Liverpool University Press
4 Cambridge Street
Liverpool L69 7ZU

British Library Cataloguing-in-Publication data

A British Library CIP record is available

ISBN 978-1-84631-061-4 cased

Typeset by Carnegie Book Production, Lancaster
Printed and bound in the European Union by Bell and Bain Ltd, Glasgow

Contents

List of Illustrations

14.1. Noemí Guzik Glantz, 'oJo aLeGrE' [Happy Eye], 27 February 2006.

14.2. Noemí Guzik Glantz, 'iNdEpEnDeNcIa' [Independence], 9 January 2006.

14.3. Noemí Guzik Glantz, 'aCto nEcEsariO' [A Necessary Act], 28 January 2006.

Acknowledgements

Firstly, we would like to thank all of our contributors for their hard work and swift responses to our editorial comments throughout the preparation of this book. Thanks are also due to the University of Leeds School of Modern Languages and Cultures Research Committee Fund and the University of Liverpool Research Development Fund for providing financial support without which this research would not have been possible; and to the Instituto Cervantes and the University of Leeds School of Modern Languages and Cultures Research Committee Fund for sponsoring the 10th Annual Symposium on Contemporary Narrative held by the Department of Spanish and Portuguese at the University of Leeds in March 2006 and dedicated to 'Latin American Cyberliterature and Cyberculture / La ciberliteratura y cibercultura latinoamericanas' – an event which provided an important forum for the contributors to discuss their ideas in the early stages of researching the project. We would like to thank the staff at Liverpool University Press, especially Anthony Cond and Helen Tookey, for their assiduous editing; Karen and Justin Charlesworth and Lynn Farthman for technical support far beyond our means; and all those people who read early drafts of individual chapters and who advised and supported us in one way or another: Ben Bollig, Anny Brooksbank Jones, Doménico Chiappe, Stephanie Dennison, Astrid Ennslin, Chris Harris, Par Kumaraswami, Alison de Menezes, Juan Muñoz, Pat Odber, Héctor Perea, Annie Polatsek (for her photos), Alejandro Riberi, Roberto Rodríguez Saona, Lisa Shaw, Blas Valdez and Claire Williams. Thea would also like to thank the staff at Quench Café in Otley, the place where she wrote and edited most of her contributions to the book. Last but not least, we would both like to thank our families for supporting us throughout: Jairo Moyano and Lara Moyano Taylor; and Haynes, Noah and Louis Collins.

Foreword

Latin American Cyberliterature: From the Lettered City to the Creativity of its Citizens

Jesús Martín-Barbero

Writing the preface for an anthology of texts written by different authors presents challenges very different from those that a book by one sole author requires, not only due to the diversity of the themes, but also of the approaches and writing styles. A preface such as this is, to some extent, forced to read the book in another way, from another perspective, or, to put it better, in another key. And the key to this book can be found, as I see it, in 'a vast process in which literary forms are being melted down, a process in which many of the contrasts in terms of which we have been accustomed to think may lose their relevance' (Benjamin 1973: 89). This key phrase is from Walter Benjamin, delivered in a speech given to trade-union leaders in Paris in 1934, and only published in 1966 with the title 'The Author as Producer'. The topic of his speech is the meaning of poetic freedom in the political Left, suggesting that the key to this liberty can be found in rethinking the 'received ideas' about written forms and literary genres, so as to arrive at 'forms appropriate to the literary energy of our time' (Benjamin 1973: 89). And since the validity of what Benjamin foresaw is so visionary and illuminating for thinking certain keys to cyberliterature, I feel it is worth clarifying. Having defined his task, Benjamin alerts us to two main obstacles. The first is the dualism that opposes the author to the reader, since 'readers are always prepared to become writers' (Benjamin 1973: 90), now that reading and writing is being displaced from the field of professional specialisation to an increasing presence of the written word in everyday life. This displacement makes it possible to give voice to work itself, to transform the social status of the author into that of producer, radically rethinking the opposition between author and reader. The second obstacle is the sheer difficulty amongst intellectuals of breaking down the barrier between writing and image. It is surprising that in the mid 1930s Benjamin was already inciting writers to make use of photography, to go beyond the bourgeois concept of the competences as barriers between these two productive forces, for 'technological progress is, for the author as producer, the base of his political progress' (Benjamin 1973: 95). That is why this applies equally to music technologies – records, radio, sound cinema – in their capacity to transform the function of the concert form, abolishing the opposition between producers and listeners.

What cyberliterature means today in Latin America is precisely the melting down (and relaunching) of the world of languages and literature, of oralities and writings, since it is taking shape in the place from which the relations between aesthetics and politics are being re-thought and re-made. An aesthetic much closer to emerging sensibilities – not only those of young people, but also of ethnic communities and marginalised or excluded populations or sexualities – than Art with a capital letter, and a form of politics much more interwoven with cultural rights and civic struggles than with the proletarian vanguard or electoral processes. And this is what makes this pioneering book especially valuable: it tackles from within the transformations that, in literature, articulate the changes which the cultural life of our countries is going through. Because just as there was a clumsy literary criticism which saw in Latin American modernism mere imitation and subjugation to European models, so today what is most prevalent over here is the criticism which sees in cyberliterary or plastic experimentation a movement that is merely submission to fashion and to the prevailing technological frivolity. This type of pseudocriticism, conformist and authoritarian in its approach, is incapable of accepting theoretical uncertainty and the instability of languages produced by the cultural mutation of our societies. In contrast to this, the research, reflections and experimentations of this book propose an alternative view; one that is marked by a strong sense of locality. We have here, thus, a situated reflection, both in terms of the sites of enunciation of the authors, and in terms of the territories of the texts studied, whether these be webmags, virtual novels, or literary blogs: the worldly globalism of the hypertextual has nothing to do with dilettante escapism, or making local problems any less important. What hypertextuality has to do with here is a new type of cultural experience in which its greatest originality lies in the capacity for interaction between writer and reader, between creator and spectator, between experiment and alternative proposals, and therefore between citizenship and political participation, between communities and cultural appropriation.

This is what the experiences narrated and studied here talk about. Several of the texts investigate what hypertextual experiments can be found, prematurely, in certain Latin American literature, starting from Julio Cortázar's *Rayuela* or Bioy Casares's *La invención de Morel*. In these writings and stories, it is not only the anticipated presence of hypertext that is important, but also its performative connections with its context. For this transformation of the written word reflects the upheavals of a society that was trying to renegotiate its relationship to the varied pasts of which it was composed. Such a transformation encourages an opening out of conventional time which is tied up with official memory, and generates an explosion of temporal continuity in history and fiction, undoing both time and space, making them reversible by detaching their temporalities and the geography of their borders and languages.

Many of the chapters in this book pose as a central question precisely what can be emancipatory in the destabilisation of borders; these borders which have always separated, in an arbitrary and exclusionary fashion, one country from the next, or the centre from the sides, edges and peripheries, in both spatial and cultural, literary and social, technological and social terms. They also investigate the creative energy which is freed when writing, oral expression and visual cultures intertwine and become hybrid, making possible new narratives which are capable of representing the turbulence and speeds, the uncertainties and the vertigos, the migrations and connections which the urban experience of the majority of inhabitants of our cities entails and interweaves.

Following the links between the webpages which various chapters cite, I have been able to prove for myself the disconcerting and fertile density of interchanges which fuel both literary practice and critical analysis. In this way, setting out from http://possibleworlds.org/ I found myself faced with the delicious irony of an expression which, coming from French *auteur* cinema of the 1960s and 1970s (the *nouvelle vague*), uproots its origin and meaning to name the most obscure relationships with its opposite: the 'telenouvelle vague'. In other words, this is the *ola telenovelera* or 'soap opera wave', in which today's Latin American genre *par excellence* is produced and circulated: the televised melodrama. But what is most striking is that the webpage in which this provocative neologism is found is itself linked to http://sabotage.tv/sabotage.html and its notion of 'another world is possible' by a writer and Net-artist. Similarly, this page, for its own part, links to http://ciberfeminista.org/, which, in a mixture of Spanish and English, of texts and images, of feminist and literary theory, and of women's narrative and art, debates a strategic topic: the transformations of corporeality and subjectivity.

The polyphony of this book, however, does not prevent there being strong points of convergence between the various voices, one of the most significant of which being the close relationship between technologies and identities, without this implying euphoria or apocalypse. In this way, a consideration of the diverse ways in which writers, artists and people in general deconstruct and reconstruct the world of the border between Mexico and the USA on the Internet becomes an exercise in understanding the very new modalities in which *mestizaje* appears today. This can be seen not only from a practical point of view, but also in terms of theory and political positioning, from which we can try to understand and transform an abhorrent social reality and a splendid cultural creativity. It involves reassessing what the masses mean – not just those of Mexico and Central America, but of the whole of the Global South – who carry on meeting up in Tijuana, in its cross-border interweavings, or the seemingly endless murders of women in Ciudad Juárez and the powerful network of solidarity and protests that gather there from the rest of the world. Put into this perspective, the Internet reveals, at the same time, all its capacity for subversion of the status quo, and its deceptive and effective ways of legitimising the current exclusionary practices of our societies. And what is worse: the new opacity of certain *mestizajes* and cybercultural visibilities means we cannot know for certain where one ends and the other begins.

I cannot end this preface without pointing out another undercurrent informing this book, and that is the profound link between the research and the political praxis of the person who writes. I am referring to the 'second opportunity' which, for those who have lived one hundred years of solitude, comes about in the convergence between their oral cultures and the new visual cultures and cybernetic writings. In this space there can be the creation of new forms of performative citizenship and mediation, which could replace the authoritarian, didactic practices of the traditional lettered cultures. For the subordination of the spoken, aural and visual cultures of the majority to the exclusionary order of the lettered is, nowadays, suffering a growing and unforeseen erosion. This stems from, on the one hand, the dislocation and dissemination of the 'traditionally modern' circuits of knowledge, and on the other hand, the new modes of production and circulation of languages and new writings which emerge from electronic technologies, especially the Internet. We thus find ourselves faced with a new cultural and political scenario which could be strategic. Firstly, this new scenario could lead to the transformation of an education system which is at present exclusionary in both qualitative and quantitative terms, and is deeply anachronistic in relation to the mutations that our everyday cultures are going through. Secondly, it could mean that the democratisation of our societies reaches the cultures of the majority, allowing populations to appropriate for themselves, within their own cultures, new knowledges, languages, and writings.

Bogotá, July 2006
Translated by Claire Taylor

References

Benjamin, Walter 1973. 'The Author as Producer', *Understanding Brecht*, trans. by Anna Bostock (London: NLB, 1973).

Notes on Contributors

Debra A. Castillo is Stephen H. Weiss Presidential Fellow and Emerson Hinchliff Professor of Romance Studies and Comparative Literature at Cornell University. She specialises in contemporary narrative from the Spanish-speaking world, women's studies, and cultural theory, and is author of several books, including *Talking Back: Strategies for a Latin American Feminist Literary Criticism* (1992), *Easy Women: Sex and Gender in Modern Mexican Fiction* (1998), and *Border Women: Writing from La Frontera* (2002; co-written with María Socorro Tabuenca Córdoba). She is also co-editor of various volumes of essays such as *Latin American Literature and Mass Media* (2001; with Edmundo Paz-Soldán). Her most recent book is *Re-dreaming America* (2004).

Doménico Chiappe was born in Peru in 1970 and brought up in Venezuela. He is a published writer and is currently studying for a doctorate in hypermedia narrative at the Universidad Carlos III in Madrid. His publications include the prize-winning collection of short stories *Párrafos sueltos* (2003), the hypermedia novel *Tierra de extracción* (1996–), the ongoing hypermedia collective novel *La huella de Cosmos* and the novel *Entrevista a Mailer Daemon* (2007).

Margaret Anne Clarke is Senior Lecturer in Portuguese at the University of Portsmouth. Her research interests include Brazilian poetry, Portuguese canonical authors, and the use of multimedia and digital applications for language learning. She is currently working on a monograph on utopian themes in Brazilian literature and culture.

Paul Fallon is Assistant Professor of Spanish at East Carolina University in Greenville, North Carolina. His research interests concern contemporary Narratives of Greater Mexico, border studies, electronic and mass media, and critical theory. His current project is a monograph on temporal representations in northern Mexican border narratives.

Stefan Herbrechter is Senior Lecturer in cultural analysis at Leeds Trinity and All Saints, UK, and **Ivan Callus** is Senior Lecturer in English at the University of Malta. Together they have edited a number of essay collections:

Discipline and Practice: The (Ir)resistibility of Theory (2004), *Post-Theory, Culture, Criticism* (2004), and *Cy-Borges* (centred on posthumanist readings of Borges, forthcoming in 2007). They are also the authors of *Critical Posthumanism* (forthcoming in 2007), which is the first volume in their new monograph series 'Critical Posthumanisms'.

Shoshannah Holdom is an Academic Coordinator at the Higher Education Academy Subject Centre for Languages, Linguistics and Area Studies. Previously she was the Modern Languages Content Editor for Intute: Arts and Humanities, a catalogue of scholarly online resources hosted by Oxford University. Her current research interests centre on the proliferation of electronic journals in Latin America, and the impact of online resources on humanities scholarship.

Geoffrey Kantaris is Director of the Centre of Latin American Studies at the University of Cambridge and Senior Lecturer in the Department of Spanish and Portuguese. He specialises in Latin American urban culture, in particular contemporary cinema, and is currently preparing a book provisionally entitled *Contemporary Latin American Cinema: The Urban Paradigm*. He has also worked on Southern Cone literature, and is author of *The Subversive Psyche: Contemporary Women's Narrative from Argentina and Uruguay* (1996).

Jesús Martín-Barbero is one of the most distinguished figures in the field of the academic study of new media in a Latin American context. He is the author of dozens of books including *De los medios a las mediaciones: comunicación, cultura y hegemonía* (1987; published in English as *Communication, Culture and Hegemony*, 1993), a volume that has influenced communication studies both in Latin America and worldwide. He was director of the Communication Studies Department at the Universidad del Valle (Colombia) until 1996, and has been invited as a visiting lecturer to universities across Latin America, the USA and Europe. He currently works at the Universidad Javeriana in Colombia.

José Edmundo Paz Soldán is Associate Professor of Hispanic Literature at Cornell University. He has published the monograph *Alcides Arguedas y la narrativa de la nación enferma* (2003), and is the co-editor, with Debra Castillo, of the volume of critical essays *Latin American Literature and Mass Media* (2001). He is also the author of seven novels, and his work has been translated into eight languages.

Thea Pitman is a lecturer in Latin American Studies at the University of Leeds. Her research interests are in the field of Latin American travel writing, postmodernism and postcolonialism in Latin American literature, and Latin American cyberliterature and cyberculture. She has published several articles on these subjects and is the author of a forthcoming book on contemporary Mexican travel writing (2008).

Rob Rix is a Research Fellow in the Faculty of Media at Trinity and All Saints College, Leeds. His research interests cover a wide range of topics in

Spanish and Latin American literature and film, including the *novela negra*, Spanish/Latin American co-productions in cinema, and the work of Julio Cortázar, the subject of his doctoral thesis (Leeds, 1982).

Lúcia Sá is Professor of Brazilian Cultural Studies at the University of Manchester. Her main research interests are the intertextual relationships between indigenous narratives and Latin American literature, discourses of identity in Latin American literature, and Brazilian popular culture. She has published the monographs *Rainforest Literatures: Amazonian Texts and Latin-American Culture* (2004) and *Life in the Megalopolis: Mexico City and São Paulo* (2007), concerning the ways in which cultural production responds to the particular context of the megalopolis.

Claire Taylor is Lecturer in Hispanic Studies at the University of Liverpool. Her research interests include Latin American women's writing, postcolonial theory in a Latin American context, and Latin American cyberliterature. She has published a number of articles on these topics, as well as the monograph *Bodies and Texts: Configurations of Identity in the Works of Griselda Gambaro, Albalucía Ángel and Laura Esquivel* (2003).

Niamh Thornton currently works as a Lecturer in Hispanic Studies at the University of Ulster. Her research interests include Latin American women's writing, the representation of conflict in Latin American literature and film and issues of (national) identity, borders and subalternity. She has published several articles on these topics, as well as the monograph *Women and the War Story in Mexico* (2006) and the edited anthology *Revolucionarias: Gender and Revolution in Latin America*, co-edited with Par Kumaraswami (2007).

Ana Cláudia Viegas lectures in Brazilian literature at the Universidade do Estado do Rio de Janeiro and in communication theory at the Pontifícia Universidade Católica do Rio de Janeiro. To date she has published a number of articles on Brazilian literature as well as the monograph *Bliss e Blue: Segredos de Ana C.* (1998), concerning the work of Brazilian writer Ana Cristina Cesar.

Introduction

Claire Taylor and Thea Pitman

The focus of this volume is, as the title states, Latin American cyberculture, with an emphasis, in the latter half of the book, on a particularly important subgenre of this: Latin American cyberliterature. The definition of these terms, and of the overarching term 'cyberspace' to which they both make reference, is still fluid, but one of the most useful is perhaps that given by Pierre Lévy, who has suggested broad outlines which take into account the potential of the new medium. 'Cyberspace', as Pierre Levy has defined it, refers as much to 'the material infrastructure of digital communications' as to the information held within, and to 'the human beings who navigate and nourish that infrastructure' (Lévy 2001: xvi). Operating within this new space, 'cyberculture' can be defined as the 'set of technologies [...], practices, attitudes, modes of thought, and values' that are thereby enabled and developed (Lévy 2001: xvi). Thus, cyberculture can be taken to mean the cultural products created for the new medium and those that address it in other more traditional media, as well as the new discourses, practices and communities that such cultural products generate.

The contributions to this volume therefore, whilst taking a predominantly arts-based approach, consider cyberculture in broad terms, examining not only cultural artefacts themselves but also new ways of engaging in (socio)-cultural practice online. At the same time, the cultural products studied by the various contributors are, in many cases, ones that maintain links with previous practices – literature, film, art, performance art, and so on. Judging by the range of cybercultural products being developed in Latin America, the most interesting and innovative work taking place is precisely at the interface between the old and the new technologies, and Latin American practitioners have much to offer in the way of reflections about emergent forms of expression on the Net.

Nevertheless, to date, Latin America constitutes something of a blind spot in terms of the analysis of cyberculture available in English. There are now a significant number of studies covering the development of cyberculture, cybercommunities, and cyber-identities in Asia and the Asian diaspora (Ho 2003; Lee and Wong 2003; Mitra 1997 and 2004) or the lack of access and/or 'cyberimperialism' prevalent in Internet provision and usage in Africa (Loader 1998; Ebo 2001). However, there is as yet no study that gives Latin America the attention that it deserves in comparative approaches to the subject covering the developing world, and there is only one recent study devoted exclusively to the region which focuses on the subject from a purely sociological perspective, exploring the importance of the Internet for development issues such as education, health and governance (Bonilla and Cliché 2004). Furthermore, while there is now a surplus of studies devoted to the performance of facets of identity such as nationality, gender, race, and ethnicity in virtual environments, very little of this material focuses on those matters as apparent in Latin American usage of the Internet.[1] The same may be said of the study of the generation of virtual communities (see, for example, Rheingold 1993; Smith and Kollock 1999).

In Latin America itself, however, interest in the subject is increasingly apparent in the number of conferences organised since the late 1990s on the subject of access and trends in usage, as well as those dedicated specifically to cyberculture and cyberliterature.[2]

[1] For nationality and race/ethnicity, see Featherstone and Lash 1999; Nakamura 2002; and Lee and Wong 2003; for gender, see Harcourt 1999; Wolmark 1999; and Flanagan and Booth 2002; and more generally, see Bell and Kennedy 2000; Bell 2001; and Trend 2001.

[2] A selection of conferences on accessibility and general issues of usage include the 'Workshop em Tecnología de Redes para America Latina e Caribe' [Workshop on Network Technology for Latin America and the Caribbean] held at the Universidade Federale do Rio de Janeiro in 1998; the series of international conferences on 'Innovación Tecnológica Informática' [Innovation and Computer Technology] held in Buenos Aires and Rosario annually since 2003; and the Association of Caribbean University Research and Institutional Libraries annual conference dedicated to 'Information and Human Rights: The Social, Cultural and Ethical Aspects of the Information Society' held in Aruba in May 2006. For more data on many similar events see Hahn (c.2000). Conferences organised on

Brief articles and research papers on the subject are also proliferating, predominantly on the web itself, and books on the subject are slowly emerging, although these tend to be limited in focus to just one country and/or just one aspect of cyberculture.[3] The current volume thus proposes to take heed of the research already done by Latin American analysts, and to produce the first anthology in English to deal with cyberculture as it manifests itself across the region as a whole. While, given the enormity of the task, there will inevitably still be lacunae in our enterprise, we hope to offer a selection of salient examples of, and innovative approaches to, the study of cyberculture and cyberliterature in Latin America, and to suggest avenues for future research on the subject. In this inevitably aleatory first sampling of Latin American cyberculture, we invite our readers to start *navegando*, to set sail, or in more customary English usage, to start surfing.[4]

i. Questions of Connectivity in Latin America

Mexican cultural critic, Carlos Monsiváis, writing in 1997, held a dim view of the potential of the Internet for Latin America (Monsiváis 1997: 13):

> For certain individuals, the Internet is the symbol and the practice of globalisation: it provides them with the possibility of reading the contents of the world's major newspapers every morning, of feeling as though they belong to a virtual

the subject of cyberliterature alone include 'El desafío de la escritura multimedia' [The Challenges of Multimedia Communication] hosted by the Universidad Católica Andrés Bello in Caracas in May 2000; the VI Congreso Latinoamericano de Humanidades entitled 'Humanidades y tecnología, una integración necesaria' [Humanites and Technology: The Need for Integration] held in Santiago de Chile in May 2003; and the two symposia entitled 'Literatura e Informática' [Literature and New Technology], held in Brazil at the Universidade Estadual do Rio de Janeiro in 2003 and the Universidade Federal de Santa Catarina (Florianópolis) in 2005.

3 On the subject of cyberculture viewed from a sociological perspective see Finquelievich 2000. On the subject of cyberliterature see Carrión Carranza 1998 and Dos Santos 2003. The Brazilian 'Literatura e Informática' symposia have also resulted in the publication of the journal *Texto Digital* (see, for example, issue 1:1, 2004). See also suggestions for further reading in this volume.

4 See conclusion to this volume for a critique of such terminology.

> community cut adrift from any traditional sense of time, of surfing cyberspace feeling like a character from a book by Jules Verne or, even better, by William Gibson.
>
> But what do those who live in the 'ranchos' (the dwellings of the poor in rural Mexico and urban Venezuela or Colombia) do? They know that this is just another episode in the infinite cancellation of options that is their lives, just another colossal social exclusion.[5]

Monsiváis' vision of the possibilities of the Internet for the traditionally marginalised sectors of Latin American society – the poor, the indigenous, the illiterate, the geographically isolated – was bleak to say the least. He conceded only that 'Subcomandante Marcos, in the Lacandón Jungle, uses the Internet to overcome isolation, and so that he can have at his disposal a global public that is not subject to the fickleness of the local censors', but concluded that, 'Strictly speaking, there are very few people who make the journey from the "rancho" to the Internet' (Monsiváis 1997: 13).[6]

Monsiváis raises concerns that are reiterated by many other commentators of the use of the Internet in/to the developing world, but these concerns need to be considered in the light of connectivity statistics for Latin America. Such statistics for Internet availability and usage are highly unreliable and quickly outdated.[7] However, it is safe to say that in 1990 there was practically no Internet access in the region and that a boom in connectivity started to occur in the second half of the 1990s (Corrales 2002: 38). This saw the numbers of users increase from half a million to 9 million in the period 1994–1999 (Corrales 2002: 38). Yet despite such a boom, the most conservative estimates in 1998 suggested that barely 1.8% of all Latin Americans had direct Internet access (Trejo Delarbre 1999: 312). Currently the

5 All translations are the work of the editors unless otherwise acknowledged.

6 Subcomandante Marcos is the spokesperson of the Ejército Zapatista de Liberación Nacional (EZLN) [Zapatista National Liberation Army] of Southern Mexico; a group that is frequently credited with having made the most innovative use of the Internet in Latin America (see chapter 4 in this volume for a revision of such claims).

7 Some of the most detailed and carefully considered studies on connectivity in the region are Trejo Delarbre 1999; Hahn c.2000; and Corrales 2002.

most generous statistics (September 2006) indicate that this figure has now risen to 15.1%, although this must be compared with 69.1% in the USA and 51.9% in the European Union (*Internet World Stats*). This is admittedly still a slim percentage of the total population of the region, although it does encompass over 83 million people.

Furthermore, growth rates are still strong. In the period 1993–1998 the countries with greatest growth rates were Mexico, Brazil, Argentina, and Chile (Trejo Delarbre 1999: 314). While the rates for these countries have now slowed down, others such as El Salvador, Guatemala, and the Dominican Republic have shown the strongest growth rates in the period 2000–2006 – in all cases this was over 1000% (*Internet World Stats*). Nevertheless, Brazil and Mexico still have the largest populations of Internet users of any of the Latin American countries – 26 million and 18.5 million users respectively – while Chile still has the highest percentage of connectivity per capita at 42.8% (*Internet World Stats*).

ii. 'Grassroots Computing' and 'The Other Internet'

Such generous figures, however, tend to obscure significant information in terms of accessibility and associated practices; information that has the power to both confirm and challenge Monsiváis' pessimistic visions. There are, for example, vast differences in accessibility between urban and rural locations (Holderness 1998: 38–41). Women also tend to have less access, with the typical Latin American Internet user being young, male, educated, and in employment (Trejo Delarbre 1999: 323–36; see also Gómez 2000). And while growth is still expected to be strong in the region, some commentators predict a ceiling forming after several years of exponential growth due to the prevailing socioeconomic and cultural conditions of these countries (Roxana Bassi, quoted in Trejo Delarbre 1999: 323). The comparatively high cost of hardware and telephone lines, the poor quality and paucity of infrastructure, particularly in rural areas, as well as poor levels of literacy and ICT-education, also continue to constitute a barrier to increasing connectivity, especially for lower-income sectors of society. Thus the Internet arguably does run the risk of accentuating the divide between sectors of society that are 'info-rich' and others that are 'info-poor', compounding traditional social exclusions and making their overturning all the more impossible, just as Monsiváis supposed it would (see, for example, Haywood 1998: 22–26).

Other commentators also warn of the possibility that there may even evolve an 'other Internet' for the developing world, or rather that the developing world will have to rely on older versions of the Internet now abandoned by the developed world – ones which are more heavily text-based and less interactive –, and that Latin Americans, for example, will thus be unable to access the more memory-heavy sites of the developed world (Belejack 1997). Or rather, in the words of still other commentators, a 'rich' Net and a 'poor' Net will evolve (Holderness 1998: 43–45). Thus the global flows of information touted by advocates of the Internet may in reality boil down to the fact that the information superhighway is more of a one-way system with the developing world being accessible to those who are interested in it in the developed world, but not vice versa.

Nevertheless, Internet access is not easy to quantify in Latin America in terms of people with direct access from a PC – the source of the statistics given above – since the predominant models for access are either through centres of education,[8] through grassroots and activist organisations or through the establishment of 'telecentros' [telecentres] which are a more community focused form of cybercafé, dedicated to the provision of access to all sorts of technology for all members of the community and, simultaneously, to the provision of the training necessary to make use of it.[9] Thus numbers of Internet users in Latin America are likely to be much higher than statistics suggest, and, even if their use of the Net is more sporadic, it is also

[8] The Spring 2006 high-school student protests in Chile may, at least with reference to their enormous scale, be attributed to the access to ICTs that the Chilean government's 'sustained investment' in secondary education since the early 1990s has facilitated. Uruguayan sociologist Ernesto Rodríguez points quite clearly to the development of the interactive online classroom www.aulalibre.cl as a contributing factor, both for its encouragement of participation, as well as for its facilitation of communications between students up and down the longest country in the world (Rodríguez 2006a). In personal correspondence, Rodríguez also confirmed the important role played by email, blogs, and mobile phones in the organisation and support of the protests (Rodríguez 2006b).

[9] For examples of 'telecentros' in Cuba see Press and Armas 1996; in Peru see Belejack 1997; and in Panama see Barrera G. 2001. For an analysis of the particular function of 'telecentros' in Latin American communities see Corrales 2002: 51–53, and Rueda Ortiz 2005.

much more likely to be strategic and productive than a leisure activity such as that suggested by the English term 'surfing'. Such models have even generated the term 'informática comunitaria' [grassroots computing] to define their function (Rueda Ortiz 2005) and it is such routes to connectivity that are providing for one of the most striking and creative features of Internet usage in Latin America – the ability to organise social activism online (see chapter 4 in this volume).

Furthermore, the chapters in this volume suggest that Latin American Internet users do not conceive of themselves as passive recipients of online information foisted upon them by the developed world but as active participants in cyberspace. Several commentators have noted the limitations of the structures of cyberspace in terms of their self-expression as Latin Americans: for example, Trejo Delarbre warns that 'the formats for making and organising websites have been determined by technology and subsequently by the customs of the biggest community of Netusers in the world; i.e. the citizens of the United States', and thus 'there is no Latin American *language* in which to express our specific content in that global hall of mirrors that is the Internet' (Trejo Delarbre 1999: 330, emphasis in original). And Carlos Monsiváis argues more generally that the Internet will force out individuality in favour of a globalised consumer culture of North American origin (Monsiváis 1997), or 'electronic Americanism' in the words of another cultural critic (Kim 2003: 182–83). Nevertheless, Rueda Ortiz, paraphrasing the Argentine critic Silvia Austerlic, argues that Latin Americans should fight this insidious cultural imperialism: 'We need to invent, identify and define our own principles of technological design; this needs to be a contribution which comes from the South as a way of avoiding being marginalised' (Rueda Ortiz 2005). Instead of making do with the scraps that are 'the other Internet', Latin Americans may well develop 'la otra Internet' as a contestatory practice to challenge the hegemony of the Internet as it has spread from the USA outwards. Furthermore, there is little evidence today that Latin American sites maintained by universities, journals, NGOs, or private individuals are substantially technologically impoverished, even if more work needs to be done to carve out a space for specifically Latin American self-expression online.

iii. *Ciberespanglish* and Linguistic Diversity Online

Allied to the cultural imperialism implicit in the design of hard- and software, the hegemony of the English language on the Internet has been the subject of much comment by speakers of other languages. Another typical trait of the average Internet user in Latin America is that they are generally proficient to some degree in English – indeed, Trejo Delarbre estimated that in early 1998 only 1.78% of the documents available on the Internet were in Spanish, while 70% of documents were in English (Trejo Delarbre 1999: 325). More recent and more generous estimates suggest that the presence of webpages in English had dropped to around 50% of the total in 2001 whereas those in Spanish stood at 5.62% and, importantly, were also estimated to have increased at a rate of 125% in the three-year period from 1998 to 2001 (Pimienta and Lamey 2001). In the same period the presence of Portuguese on the worldwide web was estimated to have increased by 238% to 2.79%. Pimienta and Lamey's conclusions on the subject of linguistic diversity on the Internet are more heartening than most assessments, but the suggestion is quite clearly that Spanish- and Portuguese-speaking states need to promote and safeguard more proactively the production of web-materials in their languages, in the same way that the French have done (Pimienta and Lamey 2001).

There is also a current debate concerning the 'quality' of a language such as Spanish online. Conservative cultural critics consider that the Internet is fostering the production of 'ciberespanglish', an impoverished form of Spanish born of the desire to make the language fit the contours of English as it is used online and peppered with all the English neologisms that define the new possibilities offered by cyberspace (see Castro Roig 2001). Even a Latin American cultural critic as predisposed to transculturation as Néstor García Canclini displays some reservations with regard to the testing of the 'semiotic and aesthetic limits' of Spanish provoked by the 'expansion of communications subordinated to commercial criteria'; an expansion in which he sees the Internet playing a leading role (García Canclini 1999: 161). Nevertheless, in terms of cybercultural and cyberliterary products, there is little evidence that this impoverishment is actually occurring, or that it is substantially different from the creative combination of Spanish and English that is seen on a massive scale in the Chicano and Latino communities of the United States.

If Spanish and Portuguese have proportionally little representation on the Internet despite their large communities of native speakers, it is no surprise that the indigenous languages of Latin America are extremely underrepresented. Nevertheless, certain organisations have made moves to promote the creation of webpages in indigenous languages. Such is the case of the Red Científica Peruana [the Peruvian Scientific Network] which hosts pages in Quechua (Belejack 1997), and there is currently a strong movement in Paraguay to ensure that all official documents on the web, as well as in traditional print form, are provided in Guaraní (Movimiento de Educadores Jekupytyrâ [para la Solidaridad] 2006).

While the director of the Red Científica Peruana, José Soriano, speaks in terms of the Internet in Latin America realising a 'latter-day version of Bolívar's dream' through its ability to include the voices of all sectors of society from the residents of Lima's upper-class suburbs to monolingual Quechua speakers living high in the Andes (Belejack 1997), the Mapuche community of Southern Chile are contesting the fact that Microsoft is trying to 'facilitate' access to IT for Mapuzungun speakers by launching a Windows software package in their language (Long 2006). Rather than seeing this as a positive move to promote access to speakers of indigenous languages, the Mapuche claim that this is a violation of their 'cultural and collective heritage' and hence evidence of cultural imperialism or at least of a patronising approach to other cultures on behalf of Microsoft and the Chilean government. Their argument rests on the fact they were not consulted about the creation of the software package. Clearly, more dialogue between Latin American communities and those with commercial interests in new technology is required in order for all to benefit.

iv. Cyberculture and Cybercommunities

Within this context, the investigation of cybercultural and cyberliterary products in Latin America must, of necessity, include a consideration of the specifics of the region. Yet at the same time, the virtual realm at first sight appears to imply a troubling of the very notion of locality. The development of cyberculture and cyberliterature challenges not only traditional media and genres – that is, it questions some of the foundations of conventional literary and cultural forms – but also the very notion of the locatedness of literature and culture within a particular nation-state framework. If utopian conceptualisations of the 'global village' – a 'virtual community of neighbors freed of geographical constraints' (Van Alstyne and Brynjolfsson 1997: 3) in which the Internet unites citizens the world over – are true, then this clearly entails a loosening of the sense of locality. As Lauren B. Lengel and Patrick D. Murphy have noted, 'the Internet is dramatically redefining the nature of social relationships between nations and challenging cultural sovereignty by creating an increased sense of borderlessness' (Lengel and Murphy 2001: 187).

Thus, while this volume proposes to examine Latin American cyberculture and cyberliterature, the Internet problematises notions of geographical fixity and specificity. Yet the issue of whether such redefinitions of borders and nationhood make the notion of locality itself, and of a specifically Latin American cyberculture, irrelevant, is far from clear. As has frequently been noted in a variety of studies, concepts of locatedness adhere in cyberspace, whose very denomination itself – cyber*space* – relies on a topographical metaphor (Stone 1999: 104). Moreover, the frequency with which cybernetic forms of communication replicate offline conceptualisations of space and locality has often been noted. Stone has observed, for instance, that in online encounters, members 'act as if the community met in a physical public space', and frequently use architectural metaphors to describe their coming together (Stone 1999: 87). In this way, whilst the conventional meanings of the nation-state may be blurred, it is not a question of the erasure of locality as such on the Internet; rather online practice is proposing new ways of negotiating locality.

Indeed, the adherence to conceptualisations of Euclidean geography in the cyberrealm can be seen in perhaps its most striking formulation in the notion of cybercommunities; a subject with which several chapters of this book concern themselves (see chapters by Fallon, Holdom, and Sá). The notion of cybercommunity provides at first sight a radical re-thinking of conventional, locality-based notions of community; cybercommunities, as theorists have argued, should be considered not through conventional affiliations of place, but through shared interests and concerns. Whilst this conception may alter the standard notion of the pastoral community, this does not mean that community *per se* is destroyed; in fact, as Wellman and Gulia have noted, the situation is much more complex since very few 'Real Life' communities in contemporary society actually do function in a strictly geographically limited space: 'communities do not have to be solidary [sic] groups of densely knit neighbours but could also exist as social networks of kin, friends, and workmates who do not necessarily live in the same neighbourhoods' (Wellman and Gulia 1999: 169). Indeed, Wellman and Gulia argue that rather than the Internet doing away with notions of community, 'the tendency of the Net is to foster participation in multiple, partial communities' (Wellman and Gulia 1999: 184). Thus, it is not the case that issues of locality are erased by the practice of forming communities in cyberspace – and indeed we may note certain examples which may actually strengthen forms of community-based identification – but these communities are now reconfigured across and beyond the confines of the nation-state. We may consider such new communities in terms of diasporic experience: one which involves flows of communication and peoples across borders, but which nevertheless retains notions of locatedness.

Moreover, it is worth pointing out that Latin American cultural practice on the Internet does not do away with concepts of locatedness. Granted, locality is re-worked and re-fashioned, and the nation-state no longer functions as the authoritative centre from which lettered culture is disseminated, as borders become transgressed and fragmented by transnational flows. Nevertheless, varying degrees of locatedness adhere, which may include new forms of thinking communities, affiliations, and geographical connections.

In Latin American cybercultural practice, from the harnessing of globalised technology in the interests of grassroots organisations (for instance, the tactics of the Zapatistas), to the use of Internet technologies to build new communities and audiences for Latin American cinema, to the expression of new collective identities which, whilst crossing national borders, nevertheless make explicit references to location and geographical space (for instance the Tijuana Blog Front), new forms of negotiation between the local and the global, and between the virtual and the real, are constantly being elaborated.[10] Such new forms do not render the notion of a *Latin American* cyberculture or cyberliterature redundant; rather, they suggest new ways of forming and understanding local, regional, and transnational affiliations.

Within this scenario of new formulations and negotiations of spaces and communities, issues of citizenship and the role of the nation-state

10 See the chapters by Pitman, Castillo, and Fallon in this volume.

come to the fore. Colombian communications theorist Jesús Martín-Barbero sees a positive role for the Internet in creating new forms of citizenship and participation (Martín-Barbero 2006a: 33):

> the Internet represents a new complexity: private contact between interlocutors which is at the same time mediated through the Net's public space in a process that simultaneously introduces an explosion of public discourse while mobilizing a large number of very heterogeneous communities, associations, and tribes. At the same time, these heterogeneous social groups can free political narratives from the multiple logics of specific life worlds, weakening the bureaucratic centralism of institutions by infusing creativity into citizenship and participation.

For Martín-Barbero, the liberating potential of the Internet lies in its capacity precisely to circumvent traditional routes of power, influence, and bureaucracy represented by the established states. Such circumventions can offer new concepts of citizenship and participation, and can perhaps be seen in some of the recent projects in Latin America which have attempted to harness the power of the Internet for democratising and participatory ends.[11] Projects such as these include that developed by the Fundación Redes y Desarrollo of the Dominican Republic which aims to create a 'cyberculture' based on solidarity and democratic participation (see Bonilla and Cliché 2004, and chapter 4 in this volume), or the Instituto Tecnológico y de Estudios Superiores de Monterrey's *Frontera* project (see Lengel and Murphy 2001 for more on this).

The potential that cyberspace offers, then, for the elaboration of new concepts of community and citizenship in a Latin American context can perhaps be summed up by Juan Carlos Godenzzi, who has noted that 'Within the space of today's multiple communicational circuits – be they rural, urban, or digital – there are important economic, political, and cultural flows of global proportions that are reshaping the place and functions of states' (Godenzzi 2006: 146). These 'multiple circuits' represent an intermingling of what are conventionally seen as

[11] See Corrales 2002 for a detailed consideration of the democratic potential of the Internet.

mutually exclusive forms of location – the rural versus the urban, and both these concrete physical spaces versus the digital or virtual. Such an intermingling, Godenzzi suggests, can provide innovative forms of negotiation, and, echoing Martín-Barbero's formulation, can imply a shift of emphasis away from the traditional powers of the state.

v. Gender, Race and Ethnicity Online

If questions of locality are complicated and problematised in the cyberrealm, other notions which have, traditionally, based themselves on purportedly essentialised conceptualisations of fixity are also troubled by their interface with technology, and, specifically, with virtualisation. One such category is that of gender, which could conceivably undergo shiftings and re-workings in cyberspace – cyberspace, as David Bell notes, being frequently posited as a realm which provides an escape from corporeality (Bell 2001: 137). Yet, even if physical appearance is not immediately manifest online, Internet-based interaction has not, in fact, erased gender-based hierarchies nor discrimination. O'Brien, for instance, reports women stating they have to 'pass as men' in order to be taken seriously online or to avoid harassment (O'Brien 1999: 91). Such comments clearly reveal that sexual discrimination takes place in the online world as much as the offline, and indicate that online gender-swapping may stem as much from negative reasons – the necessity to avoid discrimination associated with one's gender – as from any utopian desire for pleasurable fantasy in the cyberrealm.

Moreover, far from offering an idealised space free from the essentialised encodings of gender to be found in offline communications, the cyberrealm has often reinforced – in many cases, in exaggerated or stereotyped form – existing gender roles and types. Claudia Springer, for instance, in her analysis of gendered bodily images in cyberspace, notes that 'cyberbodies, in fact, tend to appear masculine or feminine to an exaggerated degree' (Springer 1999: 41) Similarly, O'Brien notes that 'far from being a wonderland of imaginative creativity, participants tend to "wear" gender features that replicate conventional gender stereotypes of sexuality and desirability' (O'Brien 1999: 87). Examples of overly sexed female characters chosen by online users – including impossibly large breasts, provocative gazes, flowing hair, and so forth – may all be virtual creations, but far from going beyond gender, they reinforce its characteristics. Thus cyberspace has a contradictory position, in that it offers its users the opportunity to swap gender at will, but frequently the alternative gender identities chosen have recourse to gender stereotypes. And Latin American practitioners are engaging with these contradictions: the work of Naomi Guzik Glantz, for instance (see chapter by Taylor in this volume), frequently interrogates the status of the body on the Net, and problematises the emancipatory claims of a free-floating, disembodied self in the virtual realm. Similarly, the Brazilian Net-art group *Corpos Informáticos* investigates some of the preconceptions regarding corporeality promised by the virtual realm, whilst recent Latin American film has engaged with – and frequently re-coded – the problematic trope of the cyborg (see the chapters by Clarke and Kantaris in this volume).

It is thus worthy of note that, although cyberspace has promised freedom from the body, this promise has yet to be fulfilled, and, in fact there are often re-essentialising conceptualisations of gender, race, and ethnicity to be found in the virtual realm. In the same way as researchers on gender in the virtual realm have noted troubling instances of the reinforcement of gendered stereotypes, so too researchers into race on the Internet have noted the frequency with which racial characteristics are reinforced or exaggerated.

Firstly, as Nakamura has noted, whilst the Internet may promise freedom from race, in its tantalising potential of a free-floating identity for the user, untied to the actual raced body of that user, in fact the real life body cannot be discounted. As Nakamura comments, lack of access to the Internet is often found along raced lines, and as such 'continues to cut particular bodies *out* of various histories in the making' (Nakamura 2002: xii). Moreover, in addition to the inequalities that issues of access clearly highlight, online practice in itself can, as Nakamura points out, end up reinforcing racist and (neo)imperialist conceptions. Noting the prevalence of images of exotic travel in the 'third world' on the Internet, Nakamura indicates how this 'reinforces the notion of the Western computer and network user as a tourist in cyberspace', and how this, in turn, is traceable back to 'earlier colonial discourses that privilege the Western gaze and the sense of freedom, expansiveness, and mastery' (Nakamura 2002: xvii). Nakamura then goes onto coin the term 'cybertype' to describe 'the distinctive ways that the Internet propagates, disseminates, and commodifies images of race and racism' (Nakamura 2002: 3), and points out that 'identity online is still *typed,* still mired in oppressive roles even if the body has been left behind or bracketed', and that 'supposedly "fluid" selves are no less subject to cultural hegemonies, rules of conduct, and regulating cultural norms than are "solid"' ones (Nakamura 2002: 4). Her examination of what she terms 'identity tourism' (Nakamura 2002: 13) in which Internet users assume a racial identity different to their own, is illustrative of precisely this phenomenon, as she notes the prevalence of white males masquerading as Asian stereotypes.

Finally, Nakamura concludes that, 'in the end, despite academic and commercial discourses, to the contrary, it does come down to bodies – bodies with or without access to the Internet, telecommunications, and computers and the cultural capital necessary to use them' (Nakamura 2002: 5). Her references to cultural capital here can be read alongside what David Bell has termed 'cyber-capital' (Bell 2001: 134), and what in other contexts has been labelled the *digerati* – the new elite group with access to and knowledge of dominant cultural forms. Issues of exclusion, therefore, relate not just to access to the actual hardware itself – in itself an important issue when considering racial inequalities –, but also to the means of using these forms.

Whilst Nakamura concerns herself with specifically Asian stereotypes in her book, many of her observations could be read in the light of racial identities in Latin America, not least with regard to issues of access as outlined in earlier sections of this introduction. In a Latin American context, Mexican-Chicano performance artist Guillermo Gómez-Peña has voiced similar concerns, arguing that the 'politically neutral/raceless/genderless/classless "territory" which provided us all with "equal access"' is nothing more than a 'feel-good utopian view' which does not reflect the real inequalities experienced in cyberspace (Gómez-Peña 2001: 285). Thus the utopian claims of a 'postracist' space on the Internet are in fact unfounded. If, as Cameron Bailey and others have argued, the cybersubject is figured as 'male, white, straight, able-bodied, and ruling-class' (Bailey 2001: 338), then the Internet clearly does not circumvent existing, offline inequalities and stereotypes.

vi. Cyberimperialism, Postcolonialism and Cyberspace

In the light of such debates, the question needs to be asked: Is there a space for the subaltern in cyberspace? Is the Internet of necessity a phenomenon of multimedia globalisation which produces a homogeneous, Westernised worldview, or are there gaps in the system from which alternative identities may speak? While this is still a relatively unexplored area, some postcolonial theorists and critics have in recent years engaged with issues of cyberculture and cyberimperialism.

Regarding the latter, Luke's comments on the new cyberspatial division of labour make important contributions to the discussion of cyberimperialism (Luke 1999: 37):

> The cyberspatial resources of global computer nets permit virtual enterprises to employ thousands of poor women in Jamaica, Mauritius or the Philippines in low-paid, tedious data entry or word-processing jobs for firms in London, Paris, or San Diego. Cyberspace permits dromo-economic entrepreneurs to virtualize segments of a core workplace at these peripheral locations.

As Luke's observations make clear, the new flows of information and capital enabled by cyberspace can often result in a new form of imperialism. The global economy in fact ends up not offering truly global equalities and access to services, but installs neo-imperialist structures in which the periphery is, once more, disadvantaged.

Similarly, a recent edited volume on cyberimperialism (Ebo 2001) looks at the impact of technology in developing countries, and examines the position of the poor and marginalised under 'cyber-capitalism'. In a seminal chapter of this volume, Lengel and Murphy have argued that 'Much of this disequilibrium of information flow and access could be labelled cyberimperialism. But [...] it must be understood as something more than simply a technological imbalance between rich and poor regions of the globe. [...] it is also a process marked by the marginalization of cultural difference' (Lengel and Murphy 2001: 189). Lengel and Murphy here stress not just access itself, but the forms of expression that take place within the cyberrealm – a formulation which recalls David Bell's claim that to talk of cyberspace is *always* to talk of cyberculture (Bell 2001: 2). That is, cyberspace must always be understood in terms of the cultural expressions it facilitates and legitimises, and must be viewed as not merely a technological feature, but rather an interface between technologies and identities.

However, despite the concerns raised regarding cybertyping and cyberimperialism noted above, cyberspace may offer room for alternative constructions. In a Latin American(ist) context, Arturo Escobar has asked whether the activism enabled by Internet technologies is 'not counteracted and vastly surpassed by the repressive powers of global technocapitalism' (Escobar 1999: 31). However, giving examples of some subaltern groups in Colombia making use of this technology (Escobar 1999: 32, 42), Escobar agrees that 'it is thus possible to speak of a cultural politics of cyberspace and the production of cybercultures that resist, transform or present alternatives to the dominant virtual and real worlds' (Escobar 1999: 32). According to Escobar's argument, provided that these resistant cybercultures show 'awareness of the dominant worlds that are created by the same technologies' and employ 'an ongoing tacking back and forth between cyberpolitics (political activism on the Internet) and [...] place politics' (Escobar 1999: 32), there is room for alternative forms of expression in cyberspace.

Similarly, we may find other examples of resistant forms of cyberexpression in the work of Gómez-Peña, for instance, whose engagement with what he terms 'ethnocyborg personae', deal with, in his words, 'cultural projections of First World desire/fear of its surrounding subcultures and the so-called "New World Other"' (Gómez-Peña 2005: 81). We may, thus, view Gómez-Peña's ethnocyborgs as an engagement – in a complicitously critical way – with the 'cybertypes' which Nakamura discussed above. Indeed, Gómez-Peña has specifically allied his performances with postcolonial aims, stating his drive to 'bypass hegemonic centers of cultural power by drafting an ever-evolving cartography that interconnects nomadic, immigrant, hybrid, and "subaltern" rebel artists from various countries' (Gómez-Peña 2005: 91). All the while aware of the possible uses and abuses of the Internet (Gómez-Peña 2005: 14), and of the reproduction of real life inequalities online (Gómez-Peña 2005: 250), Gómez-Peña nevertheless hopes to draw our attention to 'another kind of global culture, not imposed from above, but emerging organically from within grassroots communities and the streets. I'm talking about a kind of borderized proletarian *transcultura*, a hybrid culture that often resists, consciously or unconsciously, the "legitimate" forces of globalization' (Gómez-Peña 2005: 247).[12]

12 For a more detailed study of Gómez-Peña's work, see chapter by Thornton in this volume.

Meanwhile, others have looked for fruitful connections between the structures and theories of cyberspace, and postcolonial theorisations. Leda Cooks, for instance, in an article on the discourse of Panamanian identity on the listserv Panama-L, suggests ways of linking cyberspace to Homi Bhabha's concepts of the 'scattering of the people' and the 'gatherings of exiles', and indicates that there may be positive features to cyberspace in that it is a 'space that no longer holds the (ideological) claim to physical space and geographic boundary (as in the age of colonialism)' (Cooks 1999: 234). In Cooks' argument, the erosion of the nation-state which is being undertaken in the globalising flows of cyberspace may have the potential to destabilise notions of nationhood which are so central to imperialist conceptualisations. The way is thus laid open for expressions of diasporic identities online which could circumvent the traditional power structures of imperialism.[13]

Moreover, some researchers, such as Odin, have gone so far as to suggest that the terms 'hypertext' and 'postcolonial' may be interchangeable, and have posited the cyberrealm as the ideal space in which a postcolonial consciousness may be articulated. Arguing that the structures of hypertext, being non-linear, multivocal, and non-hierarchical, are 'most suited for representing postcolonial cultural experience' because they 'escape the homogenizing and universalizing tendency of linear time' (Odin n.d.: 4), Odin's argument rests on the fact that the conventional print text is seen as 'a perfect tool for propagating the universality of western patriarchal narratives' (Odin n.d.: 14). Such a formulation, mapping postcolonial and hypertextual aesthetics onto each other, may be overly optimistic in that it sidesteps aspects of both content and context, as well as avoiding issues of access. Nevertheless, Odin's comments may provide a starting point for a discussion on the portrayal of otherness on the Internet.

Indeed, this book proposes to engage in precisely such a discussion, and suggests ways of approaching the expression of alternative identities – political, literary, transnational, and so forth – on the Net. Rather than hypertext being, as Odin would have it, a privileged medium through which to articulate otherness, this book argues that hypertext can be used *strategically* by postcolonial writers, but that it is not *per se*, a postcolonial activity. Similarly, other new media technologies

[13] See also Trigo 2003 for a discussion of Uruguayan diasporic identities expressed through the website http://rodelu.com/.

– video streaming, websites, e-mags, blogs – may not, in themselves, constitute postcolonial forms of expression, but their potential can be harnessed for the expression of alternative identities. Thus, avoiding the temptation to either condemn the Internet as the imposition of global media conglomerates, or to view it as the utopian space of uninhibited expression and freedom, this book proposes instead to view cyberspace as a zone of negotiation. It is this zone of negotiation that provides the potential for Latin American cyberculture; through a strategic use of cyberspace and of globalised Internet technologies, Latin American practitioners are negotiating (temporary) spaces for the expression of localised identities.

vii. Cyberliterature: 'New Architectures of Language' and 'Different Points of View'

A key arena for the negotiation between localised identities and global forces in Latin American cyberculture is the field of cyberliterature; a field which typically comprises electronic literature – traditionally conceived works of literature in electronic format –, Internet-specific forms of literature such as hypertext, hypermedia, and blogs, as well as literature in print format which reflects on the rise of cyberculture and cybercultural products. Furthermore, Latin American experimental writers played a key role in the generation of what are often now referred to as proto-hypertexts, many years before creation of the worldwide web. Their role in this has received global recognition by hypertext theorists (see, for example, Hayles 1999; and Landow 2006); nevertheless, the 'local' origins of such authors are all too often forgotten as they are absorbed into the 'global' canon of proto-hypertextual authors. This is a perspective that we propose to rectify in the current volume through the consideration of writers such as the Argentinians Jorge Luis Borges and Julio Cortázar as Latin American avatars of cyberliterature, both world wide and in Latin America itself (see chapters in this volume by Herbrechter and Callus, and Rix).

Latin American writers have always been attuned to the development of new technology and its potential to impact on literature, both in form and content (see Süssekind 1987; and Gallo 2005), and contemporary writers have not been slow to react to the advent of the Internet and related technologies. This is apparent in Mexican writer Rosina

Conde's *La genara* [Genara] (1998), an epistolary romance using email and fax instead of letters,[14] in Bolivian writer Edmundo Paz Soldán's rather ominous *Sueños digitales* [Digital Dreams] (2000), and in the increasingly fragmented and frenzied works of Brazilian writer Luiz Ruffato (see chapter by Viegas in this volume), to name but a few. Such works approach new technologies from different standpoints, some of which coincide in certain aspects with the subgenre of science fiction literature that has been termed 'cyberpunk', 'in which computer technology is ever-present and all-powerful' (Bell 2001: 214). Nevertheless, rather than aping metropolitan literary currents, they all provide evidence of the ways in which Latin American writers are feeling the need to think through the implications that global technologies have for the writing of Latin American experience.

Despite the promising, albeit critical, start suggested by the above, many Latin American cultural critics have given the Internet and its implications for literature short shrift. For Carlos Monsiváis 'the experience of reading becomes marginalised' when it is transferred to the computer screen (Monsiváis 1997: 13): Literature with a capital L is on its way out, and, in a region where literacy is still low and technology still badly distributed, using the Internet as a way of distributing Literature and finding readers is futile. Another critic – Carlos Jáuregui – who at least concedes the existence of, and finds a role for, Latin American cyberliterature, nevertheless warns against focusing exclusively on hypertextuality as the be all and end all of literature on the Internet, arguing that hypertext constitutes little more than unreadable 'avant-garde pyrotechnics', and that in essence hypertext is not 'necessitate[d] nor constitute[d] by the electronic medium' (Jáuregui 2001: 289). He ultimately prefers to search for communities of Latin American readers and writers of 'traditional' short stories grouped around a Spanish-language literary e-magazine hosted by Princeton University. In a similar vein, still other critics argue that hypertext is by and large an Anglophone phenomenon which has had little take-up in Latin American literary circles (Perea 1998: 32).[15]

[14] For a good analysis of *La genara* see Castillo 2001. Indeed, the anthology in which said essay appears – Paz-Soldán and Castillo's *Latin American Literature and Mass Media* – is an excellent starting point for any consideration of the development of cyberliterature in Latin America.

[15] Note, too, that although there are an increasing number of publications by

Nevertheless, cyberliterature – including hypertextual forms – has been produced by Latin American writers in the years since Monsiváis, Jáuregui, and Perea made the statements cited above (see, for example, the chapter by Chiappe in this volume). A further development within Internet technologies in recent years which has led to a veritable boom within the field of personal expression on the Internet, both in Latin America and beyond, is the advent of the weblog, more commonly known as the blog. The blog format, mirrored on the diary in which entries appear in reverse chronological order, is characterised by its ease of use, and enables the user to set up his or her blog within a matter of minutes. While a variety of different sub-genres of the blog exist – the personal blog, the news blog, and so forth – this book focuses on literary blogs, and explores the ways in which such blogs are impacting on the traditional circuits of literary creation and criticism (see chapters by Fallon and Taylor, and the afterword by Paz Soldán in this volume).

Furthermore, contemporary Latin American cyberliterature has met with a more positive reception with other cultural critics in and of the region. For instance, Jesús Martín-Barbero has claimed that digital technology and the Internet are creating 'a new qualitative episteme' which promotes 'an entirely new play of interfaces, new architectures of language' (Martín-Barbero 2000: 69). But while these words augur well for the adoption of forms such as hypertext in the region, we should not ignore the subtle ways in which the production of hypertext in and/or about Latin America may differ from that disseminated from the heart of the old metropolitan centres of the First World. Another writer and cultural critic who has welcomed the advent of the Internet in Latin America, Alberto Chimal, notes of the most cutting-edge work coming out of Latin American literary e-magazines that (Chimal 2002: 80):

> It might be argued that this concern with the scraps of postmodernity, and how they react on contact with our (still extant) premodernity, is an obsession pertaining only to

Spanish or Latin American authors on the subject of hypertext, bar the statutory references to precursors such as Borges and occasionally Cortázar, the frame of reference of such works tends to be the emerging canon of hypertext works written in English (see Carrión Carranza 1998; Vouillamoz 2000; and Pajares Tosca 2004).

> the users of the Internet, who are still a minority [in Latin America]; however, although the Web necessarily imposes certain concerns, it also facilitates our access to a global culture which is evolving rapidly, not only in Mexico, but also in many other countries, and which is not identical to that global culture that we can read about in *Wired* or other supposedly alternative publications. At the very least this [Latin American] global culture confronts some of the most burning questions to do with globalisation, cultural change and new technology, from points of view that are different from those of the First World.

It is precisely the interaction between 'new architectures of language' and 'points of view that are different from those of the First World', the global and the local, that some of the chapters on cyberliterature present in this volume explore (see, for example, chapters by Pitman on hypertext and Taylor on blogs).

viii. *Latin American Cyberculture and Cyberliterature*: Examples and Approaches

The eight chapters in the first section of this book engage with the broad area of cyberculture and identity formation/preservation in Latin America, including the development of cybercommunities. Focusing on both the positive and negative aspects of new technologies for Latin American people and for cultural production in the region, the contributors investigate a range of cultural practices and products.

Debra A. Castillo's chapter on *cortometrajes* [short films] on the Internet discusses the transformation of the concept of cinema through the Internet, and argues that some of the most innovative work in contemporary Latin American cinema is to be found not in the movie theatres but on the web. Castillo explores the significance that these new technologies afford for creative exchanges between the producer and the consumer, and concludes that this new 'Flash generation' is challenging the conventions of film production, screening, and spectatorship. Continuing with the topic of cinema, Geoffrey Kantaris's chapter examines a key figure of cyberculture – the cyborg – and its manifestation in two recent Latin American films. Arguing that the presence of the cyborg in Latin American cinema reflects anxieties about the dissolution of collective memory and identity, Kantaris illustrates how, in the Mexican film *Cronos*, the cyborg functions as a microcosm of the cultural fusions and transfusions of the megalopolis, whilst in the Argentine film *La sonámbula*, it represents the socially disavowed presence of the dictatorship. Margaret Anne Clarke's chapter continues with this examination of the body and the cyborg, taking as its focus the Brazilian Net-art group *Corpos Informáticos*. Clarke examines how *Corpos* engage with the reconfiguration of the human form brought about in cyberspace, and how they suggest new and radical possibilities for interaction between the human subject, communities and networked information systems.

Thea Pitman's chapter, meanwhile, moves onto one of the most important areas of Latin American participation in the Internet, that of cyberprotest. Examining the online aspects of the 'social netwar' associated with the most prominent player within the realm of Latin American cyberprotest – the EZLN –, Pitman challenges some of the common assumptions regarding their Internet activism, and suggests a range of other activist organisations who have made important contributions to the field. Niamh Thornton's chapter which follows looks at a leading figure in Latin American cyberculture whose Net-art straddles both political and cultural expression: performance artist Guillermo Gómez-Peña. Concentrating on how Gómez-Peña explores the relationship between body, identity and nation space, Thornton gives examples of his Net-art which challenge conventional conceptions of identity and national boundaries, and which provide a tentative space for the expression of the marginalised and disenfranchised.

The final three contributions to this section all engage with the issue of community and examine the creative potential of new technologies to establish human networks across traditional boundaries. Lúcia Sá explores the creation of a 'cyberspace neighbourhood' by writers and rappers from the deprived neighbourhood of Capão Redondo, São Paulo, and reveals how they have made wide use of the Internet not only to promote their work but also to create a sense of local identity. Sá thus argues that this group creates forms of social identity that are intensely local while belonging, at the same time, to international networks related to contemporary youth culture. Shoshannah Holdom's chapter, meanwhile, focuses on the creation of virtual communities in Latin American literary and cultural e-magazines. Comparing key 'publications' from Peru, Chile, and Venezuela, Holdom examines how these e-mags forge communities based on common interests and to what extent they either encourage diverse literary communities or, conversely, reinforce conservatism and national literary canons. The final contribution to this section, Paul Fallon's chapter on border blogs, looks at the creation of a literary community through the activities of emerging border writers. Fallon explores the continuities and ruptures with traditional literature that the bloggers enact and concludes by arguing that these authors' activities enable links with limited, temporary communities that represent both shifts and continuities in reading culture.

The second section of the anthology comprises six chapters that deal with the nature of cyberliterature in all its many forms, from the legacies of proto-hypertextual writers such as Jorge Luis Borges and Julio Cortázar, to traditional print literature from the region which reflects (on) new technology, to weblogs, hypertext, and hypermedia fiction proper. The chapters endeavour both to address the aesthetic changes brought about by the advent of cyberliterary forms of narrative, and, importantly, to provide a consideration of the cultural and even technical contexts of such work.

Stefan Herbrechter and Ivan Callus consider Jorge Luis Borges as a major literary precursor of contemporary posthumanist cyberliterature arguing that Borges' speculative fictions and other prose writings offer glimpses of posthuman conditions that are more fully portrayed by writers such as William Gibson or Philip K. Dick. Borges thereby ensures that Latin American literature can stake a claim to a foundational presence within contemporary debates about the ongoing digitalisation and 'prosthesisation' of the human, and about the pervasiveness of communications systems and their reshaping of the very notion of the literary. Rob Rix's chapter considers the ways in which Cortázar's seminal 1963 novel *Rayuela* [Hopscotch] might be read as a proto-hypertext, before going on to read a selection of contemporary Latin American online hypertexts by writers from Argentina, Colombia, Venezuela and Ecuador through what he denominates a 'Cortazarian lens'. Following on from Rix, Ana Cláudia Viegas focuses her attention on the contemporary Brazilian writer Luiz Ruffato and the ways in which his work in print form not only reflects the changes in Brazilian society brought about by new technologies, but responds to innovations such as hypertext on an aesthetic level. Reading Ruffato's work through the lens of theorists such as Walter Benjamin and Pierre Lévy, Viegas argues that it represents the formation of both a new aesthetic sensibility and a 'new kind of humanity'.

Moving on to fully-fledged online cyberliterature, Doménico Chiappe's chapter offers a series of reflections on the nature of creativity in/for cyberspace, particularly for those working in groups on multimedia projects or collective novels. He also explores the changing relationship of readers and writers in cyberspace, deriving his observations from his personal experience of creating hypertext and hypermedia works online. Thea Pitman goes on to consider one of Chiappe's hypermedia fictions, along with another by Mexican writer Blas Valdez, in order to situate them within a Latin American cultural and literary context and to tease out their relationship to the theories of Latin American cultural theorist Jesús Martín-Barbero concerning the representation of space and time in audiovisual and, increasingly, digital culture.

Moving on to one of the most recent phenomena in cyberliterary production – the creation of weblogs –, Claire Taylor's chapter explores an example of a Latin American literary weblog by Mexican writer Noemí Guzik Glantz in order to consider the status of the (female) body and examine whether the emancipatory claims of a cyber-identity free of the sexed body are actualised in such works. Using a theoretical approach derived from the work of Anne Balsamo and Judith Butler, Taylor argues that conventional approaches to women's literary production are troubled when such literary production takes place in the cybernetic realm. Finally, a brief afterword to this section by Bolivian writer and blogger Edmundo Paz Soldán explores the extent to which the Internet has changed literary practice in Latin America. In particular, he suggests that, in Latin American cyberspace, the blog may well take on the key role that the chronicle, a popular Latin American literary-journalistic form, has performed in print literature in the region since the late nineteenth century.

Taken together, these chapters suggest a vibrant and varied Latin American cyberculture, and despite the inevitable newness of this cultural field, many of these projects and products represent highly sophisticated, thoughtful, and strategic responses to the new medium. Furthermore, the approaches adopted by the different authors of the chapters are evidence of the growing field of cyber-criticism and theory and how that might be fruitfully applied to and adapted for the specificities of the Latin American context.

References

Bailey, Cameron 2001. 'Virtual Skin: Articulating Race in Cyberspace' in David Trend, ed., *Reading Digital Culture* (Oxford: Blackwell), pp. 334–46.

Barrera G., Azael 2001. 'Empowering the Rural and Poor Suburban Communities in Central America: The Infoplazas Program of Panama', paper given at the International Seminar on Integrating Modern and Traditional Information and Communication Technologies for Development, 22–27 January, Mawatura, Sri Lanka. Available from http://portal.unesco.org/ci/en/files/5875/10352151720panama.pdf/panama.pdf. Last accessed 13 June 2007.

Belejack, Barbara 1997. 'Cyberculture Comes to the Americas', *NACLA Report on the Americas*, November/December. Available at: http://hartford-hwp.com/archives/40/071.html, last accessed 13 June 2007.

Bell, David 2001. *An Introduction to Cybercultures* (London: Routledge).

Bell, David, and Barbara Kennedy, eds. 2000. *The Cybercultures Reader* (London: Routledge).

Bonilla, Marcello, and Gilles Cliché, eds. 2004. *Internet and Society in Latin America and the Caribbean* (Penang: Southbound; Ottawa: International Development Research Center). Available from the IDRC at: http://www.idrc.ca/en/ev–45776–201–1-DO_TOPIC.html, last accessed 13 June 2007.

Carrión Carranza, Carmen, ed. 1998. *Nuevas tecnologías para las humanidades* (Mexico City: Universidad Nacional Autónoma de México).

Castillo, Debra A. 2001. 'http://www.LAlit.com', in Edmundo Paz-Soldán and Debra A. Castillo, eds., *Latin American Literature and Mass Media* (New York: Garland), pp. 232–45.

Castro Roig, Xosé 2001. 'El *ciberespanglish*, el español comercial y el español neutro en la red', *Panace@* 2:5, 36–41.

Chimal, Alberto 2002. 'Subir, desde abajo: el cuento mexicano en internet', *Tierra Adentro* 117/118, 76–82.

Cooks, Leda 1999. 'Negotiating National Identity and Social Movements in Cyberspace: Natives and Invaders on the Panama-L Listserv', in Marc A. Smith and Peter Kollock, eds., *Communities in Cyberspace* (London: Routledge), pp. 234–51.

Corrales, Javier 2002. 'Lessons from Latin America', in Leslie David Simon *et al.*, *Democracy and the Internet: Allies or Adversaries?* (Washington, DC: Woodrow Wilson Center Press), pp. 30–66.

Dos Santos, Alckmar Luiz, ed. 2003. *Leituras de Nós: Ciberespaço e literatura* (São Paolo: Instituto Cultural Itaú).

Ebo, Bosah, ed. 2001. *Cyberimperialism?: Global Relations in the New Electronic Frontier* (Westport, CT: Praeger).

Escobar, Arturo 1999. 'Gender, Place and Networks: A Political Ecology of Cyberculture', in Wendy Harcourt, ed., *Women@Internet: Creating New Cultures in Cyberspace* (London: Zed Books), pp. 31–54.

Featherstone, Mike, and Scott Lash, eds. 1999. *Spaces of Culture: City, Nation, World* (London: SAGE).

Finquelievich, Susana, ed. 2000. *Ciudadanos, a la Red: Los vínculos sociales en el ciberespacio* (Buenos Aires: Ediciones CICCUS, la CRUJIA).

Flanagan, Mary and Austin Booth, eds. 2002. *Reload: Rethinking Women + Cyberculture* (Cambridge, MA: MIT Press).

Gallo, Rubén 2005. *Mexican Modernity: The Avant-Garde and the Technological Revolution* (Cambridge, MA: The Massachusetts Institute of Technology Press).

García Canclini, Néstor 1999. *La globalización imaginada* (Buenos Aires: Paidós).

Godenzzi, Juan Carlos 2006. 'The Discourses of Diversity: Language, Ethnicity, and Interculturality in Latin America', in Doris Sommer, ed., *Cultural Agency in the Americas* (Durham, NC: Duke University Press), pp. 146–66.

Gómez, Ricardo 2000. 'The Hall of Mirrors: The Internet in Latin America', *Current History*, 99:634. Available from the International Development Research Centre, at: http://archive.idrc.ca/pan/pubhall_e.htm, last accessed 13 June 2007.

Gómez-Peña, Guillermo 2001. 'The Virtual Barrio', in David Trend, ed., *Reading Digital Culture* (Oxford: Blackwell), pp. 281–86.

—— 2005. *Ethno-Techno: Writings on Performance, Activism, and Pedagogy* (New York: Routledge).

González, Jennifer 2000. 'Envisioning Cyborg Bodies: Notes from Current Research', in David Bell and Barbara Kennedy, eds., *The Cybercultures Reader* (London: Routledge), pp. 540–51.

Hahn, Saul c.2000. 'Case Studies on Development of the Internet in Latin America and the Caribbean', http://isoc.org/inet2000/cdproceedings/8d/8d_5.htm, last accessed 13 June 2007.

Harcourt, Wendy, ed. 1999. *Women@Internet: Creating New Cultures in Cyberspace* (London: Zed Books).

Hayles, N. Katherine 1999. *How We Became Posthuman: Virtual Bodies in Cybernetics, Literature, and Informatics* (Chicago, IL: University of Chicago Press).

Haywood, Trevor 1998. 'Global Networks and the Myth of Equality: Trickle Down or Trickle Away?', in Brian D. Loader, ed., *Cyberspace Divide: Equality, Agency and Policy in the Information Society* (London: Routledge), pp. 19–34.

Ho, K. C., *et al.* 2003. *Asia.com: Asia Encounters the Internet* (London: Routledge).

Holderness, Mike 1998. 'Who Are the World's Information-Poor?', in Brian D. Loader, ed., *Cyberspace Divide: Equality, Agency and Policy in the Information Society* (London: Routledge), pp. 35–56.

Internet World Stats: Usage and Population Statistics 2006. September 18. http://www.internetworldstats.com/index.html, last accessed 13 June 2007.

Jáuregui, Carlos 2001. 'Writing Communities on the Internet: Textual Authority and Territorialization', in Edmundo Paz-Soldán and Debra A. Castillo, eds., *Latin American Literature and Mass Media* (New York: Garland), pp. 288–300.

Kim, Aeju 2003. 'The Geography of Cyberliterature in Korea', in Rachel C. Lee and Sau-ling Cynthia Wong, eds., *AsianAmerica.Net: Ethnicity, Nationalism, and Cyberspace* (New York: Routledge), pp. 177–92.

Kole, Ellen S. 2001. 'Between Grassroots and Netizens: Empowering Nongovernmental Organizations', in Bosah Ebo, ed., *Cyberimperialism?: Global Relations in the New Electronic Frontier* (Westport, CT: Praeger), pp. 205–21.

Landow, George P. 2006. *Hypertext 3.0: Critical Theory and New Media in an Era of Globalization* (Baltimore, MD: The Johns Hopkins University Press).

Lee, Rachel C., and Sau-ling Cynthia Wong, eds. 2003. *AsianAmerica.Net: Ethnicity, Nationalism, and Cyberspace* (New York: Routledge).

Lengel, Lauren B., and Patrick D. Murphy 2001. 'Cultural Identity and Cyberimperialism: Computer-Mediated Explorations of Ethnicity, Nation, and Citizenship', in Bosah Ebo, ed., *Cyberimperialism?: Global Relations in the New Electronic Frontier* (Westport, CT: Praeger), pp. 187–204.

Lévy, Pierre 2001. *Cyberculture*, trans. Robert Bononno (Minneapolis, MN: University of Minnesota Press).

Loader, Brian D., ed. 1998. *Cyberspace Divide: Equality, Agency and Policy in the Information Society* (London: Routledge).

Long, Gideon 2006. 'Chilean Indians take on Microsoft', *The Scotsman*, 24 November. http://news.scotsman.com/topics.cfm?tid=609&id=1741492006&bad=188567, last accessed 13 June 2007.

Luke, Timothy W. 1999. 'Simulated Sovereignty, Telematic Territory: The Political Economy of Cyberspace', in Mike Featherstone and Scott Lash, eds., *Spaces of Culture: City, Nation, World* (London: SAGE), pp. 27–48.

Martín-Barbero, Jesús 2000. 'Art/Communication/Technicity at Century's End', trans. Hugh O'Donnell, in Anny Brooksbank Jones and Ronaldo Munck, eds., *Cultural Politics in Latin America* (Basingstoke: Macmillan), pp. 56–73.

— 2006a. 'Intervening *from* and *through* Research Practice: Meditations on the Cuzco Workshop', in Doris Sommer, ed., *Cultural Agency in the Americas* (Durham, NC: Duke University Press), pp. 31–36.

— 2006b. 'Between Technology and Culture: Communication and Modernity in Latin America', in Doris Sommer, ed., *Cultural Agency in the Americas* (Durham, NC: Duke University Press), pp. 37–51.

Mitra, Ananda 1997. 'Virtual Commonality: Looking for India on the Internet', in Steven G. Jones, ed., *Virtual Culture: Identity and Communication in Cybersociety* (London: SAGE), pp. 55–79.

— 2004. 'Voices of the Marginalized on the Internet: Examples from a Website for Women of South Asia', *Journal of Communication* 54:3, 492–510.

Monsiváis, Carlos 1997. 'Del rancho a Internet', *Letra Internacional* 4:53, 4–13.

Movimiento de Educadores Jekupytyrâ [para la Solidaridad] 2006. 'Ha Guarani? Paraguái: Tavakuéra sâmbyhyhararâ jeporaravo, 19 jasypateî 2006-me / ¿Y el guaraní? Paraguay: elecciones municipales, 19 de noviembre de 2006', distributed on *latam-info* listserv, 4 November.

Nakamura, Lisa 2002. *Cybertypes: Race, Ethnicity, and Identity on the Internet* (New York: Routledge).

O'Brien, Jodi 1999. 'Writing the Body: Gender (Re)Production in Online Interaction', in Marc A. Smith and Peter Kollock, eds., *Communities in*

Cyberspace (London: Routledge), pp. 76–104.

Odin, Jaishree K. n.d. 'The Performative and the Processual: A Study of Hypertext/Postcolonial Aesthetic', http://www.postcolonialweb.org/poldiscourse/odin/odin1.html, last accessed 13 June 2007.

Pajares Tosca, Susana 2004. *Literatura digital: el paradigma hipertextual* (Cáceres: Universidad de Extremadura).

Paz-Soldán, Edmundo, and Debra A. Castillo, eds. 2001. *Latin American Literature and Mass Media* (New York: Garland).

Perea, Héctor 1998. 'De ficciones y fantasmagorías en la red', in Carmen Carrión Carranza, ed., *Nuevas tecnologías para las humanidades* (Mexico City: Universidad Nacional Autónoma de México), pp. 29–37.

Pimienta, Daniel, and Benoit Lamey 2001. 'Lengua española y culturas hispánicas en la internet: comparación con el ingles y el francés'. Paper given at the II Congreso Internacional de la Lengua Española, Valladolid, 16–19 October. http://www.funredes.org/lc2005/L5/valladolid.html, last accessed 13 June 2007.

Press, Larry, and Carlos Armas 1996. 'Cuban Networking Update {Footnote 1}', *OnTheInternet*, January/February, 46–49. Available from: http://som.csudh.edu/fac/lpress/devnat/nations/cuba/update.htm. Last accessed 13 June 2007.

Rheingold, Howard 1993. *The Virtual Community: Homesteading on the Electronic Frontier* (Reading, MA: Addison-Wesley).

Rodríguez, Ernesto 2006a. 'Movilizaciones estudiantiles: ¿Por qué en Chile y no en otros países de América Latina?', *Revista Electrónica Latinoamericana de Estudios sobre Juventud* 2:3, June. http://www.joveneslac.org/portal/000/publicaciones/revista/3/18%20MOVILIZACIONES%20ESTUDIANTILES.htm. Last accessed 13 June 2007.

— 2006b. Personal email correspondence, 1 December.

Rueda Ortiz, Rocío 2005. 'Apropriación social de las tecnologías de la información: ciberciudadanías emergentes'. Foro: comunicación y ciudadanía, *América Latina en movimiento*, 28 November. http://www.movimientos.org/foro_comunicacion/show_text/php3?key=5930. Accessed 11 November 2006.

Smith, Marc A., and Peter Kollock, eds. 1999. *Communities in Cyberspace* (London: Routledge).

Springer, Claudia 1999. 'The Pleasure of the Interface', Jenny Wolmark, ed., *Cybersexualities: A Reader on Feminist Theory, Cyborgs and Cyberspace* (Edinburgh: Edinburgh University Press), pp. 34–53.

Stone, Allucquère Rosanne 1999. 'Will the Real Body Please Stand Up?: Boundary Stories about Virtual Cultures', in Jenny Wolmark, ed., *Cybersexualities: A Reader on Feminist Theory, Cyborgs and Cyberspace* (Edinburgh: Edinburgh University Press), pp. 69–98.

Süssekind, Flora 1987. *Cinematógrafo de letras: Literatura, técnica e modernização no Brasil* (São Paulo: Companhia das Letras).

Texto Digital, 1:1 (2004), proceedings of the symposium on 'Literatura e Informática' held at the Universidade Estadual do Rio de Janeiro in 2003, http://www2.uerj.br/~textodigital. Accessed 20 April 2005.

Trejo Delarbre, Raúl 1999. 'La Internet in América Latina', in García Canclini, Néstor and Carlos Juan Moneta, eds., *Las industrias culturales en la integración latinoamericana* (Mexico City: Grijalbo; Caracas: Sistema Económica Latinoamericana: UNESCO), pp. 311–56.

Trend, David, ed. 2001. *Reading Digital Culture* (Oxford: Blackwell Publishing).

Trigo, Abril 2003. '*Cyber*nation (Or, *La Patria Cibernetica* (sic))', *Journal of Latin American Cultural Studies* 12:1, 95–117.

Van Alstyne, Marshall, and Erik Brynjolfsson 1997. 'Electronic Communities: Global Village or Cyberbalkans?', http://web.mit.edu/marshall/www/papers/CyberBalkans.pdf, last accessed 13 June 2007.

Vouillamoz, Núria 2000. *Literatura e hipermedia: la irrupción de la literatura interactiva: precedentes y crítica* (Barcelona: Paidós).

Wellman, Barry, and Milena Gulia 1999. 'Virtual Communities as Communities: Net Surfers Don't Ride Alone', in Marc A. Smith and Peter Kollock, eds., *Communities in Cyberspace* (London: Routledge), pp. 167–94.

White, Robert G. 2001. 'Implications of the Information Revolution for Africa: Cyberimperialism, Cyberhype, or Cyberhope?', Bosah Ebo, ed., *Cyberimperialism?: Global Relations in the New Electronic Frontier* (Westport, CT: Praeger), pp. 223–32.

Wolmark, Jenny, ed. 1999. *Cybersexualities: A Reader on Feminist Theory, Cyborgs and Cyberspace* (Edinburgh: Edinburgh University Press).

1

Cyberculture and Cybercommunities

1

The New New Latin American Cinema: *Cortometrajes* on the Internet[1]

Debra A. Castillo

Two years ago, when I first became interested in the phenomenon of Internet video in the Spanish-speaking world, I was able to locate over a thousand sites including articles and video projection and download sites – a large, but still manageable number. In August 2005, there were 265,000; a quick check in October turned up 700,000 (of which 18,000 were download sites). Even taking into account the vast amounts of duplication on mirror sites, I would be reluctant even to guess at the range of discrete locations that will appear by the time this chapter sees print. The well-known US-based site *Atomfilms/Shockwave* at that time reported an archive of over 15,000 films and a visitor base of over 20 million per month.[2] *Ifilm*, in its 'success stories' link, bragged about its growing importance to industry heavyweights as evidenced by the on- and offline deals with filmmakers that the site had generated. *Buscacine* was offering hyperlinked pages on filmmakers, *cortometrajes*, and even updates on unreleased *cortos* still in production stages. The

1 I want to thank video artist Grace Quintanilla for her generosity, her helpful suggestions, and for the rich conversation that helped me to formulate many of the ideas in this piece. The Spanish terms *cortometraje* and *corto* translate into English as 'short film' or 'short'.

2 Since the majority of the research for this chapter was on 'undated' although frequently 'updated' websites, it has been impossible to follow strict author–date referencing conventions throughout. Nevertheless, all websites used are listed in the bibliography, together with the date they were accessed for research purposes.

Argentine site *SoloCortos* expressed its mission in an email bulletin dated 30 September 2005 as 'to generate attention about the new creative Latin American audiovisual currents, which, thanks to the digital era, have offered greater and richer possibilities for expression to more artists, without discrimination by country, resources, and sex'.[3] Similarly, *Cortomanía* announced that it was created by a group of people who were passionate about independent film, and, they added, 'we know how difficult it is to distribute a *corto* and how frustrating it is for the creator not to be able to show his/her work; for that reason, this team took the initiative of creating this site'.

'Mejor da click' [Clicking is better], the title of an already-dated Mexican article, defines the response of many in the Spanish-speaking world when asked about national film production. Clearly, Internet video is a technology and an artistic form that has now been mainstreamed in many circles; yet it has been relatively unstudied in literary or culture studies circles despite representing a phenomenon that, in its many different and sometimes problematic forms, engages larger debates not only about the changing shape of technology, but also about comparative access, identity, and national cinema projects.

While the origins of commercial film were brief, ten-minute segments, in more contemporary times *cortometrajes* have been seen as cinema's poor stepchildren, most familiar to us in the form of television commercials, viral marketing shorts, brief documentaries, and music videos. Film-school students normally make two or three of them in the course of their studies, but with the exception of a very few festival venues, until recently few of them have been seen outside of film school screenings for faculty and fellow students. Traditionally, then, *cortos* have been thought of as a way of marking time until the filmmaker is given the opportunity to do his/her first 'real' work.[4] However, since film stock is extremely expensive and even the most prosperous Latin American countries make very few feature films per year, the ambitious filmmaker will inevitably be greatly restricted in these aspirations.[5]

3 All translations from the Spanish are my own.

4 See the comments of Carro (1997: 9), de León (n.d.), and Muñoz (n.d.).

5 Smaller and poorer countries such as Ecuador or Bolivia may make only one to three feature films a year; even the richest and most established Latin American film industries, like Mexico's, produce twenty to thirty, in contrast with the typical 160 Hollywood films in an average year.

However, a huge transformation in our concept of cinema is in the offing. On the one hand, the production situation is rapidly changing with the advent of inexpensive, high-quality DV cameras, and professional-grade PC-based editing programs such as Final Cut Pro. On the other, broadband Internet access is creating new possibilities for promotion and distribution. The creative filmmaker, thus, now potentially has all the elements needed to make high-quality films; indeed, as for many other artistic forms, the Internet seems to be a perfect transmission medium, creating a worldwide viewing audience by means of clearinghouse sites, often with internal ratings for films and feedback forums that advertise direct contact with the filmmakers. Furthermore, given the inherently conservative nature of feature films, which increasingly need to respond to the requirements of international cooperative agreements, it can no longer surprise us that some of the most exciting and innovative work in cinema in contemporary Latin America will never be found in cinemas; instead, it is available for viewing and downloading, on thousands of sites, to a wide, appreciative, if highly segmented, potential audience.

Yet access is only part of the story, though an important part, and one that needs to be more fully elaborated (see below). Increasingly, video scholars have been highlighting the specific qualities of computer-assisted production that challenge our understanding of the visual medium itself. Thus, while many *cortometrajes* retain the format and style of older conventions of cinema, albeit in miniaturised forms, other creators – many of them children of the television and video game generation – are aware of the potential for mixing conventions that earlier technologies by necessity had to keep separate. In this respect, Internet video, in its most advanced forms, offers an implicit reflection on how the codes of cinema that have become naturalised for the viewer over the last half century are in fact culturally loaded and technologically determined. Thus, media theorist Lev Manovich, in a March 2003 'self interview' about his influential book, *The Language of New Media*, comments that the new media needs to reflect on its role as the successor to cinema (which he considers the most popular art form of the twentieth century) as it prepares to become the pre-eminent cultural form of the twenty-first century. In this interview, he asks a series of crucial questions that continue to animate much of the discussion today (Manovich 2003):

> What are the ways in which new media relies on older cultural languages and what are the ways in which it breaks with them? What is unique about how new media create the illusion of reality, represent space and time, and organise human experience? How do techniques of old media – such as the rectangular frame, mobile camera and montage – operate in new media? [...] How does the shift to computer-based media redefine the nature of static and moving images? What is the effect of computerization on the visual languages used by our culture? What are the new aesthetic possibilities, which become available to us?

Manovich in this quotation focuses on the production side of the new media, on the way that new modalities offer the potential for aesthetic reflection. This line of inquiry opens onto some of the more theoretically advanced discussions around digitality. At the same time, a number of video scholars, including video scholars from Latin America, add to this discussion concerns about distribution, and the way that the interplay of distribution and aesthetics plays out in the real world today. Thus, for instance, the Internet does seem to offer more democratic and noncommercial mechanisms for distribution of short films, but the realities of download time privilege users with broadband subscriptions, and even then asks for some degree of viewer patience. Once again, the old controversies around the utopian project of Net-art return to haunt us, in almost the same terms; that Net video reinstitutes the difference between haves and have-nots, between First and Third World networks of production and distribution.

Mexican video artist and scholar Fernando Llanos makes this point clearly in a recent paper. He begins by saying that his original plan was to meditate on 'the Net as the only platform for contestatory and independent content [...]. The amplification of tools and narrative resources, tied to the scheme of multiple content generators, make a novel contribution to the aesthetic equation, but above all renew the audiovisual universe' (Llanos 2005b). However, after judging a Central American video contest, he was forced to reflect more deeply on the very real differences in the conditions affecting production in Latin America (Llanos 2005b):

> since we are peripheral, third world, developing countries, or however we want to denominate ourselves (and be dominated by others) [...] the questioning of technology requires a more critical posture, and, indeed, I suggest it is NECESSARY. In our latitudes, where we have assembly plants, where we do not produce either software or hardware, where indeed we recycle a great deal of the material exported from patrons from the capital, the understanding of digital and cable art should and ought to be other.

Surprisingly (or perhaps not) Llanos's manifesto-like language in this paper echoes the mid-century activist manifestos of the New Latin American cinema movement in its focus on the way differential access to technology must be taken into account in any fuller discussion of the particular theoretical challenges of a Latin American video practice. In order to begin to address the problematics suggested by Llanos, much less the opportunities outlined by Manovich, with respect to the Latin American context, we first need to take a step back, to look briefly at the formative cinematic tradition against which, and within which, the new media is establishing itself.

i. Old (New) Latin American Cinema and New Media

Most scholars date the New Latin American cinema movement to the period between 1968 (the date of the New Latin American Cinema festival in Mérida, Venezuela) to the fall of the major authoritarian regimes in key Latin American countries in the 1980s (see Martin 1997 and Chakravarty 1998). Overtly political, grounded in working-class and peasant realities, revolutionary in form and content, the *Zeitgeist* for the projects associated with this movement 'can be summarised as a desire to change the social function of the cinema, to transform Latin American cinema into an instrument of change and of consciousness-raising or *concientización*', and was conceived as a contestation to 'the hegemony of the Hollywood import and foreign control of cinematic institutions' (López 1997: 139). The challenge for this New Cinema, like that of the Internet video movements I have tendentiously called the 'new new cinema' in the title of this chapter (or the new media, to give it a more accurate description) remains the calculus among production costs, distribution outlets, and audience. Production technology and materials have to be purchased from abroad, at great expense to the local director; these problems are further exacerbated by distribution issues. Beyond questions of ideology and aesthetics, then, one of the central concerns of New Cinema filmmakers was gaining a foothold in national circuits of distribution (see comments by Getino, Rocha, Gutiérrez Alea, and Birri in Chakravarty 1998).

While nothing like the intense political commitment of the previous generation unifies the thousands of creative individuals currently participating in Net video projects, some aspects of the New Cinema aesthetic proposal, mutatis mutandis, can be transposed onto the motivations of video artists such as Fernando Llanos who – coming from the perspective of the Reality TV generation – is also developing low-budget films, using ordinary urban settings and people. Thus, one way of thinking about his ongoing 'videoman' project (which involves taking a portable camera and computer onto the streets to do on-the-spot filming, editing, projection, and uploading preparation) would be in relation to the earlier generation's Italian Neo-realist inspired documentary films. Llanos makes this point explicitly in the web project, 'Un día en la vida' [A Day of Life], co-produced with Argentine Martín Groisman (Llanos 2005a):

> It should be no surprise that phenomena such as reality shows resonate so much with the general public, or that photoblogs are so popular nowadays. Antecedents such as Cinema Verité, Italian Neorealism and Vertov's Cinema-Eye proposed that we should turn our gaze to look at what was going on around us, in our daily lives; that we should document and create our own characters and stories. These concepts are still valid and even necessary in our globalised and superconnected 2004.

Like the earlier generation, Llanos makes a distinction between cinematic realism and engaging reality, and proposes to expand his viewers' appreciation for spaces and faces generally ignored in mainstream Reality TV outlets. At the same time, explicitly political projects such as *Mejor Vida Corp* expand on another aspect of the New Cinema ideological project, by taking advantage of network capabilities as 'part of a series questioning capitalist economic systems. [MVC] rejects the idea of artistic production; all of the products distributed by MVC are reproducible and consumable.' Typical MVC products include

Mexico City subway tickets, a student ID card, or barcode stickers that can be downloaded and applied to fruits and vegetables in the local grocery store.

And, again, mutatis mutandis, younger artists also echo earlier concerns about technology, about distribution, and the creation of national communities. Thus, while many websites like *SoloCortos* or *Tuminuto* proudly tout their international focus and reach, there are many other sites that advertise 100% national content. Like other national organisms, IMCINE's overt project is country-specific: 'to distribute high quality Mexican films'. Llanos's website has a link entitled 'Hecho en México' [Made in Mexico], with obvious implications, as well as a second link for 'invited artists' featuring videos on Mexico by non-Mexican creators, in this way clearly delineating a particular organisational project. *Yoochel Kaaj* – an organisation and a website – announces its focus on indigenous audiovisual expression in the Maya-dominated south and southwest of Mexico, as well as the adjacent countries of Belize and Guatemala. Other sites similarly limit their reach, for example, to Argentines (e.g. *Videometrajes*, which advertises that 'the movies are 100% Argentine and all were made by people from that southern country'). Explicitly, then, such projects have community-building intentions in which the Internet serves as means of fostering conversations as well as defining a body of work.

ii. New Media: Opportunities and Limits

One of the problems of the New Cinema was that the filmmakers were often isolated, inexperienced, and initially lacked the technical expertise to fully develop the projects they had in mind. Much has changed since the 1960s. Major academic institutions in key Latin American countries have now established excellent film schools where students can train professionally in their home countries, leading to a strong professional and technologically proficient class of filmmakers, as well as incidentally creating the potential for mutual support and collaboration among young artists who are now meeting and interacting with each other in an ongoing manner. By 1995, Mexico, to take just one example, had established a multimedia program with financial support for artists and their projects, and a bachelor's degree program in video production. The academic degree provides an index for professional calibration of expertise, but is often only one factor among many for the growth in local production – the social aspect of a shared film-school experience is crucial. Collaborations begun in film school seem inevitably to give rise to other collaborations: the Mexican Cooperativa de Arte en Video, for instance, which sponsors museum exhibitions and film showings; or the clearinghouse site, *Tech-Mex*, which despite the pseudo-porn visual aesthetic on its index page gathers together a highly complex and sophisticated body of work ranging from politically engaged new Mayan documentary and fiction shorts to urban video art (see fig. 1.1).

Likewise, some of the most complete Internet sites, like the superb Argentine site *SoloCortos*, offers a wide range of downloads and feedback opportunities for the casual viewer. In addition, it is mindful of the needs of more committed scholars and practitioners. They have an impressive depth of content, and the site also features its own online journal (currently with eight issues on a variety of special topics) and courses (including online tutorials with a University of Buenos Aires professor), as well as links to academic institutions, festivals, and other venues of interest to filmmakers. Their clean-looking site, with its user-friendly tabs, is typical of the genre. While highlighting distribution of *cortometrajes* to the general public as its primary mission, it provides the more committed individual with an explicitly international community-building location to exchange information about technical matters, meditate on theoretical concerns, and develop screenplays. At the same time, it also offers the local filmmaker a useful venue for immediate needs – calls for auditions, for example, or invitations to technical crew members to participate in specific projects.

Like industry-standard sites such as *Atomfilms* and *Ifilm*, clicking on an image will bring the viewer to a short descriptive page about the chosen video; a second click will download the film for viewing or for permanent storage on a PC. Furthermore, because *SoloCortos* submits the audience's favourite film annually to the 'Noche de cortometrajes' contest sponsored by the Argentine film institute, INCAA, the siteowners have created an easy and highly accessible voting and chat system that engages the viewer and provides instant feedback to the site, while at the same time also opening up the opportunity for direct communication with the filmmakers.

New technologies then, offer new ways of imagining collaboration and distribution. Thus, one familiar response to question of the audience for local production, raised so urgently in the New Cinema era, is found precisely in the vast and growing number of websites hosting short films (or at least video samples along with images and process texts), artist profiles, and chatroom links. A second response to the question of viewership can be found in the burgeoning number of festivals and sites explicitly devoted to online contests. It would be impossible to do more than hint at the range of such sites from the Spanish-speaking world. *SoloCortos'* well-considered project of bringing together online video distribution with festival participation is but one example of how *cortometrajes* can move between media formats and sites, providing intermediary services for bringing films and audiences together. More typical, perhaps is *Tuminuto*, where every day is contest day, and international submissions are invited for one-minute, low-resolution (2MB maximum) *cortos* focused on that session's chosen theme. Audience members vote on top videos, which then receive the honour of being archived in the 'salon de la fama' [hall of fame].

If *Tuminuto* represents one end of the spectrum of contest sites, there is no shortage of richer and more prestigious prizes. IMCINE's annual call for proposals for ten-minute *cortometrajes* offers real opportunities for the film projects selected, since winners get financial and logistical support to make their films, and the finished products are promoted extensively through the 'Cortometraje ... más que un instante' [Short films ... more than an instant] project, now with eight volumes in distribution. The interested filmmaker looking for viewers for his/her film has only to go online to find other promising contest opportunities: a Santa Cruz, California community TV station in collaboration with Canal Once in Mexico has sponsored a competition in which the best ten videos were chosen for exhibition on the respective television stations in both countries. Says producer Patricia de Luna López, 'We want to unite independent filmmakers who have no idea of how to distribute their material. [...] What television allows is showing projects so that people from every social class have access at the same time' (Olivares 2005). Even the Archdiocese of Mexico has opened a contest site, with the objective of 'learning about and recognising the form by which young people live their Catholic values through short films' (Concurso 1).

iii. Emergent Practices

Lest this survey begins to sound unduly utopic, I want to take a little space to remind the reader of some of the parameters, both social and technological, that are currently framing and defining this emergent practice of Internet video by focusing on three main issues, all of which require some further elaboration: (1) the nature of the material, (2) the nature of the audience, and (3) the nature of the medium.

As Carro has pointed out, the *corto* has long been unjustly denigrated as a lower level of filmmaking. Nevertheless, 'what happens in the territory of literature can be illustrative in this sense. No one thinks that because it has a shorter extension than a novel, a short story is a minor form, nor that that short-story writer necessarily is a budding novelist.' He later adds, 'both the short fiction film and the short story require extreme rigor and condensation' (Carro 1997: 10). Other authors agree (see comments by Fernando Eimbcke and Salvador Aguirre in de León n.d.: 2–3). What all these film scholars/practitioners are pointing to is the need to rethink the form and function of the *cortometraje* in a much broader perspective, not as a poor second choice for failed artists, but as a valid and necessary genre with its own distinct challenges and aesthetic parameters.

The second point has to do with the nature of audience, especially for Internet video. The viewer in the cinema, in an art gallery, or in a museum makes a conscious decision – and often pays a substantial fee – to enjoy a film or video artwork in a public space, and has an expectation that the viewing will be shared with, and perhaps interrupted by, an indeterminate number of strangers. Even in home television viewing, the most familiar location for the television set is in a communal space, where other household members can, at least potentially, share the viewing experience. With Internet video the expectation is completely different. While Internet cafés present one popular public/private viewing option for many Latin American consumers, the video creator for Internet will generally conceive of his/her audience in the most intimate possible manner; as a solitary viewer, or – hopefully – a large number of these individuals, who each view the video on a computer screen in a more or less private manner, in a highly intimate space. As the *SoloCortos* site managers comment:

> we know that the short film is, for the creator of the short, very difficult to distribute. From here, our intention is to help them in this task so that short films have the possibility of being seen all over the world. We count on your help, the help of cinephiles who enjoy watching shorts, those who are at home surfing on the Internet.

The key phrase in this comment is 'at home'; increasingly, the Latin American video consumer is, in the imagination of the video director at least, a middle-class individual with broadband computer access at home and a restless finger on the computer mouse. This community only comes together in a virtual space through, for instance, rating links, or chatrooms devoted to specific films or sites. The general implications have already been noted in studies of market segmentation and have been endlessly explored in the explosively vast literature associated with Internet marketing. More interesting from a culture studies perspective is the significance for creative exchanges, for new aesthetic visions where the potential for an unusually close and individual relation between the producer and the consumer comes to the fore.

A third concern would involve considerations about the nature of the medium as a determinant of the discourse under elaboration. Given that the aesthetic demands of a *cortometraje* are entirely distinct from those of a longer film, that the expectations about the quality of audience participation are radically different, the creator who seriously accounts for these factors will still need to think, in this contemporary moment, about the restrictions of the medium. It requires access to separate, if often related, technologies to plan a video project for Net uploading from the outset than to use the Net to publicise work that had been previously planned for or exhibited in other venues. In the first case, Latin American artists generally feel the need to be exceptionally succinct, to plan their video very carefully, generally taking into account the specific opportunities and limits of the computer environment. For the second set of creators, the video on the filmmaker's website is often only and explicitly a teaser or a trailer. In this latter case, the Internet is serving less as a distribution method than a marketing ploy. An artist may take a video clip, reduce it in size, and post it on a website to provide a sample of work that the viewer is expected to see in its entirety in some other, perhaps public, venue.

Even more interesting from my perspective are the works that take the limitations of medium into account as part of the conception of the project. Thus, among other considerations, the filmmakers will be thinking about how the viewer will see their work in terms of computer screen size, resolution, the limits on the colour range available, as well as the parameters of what they can assume about sound quality. Thus, for example, colour saturation and pixels will change on a television screen versus a computer monitor, so the *cortometraje* filmmaker will adjust the visual balance accordingly in the editing process from DV. The soundtrack will be heard through computer-connected speaker, meaning, among other things, that the creator does not need to worry about Dolby.

The filmmaker is also aware that even the viewer with broadband tends to avoid projects with what the viewer perceives as a long download time. Interviews with filmmakers, website managers, and consumers suggest that two minutes of download time represents the very outer limit of what they imagine the audience will accept. This means, of course, that the filmmaker needs adjust his/her work to the qualities of the technology available to his/her imagined viewer. Depending on how the project is conceived artistically, s/he may exchange length for resolution. Understandably, then, the vast majority of *cortos* on Internet gathering sites tend to be four minutes or under in length, 15 frames per second, and 320 × 240 pixels, 240 × 180 pixels or even smaller in screen size, and frequently sites offer several options for larger or smaller file downloads and alternative decoders (QT, WMP, RealPlayer, DivX, etc). Some videos are even distributed through 15–20 second thumbnail video-emails (500KB). This, too, has implications for how the image is framed, including more head-shots and close-ups, since small screens and low resolution make panoramic shots almost impossible. Thus, while the discussion around *cortometrajes* as a genre has focused on the analogy to a short story, in many cases, for the *cortos* planned from initial stages for Internet distribution, the more accurate analogy might be with poetry, where the constraints of the technology could be seen as analogous to, for example, the formal constraints on the structure of a sonnet.

Finally, while there are many sites that allow and even encourage video downloads, this is still an emergent technology and a controversial one. Many filmmakers want us to buy their films, not download them – thus the prevalence of teaser sites. The Macintosh iTunes application, the hugely successful program that has set the industry standard for legal MP3 music downloads, has added video downloads to its portfolio, but the options are still limited: partial seasons of popular US television shows, Pixar shorts, and a collection of music videos. While these offerings are certain to expand dramatically, it is unlikely that iTunes or its most familiar competitors will include a strong Spanish-language or international component any time soon. Thus, while filmmakers might want to sell their compilations (again, the analogy to the short-story anthology or poetry collection is hard to miss), there is as yet no clear or consistent way for them to connect with their market. Banks in Latin America have been reluctant to accept *cortometraje* filmmakers as online businesses, so the artists who wish to sell their work tend to offer Net video teasers, and invite the viewers to go offline and snail-mail them a cheque along with a request for a film – a highly inefficient process.

While the new aesthetic possibilities opened up by Net video are legion, I want to conclude by reference to just three sites, all from Mexico, in order to provide a bit of artificial unity while still giving the reader a sense of the vast range of work now available on our computer screens. The southern Mexican collective, Yoochel Kaaj, specialises in indigenous expression. The mission statement for the project hints at the genealogical relation to the documentary and ideological thrust of the New Cinema filmmakers, and the influence of such famous people's cinema filmmakers as Bolivian Jorge Sanjinés is patent. However, in a form analogous to the shift in literary texts as they evolved from nineteenth- and twentieth-century *indigenista* works, to late twentieth century texts by indigenous people, the members of Yoochel Kaaj have taken the cameras out of the hands of the supportive non-indigenous filmmakers like María Novaro who serve as advisors and mentors to the project, and have given them to the indigenous artists. The result is that the films produced by the collective, while including documentaries in their repertoire, are not limited to that subgenre so familiar to viewers nourished on the New Cinema's 'aesthetics of hunger' (Glauber Rocha) or 'popular cinema' (Sanjinés).

In addition to the indigenous-conceived and paced documentaries, the members of the group have created Mayan-language fiction *cortometrajes*, music videos, and children's programming. Their site hosts a webzine, *Turix*, described in Spanish as 'an audiovisual magazine in indigenous languages' where there is an open and on-going call for *cortometrajes* (15 minutes maximum length) in genres that include fiction, documentaries, jokes, news reports, and music videos, all in the languages of the Mexican South and Southeast. Perhaps one of the more suggestive features of this site is the expectation that viewers will include both indigenous audiences from various Mayan language traditions, as well as audience members literate in written Spanish.

Conceptual worlds away from the Mayan site is the urban and urbane Fernando Llanos, a professor of digital art in the Universidad Iberoamericana in Mexico City, who, among other activities, sends an approximately twenty second video email every Tuesday to subscribers to his service. (Why Tuesday? 'It is the day I cannot drive because of the ecological program implemented by the government to control pollution in the city.' Why twenty seconds? 500KB 'is the limit my email account accepts for an attachment'(Llanos, 'Info Videomails').) For Llanos, then, this project has something to do with a flexing of artistic muscles and an exploration of deadline creativity. Now with over 1000 participants in the US, Mexico, Venezuela, Cuba, Argentina, and Brazil, Llanos' video-mail project has created its own viral forum through the 'reply all' function, by which individual subscribers can in turn share videos, MP3 files, photographs, or other material with the presumably interested participants on the list. Casual visitors can also click on the 'video-mail' link on his website where the 'se [sic] feliz consume video' [be happy, consume video] sign welcomes viewers to an archive of these very brief, thumbnail-size, artistically conceived videos (see fig. 1.2).

My final example is Arcángel Constantini's *unosunosyunosceros* site. Constantini, who works for the Tamayo Museum's cybercentre, has an elaborate project that from the design point on involves thinking of his audience as being actively invested in his work. Thus, from a different perspective than Fernando Llanos, he, too, is committed to explicitly working with and exploiting the possibilities of his chosen medium as an interactive technology. While the initial entry to his site has a limited Flash interface design, the various links open up onto an astonishingly rich and original exploration of hyperlink alternatives and interactive opportunities. To take a single example; the viewer who clicks on 'anime' [animate] will find a 5 × 5 grid with the text '3:00 am' on each square. Clicking on the squares will lead to looped black-and-white videos with sound tracks. The first time through the site will be a surprise, with the gratifications that uncovering the unexpected always permits us, but the viewer is also implicitly invited to return, to play with the grid, to construct varying shapes and rhythms, by choosing different patterns of image and sound. Below, as illustrations, I include screen shots of a partially uncovered and a fully uncovered grid; these still images, of course, can only suggest the pulsing rhythms of the twenty-five video loops themselves (see fig. 1.3). Constantini says that his work, including *unosunosyunosceros,* comes from his science fiction project to 'rewrite the world' [reescibir el mundo] which he further explains as 'an aesthetic, conceptual questioning of existence' ('ciberhabitat'). More crassly, we might say that Constantini has learned from video games how to combine two different logics (that of narrative flow and that of control) by creating opportunities to manipulate hot spots on an interactive screen. In a more theoretical sense, he is pointing toward the new challenges of interactive cinema as a technological opportunity, and also as an aesthetic of remixing.

Conclusion

For Ana López, the distinguishing quality of New Latin American Cinema was its tendency to 'consistently complicate the protocols necessary for [its] reception, mixing documentary and fictional modes of representation in order to alter the signifying work of the cinema and thereby engage their audiences at different levels' (López 1997: 142). The most famous projects associated with the movement were independent, artisanal films, that took on and challenged the standard parameters of fiction filmmaking primarily by exposing not the explicit qualities of Hollywood film (though they did that as well), but more importantly by asking their audiences to analyse its implicit morality and aesthetics. New Cinema filmmakers such as Tomás Gutiérrez Alea wanted their viewers to struggle with the rhetoric of their works and, fundamentally, also wanted the audience to appreciate and enjoy them. Aesthetics went hand in hand with ideology and with an understanding that cinema is primarily about entertainment. Likewise, already in 1969 filmmaker and theorist Julio García Espinosa saw the role of the New Cinema as creating an 'imperfect cinema', a kind of less polished and more attractive work that for him responded to 'a new poetics' (García Espinosa 1988: 77).

The Flash generation and the new media are once again challenging the conventions of film production, screening, and spectatorship. They are asking us to stretch our imaginations and our aesthetic understandings, to think of the ways technology binds and frees us. In 1962 Fernando Birri wrote: 'our purpose is to create a new person, a new society, a new history and therefore a new art and a new cinema. Urgently' (Birri 1998: 41). Those words ring just as presciently today.

References

Atomfilms, http://www.atomfilms.com, last accessed 13 June 2007.

Birri, Fernando 1998. 'Argentine Cinema: Cinema and Underdevelopment', in Indranil Chakravarty *et al.*, *The New Latin American Cinema: Readings from Within* (Calcutta: Celluloid Chapter), pp. 41–49.

Buscacine, http://www.buscacine.com/html/sgp85.html, last accessed 13 June 2007.

Carro, Nelson 1997. *Cortometrajes*. Mexico City: IMCINE.

Catholic Net, 'Concurso de cortometrajes', http://es.catholic.net/jovenes/299/317/ articulo.php?id=23597, last accessed 17 August 2005.

Chakravarty, Indranil *et al.* 1998. *The New Latin American Cinema: Readings from Within* (Calcutta: Celluloid Chapter).

Cine Nacional Argentino (INCAA), http://www.cinenacional.com/index.php, last accessed 13 June 2007.

ClubCultura, '¡Hay motivo!', http://www.clubcultura.com/haymotivo/videos.htm, last accessed 13 June 2007.

Constantini, Arcángel, 'Unosunosyunosceros', http://www.unosunosyunosceros.com, last accessed 13 June 2007.

——, 'Ciberhabitat', http://ciberhabitat.gob.mx/galeria/exposiciones/constantini/semblanza.htm, last accessed 13 June 2007.

Cortometrajes de América, http://cortometrajes.deamerica.net, last accessed 13 June 2007.

Cortonet: Tu portal de cortometrajes, http://www.cortonet.com, last accessed 13 June 2007.

Falcón, Héctor, http://hectorfalcon.com/video.htm, last accessed 13 June 2007.

García Espinosa, Julio 1988. 'Por un cine imperfecto', *Hojas de Cine* 3, 63–78.

Hay motivo, http://www.haymotivo.com, last accessed 13 June 2007.

Ifilm, http://www.ifilm.com/shorts/successstories, last accessed 24 August 2005.

Instituto Mexicano de Cinematografía (IMCINE), http://www.imcine.gob.mx, last accessed 13 June 2007.

Johnson, Randal 1997. 'The Rise and Fall of Brazilian Cinema', in Michael Martin, ed., *New Latin American Cinema*, 2 vols. (Detroit, MI: Wayne State University Press), vol. 2, pp. 365–96.

León, Jesús de n.d. 'El cortometraje en México funciona como ejercicio para

hacer oficio y desarrollar un estilo propio', *Consejo Nacional para la Cultura y las Artes* http://www.cnca.gob.mx/cnca/nuevo/2001/diarias/nov/071101/incime.htm, last accessed 27 August 2005.
Llanos, Fernando. http://www.fllanos.com, last accessed 13 June 2007.
— n.d. 'Info Videomails'. http://www.fllanos.com/VMesp.html, last accessed 7 September 2007.
— 2005a. 'Un día en la vida', http://www.fllanos.com/undiaenlavida/proyecto.html, last accessed 29 September 2005.
— 2005b. 'Responsabilidad creativa', http://www.fllanos.com/txt/responsbilidadcreativa.html, last accessed 13 June 2007.
López, Ana M. 1997. 'An "Other" History: The New Latin American Cinema', in Michael Martin, ed. *New Latin American Cinema*, 2 vols. (Detroit, MI: Wayne State University Press), vol. 1, pp. 135–56.
Manovich, Lev 2003. 'Self Interview for MIT Press', March. http://www.manovich.net/LNM/Q&A_Manovich.html, last accessed 10 June 2004.
Martin, Michael, ed. 1997. *New Latin American Cinema*, 2 vols. (Detroit, MI: Wayne State University Press).
'Mejor da click' 2005, *Todito*. http://www.todito.com.mx/paginas/noticias/133038.html, last accessed 4 October 2005.
Mejor Vida Corp, 'FAQ'. http://www.irrational.org/mvc/faqs/html, last accessed 27 August 2005.
Muñoz, Jaime n.d. 'Hay que mostrar lo que tiene el corto bajo la manga', *SoloCortos Escribe*. http://www.solocortos.com/RevistaSC.Asp?nroArticulo=5, last accessed 13 June 2007.
Notodo, http://www.notodofilmfest.com, last accessed 13 June 2007.
Olivares, Juan José 2005. 'Convocatoria de televisora californiana para que latinos realicen cortometrajes', *La Jornada*, 21 February. http://www.jornada.unam. mx/2005/feb05/050221/a17n1esp.php, last accessed 6 October 2005.
El Portal de los Cortometrajes, http://www.cortos.cjb.net, last accessed 13 June 2007.
Quintanilla, Grace, http://www.medusa.org.mx/grace, last accessed 13 June 2007.
SoloCortos, http://www.cortometrajes.info, last accessed 13 June 2007.
Tech-Mex, http://www.tech-mex.org, last accessed 13 June 2007.
TuMinuto, http://www.tuminuto.com, last accessed 24 August 2005.
Videometrajes, http://www.videometrajes.com.ar, last accessed 13 June 2007.
Yoochel Kaaj, http://www.yoochel.org, last accessed 13 June 2007.

2

Cyborgs, Cities, and Celluloid: Memory Machines in Two Latin American Cyborg Films

Geoffrey Kantaris

Introduction

The interdependencies between film and the city have been the object of much critical investigation.[1] Likewise, the lateral connections imposed or encouraged by urban existence have long been coded in terms of the dissolution of boundaries between the human and the machinic, with the city being understood as a technology for moulding the body to the forms of industrial manufacture and consumption.[2] Latterly, the massive emergence of cybernetic cultures has collapsed at its very base the distinction between the sphere of industry – the technological transformation of the material world – and the (ideological) sphere of representations. If representations – in the form of information, styles, and codes – have become the 'raw material' on which the cyber economy does its work, and if all transformations of the material world (even and most especially biological processes) can be coded in terms of a problem of information processing, of obtaining the 'correct' representation, model, or simulation, then cultural forms such as film, originally an imaginary nexus between the individual and the collective (particularly the city), take on a new and profoundly allegorical character. This is the case, in very

1 See for instance Clarke 1997; Shiel and Fitzmaurice 2001.

2 This is a common preoccupation of modernist thought about the city, from T.S. Eliot's *The Waste Land* (1923) to Fritz Lang's *Metropolis* (1927).

different ways, with the two principal Latin American cyborg films I shall be examining here: Guillermo del Toro's Mexican film *Cronos* of 1993, and Fernando Spiner's Argentine film *La sonámbula* of 1998. In the former, a uniquely Mexican baroque cyborg, which has its origins in narratives of colonisation, embodies the transgression of boundaries between nature and technology as a microcosm of the cultural fusions and transfusions of the megalopolis, and in particular of the vampiresque operations of multinational capitalism which threaten the loss of temporal depth and cultural memory. In the latter Argentine case, the overwhelming but socially disavowed presence of the dictatorship, coupled with a cultural current of engagement with cinema itself as the mechanical simulation of absent bodies, makes the cyborg into a figure for prosthetic, celluloid memory processes (including programmed amnesia). But before we can work out the allegorical dimension of these films, it is important to consider the specific meanings and potentialities of the cyborg figure for Latin American cultural practice.

The cyborg is generally understood, following Donna Haraway's pioneering manifesto (1991), as an ambiguous technological artefact which disturbs boundaries – between cultures, between the organic and the artificial – and which collapses temporal and spatial distinctions.[3] Having its origins in late-modern ciphers of body substitution – the mannequin and the robot, or the undead zombie and vampire, which populate the nightmares of the modern metropolis – the postmodern figure of the cyborg distinguishes itself from these in its modularity: the machine no longer substitutes for the organic as its nightmare, roboticised double; machine and organism are instead multiply interfaced in complex networks. In the entangled threads of these networks we can read, amongst many other things, dramatic stories about the technological production of nature, the conflictual implantation of global power-knowledge systems, the gendering of bodies within the reproductive and replicative scenarios of biotechnology, and the recursive materialisation and de-materialisation of bodies across the televisual information horizon. The presence of the cyborg as an object of representation in Latin American culture, from sources as distinct as Laura Esquivel's *La ley del amor* (1999) to Ricardo Piglia's *La*

3 Haraway's 'A Cyborg Manifesto: Science, Technology, and Socialist-Feminism in the Late Twentieth Century', can be found in Haraway 1991: 149–81.

ciudad ausente (1992),[4] or the films discussed here, retains the familiar features of the figure, which is unsurprising since in many senses its presence in such texts is deeply citational. Nevertheless, the Latin American cyborg seems to condense specific anxieties surrounding the dissolution of collective identities and collective memory, anxieties which connect historically to the experience of colonisation on the one hand and, on the other, to the erasure of the nation as a space of collective agency and memory, an erasure which seems to be inscribed in the very mechanisms which effect the transition from nation-state to global market.

Of course, the interspersing of normally distinct temporal frames has long been a commonplace of Latin American cultural analysis, from postulation of the Latin American Baroque as inaugurator of syncretism as a cultural process in the region,[5] to Alejo Carpentier's (1949) theorisation of temporal discontinuity as the fundamental episteme of societies forged primarily from cultural hybridity. It is therefore unsurprising that the Latin American cyborg should find fertile ground in such variegation, collapsing temporal frames and phenomena as apparently disparate as Viceregal New Spain and the globalised megalopolis, or nineteenth-century Independence and twenty-first-century prosthetic memory implants, colonial automata, late modern vampires, and contemporary bioengineering.

What seems distinctive, then, about the Latin American cyborg is the way it inhabits a spatio-temporal breach in which vampires and cyborgs, alchemy and biotech, guerrilla fighters and virtual reality can co-exist across the violently foreclosed historical narratives that might otherwise separate them. And one paradigmatic version of such a spatio-temporal breach might be the Latin American megalopolis, 'globally connected' in the words of Manuel Castells (1996) yet peripheral enough to be subject to the violent swings of speculative investment, its aggressive postmodernity cut through with the shattered fragments of a stalled modernity.

Michael Watts, citing Castells, argues that (Watts 1997: 497):

4 See Taylor 2002 and Taylor 2003 for an examination of the cyborg figure in recent Mexican literature, and Page 2004 for an account of this figure in the work of Ricardo Piglia.

5 This idea is popularised in famous essays by Octavio Paz (1950) and José Lezama Lima (1969).

> the internationalisation of post-war capitalism has produced a lived experience in which 'the space of flows ... supersede[s] the space of places'. One can productively situate [this] local-global conundrum on the wider canvas of the production of capitalist space [...]. Periods of accelerated change and reconfiguration within capitalism – the 'creative' destruction of everything it cannot use – produce what geographers have referred to as space-time convergence [...]. The erosion [...] of the glorious age of post-war Fordism, and its displacement by some form of flexible accumulation, represents in this context the most recent modulation in a recursive, wave-like pattern of space-time compressions.

At the best of times, cities in Latin America are beset by fevers of demolition and reconstruction, as new investment money tries to liquidate old assets and speculators awash with over-accumulated capital from US, European, or Asian markets, attempt to realise higher profits by making quick investments in peripheral economies, which they are just as quick to withdraw at the slightest hint of trouble. Mexican anthropologist Néstor García Canclini (1995) argues that such powerful deterritorialising forces, coupled with multiple waves of migration, split and disseminate the city's fabric into many splintered cities: the historic city, the industrial city, village cities, migrant cities, globalised information and finance cities. While the knowable community, to use Raymond Williams' term, is atomised, the dominant experience of fragmentation is compensated for, García Canclini argues, by the illusory audiovisual community of the mass media. Yet he qualifies the role of the culture industries in this re-articulation of the local and the global, claiming that these industries are implicated in the *dual* process of transnationalisation, or deterritorialisation, and the folkloric preservation of local culture through the fiction of national and supra- national difference. At the level of Latin America the marketing phenomenon of magic realism, from Gabriel García Márquez through Isabel Allende to early Laura Esquivel, might be the name of one such reading-off of Latin American difference and heterogeneity, reified as a sanctuary of pre-modern nature precisely *for* the postmodern readership of a globalised and homogenising cultural market (García Canclini 1995: 94). At the level of the city, however, paradoxically less mappable than the broad brushstrokes of magic realist Latin America, the aesthetics of the modernist *flâneur* often give way to those of the television advertisement and video clip, transcultural citation, and cultural hybridisation.

Yet such processes are not only economic. Many commentators, from British sociologist Anthony Giddens (1991) to Brazil's Renato Ortiz (1996) have stressed that the culture industries of late modernity are constitutive rather than merely reflective of deterritorialisation processes such as disembedding and time–space distanciation. In other words, audiovisual culture, which forms one of the central reflexive institutions from the mid twentieth century onwards, is complicit in the reordering of time and space which aligns the local with the global. This was certainly true of cinema in its heyday in Latin America, particularly in Mexico, where it helped in the consolidation of the post-Revolutionary nation, disembedding the popular imagination from its enmeshing with the local community and re-inscribing it within the larger framework of a newly consolidating popular national consciousness. Contemporary televisual and cybernetic cultures accelerate these processes beyond the frame of the nation, so that it is hardly surprising that the representation of the cyborg should, in Latin America as elsewhere, condense anxieties surrounding the citizen's insertion within all-encompassing televisual regimes, nor that the spatio-temporal disruptions of the megalopolis should be the stage for the cyborg's effective agency. It goes without saying that cinematic projections of such anxieties respond to a specifically reflexive moment in visual culture's thought about its own social agency.

My main thesis here is that the Latin American cinematic appropriation of US sci-fi cyborg mythologies and, in the Argentine case, cyberpunk, focuses sharply on the power structures inherent within the disciplinary regimes of global power-knowledge networks, for which the urban is the principal stage and film itself, either implicitly or explicitly, becomes a powerful synecdoche. I shall now attempt to show how this technological *mise-en-scène* is further complicated in the specific cases of films from Mexico and Argentina.

i. Mexican Cyborgs

> The vampire: the one who pollutes lineages on the wedding night; the one who effects category transformations by illegitimate passages of substance; the one who drinks and infuses blood in a paradigmatic act of infecting whatever poses as pure; [...] the one who is undead, unnatural, and perversely incorruptible. [...] For better or for worse, vampires are vectors of category transformation in a racialised, historical, national unconscious. (Haraway 1997: 216.)

Cronos is a postmodern urban vampire movie with a twist, whose title indicates an obsession with time, and whose narrative simulates the violent compression of the archaic, the modern, and the hyper- or postmodern. In this *opera prima* of 1993 by the Guadalajaran director Guillermo del Toro, the vampire co-exists with the cyborg in a spatial dimension simultaneously infused with time and bereft of temporal difference, as representational space dissolves into simulation. The film was designed from the outset for a globalised audience, being co-produced by Mexican Iguana Productions and Los Angeles-based Ventana Films, containing a mixture of Spanish and English, and using an international cast of Argentine Federico Luppi, Hollywood actor Ron Perlman, as well as Mexican actors Claudio Brook, Margarita Isabel, and Tamara Shanath. As Ann Marie Stock argues, 'Neither Del Toro nor *Cronos* is "obsessed" with authentic national culture. In fact, they flaunt their migrancy and hybridity' (Stock 1997: xxvi). Yet the film also seems to encode and play with anxieties produced in the 'pollution' of frontiers of many kinds and is an important example of the way in which post-national visual culture both reflects and partakes of aforementioned disembedding processes.

The film concerns an Argentine antiques dealer in Mexico City called Jesús Gris (Federico Luppi), who accidentally injects himself with the Chronos device. This clockwork machine, which looks like a highly ornate, baroque golden scarab, and which had lain hidden inside a statue of an angel for many years, was invented (we are told in a pre-credit sequence) around about 1536 by alchemist Humberto Fulcanelli, chief watchmaker of the Viceroy of New Spain, who also wrote a book detailing the strict rules that have to be followed in the use of the device. The credit sequence shows a series of hard cuts of a (presumed) Mexico City[6] of fast traffic, multi-lingual signposts, and the litter of Christmas shopping strewn on chaotic streets, overlain, in a typical piece of pastiche, with an Argentine tango. As the camera tilts up from street level to frame Jesús's house, we see that it is dwarfed by the modern buildings around it, an incongruous bit of the past in high-rise Mexico City. The film's obsession with antiques, with fragments of broken stories and compulsions from the past welling up through them, is coupled with a bewildering setting of uneven and unplanned urban development that leaves shards of time lying around the city's broken fabric.

But the Chronos device is not just a machine: at its very core, in amongst its intricate mechanical cogs (of which we are given several close-up shots when the device is in operation), lies a blood-sucking insect, a sort of bio-filter, that confers eternal life on the person injected by it. Such a machine, part mechanism part organism, with a body of sorts plugged into its whirling shafts and gears, already evokes, in a frightening temporal rift, a pre-modern prototype cyborg adrift in a completely irresolvable postmodern timeframe. The Chronos device seems to telescope narratives as apparently distinct as colonisation (it was invented at the dawn of the Spanish Empire in the Americas), AIDS hysteria (Jesús Gris's body decomposes the more he uses the device), the earliest forms of mechanisation (the invention of clocks which enabled synchronisation over large distances), techno-organic kinship (a kind of super dialysis machine), and biotechnology and genetic engineering (Jesús's body mutates into that of an insect).

If I insist on the biomedical paradigm, it is because it is heavily signalled in the film. Jesús, it emerges, is not the only one to know about the existence of the Chronos device. A dying capitalist millionaire, owner, it is implied, of huge industrial wealth, who has had a number of bodily organs surgically removed due to slow-spreading cancer, has found the old alchemist's book, and sends his English-speaking nephew, Ángel de la Guardia (an ironic Guardian Angel in the form of Ron Perlman), searching around Mexico City for replica angels in

6 Del Toro confirms that the setting of this vampire story in Mexico City is very important to him 'even if the geography of the city is not a determining factor' (Del Toro 2004)

the hope of finding the one with the device hidden in it, since he wants to use it to cure himself of his disease.

We first meet Ángel and his uncle Dieter de la Guardia (Claudio Brook) in the multi-storey warehouse which is the operational centre of 'Empresas de la Guardia'. This building strongly signals the allegorical dimension of urban space in this film, with its figuring of different layers of industrial manufacture and linguistic hybridity (Ángel and Dieter speak to each other in English), interlaced with religious iconography straight out of a morality play but with far less certain meaning. Ángel, standing at his desk with a computer behind him, a manual typewriter on the desk and an enormous rusty cogwheel in the background (allegorically suggestive of temporal layering and that the humans in the warehouse are analogues of the insect amongst the clockwork cogs of the Chronos device), receives a telephone call from one of his roaming agents who is out looking for angels, and has just found one in Jesús Gris's antiques shop. Speaking English, he says he will pass on the message. He leaves the desk and we follow his ascent in an industrial lift to the top floor of the warehouse. The camera gives panoramic shots of the cavernous warehouse space with showers of sparks and arcing from heavy industrial metalwork, giving way to the sterile environment of the top floor where Dieter de la Guardia lives in a hermetically sealed high-tech environment and which Ángel has to enter with a facemask and shoe covers. Inside, a travelling shot depicts several illuminated X-rays on the wall and dozens upon dozens of replica angels, all covered in polythene dust bags like so many cloned specimens, while softly diffused operatic music pervades the environment.

Cocooned in this high-tech medical bubble, the dying Señor de la Guardia is clearly a cyborg composite, dependent upon biomedical technology to keep himself alive, his body penetrated by imaging and medical technologies and openly displayed around the walls and shelves of the open-plan space, confounding interiors and exteriors. As such he is the postmodern double of the insect cocooned inside the pre-modern Chronos device, and just as the cyborg scarab vampirises those who come into intimate bodily contact with it, so, it is implied, Dieter de la Guardia vampirises Mexico's industrial wealth. The film's multilingualism, with almost all signs and forms of writing given in different languages and scripts ranging from Chinese and Arabic to Cyrillic, is evocative of a globalised, transculturally hybridised city in which the most inalienable forms of national (cultural) identity are being gradually eroded. Released on the eve of Mexico's absorption into the North American Free Trade Agreement, NAFTA, the analogies which the film draws between a cyborg-vampire whose origins lie in the colonial period and a contemporary US-Mexican businessman and his fully Anglo-American nephew, could not be clearer.

Donna Haraway makes patent the link between the 'creative destruction' of capital and vampire mythology when she writes that 'any expanding capitalist society [...] must continually destroy what it builds and feed off every being it perceives as natural – if its strategies of accumulation of wealth are to continue to push the envelope of catastrophe' (Haraway 1997: 214). *Cronos* plays with the multiple valency of vampire mythology, which encodes fears about hybridisation, racial-cum-sexual pollution, the corruption of virginal 'nature', and the transfusion of body into simulacrum, while freely vampirising the stock repertoire of horror movies both within Mexico and internationally, from the Mexican films *El fantasma del convento* (1934), *El vampiro* (1957) and *El ataúd del vampiro* (1959),[7] to Hitchcock's *Rear Window* (1954) and Cronenberg's re-make of *The Fly* (1986), from *Nosferatu* (1922) to *Videodrome* (1983). Jesús Gris takes to injecting himself regularly with the Chronos device, pleased at the rejuvenating effects it appears to have, but finds that, like any drug, it has to be used regularly and in increasing doses, and creates in the person who uses it an irresistible craving for ever larger quantities of human blood. In short, in a pastiche of social anxieties surrounding the 'pollutions' of contemporary urban society, Jesús Gris, respectable upright grandfather, finds himself transformed, by stages, into an intravenous-drug user, then a haemophiliac, until finally, his body mutating slowly into that of a monstrous insect, he becomes a simulated postmodern vampire.

The film plays on a disturbing symbology of transfusions and the pollution of cultural frontiers expressed in terms of the pollution of the boundaries of the body. Further citing Donna Haraway, one could say of this film, as she does of Lynn Randolph's artwork, that it 'uses the vampire-cyborg mythology to interrogate the undead psychoanalytic, spiritual, and mundane zones where bio-medicine, information

7 These films are cited as sources of inspiration for Del Toro by Fernández L'Hoeste (2000: 42), who in turn is referring to Rodríguez-Hernández and Schaefer 1999.

technology, and the techno-organic stories of kinship converge. This is the kinship exchange system in which gender, race, and species – animal and machine – are all at stake' (Haraway 1997: 216–17). Furthermore, Jesús's undead status clearly works over a rich Mexican popular and cinematic symbology of conviviality with the dead, which is also somewhat sent up in the sequence where his (undead) corpse is being prettified in the funeral parlour accompanied by one of the few uses of 'typical' Mexican popular music in the film. Yet the *simulated* nature of the proliferating vampire analogues in the film (for who is the vampire – Jesús Gris, Señor de la Guardia, his hypocritical nephew, or the hybrid machine-organism itself?) makes the film into a startling comment on the disembedding of local cultural practice in the face of an undifferentiated onslaught of global filmic cultural references in which richly cited local traditions and compulsively cited global ones lose their attachment to any sense of cultural authenticity in the same way that any nostalgia for the organic is unceremoniously tossed out of the window. This waning of the organic is perhaps best summed up in a moving passage of Nina Auerbach's fantastic compendium of vampire mythology, *Our Vampires, Ourselves* (to which she adds a footnote referring to *Cronos*), where she examines the sick vampires of postmodern culture with some nostalgia, seeing them as an endangered species (Auerbach 1995: 177):

> In Hambly's *Those Who Hunt the Night*, London's vampires are being murdered en masse: an amateur detective must save them from the manufactured vampire who feeds on them. In a culture turning from humanism to computers and cyborgs, in which authentic transcendence is associated not with nature or bodies, but with 'a cybernetic organism, a hybrid of machine and organism, a creature of social reality as well as a creature of fiction,' even uninfected vampires are debilitated because trapped in outmoded organicism. Originally unnatural, vampires as a species are now abandoned in a nature withering before fabricated cybernetic brains.

Finally, although representational culture, the culture of the Book, is still present in *Cronos*, in the form of the ancient alchemist's manuscript, it is peculiarly redundant as its apparently strict rules are never followed, or never seem to matter, while the old Señor de la

Guardia ends up eating its pages: 'Best meal I've had in years', he says in English to a resuscitated Jesús whose flesh he peels off like so many layers of decayed cosmetics. Meanwhile, Jesús's attempts to write a note to his wife with his semi-paralysed, stapled fingers, leads to a mountain of discarded and indecipherable jottings. Film figuring writing, and in particular failed, disturbed, or pathological writing, almost always does so as a citational image, a simulation of the breakdown of coherent narratives in the passage from representation to simulation. In *Cronos* all writing, from the alchemist's unreadable jottings in coded Latin to the palimpsest-like jumble of languages and scripts inscribed on the visible iconography of the megalopolis, has in this sense been rendered little more than the pathological citation of a system of representation which is being absorbed into an order of televisual simulation.

ii. Argentine Cyborgs

If *Cronos* expresses the spatio-temporal rifts of Mexico's insertion in the economic and televisual regimes of global power-knowledge networks, for which the megalopolis, with its uneasy temporal layering, becomes an allegorical stage, then Fernando Spiner's *noir* sci-fi homage to *Metropolis* and *Blade Runner* engages with the operations of power in a somewhat less allegorical and perhaps more allusive manner. In the case of Argentina, a tradition of cultural engagement with cinema as the mechanical simulation of absent bodies, or, in more complex terms, as the disavowal of the disappeared body behind the screen fetish of the mechanically reproduced image, becomes an available framework for interpreting the operations of power in the aftermath of the dictatorship of 1976 to 1982, with its 30,000 disappearances and some 300,000 directly affected by repression. Yet it is also the case that the experience of dictatorship tends to re-activate nostalgic narratives of repression and liberation, congealed around repressive fantasies of sexual difference. This point should come as no surprise, since we know on the one hand that power and (dis)simulation are caught in a tight bind, and on the other that fetish identities such as those built around sexual difference depend on disavowal-as-simulation, a process which promotes the proliferation of simulacra in the gender masquerade.

The legacy of this interpretative framework in Argentina is certainly traceable back to Roberto Arlt and Macedonio Fernández with their dreams of mechanical replication, of story-telling and forgery machines which would destabilise the fictions of power. But they are first perhaps linked to cinematic disavowal in the work of Adolfo Bioy Casares whose extraordinary novella, *La invención de Morel* (1940), charts, in very prescient manner, a journey from terrorised dissimulation to post-technological simulation. A strange rewriting and transformation of H.G. Wells' *The Island of Dr. Moreau* of 1896, it concerns a political refugee, escapee from life imprisonment on a trumped-up charge in Caracas, who makes his way to a secret and uninhabited southwest Pacific island. Although the island is rumoured to be the focus of some strange disease, as yet unknown to science, which kills from the outside in, causing the body to lose its substance and crumble slowly away, he prefers to take his chances there than to live a life of dissimulation and hiding, pursued by the world's police forces for a crime he did not commit.

What he finds there is a terrifying and seductive new technological invention, created by a mad scientist Morel, a 1940s televisual answer to Wells' Moreau who, we may recall, fashioned human beings out of pumas in a double allegory of science and colonisation, medicine and mission. Morel's invention – a virtual-reality machine *avant la lettre* – also transforms bodies, quite literally consuming the real to produce its hyperreal simulacrum. As such, it can now serve as a precursor for a new kind of technologically mediated perfusion – that of globalisation – and precursor of a new mode of telematic simulation. Falling in love with a simulated woman on the island, literally seduced by a simulacrum, the protagonist of the novella decides to sacrifice his real existence in order to take a place in the simulation.

One film of the immediate post-dictatorship period draws explicitly on Bioy Casares' allegory of power and simulation to encode its comments on political disavowal through the mode of cinematic disavowal. Eliseo Subiela's *Hombre mirando al sudeste* (1986) plays on the spectator's splitting of belief in cinema, the incredulity generated by the protagonist Rantés' assertion that he is a simulation, a hologram projected by an invisible machine in outer space, an artefact of extra-terrestrial technology. Rantés is a *reaparecido*, having appeared from nowhere in a Buenos Aires mental asylum, and is thus a spectral corollary of the *desaparecidos* of Argentina's Dirty War. Of course we know full well that he is a mere simulation, a condensation of the technologies of vision and of the modern regimes of power-visibility that constitute cinema and which are in turn constituted by televisual imaginaries. But we nevertheless disavow that knowledge in our willingness to invest in the regime of rational belief represented by psychiatrist Dr. Julio Denis. This inversion, whereby the reality principle is in fact the simulation and the sci-fi postulate of Rantés' status as cyborg is the strict truth, acts as a powerful critique of the mechanisms of political disavowal, the bourgeois citizenry's refusal to acknowledge the horror committed in the name of social order and morality during the dictatorship. *Hombre mirando al sudeste* was also remarkable for consciously setting up a cyborg aesthetic through reference to the now classic Ridley Scott film *Blade Runner* of 1982 as well as its literary antecedent in Philip K. Dick's novel.[8]

The other important antecedent to *La sonámbula*, is Ricardo Piglia's cyberpunk novel of 1992, *La ciudad ausente*. This is not surprising, since Piglia co-wrote the script for *La sonámbula*, and director Spiner in fact asked Piglia to be his scriptwriter precisely because of his interest in the novel. Many elements overlap between the novel and the film: the cyborg story-telling woman-machine in *La ciudad ausente* is referred to explicitly as a future Eve, an 'Eva futura', while the female protagonist of *La sonámbula*, whose visions are captured directly on a giant computer screen and seem capable of foretelling the future, is actually named Eva; both plots are set in a near dystopian future at the time of writing/filming, one in which personal and collective memory and identity have imploded along with nature itself, and one in which a post-dictatorial technocratic state has fused itself with the libidinal control systems of globalised capital.

The repressive overgrown cityscape of Buenos Aires in the film follows in the tradition of *Blade Runner*'s 'old future' in which present, past, and future seem to have collapsed, or in which the future simulates the past postmodern-style. While in *Blade Runner* the cityscape of Los Angeles in 2019 is a baroque fusion of the futuristic and the simulation of ancient pyramids, perhaps Mayan, together with an imploded Dickensian vision of industrialisation run riot, in *La sonámbula*, the cityscape of Buenos Aires in 2010 – the bicentenary of Argentine Independence – fuses churches and cathedrals with a jungle of elevated highways and skyscrapers which signify the futurist city not as future, but as citation of old sci-fi movies, principally Fritz Lang's *Metropolis* of

8 One of the characters is named Beatriz Dick. For further discussion, see Kantaris 2005: 180–82.

1927. The future is thus filtered through a past cinematic imaginary, an inversion which is aided by the fact that the entire futuristic plot of the film is shot in black and white, whereas the flashbacks to the past or present – the visions of the protagonist Eva Rey – are shot in full technicolour. Like *Blade Runner*, with its startling opening sequence in which the dystopian cityscape is reflected through the close-up mirror-like eye of Deckard, an analogue for the screen which feeds the spectator's eye, so in *La sonámbula* the eye imagery of a sequence which clearly cites *Blade Runner*'s opening (the first traversal of the city) sets in train a self-reflexive focus on the prosthetics of vision throughout the film. The eye is the interface between the organic and the technological, the point of suture between the individual and the visual media as generators of a libidinal economy of prohibition and desire and as manufacturers of memory. In this sense, the future megalopolis is, quite literally, a teleopolis.

In the world of *La sonámbula*, the Lefebvrian vision of the urban consumption of organic time, the compulsion to subsume all vestiges of natural rhythms and cycles into synthetic time and life-cycles of the commodity, has been taken to a nightmare extreme (Lefebvre 1974: 114). This has a dual focus: that of ecological disaster and the literal loss of that which links us to organic time cycles, memory itself. In the film, the two are intimately linked, since the plot concerns a future in which a huge industrial accident, probably a deliberate explosion at an experimental chemical factory in a popular district of Buenos Aires, has left 300,000 people with wiped-out memories and hence no sense of their own identity or relationship to the past. All of the affected people in the film bear a highly visible mark, either on the face or on some other part of the body such as forearm or chest, a mark which becomes a substitute for identity and even an erotic fetish within the film's self-consciously condensed dream logic. The principal protagonist, Eva Rey (Sofía Viruboff) is one such amnesiac whom we see being captured and taken in for tests and 'reprogramming' at the sinister Centre for Psychobiological Research, while the other protagonist, Ariel Kluge (Eusebio Poncela) plays an equivocal role as an amnesiac who is in the pay of the state security service, but who falls in love with Eva and helps her to escape from the city in search of the perhaps mythical subversive revolutionary called Gauna (although we never know whether Ariel intends to kill Gauna once she has found him).

The character El Duke [sic] (Norman Briski), friend and substitute father figure for Ariel, having known Ariel's real father in prison before the latter's death, and who helps Ariel and Eva to escape into the countryside, explains the politics behind this literalised vision of the postmodern consumption of memory – in which it should not be too hard to see barely veiled references to the most recent Argentine dictatorship:

> The truth is ... a silent technological explosion which affects you up here [*tapping his temple with right index finger*] ... Like the stuff they used during demos to control people, but ... on a gigantic scale! So, what do the half-arsed bastards decide to do? Conduct experiments in a densely populated neighbourhood! Boom ... And what do you think happens? The results aren't what was expected ... So ... 300,000 people are mentally affected. [*Shouting*] 300,000 people ... haven't got a fucking clue who they are!

However this 'silent technological explosion', a clear corollary for the contemporary technological explosion of televisual and cyberculture, appears in the film to have extended beyond the consumption of organic time and memory to the total consumption of nature itself. The countryside outside Buenos Aires is literally a post-industrial desert, a Borgesian-cum-Baudrillardian 'desert of the real', consumed by industrial chaos as well as by compulsive simulation as in Borges' and Bioy Casares' story.[9] Even the migration of birds as organic marker of natural time cycles has become disturbed as we are told that the huge flocks of birds which we see merely circle and circle the desert without orientation (a concept that shares a source with another cipher of mechanised nature: the one-winged mechanical bird that appears in Piglia's novel *La ciudad ausente*).

In many ways memory, with its corollary amnesia, is the key theme of *La sonámbula*. In an interview originally filmed for a making-of documentary, Piglia explains the importance of this theme (Interview edited by Luppi 1998):

9 The story is 'Del rigor en la ciencia', written as a literary forgery and collected in *Historia universal de la infamia* (Borges 1946).

> We had the idea of a science fiction film in the sense that there is an idea, a speculation about the present which is translated into the future. We took the problematics of memory, what is remembered or forgotten in Argentina, and we converted it into a future world where this is the very problem that defines life.

Indeed, throughout the film, cinema, or rather televisual culture more broadly, is self-reflexively figured as prosthetic memory, or simulated memory. The central computer screen in the film, operated by the mad scientist/psychiatrist Dr Gazzar (Lorenzo Quinteros) is represented as a giant cinema screen, with images displayed in colour as against the black-and-white of the rest of the film. The machine records telepathically, interfacing directly with the mind and reproducing thought televisually. In particular, as in *La ciudad ausente*, the machine records dreams, so that the film figures a total conflation of the spheres of the technological imaginary with the unconscious. In this, it projects forward contemporary analyses of the technological mediation of personal and collective imaginaries, of which the summary given by Jonathan Beller is fairly representative. He writes (Beller 2002: 64):

> Metz argues that 'cinema is a technique of the imaginary' [...]. However, the scope of today's (counter)revolution [...] emerges from a reversal of these very terms: *the imaginary is a technique of cinema*, or rather, of mediation generally. Such a reversal de-ontologizes the unconscious and further suggests that the unconscious is cinema's product.

But of course in *La sonámbula*, these programmed memories are a form of programmed amnesia, designed to replace memory, and they appear to be part of some ultimate experiment in social programming. In the Centre for Psychobiological Research, where the amnesiacs are brought to initiate their re-insertion into society, the rhetoric of recuperating memory is bound up with a primitive Huxleyan reprogramming with normative memories through televisual technology. We are also shown the process of rehabilitation through gender programming, as the amnesiacs are given reconstructed relationships and families, with the process revealing the coercion that underlies the everyday performance of gender norms. This is ultimately a critique of the erasure of dissident cultural identities as the intended aftermath of dictatorship in Argentina, where the dissolution of collective memory prepares the ground for a society modelled along the lines of post-industrial corporatism.[10]

Finally, *La sonámbula* self-reflexively takes up the now traditional projections onto a female figure of anxieties surrounding technology and cyborgs, for which we can perhaps find the prototype in the automaton Olympia in Hoffman's *Der Sandmann* (1816). Eva Rey as a literary/filmic figure is no different in this respect to the original android, *L'Ève future* (Villiers de l'Isle Adam 1886), the robot Maria in *Metropolis*, or the replicant Rachael in *Blade Runner*. Just like these, Eva, whom Piglia playfully claims is a kind of 'Peronist Oedipus Rex tangentially suggestive of Eva Perón' (Luppi 1998), finds herself caught in the clutches of competing patriarchal narratives, and slips out of them by adopting the traditionally assigned feminine strategy of simulation.

Is it inevitable that we should find such overtly Oedipal narratives at the heart of a film which has the potential to suggest different and emergent modes of techno-organic kinship? As Donna Haraway put it (Haraway 1991: 150–51),

> the most terrible and perhaps the most promising monsters in cyborg worlds are embodied in non-oedipal narratives with a different logic of repression, which we need to understand for our survival. [...] Unlike the hopes of Frankenstein's monster, the cyborg does not expect its father to save it through a restoration of the garden.

Wired up to Gazzar's giant computer which electronically records her dreams of the future in full technicolour, Eva becomes the epicentre of the entire filmic world, simulating the real through dreams which turn out to be the dystopian reality of the film. It is in this sense that Gazzar is able to claim, quite literally, at a moment of revelation, that 'the end of the world is a woman who wakes up'. When Eva does awake, dragging her dream-lover Ariel into the 'real world', it is precisely to restore the garden (of Eden) and the patriarch (who turns out to be one and the same as the subversive revolutionary Gauna) to their rightful roles, although this restoration is presented

[10] This is, approximately, the reading which Idelber Avelar (1999) gives of the politics of memory in *La ciudad ausente*.

very precisely in the film as the culmination of the twin logics of repression and amnesia because it leaves the dream-protagonist Ariel permanently stranded in the desert of the real.

Conclusion

The cyborgs or cyborg-ciphers in these Latin American films, set in two of the region's burgeoning mega-cities, are clearly engaging with dystopian projections of imploded social and cultural identities which condense anxieties surrounding the loss of local autonomy and cultural memory, and the reinscription of these disembedded identities within global regimes governing the circulation of goods, information and, crucially, images. Both films deploy their prototype cyborgs at the threshold of the failure of representation, on the spatio-temporal boundary where representational logic phases into and out of an order of simulation. *Cronos*, perhaps through its obsessive baroque imagery and willingness to collapse the most disparate historical narratives, suggests the more radical forms of non-Oedipal techno-organic kinship, even if it neutralises them in the end as Jesús Gris rejects the temptations of an inverted Messianism, pulls back from vampirising his granddaughter Aurora, and returns to die in the bosom of the family fold. The technologically mediated dreams of an Argentine *Ève future*, on the other hand, are self-consciously bound up with a collective dream of liberation and escape. Cyberpunk has always had a romantic relationship to dissidence, viewing, in the anarchy engendered in the interstices of the capitalist system, a dystopian mode of liberation. As the rebel Gorrión puts it to Eva, '[Gauna] is the way to total liberation. If you find Gauna, you will mark the way for all of us, do you realise that?' What is perhaps radical in this film is the suggestion in the end that the dream of total liberation is merely the flipside of total conformity, in that it fixes the rhizomatic operations of power into binary structures. It is this realisation which can perhaps suspend the erasure of dissident cultural identities initiated under dictatorship and which might allow for the circulation of new forms of cyborg kinship within global circuits of power and exchange.

References

Auerbach, Nina 1995. *Our Vampires, Ourselves* (Chicago: University of Chicago Press).
Avelar, Idelber 1999. *The Untimely Present* (Durham, NC: Duke University Press).
Beller, Jonathan L. 2002. 'Kino-I, Kino-World: Notes on the Cinematic Mode of Production', in Nicholas Mirzoeff, ed., *The Visual Culture Reader* (London: Routledge), pp. 60–85.
Bioy Casares, Adolfo 1940. *La invención de Morel* (Buenos Aires: Alianza Emecé).
Blade Runner 1982. Directed by Ridley Scott (USA: Blade Runner Partnership), 35mm/colour, 117 mins.
Borges, Jorge Luis 1946. *Historia universal de la infamia* (Buenos Aires: Emecé).
Carpentier, Alejo 1949. 'Prólogo', *El reino de este mundo* (Mexico City: Siglo XXI).
Castells, Manuel 1996. 'The Space of Flows', in *The Rise of the Network Society: The Information Age. Economy, Society and Culture*, vol. 1 (Oxford: Blackwell Publishing), pp. 376–428.
Clarke, David B., ed. 1997. *The Cinematic City* (London: Routledge).
Cronos 1993. Directed by Guillermo del Toro (Mexico: Instituto mexicano de cinematografía/Ventana Films/Producciones Iguana), 35mm/colour, 91 mins.
Del Toro, Guillermo 2004. 'Entrevista con Guillermo del Toro', *ClubCultura* http://www.clubcultura.com/clubcine/espinazo/espinazo.htm, last accessed 13 June 2007.
Eliot, T.S. 1923. *The Waste Land* (Richmond: Hogarth Press).
Esquivel, Laura 1999. *La ley del amor* (Barcelona: Plaza & Janés).
Fernández L'Hoeste, Héctor D. 2000. 'De insectos y otros demonios: breves apuntes sobre las obsesiones de Guillermo del Toro', *Cifra nueva* [Trujillo] 12 (June–December), 41–50. http://www.saber.ula.ve/db/ssaber/Edocs/pubelectronicas/cifra-nueva/anum12/articulo4.pdf, last accessed 13 June 2007.
García Canclini, Néstor 1995. *Consumidores y ciudadanos: Conflictos multiculturales de la globalización* (Mexico City: Grijalbo).
Giddens, Anthony 1991. *Modernity and Self-Identity: Self and Society in the Late Modern Age* (Cambridge: Polity).
Haraway, Donna J. 1991. *Simians, Cyborgs, and Women: The Reinvention of Nature* (London: Free Association Books).
—— 1997. *Modest_Witness@Second_Millennium.FemaleMan©_Meets_OncoMouse?: Feminism and Technoscience* (New York and London: Routledge).
Hoffmann, E. T. A. 1816 [1988]. *Der Sandmann* (Berlin: De Gruyter).
Hombre mirando al sudeste 1986. Directed by Eliseo Subiela (Argentina: Cinequannon), 35mm/colour, 100 mins.
Kantaris, Geoffrey 2005. 'Holograms and Simulacra: Bioy Casares, Subiela, Piglia', in Evelyn Fishburn and Eduardo L. Ortiz, eds., *Science and the Creative Imagination in Latin America* (London: Institute for the Study of the Americas), pp. 175–89.

Lefebvre, Henri 1974. *La Production de l'espace* (Paris: Anthropos).
Lezama Lima, José 1969 [2001]. *La expresión americana* (Mexico: Fondo de Cultura Económica).
Luppi, Nacho, ed. 1998. 'Ricardo Piglia habla de *La sonámbula*', *Mabuse*, http://www.mabuse.com.ar/mabuse/piglia.htm, last accessed 13 June 2007.
Metropolis. 1927. Directed by Fritz Lang (Germany: Universum Film AG), 35mm/BW, 153 mins.
Ortiz, Renato 1996 [1998]. *Otro territorio: Ensayos sobre el mundo contemporáneo*, 2nd ed., trans. by Ada Solari (Bogotá: Convenio Andrés Bello).
Page, Joanna 2004. 'Writing as Resistance in Ricardo Piglia's *La ciudad ausente*', *Bulletin of Spanish Studies* 81:3, 343–60.
Paz, Octavio 1950 [1981]. *El laberinto de la soledad* (Mexico City: Fondo de Cultura Económica).
Piglia, Ricardo 1992. *La ciudad ausente* (Buenos Aires: Seix Barral).
Rodríguez-Hernández, Raúl, and Claudia Schaefer 1999. '*Cronos* and the Man of Science: Madness, Monstrosity, Mexico', *Revista de estudios hispánicos* 33:1, 85–108.
Shiel, Mark, and Tony Fitzmaurice, eds. 2001. *Cinema and the City: Film and Urban Societies in a Global Context* (Oxford: Blackwell Publishing).
La sonámbula 1998. Directed by Fernando Spiner, script by Fabián Bielinsky and Ricardo Piglia (Argentina: La Sonámbula Producciones SRL and Metrovisión SA), 35mm/BW/colour, 107 mins.
Stock, Ann Marie, ed. 1997. *Framing Latin American Cinema: Contemporary Critical Perspectives* (Minneapolis, MN: University of Minnesota Press).
Taylor, Claire L. 2002. 'Body-Swapping and Genre-Crossing in Laura Esquivel's *La ley del amor*', *Modern Language Review* 97:2, 324–35.
—— 2003. 'Cities, Codes and Cyborgs in Carmen Boullosa's *Cielos de la tierra*', *Bulletin of Spanish Studies* 80:4, 477–93.
Villiers de l'Isle Adam, Auguste 1886. *L'Ève future* (Lausanne: Éditions de l'Age d'homme).
Watts, Michael J. 1997. 'Mapping Meaning, Denoting Difference, Imagining Identity: Dialectical Images and Postmodern Geographies', in Trevor Barnes and Derek Gregory, eds., *Reading Human Geography: The Poetics and Politics of Inquiry* (London: Arnold), pp. 489–502.
Wells, H.G. 1896. *The Island of Dr. Moreau* (New York: Garden City Publishing).

3

The Cyberart of Corpos Informáticos

Margaret Anne Clarke

Within the last decade there has been a vigorous response to the challenges to established orders of knowledge posed by the 'digital revolution' from Brazilian artists, theorists, and practitioners, who have gained great influence within what the US social theorist Gregory Coyne has termed the new cultural axis emerging in the Americas, extending from Florida to Brazil (Hinchberger 2004). Brazilian artists' engagement with and contribution to the international cross-fertilisation of ideas within the numerous discourses of modernity is not, of course, a new phenomenon. Practitioners of the new media in Brazil are working within a tradition that was already highly receptive to, and, indeed, foreshadowed in many ways, the possibilities of engagement, interactivity and radical embodiments, and transformations of society and self promised by the new digital media.[1] Yet the new and unprecedented opportunities for communication, dissemination and access afforded by international network systems have enabled Brazilian practitioners working with computer networks and animation, telecommunications, digital video, hypermedia and multimedia to overcome logistic, cultural and national barriers, and become key players in the international digital community.

This chapter, then, will focus on the theory and practice of one example of new media art in Brazil: corpos.org, constructed by a long-established and publicly funded group of researchers, web practitioners, and performance artists, Corpos Informáticos [Virtual

[1] For a brief history of twentieth-century precursors to the copious and exuberant production of digital art in Brazil, see Johannes Birringer.

Bodies].[2] First established in 1992 at the University of Brasilia, the group have in their fifteen-year trajectory developed a theoretically sophisticated corpus of ideas within a body of work that encompasses live art, installations, video, and performance art within broadcasting media, and have, with the creation of a website of some nine years' standing, effected a further synthesis and development of one of the central questions informing the discipline: the ontological nature and status of the human subject and its embodiment and reconfiguration in communication, information, and electronic media. Corpos Informáticos develop this principal informing question from several perspectives. Firstly, the alterity of the body, and the manner in which modified and distorted reflections of the body in print and broadcast media alter and inform our own perceptions of ourselves, our will, and our desires. Secondly, the interaction between the body and the technological artefacts and prostheses which enable humans to move, function, and create. Finally, the redimension of the individual and the community in cyberspace and the new media, through the creation of new consciousnesses and new modes of perception. Partly informed by the philosophy of Gilles Deleuze and an eclectic range of European thinkers and philosophers, Corpos nonetheless develop these perspectives further within the specific context of cyberspace and networked communications. Moreover, the group debates, and in some aspects, strongly challenges, concepts and ideas well established by Anglo-American theorists concerning the nature of human embodiment and its relation to technology. I will base a reading of corpos.org on three fundamental premises addressed in the work of Corpos Informáticos: firstly, the definition of art and the aesthetic and its renewal through the redimension of human communities in cyberspace; secondly, the ontological status and nature of the human body and its relation to the purportedly diametrically opposed spheres of the organic or the biological and the inanimate and the technological; and finally, the group's ideas concerning epistemology and concepts of evolution fundamental to Western thought.

2 For a complete list of the group's researchers, participants, and collaborators, see Medeiros 2003.

i. The Aesthetic within Webmension

The challenge to modern and post-Enlightenment concepts of human civilisation brought about by the integration of 'digital technologies' – an encompassing term for a large and ill-defined complex of electronic networks and communication systems – into economic, political, and social institutions, must also entail also a corresponding transformation in the artistic sphere, and the creation of cultural artefacts. Although no unified theory of the 'digital aesthetic' may be said to exist (Gianetti 2002), some common assumptions still surround the inherent characteristics of Internet art. To begin with, the potential inherent in the almost infinite combinations possible within network systems, multimedia, and digital simulation have led, in particular, to a shift away from the 'paradigm of representation' – that is, artwork based on mimesis requiring distanced attention on the part of the viewer – and towards a process of 'virtualisation', a more interactive mode required from the viewer, who becomes also a participant and fellow-creator. The viewer-participant is now positioned at the interface, and situated at the point of assimilation into the artwork: within this enhanced zone of interactivity there is the generation of mutual feedback, and the potential for the viewer, or *internaut,*[3] to stimulate their own interpretations or reconfigurations of identity in conjunction with the networked art form and its original creators. Moreover, if, as Rabinowitz and Geil (2004: 4–5) suggest, the positive effect of digital and networked communications is to facilitate expanded interaction between communities and to furnish new configurations of communication between individual human subjects, then any fundamental definition of digital and networked culture must entail, in some form, a transformative effect on both the community and the individual, having further impact on ideas concerning the process of artistic creation and the cultural meaning of technology in social, political, and aesthetic terms.

Thus by what means heterogeneous multimedia and information systems produce a qualitatively different experience for those who view, use, and are immersed in these networks is a key question informing the Internet art of Corpos Informáticos. The fundamental role of the new media artist or practitioner is to engage with the human

3 From the Portuguese term for Internet user, 'internauta'.

and the aesthetic, to reclaim information technologies and human societies from institutional and corporate agendas, reasserting diverse identities and voices which interact through mediated technologies, within a daily life which, as Bia [Maria Beatriz] Medeiros, the group's co-ordinator, puts it, is 'overblown with technology' and where 'spaces are filled with electronic images and virtual places, [where] the mediated body [is] trespassed by technologies' (Medeiros, 'Tenuous Border').

The central concern here, then, is to examine and develop a definition of the aesthetic within the new and radical possibilities for interaction between the human subject, communities and networked information systems. A precondition for this is the denial of the linearity, separation, and alienation inherent in the Enlightenment and Cartesian conception of the self: autonomous, guided by rational faculties privileged above emotion and instinct, and within one homogenous and self-contained body. According to Corpos Informáticos, the natural impulse of the human is in fact to strive incessantly towards a state of heterogeneity and towards the other. Drawing on the unpublished work of French philosopher, Jean-Marie Doguet, Corpos expound a concept of *nous originaire*, distinguishing three categories of the 'self': firstly, the referential 'us'; then the representative 'us' of a collective such as Corpos; and finally the 'us' that emerges in communication and interlocution with others – the 'intersubjective relation' within which the 'I' can recognise itself as a subject and the other can, in turn, recognise and convert the other into an interlocutor. Within this schema, the aesthetic returns to the original Greek sense of the word, which suggests that 'an aesthetic experience involves a transfer of knowledge which takes place in both the object and the observer' (Briggs 1992: 30). The heightened awareness and proximity to the other within networked communication, the reciprocal reflection on the other's image and mutual desire to know may indeed generate aesthetic pleasure (Medeiros 2000):

> in this possibility of sharing, in this possibility that there is an aesthetic *sensus communis*, the subject [...] feels, and wants, to be a member of a community with the same taste, and for this to happen, elevates the other to the same status attributed to himself, that is, he sees the other ('you') as part of the 'us for interlocution' – or, in other words, through the sense of beauty,

> the 'I' feels pleasure, a pleasure that is felt as universally shareable, and consequently this 'I' recognises itself as part of humanity, part of *nous originaire*.

The starting point for the creation of the aesthetic within corpos.org is virtual space, which also renders problematic the common idea of dimension, usually and erroneously taken to mean a two-sided or dual entity, but, in fact, a word of Latin origins originally denoting 'movement towards different or multiple sides' (Pickover 1999: 21). Virtual space, or 'webmension' as Corpos define it, provides an almost infinite space of possibilities within which the concept of *nous originaire* and the possibility of unity through heterogeneity can be realised: 'freedom loves the interstices, the dispersions, but also the infinite, features that are impregnated by the idea of "webmension" (the n-dimension of virtual space)'. Nonetheless, 'communication technologies' such as one-to-many broadcasting media and television channels which function as the purveyors of information in the form of 'news' and the relentless advertisement of consumer goods, or the type of Internet navigation which entails the clicking on conventional linear hypertext links in a continuous sequence, do not in themselves facilitate any genuine interaction between individuals or their communities. Only within communication networks whose design enhances or brings about 'the spectral presence of others in real time' can there be a genuine means and outlet to realise *nous originaire*. The overriding aim which underpins the design of the group's site is the creation of a new affective relation between viewers and participants, a '"mise-en-scène" of the instincts'.

This means, first of all, divesting the site of the usual paraphernalia associated with desktop interfaces – no buttons, windows, scroll bars or icons are visible on the opening page of the site, nor designs associated with traditional print media remediated in computer networks, nor any other feature which might present the site as 'a digital medium interposing itself between the viewer and an apparently simple and unitary physical world' (Boulter and Grusin 2001: 216). Rather, on opening the site, the internaut encounters what Mark Hansen describes as an 'affective interface', that is, a digitally generated close-up image of a human face, which functions as a 'medium for the interface between the domain of digital information and the embodied human' (Hansen 2004: 128). When the cursor is moved over the face/interface, the internaut is offered random access through a number of hotspots, displaying hidden and simultaneous views of multiple destinations: five sites within the site, each offering a different interpretation of the human body and its interactions within electronic media.

The overall design of the site highlights the tension between the potential for communication and networked technologies to facilitate the interaction, growth and transformation of human identities and their communities on the one hand, and the power of the same technologies in the hands of corporate and monopoly interests to control, manipulate, and fragment the individual consciousness and its body. Thus Corpos employ contrasting design media and text to negotiate this dilemma, to comment on the potentially negative and destructive social effects of technological communication, and to present radical alternatives. For example, the area entitled 'quecorpo' [which body] critiques in image and hypertext prose the commodification and reification of the body by commercial and broadcasting media, and the alienation brought about by the imposition of wholly bogus aesthetic norms in commercial contexts (see fig. 3.1). The site presents a static arrangement of blurred images which, when opened, present vivid portraits drawn from the group's live art performances of 'bodies bent awkward, atrophied, hideous and distorted':

Bodycutexhaustedwoundedinvadedbytechnologiesblind
Feels
Aesthesis
Bodycutexhaustedwoundedinvadedby technologiesblind
Don't fear
TEAR
Expressionwillbefightandshout.

In striking contrast to 'quecorpo', the area entitled 'telepresence' presents a hypertextualised collage of nine hundred images again drawn from the group's performance art exhibitions and installations (see fig. 3.2). The page, once opened, rapidly fills with flickering images, each one measuring 18 × 24 pixels, either static or revolving at several velocities, of individuals, bodies, and spaces of all kinds drawn from the natural and built environment. This interpenetration of images, their juxtaposition, overlap, and multiplication, is inspired by Deleuze's argument that a body must be understood, not in terms of its form or functions, but in terms of its relations: longitudinal relations of speed and slowness, and its latitudinal capacity for affect and proximity to others. Thus 'telepresence''s metonymical representations illustrate the relations between the myriad components of bodies, selves, and identities as a state of process, or 'becomings, which have neither culmination or subject, but draw one another into zones of proximity' (Deleuze and Guattari 1988: 507). Such a process is a perpetual interplay of flows, interstices, and interchanges, with no principal axis of organisation, according no special privilege or status to any one race, gender, or identity, and in a constant state of interaction with the physical and natural environment. The visual arrangement is complemented by a soundtrack of multiple voices heard as textures of sound, which may represent positive feedback that derives from infinite human interaction. This 'spatial dynamic' can also be infinitely decentred and recentred by the internaut: any one of the 900 images opens as a separate window which can be moved around the screen at will, and thus any one image serves as an entrance to the site and can be connected by the internaut's agency to any other point.

ii. The Body, Technology and the Cyborg

Corpos Informáticos also engage with the constant redefinitions and debates which have taken place in Western philosophy and thought concerning the ontology of the body itself and its relations with its physical and organic environments. From the advent of modernity onwards, a fundamental contradiction has informed the concept of the 'human', or, rather, the relation of the human subject with the organic natural realm of the biological, of which the human body is held to be inherently a part, and the technological artefacts constructed by human agency and skill from inorganic matter and energy. These artefacts are the means by which human subjects and the civilisations they create may assert their dominion over the natural realm. The individual consciousness, and in particular the body it inhabits, is positioned awkwardly and in a somewhat ill-defined way between these two domains. This double bind is, in fact, at once 'an outgrowth of Enlightenment thought and of its steady erosion' (Rabinowitz and Geil 2004: 7). The fear expressed by Corpos in 'quecorpo' and at other points on the site is that living organic bodies and their consciousnesses exist in a state of threat from the potentially dehumanising effects of technological networks and information systems, which, far from existing in a state of harmony with the needs and aspirations of human life and its environment, are in danger of suppressing them altogether with one 'wholly fabricated by human beings that feeds on itself' (Mitcham and Casey 1994: 46). Not only is the pressure on human life disorienting in itself, but technological media which are controlled or manipulated by institutional or corporate authority must also by definition stand in opposition to the human subject, its self and its body: 'during the past two centuries, to be a self is to be under relentless pressure to catch up' (Radcliff 2004: xiv).

On the other hand, the promise is also held out to us that at this juncture in twenty-first century civilisation, myriad combinations of communication, information, and biomedical technologies are bringing human bodies to the point of imminent liberation from the exigencies of nature, mortality, and even the constraints of time–space. Thus it is still difficult to conceptualise the ordering of the human being in either the organic realm or the inorganic physical realm except in terms of 'an increasingly untenable anthropocentrism' which elevates or positions us as 'the human' at the apex of both the natural and inorganic worlds, their orderer or master (Mackenzie 2002: 1).

The search for an answer to these contradictions is encountered in one of the central precepts at the heart of the numerous debates concerning the relation of the human subject with its world, origins, and technologies: that the boundaries between the spheres of the body, the physical, the technological, and the organic, formerly rigidly demarcated by Enlightenment doctrine, now exist in a state of transgression, overlapping each other. This does not just entail the creation of a hybrid effected through the implantation or incorporation of technological artefacts or artificial prostheses into living bodies. The theory most notably propounded by such Anglo-American theorists as Donna Haraway (1991, 1997) and which has appeared in numerous other cultural, social, and theoretical contexts also, is the narrative of the cyborg. This theory proposes that the shifting, ordering, and transformation of the human and the human body into other spheres has, by the same token, effected a transformation of the human body into an essentially hybrid entity: a dynamic synthesis of the organic human sphere as subject and the inorganic material sphere as object. According to Donna Haraway, 'what we take to be a body is not only inseparable from technologies (or "technoscience") but is dynamically engendered in the interplay of disparate actants – historical, natural, technical, discursive and material entities' (Haraway 1997: 209). Notwithstanding the various means by which this synthesis may be effected, however, it is still difficult to overcome the underpinning dualism that is at work within this schema: the inorganic, *techne*, and the body in some way still preserve the autonomous integrity of their respective spheres. This assumption is still apparent in the 'classic' definition of the cyborg as provided by Dyens (2000), and as generally conceived in Anglo-American theory, culture, and literature: the cyborg is 'not a model of a denatured body, but one of an overnatured body, i.e. a body whose definition cannot exclude technology'. Nonetheless, several contradictions still remain inherent in the conceptualisation of the cyborg figure, the most salient of which is the implication that the cyborg, or cybernetic mechanism, however it may be constructed or synthesised, still entails an amalgam or merger of diverse elements from domains that, in post-Enlightenment Western civilisation, have been preserved as opposites. According to Chris Hables Gray, 'the concept of the cyborg both strengthens and explodes these binary concepts – because the cyborg only exists in this union of supposed opposites. These opposites are defined and clarified in the naming of them' (Hables Gray 1998). More recently still, in an effort to develop a resolution of these inherent contradictions, such Anglo-American theorists as N. Katherine Hayles (1999) have postulated the concept of the 'post-human': that is, a fundamental rethink of the concept of the human's embodiment as an autonomous and self-contained thinking subject. Rather than consisting of an amalgam of elements from diverse spheres, the human essence and its consciousness is distributed across biological and technological systems. This, in turn, has called into question the entire status of the 'biological' as the fundamental matter of which the human and its body is composed, and thus the principal component of the ontological status of the human. 'Post-biology' as proposed by Roy Ascott (2000) and others, conceptualises the body as a 'mosaic of biological, viral and political dynamics, all meshed into one stable pattern' (Dyens 2000). Thus, not only is the traditional definition of the body as a structure embodied within a biological or organic substrate called into question within philosophies of the 'post-human'; the constant and encroaching convergence between technology and living organisms means that human consciousness itself cannot be confined to the strictly delineated zone of the human body. Nonetheless, the post-human subject is still in its essence an amalgam (Hayles, 1999: 3), still composed of components, albeit in a state of ongoing construction, reconstruction, and flux.

Corpos Informáticos, on the other hand, display a considerably more measured attitude to claims that the ontological status of the body or its fundamentally organic nature has been profoundly transformed by its incorporation into 'new' technologies and information systems. To begin with, the concept of 'new' technologies, and their role in the changing ideas concerning what it is to be human, implies something that did not exist prior to their invention, although those information technologies which are in use at present may be renewed at several points, or reconfigured in various ways. Technological artefacts and the information they convey are brought about or come into being through poeisis or the craft of making; they are an inherent characteristic of the human, and reside, latent and immanent, within the domains of the natural and the inorganic. In Bia Medeiros' words, 'anthropogenesis and technogenesis happen simultaneously, and if we accept the existence of new technologies, we would have to acknowledge the existence of a new mankind, which, we are certain, is not true' (Medeiros 2000).

Moreover, although the redimension of the body within information technology networks may lead to an enhanced awareness of a body which perceives itself as refracted or reflected in others, the 'expansion' this entails, according to the group, is metaphorical in nature only, and does not entail the redimension of the physical body, which retains its integrity as an organic entity and what should be its fundamental harmony with the natural world and the ecological sphere. According to Bia Medeiros (Medeiros 2000):

> Consciousness is being redimensioned by technologies; however, the repetition of the body extended by technologies [...] bothers me intensely ... With a redimensioned consciousness, with the symbolic ecology of the individuals and society in general, the real body is still the one that makes me conscious of my being, the other and of the world. On the other hand, we are becoming more conscious of the complexity of the Web, of the *time arrow* (Ilya Prigogine), of the hypertextual complexity, of the multidirectionality of human thought, of the non-linearity of the real and of imagination, of the development of scientific thought, of the eco-system and of time. Thus I realise how

> inappropriate is the term 'post-biological era'. 'Post-biological' would imply, on the one hand, linearity, and on the other hand the overcoming of the biological. We propose, then, the era of foldings [...] and we confess our Deleuzean inspiration: in this era ecology folds upon chemistry, mathematics folds upon physics, philosophy upon psychoanalysis, and the arts upon technology. All of them become unstable, permeable, penetrable layers, capable of new interactions; layers of thought, sensations over individuals.

Moreover, the teleology implicit in the phrases 'post-biological' or 'post-human' implies a trend towards linear progression rather than a dynamic process immanent in the world and the self which is represented in corpos.org. Any word, image, or concept which implies 'progress' in the Enlightenment, positivist manner, and thus linearity, is abjured and challenged as far as is possible in the website. Thus, as the quotation above suggests, Corpos Informáticos attempt to transcend this debate altogether and do not inform their theory and practice by amalgams or syntheses between several domains. Rather, the group focuses instead on the co-operating and dynamic substrates underlying the spheres of the organic and the technological which give rise to the evolution of forms apparent in biological, social and cultural structures, and manifest also in corpos.org. Following the body of theory formulated by the physicist Ilya Prigogine (1984), Corpos frame their web-art around the distinction between systems, rather than domains: between closed systems, mechanistic and self-contained, which reduce nature – and the human – into a few quantifiable laws, and open systems, consisting of dissipative structures which are informed by a fundamental desequilibrium and instability in their nature and the internal reinforcement of fluctuations. Dissipative structures have several characteristics. Firstly, they are continually engaged in a fluctuating exchange of energy, matter, or information with their environment. Secondly, dissipative structures are non-linear: that is, the quantity and nature of energy, matter and information these systems transmit to and from other forms, and what these will create in the future, is unpredictable and indeterminate. Thirdly, open systems are dependent on feedback processes for their growth and dynamism: the folding and refolding of feedback in 'transition areas' magnifies small fluctuations and amplifies them into transformations that change the global complexity of the systems in ever-broadening orbits (Briggs 1992: 19–21). Thus the macroscopic world is constantly in a state of process (Porush 1992: 286); in a state of *becoming*. The principles informing open, dynamical systems, then, collapse the distinction between the living and the inanimate, the natural and artificial, and the organic and mechanical (Porush 1992: 294). Rather, what we have here is a system of co-evolution and dynamic exchange at all levels, the co-evolution of micro- and macro-cosmos (Jantsch 1980: 73) of which digital technology, communicative and information systems form but one component. In this context also 'life no longer appears as a thin superstructure over a lifeless physical reality, but as an inherent principle of the dynamics of the universe' (Jantsch 1980: 19).

The group extend this fundamental premise to culture, thought, and conceptualisation itself, based on the Deleuzian concept idea of 'folds' or 'dobradura' in Portuguese (Deleuze 1993). Ideas interact, they mix, they are tied together, they fragment and transform. Indeed, the group conclude by challenging common assumptions surrounding the idea of 'evolution' of life and society, if by 'evolution' we mean any process though which something – be it human, biological, or mechanical – passes by degrees to ever more advanced stages, 'going from the least to the most differentiated' (Deleuze and Guattari 1988: 1). In another area contained within corpos.org ('dobras'), we read:

> We understand the time continuity as 'volution': neither evolution nor involution but 'volution' as in the radical 'voluta' (1545; it). *Voluta*, the Latin word from *volutes, de volvere*, 'to roll in', time continuity, *volvimento* of the scientific, philosophic and artistic knowing. This process is achieved by the folding of layers [...]. These layers are permeable, allowing the merging between the primitive static fields of knowledge [...]. The scientific permeates the philosophic, the artistic interferes in the scientific and mathematics is mixed with ecology. Secretions of linguistics, music and computing contaminate sociology.

Reading corpos.org in the light of this conceptual structure reveals new insights and interpretations. As an open cybernetic structure in a state of process, the site draws in feedback from the continuous fluctuations of its immediate cultural environment, its constructors and contributors and, of course, the internaut's experience of his or her mind and language, and organises the site at the 'transition points' of the internaut's navigation, into dynamic configurations and folds.

The opening page of the site illustrates the fractal dimension engendered by dynamical open structures, or 'mension' which, according to Corpos, suggests the infinite and immeasurable, excluding any possibility of linearity or teleologies of whatever sort, and emphasising process and interaction. This holism, or 'symbolic ecology' as Corpos have it, within which all the different components feed into one another, generates images whose patterns show scaling detail. The pixelated form of the page, revealing the self-similar details of a human face in muted black and green tints – which also serve to emphasise the fundamental kinship of the human with the natural realm – contains what is potentially an infinite amount of image detail, and thus acts as a metaphor, or introduction to the site's structure as a dissipative system, which evolves and interacts continuously at every scale and at every dimension (Briggs 1992). This illustration of scaling is accompanied by another corresponding pattern of the dynamism of dissipative systems: self-similarity. That is, the shapes seen at one scale are similar to the shapes seen in the detail at another scale. The images thus invite the internaut to reflect on our reality as a place composed of folding worlds within self-similar worlds, of worlds folded between dimensions.

The principle of simultaneous, dynamic, and interacting co-evolution or 'volution' is illustrated in the 'dobras' section (see fig. 3.3). The opening page of the section is organised around a central panel drawing the reader into a brief account, quoted above, of the group's philosophy concerning the nature of knowledge and the nature of evolution. At either side of the central panel lie two parallel windows, representing Deleuze's 'outer façade of reception and the inner rooms of action [...] the extrinsic fabrication of material partitions, and the two poles, one toward which all principles are folding themselves together, the other toward which they are all unfolding in the opposite way' (Deleuze 1993: 35). The parallel windows portray assemblages of photographs and hyperlinked text, divided along horizontal axes, inviting the internaut to break into, decode, and recompose this ecology of different media, in a continuous process of involution-evolution. Thus the site is developed ever further by positive feedback from the viewer: pressing on the transition points of the discreet hyperlinks within the two parallel windows opens up successive windows within frames, to the point where the screen is crowded with a concatenation of frames. Lying concealed within these are comments, fragments of texts, citations contributed by different members of the group further emphasising that 'nothing is realised by one individual; above all it is a continual process which is always a result of a relation with the other' (Medeiros 2000). The proximity and crowding of the unfolding frames also serve to break up the normally homogeneous space of user interfaces, revealing a potential infinity of new dimensions and spaces within 'webmension' refracted against each other, and revealing to the viewer also the 'heterogeneous genesis' (Munster 2001) of both technological systems and cultural artefacts, triggered by feedback from the human viewer-participant. Clicking on the line 'Era of Folds' repeats the entire process in a separate window, and again for as long as the screen will support the frames, and potentially, as the site suggests, all the way to infinity. Thus to both construct and use the interface is not to transform, but simply to reveal that which has been suppressed under the sovereign concepts of Enlightenment dualisms and Cartesian schisms. The modes of composition used by Corpos, whether pixelation, looping flash, hypertext at revolving velocities, framing, and the construction of windows, as in 'dobras', serve to illustrate the utopian space of 'webmension' through which the boundaries between human subjects and their others, worlds, and spheres may dissolve, transform, and be transfigured again, within multilateral communication networks and the interfaces where the evolution of life, technogenesis, and human practice are revealed as one and the same.

References

Ascott, Roy (ed.) 2000. *Art, Technology, Conciousness: mind@large* (Portland, OR: Intellect).

Birringer, Johannes. 'RePerCute: reflexiones sobre performance, arte y tecnologia', *AlienNation Projects*, http://www.alienationcompany.com/projects/redial2.htm, last accessed 25 March 2006.

Boulter, Jay David and Richard Grusin 2001. *Remediation: Understanding the New Media* (Cambridge, MA: MIT Press).

Briggs, John 1992. *Fractals: The Patterns of Chaos: Discovering a New Aesthetic of Science, Art and Nature* (London: Thames & Hudson).

Corpos Informáticos. http://www.corpos.org, last accessed 17 June 2007.

Deleuze, Gilles 1993. *The Fold: Leibniz and the Baroque*, trans. Tom Conley (Minneapolis, MN: University of Minnesota Press).

—, and Félix Guattari 1988. *A Thousand Plateaus: Capitalism and Schizophrenia*, trans. by Brian Massumi (London: Athlone).

Dyens, Oliver 2000. 'Cyberpunk, Technoculture and the Post-Biological Self', *CLCWeb: Comparative Literature and Culture: A WWWeb Journal,* http://clcweb-jouranl.lib.purdue.edu/clcweb00–1/dyens00.html, last accessed 30 March 2006.

Gianetti, Claudia 2002. 'Digital Aethetics: Introduction', *Media Net Art,* http://www.medienkunstnetz.de/themes/aesthetics_of_the_digital/editorial/1/, last accessed 30 August 2007.

Hables Gray, Chris 1998. 'Cyborgs, Attention and Aesthetics', *Cyborg Citizen.* September, http://www.routledge_ny.com/ref/cyborgcitizen/cycitpgs/kunst.html, last accessed 30 March 2006.

Hansen, Mark 2004. *New Philosophy for New Media* (Cambridge, MA: MIT Press).

Haraway, Donna J. 1991. *Simians, Cyborgs, and Women: The Reinvention of Nature* (London: Free Association Books).

—— 1997. *Modest_Witness@Second_Millennium.FemaleMan©_Meets_OncoMouse?: Feminism and Technoscience* (New York and London: Routledge).

Hayles, N. Katherine 1999. *How We Became Posthuman: Virtual Bodies in Cybernetics, Literature and Informatics* (Chicago, IL: University of Chicago Press).

Hinchberger, Bill 2004. 'São Paulo Biennal of Art: A Short History of the Bienal International de São Paulo', *Brazilmax.com.* http://www.brazilmax.com/news3.cfm/tborigem/pl_southcentral/id/lb, last accessed 4 March 2006.

Jantsch, Erich 1980. *The Self-Organising Universe: Scientific and Human Implications of the Emerging Paradigm of Evolution* (Oxford: Pergamon).

Mackenzie, Adrian 2002. *Transductions: Bodies and Machines at Speed* (London: Continuum).

Medeiros, Maria Beatriz de 2000. 'Actualizations of the Human Being: Reflections Concerning Some Contemporary Artistic Languages from the Practices of the Research Group Corpos Informáticos', http://www.corpos.org/papers/performativesites.html, last accessed 17 June 2007.

—— 2003. 'Performance Art and Digital Bodies (Corpos Informáticos)', *Body, Space and Technology Journal,* 3:2, http://people.brunel.ac.uk/bst/vol0302/mariabeatriz.html, last accessed 17 June 2007.

——. 'Tenuous Border of the Performance Artistic Language, Its Possibilities within Technological Means', http://www.corpos.org/papers/performancestudies.html, last accessed 17 June 2007.

Mitcham, Carl, and Timothy Casey 2002. 'Toward an Archaeology of the Philosophy of Technology and Relations with Imaginative Literature', in Mark L. Greenberg and Lance Schachterle, eds., *Literature and Technology* (London and Toronto: Associated University Press), pp. 31–65.

Munster, Anna 2001. 'Digitality: Approximate Aesthetics', *CTheory.net,* http://www.ctheory.net/articles.aspx?id=290, last accessed 17 June 2007.

Pickover, Thomas 1999. *Surfing through Hyperspace* (Oxford: Oxford University Press).

Porush, David 1992. 'Literature as Dissipative Structure: Prigogine's Theory and the Postmodern "Chaos" Machine', in Mark L. Greenberg and Lance

Schachterle, eds., *Literature and Technology* (London and Toronto: Associated University Press), pp. 275–306.
Prigogine, Ilya, and Isabelle Stengers 1984. *Order out of Chaos: Man's New Dialogue with Nature* (New York: Bantam).
Rabinowitz, Lauren, and Abraham Geil, eds. 2004. *Memory Bytes: History, Technology and Digital Culture* (Durham, NC: Duke University Press).
Radcliff, Carter 2004. 'Foreword' to Margot Lovejoy, *Digital Currents: Art in the Electronic Age* (London: Routledge), pp. xii–xiv.

4

Latin American Cyberprotest: Before and After the Zapatistas

Thea Pitman

Despite the very real concerns about the politics of connectivity in Latin America (outlined in the introduction to this volume), in this chapter I intend to challenge such pessimistic visions, arguing that, by hook or by crook, grassroots and activist organisations in the region have contrived to make strategic use of the Internet – and earlier, more localised networks – for pro-democratic networking and consciousness-raising activities, as well as some hactivism proper, since the late 1980s. In so doing, I thus hope to counter the prevailing misconception that only the educated and wealthy elites of such countries have access to the Internet, as well as the misconception that corporate interests preclude democratic uses of the new medium. Ultimately, I will argue that this kind of Internet-based activism is Latin America's most important contribution to global cyberculture, and, although far from being the only, the first, or even the most innovative activist group in the region, it was the Ejército Zapatista de Liberación Nacional (EZLN) [Zapatista National Liberation Army] of Southern Mexico – or the Zapatistas as they are more informally known – who turned themselves into a household name through such means, to the extent that Zapatismo and Internet-based activism have come to be seen as practically synonymous.

i. Social Netwar, Cyberprotest and Other Neologisms

Before embarking on a critique of the Zapatistas' contribution to Internet-based activism, it is worth exploring the plethora of often overlapping and confusing neologisms that have sprung up to define the conjunction of the Internet with a range of activities from the non-violent expression of alternative political ideas, to civil disobedience, and to out-and-out terrorism.

Some of the first terms to be coined in the field were David Ronfeldt and John Arquilla's 'cyberwar' which was used from as early as 1993, thus predating the Zapatista Uprising of 1994, and 'social netwar' which they have used in publications from 1996 onwards, almost exclusively in conjunction with analyses of the Zapatistas' strategies (see Ronfeldt *et al.* 1998).[1] Ronfeldt and Arquilla (and their colleagues) define 'cyberwar' as a 'concept that refers to information-oriented military warfare' (Ronfeldt *et al.* 1998: 8), the best example of which is perhaps the conduct of the war in Kosovo in 1999, where both sides used the Internet for the purposes of spreading propaganda and disinformation, as well as to hack into each other's computer systems (Denning 1999). Although these analysts wish to dispel the misconception that 'cyberwar' is characterised only by this kind of 'strategic information warfare' (Ronfeldt *et al.* 1998: 8), the potential for large-scale hacking activity is what has captured the imagination of the general public, and a whole host of more memorable related terms have been coined. When not occurring in the context of declared situations of war between recognised states, 'strategic information warfare' may also be referred to as 'hactivism' – large-scale computer hacking generally harnessed to the cause of non-violent activist groups – or even 'cyberterrorism', when used by those defined as terrorists, although arguably, depending on one's politics, there is a fine line to be drawn between many of these terms.[2]

1 Ronfeldt and Arquilla did, in fact, coin the term 'netwar' in advance of the Zapatista Uprising in their seminal article, 'Cyberwar Is Coming!' (Arquilla and Ronfeldt 1993). However, the term 'social netwar' is particular to their analysis of the Zapatistas.

2 It should be noted that terrorist uses of the Internet are not only confined to 'cyberterrorism' which, while it has captivated the public imagination, according to Weimann has yet to manifest itself in any significant way. Typically, terrorist groups use the Internet for 'communicative' purposes – to inform the world of their cause – and, importantly, for 'instrumental' purposes, as a means of fund-raising, recruiting, and organising themselves in order to conduct terrorist acts in the real world (Weimann 2006). This communicative and instrumental use of the web is clear in the sites belonging to the FARC (Fuerzas Armadas Revolucionarias de Colombia) [Revolutionary Armed Forces of Colombia],

On the other hand, 'netwar' is defined as 'an emerging mode of conflict (and crime) at societal levels, involving measures short of traditional war, in which the protagonists use network forms of organization and related doctrines, strategies, and technologies attuned to the information age', and it may be conducted by criminals, terrorists, or members of civil society, hence the coining of the more specific term, 'social netwar', to define the latter (Ronfeldt *et al.* 1998: 9). With respect to 'netwar''s use of high technology, the authors also stipulate that 'the new technologies, however enabling for organizational networking, may not be the only crucial technologies for a netwar actor. Old technologies, like human couriers, and mixes of old and new systems may, in some situations, do the job' (Ronfeldt *et al.* 1998: 11). In short, social 'netwar is not simply a function of "the Net"' (Ronfeldt *et al.* 1998: 11), but a new form of social protest developed by groups working in non-hierarchical networks that inevitably finds the Internet a useful tool, both for communicative and instrumental (organisational) purposes.

Nevertheless, there are clearly aspects of 'social netwar' which are particular to cyberspace. These aspects, including mild forms of 'hactivism' – ones which do not endanger human lives or exploit individual citizens –, can also fall under the umbrella terms of 'Internet activism' or 'cyberprotest', which, as the names suggest, use the Internet to conduct lobbying activities and acts of civil disobedience, as well as the expected communicative and intra-group instrumental uses. Such acts of hactivist civil disobedience may include 'virtual sit-ins' of websites, email-bombing campaigns, the spreading of viruses and worms, the graffitiing or parasitical usurping of websites belonging to others and many other disruptive, but creative, uses of new technology which some practitioners consider to be a form of conceptual Net-art (Domínguez c.1998).[3]

Although Ronfeldt and Arquilla are military strategists and US government advisors whose main interest in the subject of 'social netwar' is how best to curb such activities, the term in itself is useful and has been taken up by many, often more sympathetic, analysts

which Weimann defines as 'an impressive example of media-savvy Internet use by a terrorist group' (Weimann 2006: 75).

[3] For more information on the varieties of hactivism and cyberprotest see Denning 1999, Van de Donk *et al.* 2004.

of the Zapatistas and other contemporary social protest movements. Nevertheless, as we shall see below, these terms have become distorted and confused with overuse.[4]

ii. The Zapatistas and Social Netwar

Any search for information on the conjunction of Latin America and the Internet almost exclusively brings up material related to the Zapatistas. Nevertheless, the conception that the Zapatistas' use of the Internet to fight their battles is innovative *per se* and the exact nature of their 'netwar', social or otherwise, are both areas that have too often been taken for granted, assumed or even wilfully mythologised. It is my contention that these issues need further probing.

Without rehearsing all the details of the Zapatista Uprising of 1 January 1994, suffice it to say that the group very swiftly moved from violent protest which left around 150 people dead in the first few days and tens of thousands of people displaced (Bob 2005: 125), to 'social netwar' in the fullest sense of Ronfeldt and Arquilla's definition of the term. Although, as we have seen, 'social netwar' is not only about the use of Internet to achieve social change, very early on in the conflict and subsequent negotiations, popular opinion confused Ronfeldt and Arquilla's terminology such that 'cyberwar' and 'netwar' became synonymous and both came to mean exclusively 'war conducted on the Internet'.[5] Popular opinion has furthermore presumed that this kind of activity comprises the bulk of what the Zapatistas do and that the Zapatistas are directly responsible for all of this Internet activism.

These misconceptions were fostered by numerous sensationalist and sometimes confused journalistic reports on 'cyberwar', 'netwar', or '"high-tech" guerrilla warfare' and often indulging in the myth of Subcomandante Marcos and his laptop with wi-fi access in the Lacandón Jungle.[6] Furthermore, even senior Mexican government

4 See Hables Gray 1997 for an informed critique of these terms.

5 For a slightly confused use of the term in a Spanish context see De Ugarte (2004). Despite having read Ronfeldt and Arquilla, De Ugarte uses 'netwar' to refer both to terrorist networking/cyberterrorism and to encourage people to resist such activities via 'social netwar'.

6 See those mentioned by Iturriaga 1996, Vegh 2002 and Cleaver 1998: 88. The myth is even repeated in academic studies such as Weimann (2006: 211).

officials have contributed to the hype regarding the Zapatista's Internet-based war: in 1995 José Ángel Gurria, then Mexican Secretary of State, defined the Uprising as a 'war of ink, of the written word and a war of the Internet' (quoted in Cleaver 1998: 93). And finally, internationally acclaimed scholars such Manuel Castells have lent their weight to the easy conflation of Zapatismo and the Internet: in the context of a very brief analysis of the Zapatistas' use of the Internet he pronounced that, 'The success of the *Zapatistas* was largely due to their communication strategy, to the point that they can be called the *first informational guerrilla movement*' (Castells 1997: 79). Harry Cleaver has similarly left the impression, largely by dint of his numerous publications on the subject, that the 'electronic fabric of struggle' is one of the defining features of the insurgency and that this is key to the Zapatistas' phenomenal success in gaining the attention of the world media and thus in furthering their cause (see, for example, Cleaver 1994, 1996–2003, 1998).

Nevertheless, a close reading of Castells' and Cleaver's work, together with other more recent appreciations of the Zapatistas' achievements such as that by Clifford Bob (2005), reveals several facts that have too often been overlooked: (1) that the Zapatistas did not really start the 'war of the Internet' themselves, even though they have since capitalised on it; (2) that there are other reasons than web-presence that have accounted for the massive popularity of the Zapatistas, particularly on an international level; (3) that the Zapatistas have not only fought their 'social netwar' online; (4) that, in terms of its innovative nature, 'the war of the Internet' was, in the early stages at least, rather more about the traditional dissemination of (dis-)information and about networking via electronic means rather than about Internet-specific forms of activism; and (5) that other activist groups in Latin America, even some armed ones, had already set a precedent for Internet activism.

In the first case, 'the electronic fabric of struggle' that Cleaver mentions is by and large orchestrated by individuals and groups with pro-Zapatista sympathies rather than by the Zapatistas themselves. Cleaver outlines in some considerable detail how, at the time of the initial Uprising, interested parties gleaned basic information from the Mexican press and then proceeded to transfer that material to sympathetic listservs, newsgroups, and websites, and that it was the subsequent activities of these sympathetic Netizens that carried the

Zapatista message around the world, orchestrated mass demonstrations, sent international observers to the region and so on (Cleaver 1998: 82–88). Elsewhere he specifically cites the development of anti-NAFTA and anti-neoliberalisation networks on Peacenet, Usenet, and on the Internet itself as a key to the rapidity, 'political responsiveness and militancy' of the online response to the Zapatista Uprising (Cleaver 1994). Castells also makes specific mention of the pro-Zapatista sympathisers' use of Laneta, Mexico's alternative computer communications network, to disseminate information (Castells 1997: 80). And as noted by Clifford Bob in his study of 'the marketing of rebellion' (Bob 2005: 137–38):

> The Zapatistas did not have their own Web site until 2001, only establishing one for the March for Indigenous Dignity. Especially in the early days of the revolt, their communiqués made their way onto the Internet sluggishly, most after hand delivery to and initial publication in *La Jornada*. Thus, as an initial matter, the electronic aspects of the Zapatistas' 'netwar' were a consequence, not a cause, of their gaining critical support from technologically adept third parties.

Even Subcomandante Marcos, the Zapatistas' spokesperson, has emphasised the consequential nature of the Zapatistas' use of the Internet in the first instance: in interview with Yvon Le Bot, when questioned about José Ángel Gurria's definition of their 'war', he commented that '*People* put us on the Internet and thus Zapatismo came to occupy a space that no-one suspected it would', although he also conceded the efficacy of the Internet in furthering their cause (Le Bot 1997: 349, my italics).[7]

However, because of the efficacy of the Internet in keeping them in the media spotlight, in the years since the 1994 Uprising, the Zapatistas have moved to embrace the general public's conception of them as high-tech guerrillas with laptops. For example, they actively condoned the use of the words 'ezln.org' in the URL of the *¡Ya Basta!* [Enough's Enough!] website, thus leading the general public to believe they had an official website well before they actually did – the site was set up by a US university systems administrator as early as spring 1994

7 All translations are my own unless otherwise stated.

(Bob 2005: 133).[8] Since 2001 they have had a *very nearly* official web-presence through the website of the Centro de Información Zapatista [Zapatista Information Centre]. The centre is physically based in San Cristóbal although not run by the EZLN itself, and the website was set up in order to support the Marcha por la Dignidad Indígena [March for Indigenous Dignity] from Chiapas to Mexico City in early 2001. It is the only website where Marcos has had any kind of interactive web-presence, providing responses to certain frequently asked questions (Olesen 2005: 65).

Since December 2005, as a means of supporting the forthcoming 2006 La Otra Campaña [The Other Campaign] tour of Mexico which was designed to suggest an alternative to the then competing presidential campaigns, the EZLN has maintained its own official website – *Ejército Zapatista de Liberación Nacional* –, taking over the original 'ezln.org' URL from *¡Ya Basta!*, which has now ceased to exist, and adding 'mx' at the end (see Morello 2007: 64–65). This site is split into two main branches: *Zezta Internacionale* [Sixth International] deals with international aspects of the EZLN's campaigns and *Enlace Zapatista* [Zapatista Link] with national aspects. Both are sophisticated and slick, offering a complete multimedia experience, and taking advantage of the full potential of the web for communicative, instrumental, and dialogic purposes (see fig. 4.1 for *Enlace Zapatista*'s homepage).

In his communiqués on the subject of the Centro de Información Zapatista, and later on the creation of the new official Zapatista website (cited by Olesen 2005: 65 and Morello 2007: 64–65, respectively), Marcos is quite emphatic that these are the correct channels through which the public should contact the leadership of the EZLN. The Internet has thus come to be absolutely central to the EZLN's mode of organisation both internationally and within Mexico itself. Nevertheless, the EZLN continues to endorse other semi-official and support sites such as *La Otra Información*, which is housed on border-hactivist Fran Ilich's *Possible Worlds* server and, like the official EZLN site, was also set up in 2005–2006 to support La Otra Campaña with some hint of official EZLN support (Ilich 2006). What one should retain from this is that it is precisely this proliferation of overlapping

8 This resource is no longer available and the URL now redirects Netusers to the Zapatistas' official website.

official, semi-official, and support sites which constitutes the effective use of the Internet made and/or provoked by the EZLN.[9]

The second misconception about the Zapatistas' use of the Internet is that this is the primary reason for their popularity. Backing up his claims that 'the electronic aspects of the Zapatistas' "netwar" were a consequence, not a cause, of their gaining critical support from technologically adept third parties' (Bob 2005: 137–38), Bob explores the impact of other factors than the Zapatistas' media-savvy manipulation of the Internet as a tool to keep them in the international media's spotlight. According to Bob, significant factors affecting the resonance and popularity of the Zapatistas, both at home and abroad, include the 'spectacular' and very well staged performance events of the January 1994 Uprising itself, despite the actual bloodshed.[10] Both timing and location were chosen well. San Cristóbal is a tourist destination on the international circuit for those interested in indigenous cultures, thus an international audience of the right political pedigree was guaranteed, as was easy access for journalists. The 1 January 1994 was not only a holiday but also the day that the North American Free Trade Agreement (NAFTA), a major event in the neoliberal agenda, came into force (see also Cleaver 1994). Thus the Uprising tapped into the broad international currents of anti-neoliberal, anti-globalisation sentiment, as well as speaking to those concerned specifically with the question of indigenous/human rights. Furthermore, Subcomandante Marcos, the soft-spoken, unassuming intellectual in a balaclava who smoked a pipe, read García Márquez, and wrote fables and short stories alongside communiqués quickly became something of a sex symbol, reviving the aura of past *guerrilleros à la* Che Guevara, even if the movement was also considered by many to be the first post-communist uprising (see, for example, Fuentes 1994). And finally, according to Bob, the Zapatistas' success in gaining international media attention was due to their willingness to modify their aims to suit the international 'mood': they laid down arms and pursued – non-violently – the indigenous rights and anti-neoliberalism causes favoured by the international community (Bob 2005: 139–61). In all

9 I would like to thank Paul Fallon, Paul Chatterton, and Edgar at *La Otra Información* for their help with identifying the official status of some these sites.

10 Marcos himself referred to the Uprising as 'spectacular' (quoted in Bob 2005: 128).

the reasons advanced above, the only role that the Internet played was secondary – once the audience was created, the Internet was used to supply the text and images required to propagate the image and the ethos.

The third misconception presumes that the Zapatistas have used the new medium to the exclusion of all other forms of communication to attract attention to their cause. However, according to Bob, they have exploited profitably any means of communication they could including print media; face-to-face contacts via invitations to the Selva, a phenomenon that came to be known as 'Zapaturismo' [Zapatourism]; and radio to access indigenous communities elsewhere in Mexico (Bob 2005: 133–37). Cleaver also notes their willingness to use other media (Cleaver 1998: 99, n.3). Furthermore, it should, of course, be noted that the people with whom the EZLN most immediately needs to network in order to continue to exist as a social movement are its own adherents among the indigenous communities of Chiapas, and these are the people least likely to have access to the technology necessary to access the Internet. Certainly the Internet can significantly help groups who are censored by their governments and denied a traditional public forum, such as the press, to have their say, but the EZLN was not strictly speaking in this position – their communiqués were published in Mexican newspapers and their lack of coverage on certain television channels was their own decision (Bob 2005: 137). Thus the Internet is only one communication tool among many used by the Zapatistas, and its maximum function is perhaps to facilitate networked support activities among the wider national and, particularly, international communities.

Fourthly, the concept that the Zapatistas did something inherently innovative in their use of the Internet – an 'impression' largely created by Harry Cleaver – is widespread. Even Marcos has had to dispel it: in interview with Yvon Le Bot, after conceding that the Internet had been of substantial use in strategic terms, he went on to say that: 'The novelty of the EZLN is not in the fact that they have used satellite communications such that people claim today that the Zapatistas are more cybernauts than real guerrillas. It's actually in the resemanticisation of political discourse which, paradoxically, looks to the past for inspiration' (Le Bot 1997: 349). The concept continues to circulate today, resurfacing most recently, even if carefully framed, in Steve Wright's work on information and communication technologies (ICTs) and anti-capitalist movements (Wright 2004) and Chris Atton's *An Alternative Internet* (2004). Both Wright and Atton are at pains to define the exact relationship of activist groups to new media technologies and cite the myth of the Zapatistas' innovative use of the new medium in order to revise it. Atton, for example, starts by noting that, 'the most widely cited example of radical Internet use by new social movements is that employed by *the Zapatistas*' (Atton 2004: 29, my italics). Yet Wright quickly notes that 'Cleaver [...] has written eloquently of the "electronic fabric of struggle" woven around the Zapatistas, while himself playing a pivotal role in establishing and maintaining that fabric' (Wright 2004: 81). Indeed, Cleaver orchestrated the *Chiapas95* mailing list and made the archives available online from the Autumn of 1994 (Bob 2005: 132; see also *Chiapas95*). He was also a key player in the *Acción Zapatista* [Zapatista Action] group and associated website (Bob 2005: 132; see also *Acción Zapatista*).

But even if one were to acknowledge that the bulk of 'Zapatista' Internet use is by pro-Zapatista sympathisers such as Cleaver and others, what do they do that is innovative in their use of the Internet? A close reading of Cleaver (especially Cleaver 1998) reveals that the vast majority of cyberspace dedicated to Zapatista affairs, at least in the period immediately following the Uprising itself, was simply given over to text and images – materials that were transferred straight from other media such as the press and then made massively available online via listservs by dedicated supporters such as Cleaver. Arguably, the use of the Internet, even for purely communicative purposes such as these, was innovative to some extent because of its speed and scale alone (see Halleck 1994: 32), and because of its ability to circumvent censorship and to offer views from across the political spectrum side by side, thus encouraging readers to make up their own minds about events.

Wright, quoting Mario Diani, also observes that the use of ICTs in activist organisations is often of an instrumental order, in order to 'reinforce face-to-face acquaintances and exchanges' (Wright 2004: 82). Indeed, this tacking back and forth between the real and the virtual is seen by many activists as essential if the advent of ICTs is not to be detrimental to the concept of activism *per se* (see, for example, Escobar 1999: 46). And indeed, very quickly following the basic communicative Zapatista web-presence mentioned above, instrumental use of the Internet for organisational purposes became apparent. Both the *¡Ya basta!* and *Acción Zapatista* sites include(d) 'How you can help' or similar sections which recruit(ed) supporters for traditional activist activities as well as a few Internet-based ones such as website maintenance (for a good overview of these sites in their heyday see Iturriaga 1996 and Cleaver 1996–2003).

Thus, with the exception of the call for website maintenance, both communicative and instrumental uses of the Internet constitute simply the transference of traditional activism to the new medium. But what, if anything, does the pro-Zapatista web-presence do that pre-Internet-age forms of social networking and activism could not? Even if one concedes that the Zapatistas' 'social netwar' in terms of the spread of information was successful in spontaneously attracting people of all walks of life to defend them and in so doing, strengthening the role of civil society in Mexico, is there anything specifically related to the new opportunities afforded by cyberspace in their online presence?

Internet activism proper is perhaps most evident in the Zapatistas' increasingly marked exploitation of the dialogic potential – the interactivity – of the Internet. Atton claims that the really innovative aspect of the Zapatistas' use of the Internet and the reason they have inspired other movements across the globe 'not only to act in solidarity with each other, but to act together, publishing and protesting as networked "affinity groups"' is because of their dialogic approach to the medium and to activism in general. He goes on to define this as 'an anarchist model of organising' (Atton 2004: 30). Deedee Halleck backs this up with her hands-on observation that (Halleck 1994: 32):

> A vital part of any revolutionary movement is the degree of hope that is mobilized. Perhaps the most effective outcome of Chiapas on-line has been the boosting of psychological morale of Latin American activists, anti-GATT cadre and human rights workers. [...] [During the early days of the Uprising] there was a sense of direct connection, of an authentic 'interactive' movement, as groups and individuals forwarded messages, excerpted passages, pinned up tear sheets and posted their own comments on-line.

However, since January 1998, there is also evidence of hactivism associated with the pro-Zapatista movement: sympathetic groups such as the Electronic Disturbance Theatre have conducted high-profile 'virtual sit-ins' of the websites of Mexican banks, the Mexican stock exchange, and the Mexican president's office, in support of the Zapatistas (Domínguez c.1998; Denning 1999; Atton 2004: 20–21). Such activities, now aided by the advent of 'FloodNet' software, seek to deny other users access to a particular website by 'deluging' it with hits, thus limiting the ability of that website to conduct its business. It is this kind of activity that one of the co-founders of the Electronic Disturbance Theatre, Ricardo Domínguez, refers to as 'digital zapatismo' (Domínguez c.1998). The measure of the impact of such activities is indicated by the fact that some commentators even trace the advent of hactivism specifically to the Zapatista Uprising (Wolf 2000). Furthermore, the term 'digital zapatismo' has also been used to describe acts of electronic civil disobedience 'in the spirit of Chiapas' rather than those for specifically pro-EZLN activism (Domínguez c.1998; Weimann 2006: 211), thus indicating, once again, the blurring in the popular imagination of Zapatismo with the field of Internet activism.

In all of the above it is apparent that a real 'social netwar' of networked groups of civilians putting pressure on state institutions for social change did spring up around the Zapatistas, and its achievements have been really quite considerable. However, one should be careful to note that this 'social netwar' was not achieved through electronic means alone and that any reference to the 'Zapatista social netwar', as in the title of the book by Ronfeldt *et al.*, needs to be nuanced to encompass the understanding that it was a 'social netwar' orchestrated by Zapatista sympathisers and not just members of the EZLN itself, even if the Zapatistas actively endorsed and encouraged such efforts.

iii. Before the Zapatistas

Based on a generous interpretation of all the above, one might, nevertheless, presume that Zapatista sympathisers were instrumental in introducing specifically Latin American new social movements to the technology of the Internet. To their credit they certainly have put Latin America on the map for innovative social protest movements – according to Denning, 'the Zapatistas were chosen by Wired as one of the twenty-five most important people [sic] on-line in 1998' (Denning 1999). Furthermore, they certainly have promoted 'social netwar' both on- and off-line to a degree not previously seen in the region or indeed beyond, but they really are just the most familiar name in the field. They did not start alternative/activist networking in the region, not even on a global scale, and nor were they the first activist group to use the Internet in the region. Indeed, Laneta, as we have seen, was already there to support their electronic networking needs.

In 'The Electronic Fabric of Struggle', Cleaver referred briefly to an article by Sheldon Annis, which, as early as 1991, made substantial claims for the role that the Internet was playing among Latin American NGOs and grassroots organisations. For Cleaver this was simply proof of policymakers' on-going interest in NGOs' use of new technology rather than a source of information on pre-Zapatista uses of the Internet itself.[11] But the article itself merits further attention. In Autumn 1991, two and a half years prior to the Zapatista Uprising and at a point in time when most analyses of Internet usage in Latin America suggest it was still extremely minimal (the boom coming in the mid-1990s – see introduction to this study), Annis argued that (Annis 1991: 93):

> A wave of empowerment is sweeping Latin America. Its poor are increasingly bound into new, complex networks of civic organizations – and more recently into social movements that transcend political boundaries and traditional class lines. While poverty once implied physical and cultural isolation, the poor today – while more numerous and poorer than ever before – are connecting with each other and with the outside world.
>
> Driving this evolving 'connectedness' is an information revolution. An explosion of electronic information is penetrating poverty, giving it a new social character and forcing us to reassess what 'poverty' actually implies.

Although looking at a range of new technologies rather than just the Internet, Annis goes on to assert that, even if individual 'poor people' from across Latin America do not have PCs, modems, ISPs, and the

11 Cleaver was even somewhat unfair in his definition of Annis as one of the policymakers – Annis is an academic and research associate at the Overseas Development Council, thus writing for policymakers but not strictly speaking a policymaker himself.

like, the decreasing cost of hardware, the increasing transportability of the same, and an increase in the user-friendliness of software which mitigates the need for specialised computer literacy, although not for literacy *per se*, have meant that organisations that represent the poor across the continent do now have access to computers and to the Internet and are using this facility to striking effect (Annis 1991: 98). Indeed, demand for the use of email and other Internet services has actually been a South–North phenomenon, whereby southern NGOs have put pressure on ones in the North to start to use the new technologies, given the unreliable postal service and high cost of long-distance telephone calls in the South (Burch 1999: 200; Bissio, in APC 2000: 25)

Annis notes that Brazil was the most 'connected' nation in Latin America in 1991 and outlines the resultant connectivity for NGOs and grassroots organisations via the Brazil-based alternative network AlterNex which originally linked with the US-based network PeaceNet. Thus news of the murder of the Brazilian rubber-tapper Chico Mendes was circulated electronically 'within minutes' of its happening. This, in turn, influenced traditional media reporting as well as inspired protests among members of civil society across the world in a way which clearly pre-empts the media and civil-society responses to the Zapatista Uprising (Annis 1991: 99).

Another phenomenon not mentioned by Annis, but of perhaps more bearing on the Zapatista case, was the burgeoning Pan-Mayan activist network in Mexico and Central America which stemmed from the First Continental Encounter of Indigenous Peoples held in Ecuador in 1990. Evidence suggests that these (pro-)Mayan activists were already using the Internet prior to 1994: indeed, O'Donnell and Delgado document the phenomenon of 'Mayan hackers' in Guatemala in the early 1990s (O'Donnell and Delgado 1995: 38).[12]

To return to Annis' survey of the benefits of the Internet for the poor of Latin America, he specifically emphasises his view that 'the most important change is that the poor are increasingly able to

12 One might also mention the 'prolific endeavours of Central American organizations, in the late 1980s and early 1990s, to reach out to peace and solidarity groups in the US' (Burch 1999: 201). See Ronfeldt *et al.* on the 'social netwar', including electronic aspects, associated with CISPES – the Committee in Solidarity with the People of El Salvador (1998: 39–40). See also Gómez 2000.

manipulate the media, instead of just receiving messages' and he notes the key role played by the new 'conferencing' facilities provided by the Internet in allowing Latin Americans to respond to the media and/or to link up with each other to help fight their battles (Annis 1991: 95–99). Other analysts of the rise of Internet activism in Latin America such as Sally Burch concur with Annis on this (see Burch 1999). Burch cites the conferencing work that was being conducted in the run-up to the Fourth United Nations World Conference on Women held in Beijing in 1995 and which benefited from the participation of many Latin American delegates; Annis, that which paved the way for the United Nations Conference on Environment and Development – the 'Earth Summit' – held in Rio de Janeiro in June 1992, one of the largest such events ever held.

Indeed, 'the Earth Summit' counts as something of a watershed in the conjunction of activism and ICTs both within Latin America and worldwide, and has attracted critical attention specifically for this aspect of the event. Shelley Preston, for example, underscores the fact that such key international conferences held since the beginning of the 1990s have almost always explicitly focused on how they intend to use the Internet to support the event itself, as well as on how the Internet might be harnessed for the benefit of the less 'connected' and 'informed' members of global society (Preston 1994). The same is true of the Beijing Women's conference. In the case of both conferences the information dissemination and networking activities were managed by the Association for Progressive Communications (APC), a network organisation with associated member groups worldwide and particularly strong connections in Latin America which petitions for better access to communications technology.

Although the APC evolved in the mid-1980s, it was officially founded in 1990 by the US-based Institute for Global Communications (previously PeaceNet and EcoNet) and the UK-based GreenNet, together with five other networks including two from Latin America (Brazil's AlterNex and Nicaragua's Nicarao/CRIES) (APC 2000: passim; Rheingold 1993: 266). These original members were shortly joined by other networks including ones in Uruguay, Ecuador, and Mexico (Laneta).[13] Its mission

[13] The strength of the APC's Latin American links should not be underestimated: 'early APC visionaries' include the Brazilian Carlos Afonso, one of the original founders of the APC, and the Uruguayan Roberto Bissio, 'APC's voice in United

is expressly to 'empower and support organizations, social movements and individuals in and through the use of information and communication technologies' in order to promote democracy, human rights and related issues (APC 2000: front cover), and its work has moved in the period 1990–2000 from 'primarily facilitating technical interconnection' to the use of ICTs to promote 'justice and development' (APC 2000: 4). Given its remit and its scope the APC really deserves far more attention than the EZLN for its achievements in the field of Internet activism. Its use of the Internet is much more central to its activities and conceptually innovative than the Zapatistas' use of the same: the APC's focus is on activism which is directed at campaigning for better Internet access and activism which simultaneously uses the Internet to achieve its objectives.

The 1992 'Earth Summit' was the APC's first big challenge. Its members negotiated for several years in advance of the summit in order to situate the Association as the providers of a communications network for the conference, posting information about the various forums in online conferences and news bulletins on behalf of the UN, who at that time had no means of its own of distributing electronic information widely. And through its unique position of being able to offer the only international, civil society communications network at that point in time, the APC was able to enhance significantly the access of NGOs to the activities of the summit, both on the ground and via its online postings.

The APC continued this work in the run-up to the 1995 Beijing conference, and it continues this work today, participating most recently – with a 'noisy' Latin American contingent – at the 2006 Athens Forum on Internet Governance (APC 2006). It also promotes the creation of web content to represent traditionally marginalised sectors of Latin American communities and offers prizes for those making efforts to make free and open-source software accessible to all. Proof of its phenomenal success and scope is that the APC.org site ranks currently among the top 15,500 sites globally in terms of traffic – only one .org site in the world ranks higher (APC 2006).

Of course, the increasing importance of such 'infrastructure-building NGOs' and network organisations, including the APC and its

Nations processes in the early days' and today an advisor for the Association (APC 2000: 15).

contribution to the 'Earth Summit', did not go unnoticed by Ronfeldt and Arquilla in their survey of the social conditions and networks which paved the way for the Zapatistas, albeit indirectly (Ronfeldt *et al.* 1998: 36–39). Such developments were key to facilitating access to cyberspace for NGOs working in the region at the time of the 1994 Uprising and key to the instant retransmission of the Zapatista message round the globe in the hours after the Uprising to a sympathetic networked audience.[14]

iv. After the Zapatistas: New Social Netwars?

But even if the Zapatistas and their sympathisers were not the first in Latin America to exploit the Internet for activist purposes, one might still suppose that they have been massively influential in their use of such tools, and that even pre-existing organisations such as the APC might recognise the 1994 Uprising as a landmark in the field of Latin American Internet activism. Nevertheless, in their account of their development and influences, the APC make no mention of the Zapatista Uprising or ensuing social netwar (see, for example, APC 2000). Another commentator from an APC-affiliated network simply mentions the Zapatistas in passing, as a 'more recent' example of such activities (Burch 1999: 201), thus implicitly denying any sense that the Zapatistas and sympathisers have done anything that other groups were not already doing before them, or at least simultaneously with them, and also that their successes in the field have had any impact on the Internet usage/tactics employed by other activist organisations.

Such important groups as the APC and affiliated networks constitute a rather impervious before and after of the Zapatistas in terms of Latin American Internet activism. Arguably, it is groups such as these that have fought battles – albeit of an infrastructural and hence less 'sexy' nature for the world's media – that will have positive effects on the lives of more people across the region than the Zapatistas. And it is groups such as these whose tactics with respect to the Internet most clearly display the traits of a 'double type of activism' that anthropologist Arturo Escobar sees as the most characteristic of the developing world's creation of resistant cybercultural actors: activism which displays an

14 Other commentators who have also noted the importance of the role played by the APC in Latin America include Belejack (1997) and Gómez (2000).

awareness of the nature and the governance of the Internet itself, in tandem with activism associated with more traditional 'real' issues such as women's rights or environmental concerns (Escobar 1999: 33–34). And, indeed, such groups' particular 'meta'-focus on questions of access to and use of information technology for traditionally marginalised sectors of society, linked to issues such as the fight for democratic change, the existence of cultural specificity and linguistic pluralism online, has come to be a particularly distinctive characteristic of Latin American Internet activism. The term 'informática comunitaria' [grassroots computing] has even been coined to define the phenomenon (Rueda Ortiz 2005).

Two paradigmatic examples of this kind of double Internet activism are the Ecuador-based Agencia Latinoamericana de Información (ALAI) [Latin American Information Agency] whose activities date back to 1977 (off-line) and the late 1980s (online) (Burch 1999: 198–99), and the Dominican Republic-based Fundación Redes y Desarrollo (FUNREDES) [Networks and Development Foundation], which has been in existence since 1993. ALAI, led by Sally Burch and Eduardo Tamayo G., is a long-standing member of the APC. Although defining itself as an organisation 'committed to the full respect of human rights, gender equality and people's participation in development and policy making in Latin America', the bulk of its mission statement is very similar to that of the APC (ALAI). Nowadays its main website currently places greater emphasis on the reporting of news regarding Latin American social movements; its 'sister' site *América Latina en Movimiento* [Latin America in Movement] is devoted to 'facilitat[ing] the circulation and exchange of information, particularly over the Internet' (ALM), publishing new research in the field as well as promoting participation in events lobbying for better access.

The remit of FUNREDES, a slightly younger member of the APC, headed by Moroccan-born French citizen, Daniel Pimienta, is very similar to that of ALAI, although it has traditionally had a more technical, and less news-orientated bent: it is an NGO dedicated specifically to facilitating access to ICTs in Latin America and the Caribbean. Prior to the official constitution of FUNREDES in 1993, Pimienta helped set up computer networks in Peru, the Dominican Republic, and Haiti, although the latter is still the last remaining Latin American country with no real public access to the Internet because of government repression. He also ran computer literacy and web-design programmes. However, FUNREDES proper is now focused on new technology for communicative purposes rather than issues of basic connectivity, and, in particular, it seeks to lobby governments across the region for better access to ICTs, and to promote cultural and linguistic diversity online, having experimented with various models to offer on-going translation services for documents posted online and conducted research into the presence of both Spanish and French online (see the introduction to this volume).

Nevertheless, one might well argue that organisations conducting meta-Internet activism such as ALAI and FUNREDES, no matter how idiosyncratically Latin American, are a different kettle of fish to those such as the EZLN that campaign for 'real' issues and simply make strategic and very effective use of the Internet. In the case of the second group of activists, the Zapatistas' use of 'social netwar', including electronic aspects, may be demonstrated to have been of some considerable influence. Furthermore, meta-Internet activist organisations might provide the networks that allow for social netwars to take place, but the activism that really captures the attention of the general public around the world and which can thus evolve into a fully fledged social netwar is that which follows the pattern of the Zapatista Uprising with its apposite combination of traditional weapons and ICTs, and the pathos of its David versus Goliath narratives.

Eduardo Tamayo G., co-director of ALAI with Sally Burch, is more positive in his evaluation of the Zapatistas' influence. He considers them to be 'pioneers' in the field and, although without providing any proof of direct Zapatista influence, goes on to list other subsequent 'social netwars' that have made strategic use of the Internet: the 'cacerolazos' [lit. 'banging on pots and pans'] that resulted in the ousting of Argentine president Fernando de la Rúa in 2001;[15] the public response to the coup d'état against Venezuelan president Hugo Chávez in the same year; and the civil unrest which lead to the removal of Bolivian president Gonzalo Sánchez de Lozada in 2003 (Tamayo 2005).[16] In all of these scenarios the Internet may be

15 The associated website was named *Cacerolazo.com* (Corrales 2002: 39).

16 Trejo Delarbre also considers the Zapatistas' example to have had some influence over the creation of websites by the Peruvian Sendero Luminoso [Shining Path] group and the Fuerzas Armadas Revolucionarias de Colombia [Revolutionary Armed Forces of Colombia], although absolute proof of this is not given (Trejo Delarbre 1999: 336).

demonstrated to have played a key role, although, as is typical of its usage in Latin America, this almost always happened in conjunction with other forms of media and communications tools such as radio and mobile phones.[17]

Within Mexico itself, the current (Autumn 2006) uprising by teachers and their sympathisers in the state of Oaxaca under the name of the Asamblea Popular de los Pueblos de Oaxaca (APPO) [Popular Assembly of the Peoples of Oaxaca] has shown signs of triggering a new 'social netwar' very similar to that started by the Zapatistas. On the 'electronic' front alone, the APPO already have an extremely sophisticated website – although parts of it are still under construction – and they have integrated into the site the community radio broadcasts – from Radio Plantón [Tent-City Radio] – which are the mainstay of their communications strategy in Oaxaca itself (see fig. 4.2 for APPO's homepage). Furthermore, the international activist community has taken up their cause and is 'swarming' in the same way that it did around the Zapatistas in 1994. International NGOs and other watchdogs are distributing news and requests for donations and support via listservs and their own websites.[18] The Electronic Disturbance Theatre is already organising virtual sit-ins in support of the teachers (EDT). Journalists and cameramen who are affiliated with Indymedia – the online network of Independent Media Centres central to the development of radical online journalism – are reporting from the conflict zone – indeed, one Indymedia cameraman has been reported dead thus far ('Zapatista'). And finally, the most compelling evidence to suggest Zapatista influence are the references to La Otra Campaña on the APPO website and those to APPO on the Zapatistas' *Enlace Zapatista* website. The international media are endorsing this genealogy of struggle – on the UK Indymedia website

[17] Other critics have also underscored the way in which, in Latin America, the Internet necessarily has to work in conjunction with other media such as radio in order to reach all parts of the population, and that Internet activism entails complex movements between on- and off-line environments (Burch 1999: 202). On a related point, Rueda Ortiz also notes the fact that the Internet's ability to incorporate sound, such as radio broadcasts, is useful in that even cultures that traditionally prefer oral communication, or that have high rates of illiteracy, can derive benefit from online materials (Rueda Ortiz 2005).

[18] For example, the International Relations Center (IRC) distributes its news bulletins to the *latam-info* listserv.

the 'Zapatista' archive includes, as its most recent entries, news reports of the solidarity efforts in support the APPO ('Zapatista'). That Zapatista influence should be felt in a contiguous state in Mexico is hardly surprising. Nevertheless, the similarities in communications strategy are striking – indeed, APPO seem to have learned many a lesson from the EZLN's experiences in this respect.

Conclusion: 'Another World Is Possible'

As is evident from the preceding discussion, the use of the Internet by NGOs and other activist groups has been of considerable significance in Latin America, as in other developing countries, and provides a substantial counterbalance to corporate capitalisation on, and, to a lesser extent, state control of the new medium, despite attempts by such powerful actors to limit the development of alternative and activist uses of the Internet.[19] Indeed, it is Latin America's ability to develop in this field which, according to some commentators, suggests the region's most significant contribution to global cyberculture and which also promises positive benefits for democracy in the region itself: access to information technology is fast coming to be considered a marker, as well as a promoter, of democracy (Annis 1991: 93; Corrales 2002: 37), as well as a basic human right (ALAI, 1994, quoted in Mastrangelo Gittler 1999: 97). To adopt the optimistic catchphrase of the notorious Mexican hactivist Fran Ilich, 'Another world is possible' (Ilich 2006–).

References

Acción Zapatista Austin Texas 1994–? http://www.utexas.edu/ftp/student/nave, no longer available online.

ALAI (*Agencia Latinoamericana de Información* [Latin American Information Agency]). Website available in Spanish, Portuguese, and English. http://www.alainnet.org, last accessed 17 June 2007.

ALM (*América Latina en Movimiento* [Latin America in Movement]) 2000–. http://www.movimientos.org, last accessed 17 June 2007.

Annis, Sheldon 1991. 'Giving Voice to the Poor', *Foreign Policy*, 84, 93–106.

Arquilla, John, and David Ronfeldt 1993. 'Cyberwar is Coming!', *Comparative Strategy*, 12:2, 141–65, reprinted in John Arquilla and David Ronfeldt,

[19] For reasons of space, such interventions have not been covered in any detail in this chapter. They merit further research.

eds., *In Athena's Camp: Preparing for Conflict in the Information Age* (Santa Monica, CA: RAND, 1997), pp. 23–60.

APPO (*Asamblea Popular de los Pueblos de Oaxaca*) 2006–. http://www.asambleapopulardeoaxaca.com, last accessed 17 June 2007.

APC (Association for Progressive Communications). Website available in English, Spanish, and French, http://www.apc.org, last accessed 17 June 2007.

—— 2000. *1990–2000: Looking Back on APC's First Decade*. Annual Report. Available from http://www.apc.org/english.about/history/apc_ar_2000.pdf. last accessed 20 November 2006.

—— 2006. 'Internet and ICTs for Social Justice and Development News', http://www.apc.org/english/news/index.shtml/, last accessed 3 November 2006.

Atton, Chris 2004. *An Alternative Internet: Radical Media, Politics and Creativity* (Edinburgh: Edinburgh University Press).

Belejack, Barbara 1997. 'Cyberculture Comes to the Americas', *NACLA Report on the Americas*, November/December, http://hartford-hwp.com/archives/40/071.html, last accessed 17 June 2007.

Bob, Clifford 2005. *The Marketing of Rebellion: Insurgents, Media, and International Activism* (Cambridge: Cambridge University Press).

Burch, Sally 1999. 'ALAI: A Latin American Experience in Social Networking', in Wendy Harcourt, ed., *Women@Internet: Creating New Cultures in Cyberspace* (London: Zed Books), pp. 197–205.

Castells, Manuel 1997. *The Information Age: Economy, Society and Culture*, 3 vols, vol. 2: *The Power of Identity* (Oxford: Blackwell Publishing).

Centro de Información Zapatista 2001–. *Con el EZLN al DF*, http://www.ezlnaldf.org/, last accessed 17 June 2007.

Chiapas95 1994–. http://www.eco.utexas.edu/~hmcleave/chiapas95.html, last accessed 17 June 2007.

Cleaver, Harry 1994. 'The Chiapas Uprising and the Future of Class Struggle in the New World Order'. First published in Italian in *RIFF-RAFF: Attraverso la produzione sociale*, March, 133–45. Available from http://www.eco.utexas.edu/facstaff/Cleaver/chiapasuprising.html, last accessed 17 June 2007.

—— 1996–2003 (last updated). *Zapatistas in Cyberspace*, http://www.eco.utexas.edu/~hmcleave/zapincyber.html, last accessed 17 June 2007.

—— 1998. 'The Zapatistas and the Electronic Fabric of Struggle', in John Holloway and Eloína Peláez, eds., *Zapatista!: Reinventing Revolution in Mexico* (London: Pluto Press), pp. 81–103.

Corrales, Javier 2002. 'Lessons from Latin America', in Leslie David Simon *et al.*, *Democracy and the Internet: Allies or Adversaries?* (Washington, DC: Woodrow Wilson Center Press), pp. 30–66.

Denning, Dorothy E. 1999. 'Activism, Hacktivism, and Cyberterrorism: The Internet as a Tool for Influencing Foreign Policy', paper given at the Internet and International Systems: Information Technology and American Foreign Policy Decisionmaking Workshop, Nautilus Institute, San Francisco, CA, 10 December, http://www.nautilus.org/archives/info-

policy/workshop/papers/denning.html, last accessed 17 June 2007.
De Ugarte, David 2004. *11M: Redes para ganar una guerra* (Barcelona: Icaria).
Domínguez, Ricardo c.1998. 'Digital Zapatismo', *Electronic Civil Disobedience*, http://www.thing.net/~rdom/ecd/DigZap.html, last accessed 17 June 2007.
Ejército Zapatista de Liberación Nacional (EZLN) 2005–. Official website, http://www.ezln.org.mx, last accessed 17 June 2007.
Electronic Civil Disobedience. http://www.thing.net/~rdom.ecd/ecd.html, last accessed 16 November 2006.
Enlace Zapatista 2005–. http://www.enlacezapatista.ezln.org.mx, last accessed 28 October 2006.
Escobar, Arturo 1999. 'Gender, Place and Networks: A Political Ecology of Cyberculture', in Wendy Harcourt, ed., *Women@Internet: Creating New Cultures in Cyberspace* (London: Zed Books), pp. 31–54.
FUNREDES (*Fundación Redes y Desarrollo*) 1993–. Website available in Spanish, French, and English, http://funredes.org, last accessed 17 June 2007.
Fuentes, Carlos 1994. 'Chiapas: Latin America's First Post-Communist Rebellion', *New Perspectives Quarterly*, 11:2 (spring), 54–58.
Gómez, Ricardo 2000. 'The Hall of Mirrors: The Internet in Latin America', *Current History*, 99:634. Available from the International Development Research Centre, at http://archive.idrc.ca/pan/pubhall_e.htm, last accessed 17 June 2007.
Hables Gray, Chris 1997. *Postmodern War: The New Politics of Conflict* (London: Routledge).
Halleck, Deedee 1994. 'Zapatistas On-Line', *NACLA Report on the Americas*, 28:2 September/October, 30–32, 44.
Ilich, Fran 2000–. *Possible Worlds*, http://www.possibleworlds.org, last accessed 17 June 2007.
—— 2006. 'Historia', http://possibleworlds.org/?page_id=3, last accessed 17 June 2007.
Iturriaga, Markus 1996. 'The War of Ink and Internet: The Zapatista Rebels in Mexico and the Electronic Revolution', Masters Dissertation, University of Tennessee. http://www.cs.utk.edu/~miturria/project, last accessed 17 June 2007.
Le Bot, Yvon 1997. *Subcomandante Marcos: El sueño zapatista* (Barcelona: Plaza y Janés).
Martín-Barbero, Jesús 2000. 'Art/Communication/Technicity at Century's End', trans. by Hugh O'Donnell, in Anny Brooksbank Jones and Ronaldo Munck, eds., *Cultural Politics in Latin America* (Basingstoke: Macmillan), pp. 56–73.
Mastrangelo Gittler, Alice 1999. 'Mapping Women's Global Communications and Networking', in Wendy Harcourt, ed., *Women@Internet: Creating New Cultures in Cyberspace* (London: Zed Books), pp. 91–101.
Morello, Henry James 2007. 'E-(re)volution: Zapatistas and the Emancipatory Internet', *A Contracorriente: A Journal on Social History and Literature in Latin America*, 4:2, 54–76.

O'Donnell, Susan, and Guillermo Delgado 1995. 'Using the Internet to Strengthen the Indigenous Nations of the Americas', *Journal of Media Development*, 42:3, 36–38.

Olesen, Thomas 2005. *International Zapatismo: The Construction of Solidarity in the Age of Globalization* (London: Zed Books).

La otra información 2006–. Site hosted on www.possibleworlds.org server maintained by Fran Ilich. http://www.laotrainformacion.org, last accessed 17 June 2007.

Preston, Shelley 1994. 'Electronic Global Networking and the NGO Movement: The 1992 Rio Summit and Beyond', *Swords and Ploughshares: A Chronicle of International Affairs*, 3:2. Available from http://www.globalpolicy.org/ngos/role/policymk/internet/2000/131100.htm, last accessed 17 June 2007.

Rheingold, Howard 2000. *The Virtual Community: Homesteading on the Electronic Frontier*, 2nd edn. (Reading, MA: Addison-Wesley).

Rodríguez, Ernesto 2006. 'Movilizaciones estudiantiles: ¿Por qué en Chile y no en otros países de América Latina?', *Revista Electrónica Latinoamericana de Estudios sobre Juventud*, 2:3, June. http://www.joveneslac.org/portal/000/publicaciones/revista/3/18%20MOVILIZACIONES%ESTUDIANTILES.htm, last accessed 25 July 2006.

Ronfeldt, David, *et al.* 1998. *The Zapatista Social Netwar in Mexico* (Santa Monica, CA: RAND).

Rueda Ortiz, Rocío 2005. 'Apropiación social de las tecnologías de la información: ciberciudadanías emergentes', Foro: comunicación y ciudadanía, *América Latina en movimiento*, 28 November. http://www.movimientos.org/foro_comunicacion/show_text.php3?key=5930, last accessed 17 June 2007.

Tamayo G., Eduardo 2005. 'Globalización, comunicación y movimientos sociales', Foro: comunicación y ciudadanía, *América Latina en movimiento*, 29 November. http://www.movimientos.org/foro_comunicacion/show_text.php3?key=5932, last accessed 17 June 2007.

Trejo Delarbre, Raúl 1999. 'La Internet en América Latina', in Néstor García Canclini and Carlos Juan Moneta, eds., *Las industrias culturales en la integración latinoamericana* (Mexico City: Grijalbo; Caracas: Sistema Económica Latinoamericano; UNESCO), pp. 311–56.

Van de Donk, Wim, *et al.*, eds. 2004. *Cyberprotest: New Media, Citizens and Social Movements* (London: Routledge).

Vegh, Sandor 2002. 'Hactivists or Cyberterrorism?: The Changing Media Discourse on Hacking', *First Monday*, 7:10, http://firstmonday.org/issues/issue7_10/vegh/index.html, last accessed 17 June 2007.

Weimann, Gabriel 2006. *Terror on the Internet: The New Arena, the New Challenges* (Washington, DC: United States Institute of Peace Press).

Wolf, Jim 2000. '"Hactivism" Credited to Zapatistas', 2 November. Reuters. Available from *Electronic Civil Disobedience*, http://www.thing.net/~diane/ecd/ZapsFirst.html, last accessed 16 November 2006.

Wright, Steve 2004. 'Informing, Communicating and ICTs in Contemporary Anti-Capitalist Movements', in Wim van de Donk *et al.*, eds., *Cyberprotest: New Media, Citizens and Social Movements* (London: Routledge), pp. 77–93.

¡Ya basta! 1994–c.2001. http://www.ezln.org, no longer available online.
'Zapatista'. *UK Indymedia*, http://www.indymedia.org.uk/en/topics/zapatista, last accessed 17 June 2007.
Zezta Internazionale 2005–. http://www.zeztainternazionale.org, last accessed 21 November 2006.

5

Body, Nation, and Identity: Guillermo Gómez-Peña's Performances on the Web

Niamh Thornton

The Internet is frequently heralded as a positive alternative space for the exploration of new identities, allowing the imaginative creation of a new self – or selves – that may or may not be carried through into everyday life (Laurel 2001: 110). The artist Guillermo Gómez-Peña invites Net-users to project themselves imaginatively onto others' lives, to explore alternative life narratives and purge their demons through his different projects. Through his work as a multimedia artist working both on- and off-line, he aims to make others aware of issues such as race, class, gender, and national allegiances, using multiple – often ludic – methods, in order to achieve radical social change. In this chapter, I shall examine some of the games, identities, and techniques used by Gómez-Peña as an online performer and consider his stated aims.

i. Techno-Razcuache Border Artist

Gómez-Peña was born in Mexico City and moved to the USA in 1978 where he works as a performance artist and writer. In terms of his artistic practice, he describes himself as a 'migrant performance artist' (Gómez-Peña 1994: 211) and 'an interdisciplinary intellectual' (Gómez-Peña 2005: xviii), and, with respect to his relationship to new technologies, as a 'webback' (Gómez-Peña 2005: viii), an unwilling 'cyber-vato' and an 'information superhighway bandido' (Gómez-Peña

2001: 281).[1] In general terms, he tackles issues of the locatedness of cultures and the significance of borderlands, through an interrogation of the concept of a fixed nation space and an exploration of identity issues associated with such a conceptualisation of space. In particular, he makes use of new technologies to challenge the construction of new 'digital borders' (Gómez-Peña 2001: 285) and, in his work with fellow performance artist Roberto Sifuentes, to engage in 'Aztec high-tech' and 'techno-razcuache art', where they see themselves as fighting against US images of Mexicans and other Latina/os as unable to 'handle high technology' (Gómez-Peña 2001: 283–84).

The term 'razcuache', although not commonly found in standard dictionaries, has been popularly defined as referring to 'our people' (derived from 'la raza'), and is used principally by Chicana/os to identify other Chicana/os (Weber State University). Gómez-Peña's use of the term is, in part, a recycling and re-appropriation of the Mexican word 'rascuache', which is associated with the perspective of the subaltern, the poor, and the disenfranchised. In a US context, it suggests a specifically Mexican-inflected, resistant, outsider, *mestizo* sensibility. José Anguiano has considered the cultural significance of 'rasquachismo' with specific reference to Chicano and Mexican rap music, stating that the basic elements of 'rasquache' aesthetics include, 'tackiness', 'satire', and the 'use of code-switching' (Anguiano 2003). All these are evident in Gómez-Peña's web-based performances, and his appropriation of typically 'rasquache' referents can be seen in his description of his decorated and dated Apple Mac laptop as a 'lowrider' (Gómez-Peña 2001: 282). In the same way that *cholo* youths re-model out-of-date, US cars and turn them into 'lowriders', Gómez-Peña implies that he ironically re-uses and re-appropriates hand-me-down technologies.[2]

The aims and aesthetics of *techno-razcuachismo* can be found in Gómez-Peña's expressed intention to increase the web presence of Chicana/os and Latina/os. His professed aim in his engagement with technology is to: '"brownify" virtual space; to "spanglishize the net"; to

[1] 'Webback' is a neologism that combines a reference to the worldwide web with the term 'wetback', the derogatory word used to refer to illegal Mexican immigrants in the USA, and thus implies that Mexicans and Latin Americans are equivalent to illegal immigrants in their presence on the web. *Vato* is a commonly used Mexican and Chicana/o slang term meaning 'guy' or 'dude'.

[a/2] A *cholo* or *chola* is a Chicano or Mexican member of a street gang.

"infect" the lingua franca; to exchange a different sort of information – mythical, poetical, political, performative, imagistic; and on top of that to find grassroots applications to new technologies and hopefully to do all this with humour and intelligence' (Gómez-Peña 2001: 286). Gómez-Peña's implied vision of the Internet as a white, English-speaking, homogeneous zone may be inaccurate – the significant web presence of the Zapatistas and their supporters since 1994 is but one example (see chapter 4 in this volume). However, what Gómez-Peña is doing here is drawing attention to the power of the web as a tool for activists, and suggesting alternative practices through the playing with identity, space and realities online. It is his belief that the Internet can be a powerful space to enact not only our fantasies of a better world, and expurgate our terrors, but also to learn about others and ourselves in order to fulfil those ideals.

ii. Politics and Art

Implicit and explicit references to politics are always integral to Gómez-Peña's projects and there is a fluid and consistent conceptual and imaginative flow between his writing on the Internet and elsewhere. In his 1994 essay, 'The Free Art Agreement / El tratado de libre cultura', he unpicks the relationship between body, identity and nation space, and examines art and the artist's role in social change: 'The job of the artist is to force open the matrix of reality to admit unsuspected possibilities. Artists and writers throughout the continent are currently involved in a project of redefinition of our continental topography' (Gómez-Peña 1994: 212). Gómez-Peña's references to mapping allude to both the creation of images of a country based on topography, and also to corporeal mapping. Thus, in his creative output, body and space are congruent, and the nation space that is mapped can be visually reconstructed through performance on the body.

Examples of such online aesthetic and political practice can be found on the *La Pocha Nostra* [Our Impurities] [3] website created by Gómez-Peña and his egalitarian collective of performance artists, La

[3] According to Gómez-Peña the term *La Pocha Nostra* is a 'Spanglish neologism' meaning either 'our impurities' or 'the cartel of cultural bastards' (Gómez-Peña 2005: 78). A *pocho* or *pocha* is an Americanised Mexican. The term is often used disparagingly to suggest someone who has lost their Mexican cultural roots. It can also refer to the 'Spanglish' spoken by Mexican-Americans.

Pocha Nostra.[4] They have a detailed 'ever-evolving manifesto' of their objectives and define themselves as 'neither an ensemble nor a troupe. We are more of a conceptual "laboratory" – a loose association of rebel artists thinking together, exchanging ideas/aspirations, and jumping into "the abyss" together' (Gómez-Peña 2005: 78).

The layout of the website is often confusing, and comparisons with an older site of the same name suggest that this is deliberate.[5] The previous site was easy to navigate, highly text-based, with links to visuals. The current site has adapted to developing technology, with increased integration of images and the incorporation of audio features in some of the links. The site has certain other peculiarities which make it more difficult to navigate, such as the green font against a black background which can be difficult to read. And in a playful – and somewhat sinister – reference to current US foreign policy, the cursor turns into a gun-sight when it hits on a link. Through what is called the 'Main Pocha Entry', the viewer must move the cursor across the screen in order to happen upon the subsequent links, most of which are not obviously marked.

One of the clearest examples on the website of Gómez-Peña and La Pocha Nostra's political and artistic goals is a piece entitled 'Performance Art Definition 2539A' (Gharavi). Further clicks reveal an image of a beating heart. A syringe appears from the right of the screen and is plunged into the heart, extracting all of its blood, and making it disappear. The syringe then squirts the blood at the viewer and the definition 'an emergency procedure performed on the body politic' together with the artist's name, Lance Gharavi, appears in green font against this dramatic red background.[6] The heart acts as a synecdoche for the physical body, which is made visually co-terminous with the body politic, thus exploring the relationship between politics and the body. There is a disturbing violence in the squirting of the screen, as the syringe is directed towards the viewer.

'The Chica-Iranian Project' and 'The Fourteen Commandments' are

4 Gómez-Peña is the one core continuous member, which gives the group its public coherence. He has also been part of several other troupes (for more detail on his working career to date, see Gómez-Peña 2005: 260).

5 The current site was created in 2005; however, the older site can still be accessed through it.

6 Lance Gharavi is a performance artist and collaborator with La Pocha Nostra.

two other areas on the website in which Gómez-Peña, and his collaborators, explore the representation of ethnic identities online and the challenges faced by subalterns in a highly stratified society in the digital age. Both are presented as games. The clever combination of ludic elements and popular referents enables them to explore serious political issues. Their manipulation of navigational and interface design tools, alongside the sometimes controversial and challenging content, push out the artistic boundaries and demonstrate some of the range of possibilities available to performance artists on the web.

iii. 'The Chica-Iranian Project': Ethnic Identities Online

In Gómez-Peña and Ali Dadgar's 'performance photo essay on the dangers of ethnic profiling in the post 9/11 era' entitled 'The Chica-Iranian Project – Orientalism Gone Wrong in Aztlan', various artists, from Gómez-Peña who describes himself as 'post-Mexican', to others of mixed Hapa-Japanese heritage, to Iranians and Chicana/os, 'exchanged identities' and 'altered each other's identities with props and costumes and constructed a dozen performance personas in ethnic drag' (Gómez-Peña and Dadgar 2005). The 'viewer', as the visitor is named in this cyberspace environment – a reminder of the voyeuristic nature of his/her position in this site – must match the character to the name with only their racial/cultural description as a clue.

This game of 'Guess Who?' provides the viewer with a ludic exploration of some of the racial issues that have come to the fore in post-9/11 USA, alongside a radical reconstruction of identity and a play on stereotypes. The player must decide who is performing the 'Typical Arab Chola' or 'El Spaghetti Greaser Bandit' or the 'Palestinian Vato Loco' – to name just the first three characters – having only been given their racial/cultural self-identification. Is the butch 'Spaghetti Greaser Bandit' with his corny Western/mariachi–inspired outfit the post-Mexican Gómez-Peña? Or could he be the Iranian Ali Dadgar? Or one of the other individuals listed and categorised on the site? What is the viewer really being asked to do? The suggestion is that perhaps s/he must guess based on stereotype, or on a corruption of that stereotype, or simply based on a 'wrong orientalism' as the title suggests.

The viewer's, and, implicitly, US society's preconceived notions of what a person with the various self-identifications listed should do/ look like, are the objects of this game. The aim is thus both pedagogical and political. It challenges accepted racial and cultural performances which are framed as deeply political acts in a racially divided US. Yet it does so with irony and humour. Not only are the images amusing parodies and subversions of popular and iconic imagery, there is also a definite political subtext. Once the game is completed, the following words appear on the screen: 'Bravissimo. Thanks for participating in our (non)objective risk classification exercise. You've added greatly to our store of intelligence. We feel much safer now' (Gómez-Peña and Dadgar 2005). The humour is tinged with a political edge by alluding to the climate of fear and paranoia that is current in post-9/11 US, as the words mock the establishment which uses this discourse of safety and intelligence.

Gómez-Peña and Dadgar's project here aligns itself with the online, alternative media's critical engagement with dominant political discourse. The mixture of the serious and the humorous allows them to explore new identities, and challenge the old stereotypes, which, through their performance, have been rendered ridiculous. Their *razquachismo* – the re-appropriation of old models and Mexican terms of reference, alongside what could seem to be magpie-like appropriation of other cultural referents – thus speaks to a wide audience.

iv. 'The Fourteen Commandments': Life in a Digital Age from a Subaltern Perspective

The second game is entitled 'The Fourteen Commandments' and is a primarily textual game in which the viewer is taken through an alternative set of commandments. The entry point in itself is difficult to access, and in recognition of this fact the opening window states: 'Congratulations, only 3 out of 10 make it this far! To become a true borderless citizen, please read and agree with the following.' Flattery is used to draw the viewer in, mixed with a very definite political challenge. In the next window there is a phallic-looking switch accompanied by the phrase: 'Yes I promise to obey.' This relatively simple juxtaposition of image and apparently banal statement bears multiple layers of meaning. The statement promises obeisance, which suggests the rescinding of power by the viewer, but it is never made clear to whom – although the word 'commandments' clearly implies a deity. In order to satisfy curiosity and continue with the game, the viewer must become complicit and obey.

Once the viewer flicks the lever, the first commandment appears on the screen: 'Practice responsible hedonism, vindicate the sacred right to party, fight Puritanism in all its forms. It is a subtle form of political control'. However, subsequent commandments are not arranged in ascending numerical order. This non-linear presentation of the commandments suggests a non-hierarchical sequence, although there is an evident logical development and relationship between the commandments. Each commandment is then followed by two phallic-looking switches – 'Promise' and 'Fuck off' – which both make sounds resembling ricocheting gunshots. If the viewer clicks 'Promise', s/he continues smoothly through the piece, and continues to access the commandments in the non-numerical order detailed above. If the viewer selects the 'Fuck off' switch, responses include: 'Ok pendejo we forgive you this time',[7] 'La nostalgia will protect you … for a time', and 'America, ca, ca, ca-put! Digital mortis!' After several return visits it became apparent that, at random, the only option available to the viewer is ultimately the 'Fuck off' switch, with its increasingly lewd and provocative statements.

This piece is highly stylised and playful, yet it also has the political aim of challenging the viewer to consider their position with regard to these statements. It also plays with the expectations of the viewer not only through the jumbled ordering, but also through the forced obeisance. Because it is difficult to navigate, the viewer either becomes frustrated and leaves, or alternatively, on completion, derives satisfaction and feels part of this group of radical artists and free-thinkers.

The content of the commandments in themselves reflects Gómez-Peña and La Pocha Nostra's aims with regard to the Internet. Commandment number twelve echoes the earlier quotation where Gómez-Peña stated that he wishes to 'brownify' the Internet: 'Go high tech we have no option, if you don't participate in the net and expropriate the new digital technologies for humanistic purposes, you will soon be out of the game.' Here, the pronoun change from 'we' to 'you' is significant, as it implies that La Pocha Nostra (we) are aligning themselves with the viewer (you). 'We' suggests solidarity and 'you'

7 *Pendejo* or *pendeja* is a term in Mexican and Chicano slang which is often used as an insult, meaning idiot or fool. It can also be used with a more positive connotation as a way of referring to a friend, as a substitute for the term *vato*.

responsibility, as the Internet is posited as a powerful tool that must be accessed and exploited.

Commandment number four, meanwhile, continues with this demand for action on the part of the viewer: 'Go out of your way to remain informed and distrust mainstream media. Subscribe to various alternative magazines, scan the net regularly, read the foreign press as often as possible, welcome other points of view.' Here, the Internet is presented as an important source of information, in opposition to the untrustworthiness of the traditional media. Yet this is, clearly, a utopian vision, emphasising the positive aspects of the Internet as a source of reliable information, and ignoring the existence of dubious or untruthful websites. To acknowledge these failings would fall outside of the vision and anti-censorship spirit of the commandments, and, in this way, the commandments betray their idealistic view of Internet technologies.

Two further commandments provide a key to Gómez-Peña and La Pocha Nostra's use of Internet and Internet-based identities:

> 2. Avoid simplistic binary oppositions: us/them, good/bad, oppressive/oppressed, first world/third world. Things have become logarithmically more complex. New conceptual models to understand and explain our times must be fluid, open-ended and multi-dimensional.
>
> 11. Fight self-marginalization. Be an outsider/insider. Be a temporary member of multiple communities, we need to be everywhere in the media, in the major institutions, as well as in community-based ones.

These appear sequentially, and show that, although the numbers are not consecutive, the development of ideas is. Commandment two makes reference to the contemporary political polarisation in a post-9/11 USA whose president is waging a 'war on terror' and encouraging such binary thinking. References to refusing 'simplistic binary oppositions' and becoming 'a member of multiple communities' suggest the identity games Gómez-Peña and La Pocha Nostra play, both on their website and in other performance spaces. In the interaction between the visual images seen elsewhere on the site, from the homepage through to other links, and the statements within this section, the layered meaning of La Pocha Nostra's endeavour becomes apparent.

The examples of non-linearity, mis-numbering and subverted chronology that can be found in this site can be usefully read in the light of Gabriela Coronado and Bob Hodge's comments on chaos theory. Coronado and Hodge define chaos as anything that cannot be described in linear terms (Coronado and Hodge 2004: 31), and argue that a networked medium such as the Internet is an ideal medium for chaotic creativity since it 'has neither a beginning nor an end, and neither its centre nor its limits are clearly defined or fixed' (Coronado and Hodge 2004: 72). Gómez-Peña and La Pocha Nostra's identity games can thus be seen as examples of this combination of chaos and creativity, as they use these strategies to political ends.

v. 'El Webback''s Confession: The Pitfalls of Online Identities and Communities

Whereas much of Gómez-Peña's writing is celebratory of the possibilities for identity and community offered by the Internet, at times he does tire of it and draws attention to its pitfalls. In *Ethno-Techno: Writings on Performance, Activism, and Pedagogy* (2005), after the title page and dedication, there is poem signed by 'El Webback' and entitled 'Confession' (Gómez-Peña 2005: viii):

> Today, I'm tired of ex/changing identities on the net.
> In the past eight hours,
> I've been a man, a woman and a s/he.
> I've been Black, Asian, Mixteco, German,
> and a multi-hybrid replicant.
> I've been ten years old, twenty, forty-two, sixty-five.
> I've visited twenty-two meaningless chat rooms
> I've spoken seven broken languages.
> *(I speak in tongues)*
> As you can see, I need a break real bad;
> I just want to be myself for a few minutes.

This poem inspires many questions. Firstly, the title itself, 'Confession' could imply that the writer is playing out a form of Catholic guilt and shame over what has been performed online.[8] Equally, the term could also indicate the lie of the performer, guilty of pretending to be something else in spaces where others honestly share intimate, personal details about their lives. On the topic of confession, Gómez-Peña has written that public confession is part of a Protestant tradition alien to him, but he has also described it as a 'Catholic format' used to invite 'Americans to "confess" to us [Gómez-Peña and Roberto Sifuentes] their cyber-cultural sins in a completely safe environment', that is, on the Internet (Gómez-Peña 2000: 241). Evidently, here he presents contradictory readings of the function of confession in his work, as well as its origins, and his own ambivalences with this form. However, it is clear that he puts the autobiographical to the forefront, 'in the hope that some readers will see their lives, faces and ideas reflected here and there in the multiple shifting (and cracked) mirrors of these texts' (Gómez-Peña 2000: 7).

The poem also raises further questions relevant to the role and function of the Internet for Gómez-Peña. If all of this is a performance, and, indeed, Gómez-Peña presents the everyday as performance, who is the writer's true self, and how is that easier to perform than these others? Which of these components of identity mentioned – age, gender, language, ethnicity – define and are owned by the self? Gómez-Peña thus simultaneously challenges his reader/viewer to question the utopic vision of the Internet presented by many, but also to consider its strength as a space for exploration of these many selves. He thus both celebrates the Internet and its potential as a space to explore other selves, and yet indicates its limitations in one brief poem.

Conclusion

La Pocha Nostra and Gómez-Peña are highly skilled creators who are aware of their audiences. They challenge existing models of identity – in particular, formulations of national identity – with their shifts in characters and identities and their ever-evolving creative output and international collaborations. In a recent blog exchange with the

8 Through its website, La Pocha Nostra has played with the notion of the confessional, juxtaposing it with the anonymity of the web, a combination which allows contributors considerable freedom to express their fears, hatred and desires. For samples of these confessions see 'A Selection of Internet Confessions' (Gómez-Peña 2000: 58–60).

London-based Argentine curator Gabriela Salgado, Gómez-Peña has described all ex-centric artists – as he frequently describes himself – as (Gómez-Peña and Salgado):

> post-national artists in search of a new conceptual nation capable of containing our aspirations and complex identities; our rage and *locura*. We are an unusual milieu of border-crossers, exiles, nomads and hybrids of sorts. And our job is to smuggle ideas from one community to another; from one country to another; and from the streets into the museum and back [...]. Performance art is our common language; our lingua franca.

It is this energy and anger that fuels Gómez-Peña's work. La Pocha Nostra's engagement with the Net is based upon its existence as a medium with wide distribution and access. That said, the issue of accessibility is a thorny one, and although Gómez-Peña wants to see subaltern presence online, his work online is not necessarily accessible to everyone. The Pocha Nostra site uses increasingly memory-heavy elements which presuppose that the user has a high-frequency connection, as well as challenging the user's know-how and patience. It is deliberately complicated to navigate, both in terms of colour scheme and use of changing cursor design; no extra information is given to inform (warn) the user as to what is ahead; and many visual and verbal elements may alienate as much as they attract. Therefore, there is a danger that this website speaks only to the converted: multicultural, fluid, gender-blending, media-savvy individuals, rather than the disenfranchised subaltern he purports to address.

Nevertheless, Gómez-Peña's aim is a democratising one: a wish to capture a space in which to explore his own ideas and provide others with a forum. This space can function as an unconventional, multicultural community, or as an alternative to the national boundaries that exist; a community for the marginalised and disenfranchised; and a place where they and others can be empowered. Whether it is through expressing their own wishes, desires, theories or ideas, or performing those of others, the Internet has provided Gómez-Peña the possibilities to reach a wider audience.

References

Anguiano, José 2003. 'Rasquachismo in the Mix: A Case Study of the Rasquache Sensibility in Chicano and Mexican Rap Music', *Berkeley McNair Research Journal*, 11, http://www-mcnair.berkeley.edu/2003journal/JAnguiano.html, last accessed 19 September 2006.

Coronado, Gabriela, and Bob Hodge 2004. *El hipertexto multicultural en México posmoderno: Paradojas e incertidumbres* (Mexico City: Porrúa).

Gharavi, Lance. 'Performance Art Definition 2539A', http://www.pochanostra.com/#Scene_142, last accessed 20 June 2007.

Gómez-Peña, Guillermo 1989. 'A New Artistic Continent', in Arlene Raven, ed., *Art in the Public Interest* (Ann Arbor, MI: UMI Research Press), pp. 105–17.

—— 1994. 'The Free Art Agreement / El tratado de libre cultura', in Carol Becker, ed., *The Subversive Imagination: Artists, Society, and Social Responsibility* (New York: Routledge), pp. 208–21.

—— 2000. *Dangerous Border Crossers: The Artist Talks Back* (London: Routledge).

—— 2001. 'The Virtual Barrio @ The Other Frontier (or the Chicago Interneta)', in David Trend, ed., *Reading Digital Culture* (Oxford: Blackwell Publishing), pp. 281–86.

—— 2005. *Ethno-Techno: Writings on Performance, Activism, and Pedagogy* (New York: Routledge).

—— and Ali Dadgar 2005. 'The Chica-Iranian Project – Orientalism Gone Wrong in Aztlan (sic)', http://www.pochanostra.com/#Scene_14, last accessed 20 June 2007.

—— and La Pocha Nostra. '14 Commandments', http://www.pochanostra.com/#home, last accessed 20 June 2007.

—— and Gabriela Salgado. 'Performing (or Making Art) in "The Zones of Silence"', http://www.pochanostra.com/dialogues, last accessed 20 June 2007.

Laurel, Brenda 2001. 'Computers as Theatre', in David Trend, ed., *Reading Digital Culture* (Oxford: Blackwell Publishing), pp. 109–14.

Weber State University, *Visual Arts Glossary*, http://faculty.weber.edu/chansen/humanweb/assignments/artglossary.htm, last accessed 20 June 2007.

6

Cyberspace Neighbourhood: The Virtual Construction of Capão Redondo

Lúcia Sá

Cyberspace is most often placed by urban theorists in opposition to more traditional ideas of space, like neighbourhood or 'local community'. For although the term 'community' appears frequently in Internet rhetoric, it is used to describe groups that establish 'virtual' connections based on affinities other than living near each other – professional, intellectual, leisure, and consumption affinities being the most common ones. Discussing the modern megalopolis, Néstor García Canclini states that 'social identification is more and more based on semiotic models provided by the culture industry rather than on the signifying structures or the temporality of the neighbourhood' (García Canclini 1998: 27). Manuel Castells, in turn, points to a social division between the two types of communities in his description of the contemporary megalopolis as a 'dual city', where the elites establish network connections with the whole world, leaving the poor and displaced to develop internal networks of survival (Castells 1989: 227–28).

The youth from Capão Redondo, a poor neighbourhood on the south side of São Paulo, defy such oppositions. They create forms of social identity that are intensely local while belonging, at the same time, to international networks related to contemporary youth culture in many of its manifestations: hip-hop, video and computer games, 'marginal literature', and cyberspace. This chapter will focus on the website www.capao.com.br (hereafter referred to as *Capao.com*) founded in 2000 by the brothers Leonardo and Allan Lopes to inspire pride in the neighbourhood. Since this website is intimately connected with hip-hop and the 'marginal literature' of Capão, it will be discussed as part of a growing phenomenon that began towards the end of the 1980s, when a few hip-hop groups began to appear in Capão Redondo. The most successful of these was Racionais MCs, whose fourth record, 'Vivendo no inferno' [Living in Hell] (1993) sold millions of copies to listeners from all social classes and from all parts of the country, and received many prizes. In 2000 Ferréz, himself a rapper, published the novel *Capão pecado* [Sin Capão] which describes everyday violence in Capão Redondo. The novel includes vignettes introducing each chapter by many of the most important rappers from the region, among them Mano Brown, from Racionais MCs, and Conceito Moral [Moral Concept]. In 2003 Ferréz published a second book, *Manual prático do ódio* [A Hands-On Guide to Hatred], and has become the editor of a page of 'marginal literature' published more or less regularly in the leftist monthly *Caros Amigos* [Dear Friends]. His books have also sold large numbers of copies and his name appears quite frequently in mainstream dailies such as *Folha de São Paulo* and *Jornal do Brasil*.

What Ferréz calls 'marginal literature' – the publication of texts by *favelados* [shanty town residents], landless workers, prisoners, and semi-literate people – is connected to a recent interest, in Brazil and Spanish America, in such genres as testimonial literature, prison diaries, and texts written amid violence or from within the most disadvantaged sectors of society. In the case of Ferréz, literary production goes hand in hand with attempts to recreate Capão Redondo as a space of resistance, starting with his own pen name, Ferréz: it combines the first syllable of Ferreira – surname of the revered *cangaceiro* [bandit] Lampião from the Northeast – and the first letter of Zumbi, the leader of the largest *quilombo* [maroon runaway slave community] in Brazil. For that reason, Ferréz's writing has to be seen as interconnected with other 'resistant' Capão phenomena such as hip-hop and the website. In fact, the protagonists of each group often participate in each other's works, have joint projects, or advertise each other. Their activities also extend into social projects.

Hip-hop groups such as Racionais MCs and Conceito Moral organise themselves in posses, that is, agglomerations of more than one music group that meets regularly to discuss social issues and offer services to the community, such as music and dance classes, libraries, sexual education, soccer schools, and so on. Ferréz and several contributors to the website collaborate with different posses, and have, as well, their own social activities that complement or resemble those of the posses.

In social and economic terms it should not come as a surprise that the youth of Capão Redondo define their local space with the help of global media. As in many other cities of Latin America, a lack of job opportunities and a dysfunctional education system are driving young men to work in the drug trade – an underground and illegal industry that uses local labour but is also entirely dependent on well-organised, international networks that make ample use of modern technologies and communication systems. In most places drug traffic is also connected to the illegal traffic of weapons: in the *favelas* of most Brazilian cities, gang and drug-related deaths often happen with the use of extremely modern and sophisticated weapons that can only reach those localities thanks, again, to well-organised international networks. Moreover, many of these youths die in pursuit of consumer goods that are iconic representations of globalised capitalism: brand-name tennis-shoes and clothes, expensive watches, and cars. Thus, in social terms, these young men belong both to extremely disadvantaged communities, which often lack basic services such as underground sewage, and to modern, international networks that are, albeit illegally, a definite part of international capitalism. Their music is hip-hop.

Of course, in itself hip-hop is not linked to drug traffic or other illegal activities. In these poor urban neighbourhoods, however, both hip-hop and drug trafficking are a common part of life. Thus, rap songs often have lyrics that comment on drug-related activities and deaths – in fact some critics have lamented the way they glorify violent death. Others see hip-hop as an alternative to drug trafficking, a remedy even, a tool to educate youth to keep away from crime, with songs that nevertheless still have drug-related violence as their central theme. The same happens with the literature that has come out of Capão, and the contributions to the website *Capao.com*, most of which also deal, one way or another, with drug violence.

Capão Redondo, a *bairro* of 200,000 people, appears frequently in the national press, where it is referred to as one of the most violent places in the city of São Paulo, which, in turn, is one of the largest urban conglomerations in the world. According to some sources, the probability of a person dying a violent death in Capão Redondo is forty-six times higher than in the richer areas of São Paulo (Teresa

2005). It is also considered the birthplace of São Paulo hip-hop. In the 1960s and 1970s, Capão Redondo and other neighbourhoods in the *periferia* of São Paulo became home to many immigrants from the Brazilian northeast, who came to live in *favelas* or government-funded housing. Capão Redondo is therefore a neighbourhood where most of the inhabitants came from somewhere else: it is a neighbourhood of displaced people who, because of their origin and skin colour, suffer strong prejudice from other *paulistanos* [residents of São Paulo].

On the website as well as in the hip-hop songs and in Ferréz's works, Capão Redondo is portrayed as part of the generally poor Zona Sul (the south side of São Paulo) and more amply, of the *periferia*, that is, the neighbourhoods in the outer areas of São Paulo where public services are more precarious and most of the *favelas* are located. As a matter of fact, Zona Sul has many wealthy neighbourhoods, and some expensive condominiums have been built not far from *favelas* in some parts of the region in the last few years. The use of the term 'Zona Sul' to denote an exclusively poor region of São Paulo is part of these groups' strategy to reclaim the space and to make it their own. The expression appeared in one of the first songs by Racionas MCs, 'Pânico na Zona Sul' [Panic on the South Side], which dwelt on police brutality in the area. On their third record, the song 'Fim de semana no parque' [Weekend in the Park] compared a weekend in a middle-class park in São Paulo to the environment of danger and lack of available leisure options in Zona Sul, but concludes as well that 'the number one in low income in the city / South side community is dignity'. Forging the number '1' into a collective self, in 1999 Ferréz launched the movement '1 da Sul' [1 from the South], which attempted to foster pride in coming from this poor, marginalised area of São Paulo. The expression appears on the T-shirts (worn by young men) seen in the photographs of Capão Redondo which complement the text of *Capão pecado*. This same pride in being from Capão prompted the creation of the website *Capao.com*.

According to Leonardo Lopes, the founding of the site was motivated by the desire to show the 'good side of Capão' (*Capao.com*). Later, it started to post useful information, and now, in its third phase, the site has an open format and invites responses, comments, stories, poems, and thoughts, as well as publicising bands, events, meetings, open days, help programs, and so forth. In its current format (May 2006), the homepage of *Capao.com* has at its centre an explanation and history of the site itself (see fig. 6.1). To the left we can see a list of collaborators,[1] and at the top a list of topics: articles, events, our art, humour, dialect, 'o comédia e o truta' [the clown and the buddy – a service for posting public messages to friend and foe], and 'stories from the ghetto'.[2] Not all collaborators claim to be from Capão, and some give no personal details. Among those who do describe themselves, we can see certain variations in their social and educational backgrounds: some collaborators have gone or are going to college, while others have had little formal education. This variety is perhaps the most relevant aspect of the website, as it points to the novelty of the Internet as a producer of genres. For the first time in the history of the West, people who would never before have had access to publishing have gained access, and the texts they write are reaching impressive numbers of readers. As Ananda Mitra puts it (Mitra 2004: 492):

> The Internet has transformed popular culture by providing a virtual forum in which different communities and groups can produce a 'presence' that might have been denied to them in the real world. This presence can be obtained in cyberspace by appropriate use of one's voice to articulate the specific narratives and discourses about one's group or subculture.

Since the postings on *Capao.com* are not edited or corrected they give us a fresh feel of *paulista* slang and syntax. Surprisingly, perhaps, this vernacular varies little between people who claim or appear to have minimal formal education and those who boast a college degree. Exceptions are rare, and involve one or two contributors who write professionally for local newspapers and blogs. The overwhelming majority of the texts reveal the characteristic traits of *paulista* oral language: the suppression of plural markers and the lack of grammatical agreement between subject and verb. The linguistic analysis of these contributions requires a specialised study that goes beyond the scope of this chapter. However, for the first time in history these traits are gaining a significant written register. It is of course too early to

1 This list of collaborators was no longer present when the image of the homepage was captured, although it still appears on many other of the site's pages.

2 All translations are my own unless otherwise noted.

predict how this alphabetic record might impinge on *paulista* language norms and literature, but it is hard to imagine that either will remain unaffected. Already it is redefining the difference between the 'two languages of São Paulo' – the spoken and the written – famously observed by the character Macunaíma in Mário de Andrade's novel of the same name (1928).

As for content, the open format of the website also makes for a more varied and at times contradictory view of Capão Redondo, which differs from the image of the area projected by the other cultural manifestations to which it is otherwise tightly connected: the hip-hop songs and the local literature. Many sections on the website are dedicated to the local heroes: rappers, writers, and footballers who, thanks to their fame, are lights on the horizon. Indeed, most texts consist of histories of hip-hop and home-grown groups, especially Racionais MCs. There are interviews with Mano Brown and other successful rappers, commentaries on hip-hop songs, positive reviews of Ferréz's books and interviews with the author himself. A sample of such contributions is Leonardo Lopes's description of the musical group Banda Tecora. After classifying their musical genre as a mixture of the 1960s sound with 'ghetto music', he goes on to make a strong spatial claim: 'They have their feet firmly placed in the *periferia*, the southern end of São Paulo, Capão Redondo, but have a global view of the poverty and deprivation that most of the Earth's population is subject to' (*Capao.com*). That is, Lopes sees Banda Tecora as both rooted in Capão Redondo and belonging to a global economy that causes 'poverty and deprivation'. Local identity, in other words, is created through a global discourse, not in opposition to it.

In language that is both vernacular and grandiose, Alexandre M.O. Valentim reviews the names of Capão's famous offspring, in the article 'Periferia: berço de valores' [*Periferia*: Cradle of Values]. He notes that those who have made a name for themselves in Capão Redondo have had to 'overcome prejudices, resentment, lack of support, poor economic conditions and all kinds of obstacles', and wonders what more could have been done if there had been 'minimum support for and investment in these worthy people?' (*Capao.com*). The names he lists are: Mano Brown, André Luiz de Souza (filmmaker, now resident in France), Ferréz, Natarja Turetta (actress), Cafú (footballer), Lucila (city representative), and Father Jaime Crowe (an Irish priest who fights for human rights). Most of these names come from the arts and sports, swelling the emphasis on creativity as the best – and sometimes only – job option for young people in the *periferia* – an emphasis reiterated elsewhere on the website, in the hip-hop songs, and in Ferréz's novel. This last, for instance, paints a bleak picture of Capão: the main characters – a group of young men who used to gather every day by a particular lamp-post – all die violent deaths. Countering such pessimism are the vignettes by the rappers – since the reader knows they are alive and that they have succeeded – and some of the dialogues. One of the young men, Narigaz explains to his friend Matcheros how they can compete with the 'playboys' (in English in the vernacular; meaning young white men from the richer areas in the city): 'know what I mean? The playboys have more options, but in my opinion we have to beat them with our creativity, you with me? We have to destroy the sons-of-bitches with the best thing we've got: our talent' (Ferréz 2000: 118). The website's emphasis on hip-hop, other sorts of music, and writing, reinforces that idea, as indeed do many of the social initiatives that it describes and promotes: soccer and hip-hop workshops, and nothing less than a 'fábrica de criatividade' [creativity factory].[3]

On the one hand this emphasis on 'creativity' reflects the social/economic predicament of current capitalism, where jobs are scarce and badly paid, leaving young people in poor neighbourhoods with little hope of a future. It reflects, as well, the specific situation of places like Capão Redondo, where the majority of the young people are black and will have to face racism when trying to get accepted in the job market. In the Racionais MCs song 'Negro Drama' Mano Brown comments on that fact, being ironic about his own success: 'Crime, football, music / I didn't manage to escape that either / Count me in' (*Nada como um dia depois do outro dia*) [Nothing Like One Day after the Other].

Yet, through this very creativity, these young men have been able to forge their own idea of place. Elias Lubaque, an avid contributor to the website, quotes fellow citizen Roberto Teixeira Barbosa, who says (*Capao.com*):

> living in a *bairro* like Capão Redondo may be dangerous but

[3] Brazilian soccer is also described in the national press and popular culture as being more 'creative' than its European counterpart.

> it is also gratifying because the *bairro* is making history and gaining space and a voice in society after almost one hundred years of existence. It is not much, but we have to fight to achieve more. Artists and other people who are respected in the 'system' came from here, and this no doubt is a sign that things are going to change.

Capão is 'making history', that is, it is becoming a recognised place, a well-known neighbourhood, because of the rappers and writers, because of the 'creativity' of its citizens. It is not only that Capão inhabitants can now feel proud because their place is home to famous and successful people. More specifically, the famous and successful people from Capão, particularly the rappers and writers, sing about Capão, write about Capão, live in Capão, and are socially involved in Capão – in other words, they are actively engaged in producing their own idea of Capão. They do this not by offering conventionally positive views of the neighbourhood. On the contrary, their strategy is to turn their own weakness into strength: by talking about crime, violence, and drugs, they manage to attract attention from other sectors of Brazilian society at the same time as making themselves understood by the local youth. They repeat the much propagated view of Capão as a violent, dirty and ugly place, yet reaffirm their pride in being from there. A clear example of this can be seen in the following vignette by Mano Brown, published in Ferréz's *Capão pecado* (Ferréz 2000: 24):

> Capão Redondo is poverty, injustice, unpaved streets, open-air sewage, children barefoot, crowded police stations, vans from the morgue combing the streets, tension and smell of marijuana all the time.
>
> São Paulo is not the wonderful city[4] and Capão Redondo on the south side of the map, even less.
>
> Here, crime stories have no romanticism no heroes.
>
> But so what? I love this fucking place.
>
> In the great big world I am nobody, but in Capão Redondo I have my place guaranteed, do you get it brother?

4 'Cidade maravilhosa' is the epithet usually applied to Rio de Janeiro.

This pride of being from Zona Sul, from Capão Redondo, from the periphery, is not accompanied by any positive material references to those places. What makes Capão positive is firstly the fact that, as the Racionais song 'Fim de semana no parque' states, the *periferia* 'is where my brothers and my friends live / and most people look like me'. That point is repeated again and again in Ferréz's book and in many of the songs and vignettes by rappers from the region. In all of them Capão is described as being ugly, violent, dangerous, and lacking all of the basic services that are available in other parts of the city. Yet, none of those songs talks about leaving the Zona Sul because it is their place, the part of the city where they belong and where their friends and brothers are. For these young men, the great majority of whom are the first generation in their families to be born in Capão – or not even that in some cases, as several of these young men were themselves immigrants – the sense of belonging to a place does not come from a long line of ancestors or historically deep cultural connections. It comes from their own activities, from what they believe they are building at the present moment, from the networks of solidarity that they themselves are constructing. The fact that, according to Mano Brown, in Capão most people look like him is perhaps one of the most important elements in this construction of a local identity. Mano Brown and Racionais MCs are committed to an idea of *bairro* that is strongly centred on race: their songs emphasise the fact that most inhabitants in the poor areas of São Paulo are black, and are discriminated against because of their race.

Though more common now than it was five decades ago, this view of race in Brazilian society still meets with a lot of resistance from the general public and academics alike, who often claim that in Brazil prejudice and social discrimination have to do exclusively with class. In fact, the rappers are often accused of trying to import a US version of race into Brazilian society.[5] However it may be, their race-centered approach to discrimination and inequality has now become more widely accepted in Brazil. The Black Movement has gained strength in the last two decades, thanks largely to groups like Racionais MCs. But if rappers have imported their musical rhythms,

[5] A recent example of this type of accusation can be seen in an interview with the pop star Caetano Veloso in the monthly magazine *Cult* (Veloso 2006: 13).

dance techniques, and some of their notions about race from the US Black Movement and youth culture, they have also engaged deeply with Brazilian history. Ferréz's choice of the names of Zumbi and Lampião to compose his own artistic name signals a deep commitment to the history of resistance in Brazil. The same can be said about the importance of Zumbi more generally in the hip-hop movement, and about the rappers and writers' refusal to accept the official date of Abolition (13 May 1888) as the date of liberation for black people.

Their point is that blacks have never been truly liberated in Brazil, and that, in spite of Abolition, slavery remains untouched in the current social system, which continues to favour whites and the wealthy. Not only that, but the consumerism that is imposed by the capitalist system is, in their view, a form of slavery that drives young black men to become seduced by drug trafficking and violence. As Racionais MCs' song 'Negro Drama' states: 'Hey Master / I know well who you are / alone you're afraid / You said what was good / and the favela heard it / whisky, Red Bull, Nike tennis-shoes, machine guns' (*Nada como um dia depois do outro dia*).[6] Many contributors to the website make the same point. Tiago Aparecido da Silva, for instance, complains that 'we live in a country where boys and girls from the *periferia* want to be rich, drive motorcycles, cars, wear brand-name tennis-shoes. [...] it has contaminated my *bairro* as well, even friends of mine, people who have nothing and want it all' (*Capao.com*). The banalisation of violent death as part of the drug trafficking in Capão Redondo and other Latin American *periferias* can be described, after all, as consumerism taken to its most extreme consequences, as Jean Franco has said: 'contract killers take consumer society to its extreme: they turn life (their own and that of their victims) into a commodity to deal in, into a disposable object' (Franco 2002: 223).

Racionais MCs, Ferréz, and many of the contributors to the website call Capão Redondo a ghetto – an expression that aggressively denies the idea, widespread in Brazilian society, that as 'melting pots' Brazilian cities have no ghettos because blacks, whites, and other races have tended to mix. They also use the term *quilombo* [maroon runaway slave community] to refer to the neighbourhood, giving it a clear sense of a space of resistance – a space where blacks can create their own society. Their idea of space exposes the isolation of the *periferia*,

6 For an excellent analysis of Racionais MCs' lyrics see Zeni 2004.

its status as a ghetto, the actual brutal separation between races and classes in Brazil, and at the same time recreates it as a new space of resistance and brotherhood. Their efforts can be described, to use Edward Soja's words, as an attempt to 'take greater control over the making of geography' (Soja 2000: 281):

> If traditional equality politics mobilizes its radical subjectivity most expansively around taking collective control over the 'making of history', then the new cultural politics of difference, identity, and representation, without lessening the power of its historically inspired strategies, adds a new source of mobilized consciousness rooted in the more immediate collective struggle to take greater control over the making of geography – the social production of human spatiality. This involvement in producing and in already produced spaces and places is what all those who are oppressed, subordinated, and exploited share, and it is this shared consciousness and practice of an explicitly spatial politics that can provide an additional bonding force for combining those separate channels of resistance and struggle that for so long have fragmented modernist equality politics.

The website *Capao.com* shares with the rappers and with writers such as Ferréz this attempt at the 'social production of human spatiality'. By celebrating, as we saw, its local artists, it can create a sense of community based on creativity – a community that its own contributors can then join.

The image of Capão as a ghetto appears frequently on the website: not only in the references to rappers and writers, but also in the repeated descriptions of the Zona Sul as an isolated place. Marco Garcia, a twenty-eight year old journalist who has lived for twenty years in the Zona Sul, emphasises the physical division between the wealthy parts of the city and the Zona Sul in a story entitled 'Um novo muro de Berlim' [A New Berlin Wall], which points to the idea of a constructed socio-political barrier that keeps the two sides from understanding each other. But the river that divides them – Pinheiros – is the image most often used to indicate the separation between the two sides. Jack Arruda Bezerra, for instance, claims that 'to live on this side of the river one has to kill a lion a day' – a reference to the bravery that the 'asphalt warriors' or 'urban warriors' have to demonstrate in order to survive in the Zona Sul (*Capao.com*). The expression 'this side of the bridge' also provides the title to one of Racionais MCs songs, 'Da ponte pra cá', which talks specifically about Capão, noting that 'life is different on this side of the bridge' (*Nada como um dia depois do outro*).

Like the rappers, too, a contributor called Renato explains why he refused to leave his Zona Sul neighbourhood, Jardim Macedônia, to live in Butantã, a middle class neighbourhood on the west side of the city: 'it didn't look like my kinda place', or more literally, 'it didn't look like me' [não era a minha cara]. The expression 'não era a minha cara' seems to point to the same racial definition that helps Mano Brown, as we saw, construct an idea of Capão. But the racial outline here is slightly more complicated, as Renato describes himself as being light-skinned and the son of a black father, and as 'loving everybody; blacks and whites are the same to me' (*Capao.com*). The statement is in clear contrast to one of the contributions by Hermes Augusto M. da Fonseca, who complains that when registering for the compulsory military service he saw a dark man declare himself to be white: 'has this guy listened to the music of 2PAC or Racionais? Has he heard the words of Malcolm X? Has he studied the history of Zumbi or Mandela?', he asks (*Capao.com*). A more controversial note appears in a contribution by someone called Washington, who accuses Mano Brown of racism against whites (*Capao.com*). This implicit debate shows a racial construction of Capão that differs from the all-black neighbourhood seen in the hip-hop songs.

That said, in the section of the webpage called 'Stories from the ghetto', most of the narratives talk about events that are very similar to those described in the rap songs and in Ferréz's novels. They concern young men who get involved in crime and drug trafficking and are killed; or those who nearly get involved but manage to escape; or those who know somebody who got involved and got killed. Examples of this include Eder Paulo Kogus's short text 'Será que tenho anjo da guarda?' [Do I have a Guardian Angel?], which discusses a shoot-out at a party, or Fábio Calvisio Rodrigues's story, 'A vida não é conto de fada' [Life Is Not a Fairy Tale], which relates how he became involved in crime after his parents separated but was saved by a girlfriend.

The message arising from these narratives repeats itself and coincides, too, with those coming from the hip-hop songs and Ferréz's novel: every young man in Capão and the *periferia* lives too close to drug trafficking and crime and is going to be, at some point in his life, tempted to join in. But crime always ends in early death and should be avoided at all costs. Although some of these stories claim to be real and others fictitious, all of them are in one way or another narrated from the point of view of survivors: writing in the first person, after all, can be done only by those who have survived. Read as a collection, these stories provoke the same feeling one has when reading Ferréz's *Capão pecado*. In the novel a young man becomes an alcoholic after being abandoned by his wife, kills her lover and ends up being killed himself in prison. This melodramatic central plot is, as it were, superfluous, since the strength of the novel lies in the beautifully monotonous repetition of the young men's attempts to stay alive. The main character in the web narratives is, as in the novel, the attrition of everyday life in the São Paulo *periferia*. Through the repetition of similar incidents and personal tragedies, the web stories, along with the rap songs and Ferréz's novels, create a sense of community that is at once virtual and geographically bound. It is as if the contributors were saying to each other: 'I can understand your story because I live in the same place as you, and because I live there, I can also tell a story that is similar to yours.' Together, they form a kind of 'hypernarrative' which tells the life and death of a young man from the South side of São Paulo. The sense of place created by this hypernarrative stems from the conditions of production and consumption in present-day capitalism: on the one hand, massive unemployment, especially for unqualified young men; on the other, massive pressure for consumption through globalised media. Rather than celebrate a proletarian hero, this hypernarrative tells the tale of the unemployed anti-hero: a young man who sooner or later will be tempted to join a life of crime.

But here we find, once again, an important difference between the web narratives and the novels and songs to which they are so closely connected. In Ferréz's novels and in the rap songs, crime is always inevitable, or it is to be escaped only by those who manage to become conscientious writers and rappers (or, to use Mano Brown's expression: those who turn from 'flesh' into 'razors'). The multiplicity of voices that characterises the Web narratives – a heteroglossia in the Bakhtinian sense[7] – puts this hypernarrative in dialogue with another

7 For a discussion of heteroglossia on the web, see Mitra 2004.

tale: that of the average young man who is strong enough to avoid the world of crime. These are hero stories in which the heroic act is seen as choosing the 'good way' (studying, working, and in some cases joining a religion) and resisting the temptation of falling into drug traffic and crime. Thus, the Capão Redondo that arises from the website is at once a celebratory affirmation of the neighbourhood created by the raps songs and Ferréz's novels, and a rewriting of it into a more nuanced geography.

But the greatest difference between the Capão constructed by the website and the Capão of the hip-hop songs and Ferréz's novels is in the treatment of gender issues. The space of resistance created by the rappers and by Ferréz's *Capão pecado* is a masculine utopia, where women are treated with contempt except when they are the artists' or protagonists' own mothers, or their 'brothers" mothers. Some of Racionais MCs first lyrics were overtly misogynistic: the song 'Mulheres Vulgares' [Sluts], for instance, is frequently quoted as a major example of anti-female rhetoric in Brazilian hip-hop. It criticises women for using a feminist discourse and being, at the same time, only interested in men with money and power. Similar ideas appear in the songs of many other rappers in Brazil, and in spite of a growing number of female composers and performers, hip-hop remains a pervasively male field.

Given the fact that more than 90 per cent of the victims of violent death in the Brazilian *periferias* are young men, and that young men are also the main perpetrators of those murders, one could say that violence in Brazilian (and Latin American) cities is gendered. Of course women are also victims of violence in these neighbourhoods, but rarely do they suffer violent death. The general ethics behind this violence is also masculine, appealing to ideas of honour, manly courage, and bravery before death. Texts such as 'Mulheres Vulgares' and *Capão pecado* blame women for the fact that men are tempted into crime and die so young. In the Racionais MCs song, their message to the brothers is clear (Racionais MCs):

> Don't fall into this trap
> Be smart with the world and pay attention to everything and nothing
> Women want or prefer only what favours them
> Money and possessions, they forget you if you don't have it

> We are *Racionais* [rational], different, if not the same
> Sluts, only for a night and nothing more.

Similarly, Rael, the protagonist of *Capão pecado* is driven to alcoholism, crime, and an early death because his wife left him for their boss; that is, she chose the richer man.

In a society where they are displayed (often semi-naked) everywhere on advertisements on billboards, magazines, and television, it is not surprising that women are seen as a consumer product – a product that, like Rolex watches and expensive cars, may drive men to commit crimes in order to obtain it. But women are also consumers, and one of the commodities that they consume is men: what the Racionais MCs song and Ferréz's story complain about is precisely the fact that women can dispose of men when they find them useless: when they no longer provide them with the goods. In other words, what makes men desirable as commodities, according to these texts, is the fact that they enable women to obtain more and more commodities. Men are, in that sense, the ultimate commodity. What seems to haunt these authors is, in other words, a fear of being turned into a mere consumer item by women. No wonder, then, that the Racionais MCs' recommendation to the brothers is not to allow themselves to be consumed and, instead, be the consumers: 'Sluts, only for a night and nothing more' (Racionais MCs).[8]

Although this view of gender issues is not entirely absent from the website (one example is Marcos Lopes's story, whose protagonist also becomes a criminal because of a woman), the multiplicity of voices that can be heard on *Capao.com* allows for the existence of a more complex view of the relationship between the sexes. Simone, for instance, tells a story of violence, which at first appears a mere repetition of the stories quoted above in its focus on infidelity and betrayal. However, this story has the crucial difference of being told from the point of view of the woman, 'a young mother of only twenty-four whose only desire was to live a great romance', but who ends up being a victim of violence (*Capao.com*).

Similarly, Marco Garcia in 'A invenção' [The Invention] lists the

8 See Jean Franco for an excellent discussion of the relations between consumerism and a crisis in masculinity in Latin American cities (Franco 2002: 222–33).

numerous ways in which women are superior to men, while Karen Dias overtly attacks *machismo* in the form of men who get drunk and treat women badly. Meanwhile, Ananda, a young hip-hopper, reveals a determination that goes far beyond consumerism, and reaffirms, in beautifully stylised *paulista* slang, her own desire to go on making music. Moreover, we should not forget that in the story by Fábio Calvisio Rodrigues it is the woman who saves the young man from crime. In this way, *Capao.com* reworks the highly masculinised community elaborated by Ferréz and others by opening up a dialogue with feminine and feminist voices.

In this way, the Capão Redondo website reworks both traditional senses of community and the highly masculinised community elaborated by Ferréz and others. It is not an exaggeration to say that hip-hoppers like Racionais MCs and writers like Ferréz have reinvented Capão Redondo, fusing a strong sense of locality with concepts – and rhythms – drawn from international youth and consumer culture. For its part, the website *Capao.com* is reinventing this place once again, by pluralising it and disclosing its inner contradictions, thus complicating received ideas of resistance. The evidence of locatedness in this experience may cause us to conclude that besides forging virtual online communities, the Internet might be capable of creating off-line worlds after all.

References

Andrade, Mário 1965. *Macunaíma, O Herói sem Nenhum Caráter* (São Paulo: Martins Fontes).
Castells, Manuel 1989. *The Informational City: Information Technology, Economic Restructuring and the Urban-Regional Process* (Oxford: Blackwell Publishing).
Capao.com, http://www.capao.com.br, last accessed 20 June 2007.
Ferréz 2000. *Capão pecado* (São Paulo: Labortexto).
—— 2003. *Manual prático do ódio* (Rio de Janeiro: Objetiva).
Franco, Jean 2002. *The Decline and Fall of the Lettered City: Latin America in the Cold War* (Cambridge, MA: Harvard University Press).
García Canclini, Néstor 1998. 'Las cuatro ciudades de México', in Néstor García Canclini, ed., *Cultura y comunicación en la ciudad de México* (Mexico City: Grijalbo), pp. 19–39.
Mitra, Ananda 2004. 'Voices of the Marginalized on the Internet: Examples from a Website for Women of South Asia'. *Journal of Communication*, 54:3, 492–510.
Racionais MCs 1994. *Racionais MCs* (RDS Fonográfica).
—— 1998. *Sobrevivendo no Inferno* (Cosa Nostra. RA 001).

—— 2002. *Nada como um dia após outro dia* (Zâmbia. ZA 50).
Soja, Edward 2000. *Postmetropolis: Critical Studies of Cities and Regions* (Oxford: Blackwell Publishing).
Teresa 2005. 'Universo paralelo no Carta Capital', *Depois do tiro*, http://depois-dotiro.blogspot.com, last accessed 20 June 2007.
Vallejo, Fernando 1994. *La virgen de los sicarios* (Bogotá: Santillana).
Veloso, Caetano 2006. 'Caetano Veloso é verbo e adjetivo (entrevista)', *Cult*, 105:9, 11–17.
Zeni, Bruno 2004. 'O negro drama do rap: entre a lei do cão e a lei da selva', *Estudos Avançados*, 18:50, 225–41.

7

Literary E-magazines in Latin America: From Textual Criticism to Virtual Communities

Shoshannah Holdom

Communications theorist Joaquín María Aguirre Romero surmises that 'the digital magazine cannot be an object in itself but rather an instrument servicing the diffusion of worthy content' (Aguirre Romero 1999). Emphasising the new opportunities afforded by digital media, he calls for authors and editors of electronic publications to bear in mind the 'important mission' of e-publications, that of dissemination of information and widening access, and to approach new digital media with a 'new mentality', conceiving of e-magazines within new media itself, as opposed to traditional print models, and taking advantage of all the resources on offer. As Internet connectivity has increased rapidly across Latin America (Everett 1998; Stinson 1998; Muñoz 1999), so too has the development of new online publications. Individuals and groups in certain countries across the region are now working to take advantage of new technology and harnessing otherwise unavailable opportunities for information access and dissemination by means of e-magazines in particular. Elsewhere (Holdom 2005) I have argued that electronic publication has been notably embraced by the Latin American academic world: scholarly e-journals proliferate in Chile, Brazil, Argentina, Mexico, and Venezuela, for example, and publication of research in electronic form has overtaken that of some Western countries where a greater percentage of the population will be Internet users. In short, e-publication for a variety of fields – cultural and scientific – is booming in Latin America.

The literary e-magazine is a notable example of this boom. From

Cuba to Argentina, fiction writers and literature fans are realising the extraordinary opportunities afforded by the Internet in terms of publishing original work, sharing expertise, reaching a global audience, and fostering a sense of community wherein individuals share the roles of writer, reader, and critic, all for relatively little cost. It is here in particular that e-magazines start to fulfil Aguirre Romero's expectations in moving beyond the boundaries of self-contained cultural artefact to become an instrument of communication.

This chapter seeks to explore how online publishing can generate much more than the static object produced by the printing press, where e-publications can be understood as facilitators of virtual communities. Drawing upon critical debate prevalent in new media studies on the notion of virtual communities, this chapter takes three very different literary e-magazines – from Peru, Venezuela, and Chile – as case studies against which Aguirre Romero's theory will be tested. While the magazine editors all affirm that the idea of virtual community is central to their work, these publications correspond to or redefine accepted definitions of virtual communities in different ways.[1] Furthermore, the strategies employed by each publication, be they structural, functional, or linguistic, to generate and sustain virtual communities will be analysed and the relative effectiveness assessed. This chapter proposes some initial steps in analysing the diverse aims and directions of Latin American literary e-magazines, in the light of the indisputable boom in e-magazines and what it may represent.

i. Virtual Communities

The term 'virtual community' pervades new media, Internet and Web studies, 'virtual' being used to denote anything mediated by technology. A virtual community is understood as people coming together and interacting via technology as a consequence of affinities, shared interests, and common values, as opposed to traditional understandings of communities as defined by geographical proximity and kin (Ridings and Gefen 2004). Howard Rheingold was the first

[1] I would like to thank the editors of the e-magazines under consideration here for their kind and helpful comments and particularly for the generous provision of information relating to their work: Mario Granda Rangel and Giancarlo Stagnaro Ruiz of *El hablador*; Jorge Gómez Jiménez of *Letralia*; and Ernesto Langer Moreno of *Escritores.cl*.

to bring 'virtual community' into currency, optimistically predicting that 'the technology that makes virtual communities possible has the potential to bring enormous leverage to ordinary citizens at relatively little cost – intellectual leverage, social leverage, commercial leverage, and most important, political leverage' (Rheingold 1993: 5). While a number of caveats persist, such as the need for the Internet to be used intelligently by an informed population, and the fact that a bright future of global equal access to the information highway remains emphatically out of reach, Rheingold's positive premise underpins much of the late–1990s thinking about virtual communities.

Watson suggests 'commune-ity' as a way to describe a social group facilitated by technology: a group communing on issues of shared concern (Watson 1997: 104). Rheingold also emphasises this communing nature by defining virtual communities as 'social aggregations that emerge from the Net when enough people carry on those public discussions long enough, with sufficient human feeling, to form webs of personal relationships in cyberspace' (Rheingold 1993: 5). The notion that the more users are involved in the sustenance of a site, the more fame and respect that site is likely to achieve finds particular resonance in the context of the Latin American e-magazines under consideration here.

Further factors crucial to the understanding of virtual communities include the persistence and permanence of participants (Ridings and Gefen 2004; Mitra 1997: 55). Virtual communities consist of 'persistently interacting individuals' (Smith 1999) who feel part of a larger group and share common values, unlike some online discussion groups and chatrooms which are simply places to meet without any sense of permanence and commonality (Q. Jones 1997). Furthermore, it is suggested that virtual communities must have 'compelling content' to survive (Sreenivasan 1997), ideally created by users themselves in order to generate a sense of ownership and belonging (Hagel and Armstrong 1997). It is the sharing of information and knowledge which is central to the idea of the virtual community.

While virtual communities exist in many forms, I choose to follow Gauntlett by examining those communities that spring up around similarly themed websites or e-publications (Gauntlett 2004: 16). The scholarly electronic journal, for example, provides a platform for online discussion of research and the non-static nature of e-publishing permits new, dynamic forms of research in the shape of hypertext articles

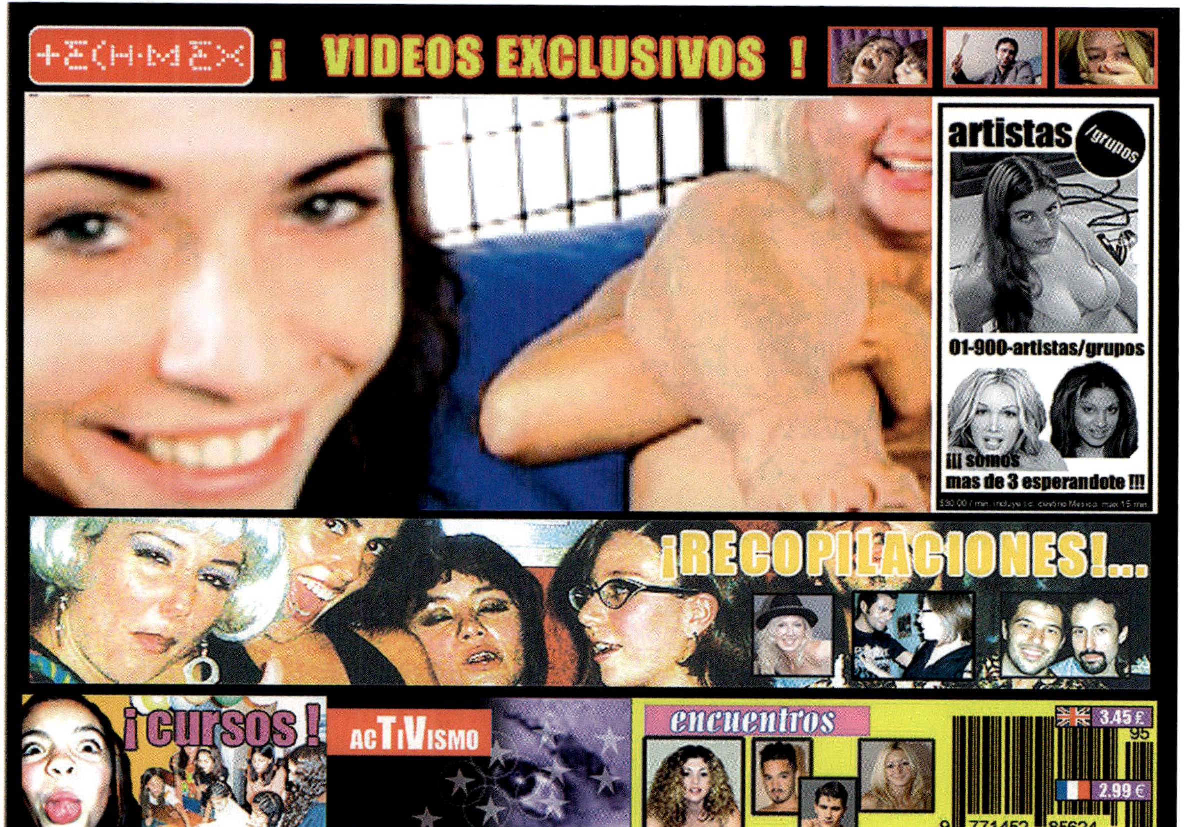

1.1. *Tech-Mex*, the Mexican digital-video clearinghouse site.

1.2. Fernando Llanos, 'seFELIZconsumeVIDEO' [Be Happy, Consume Videos].

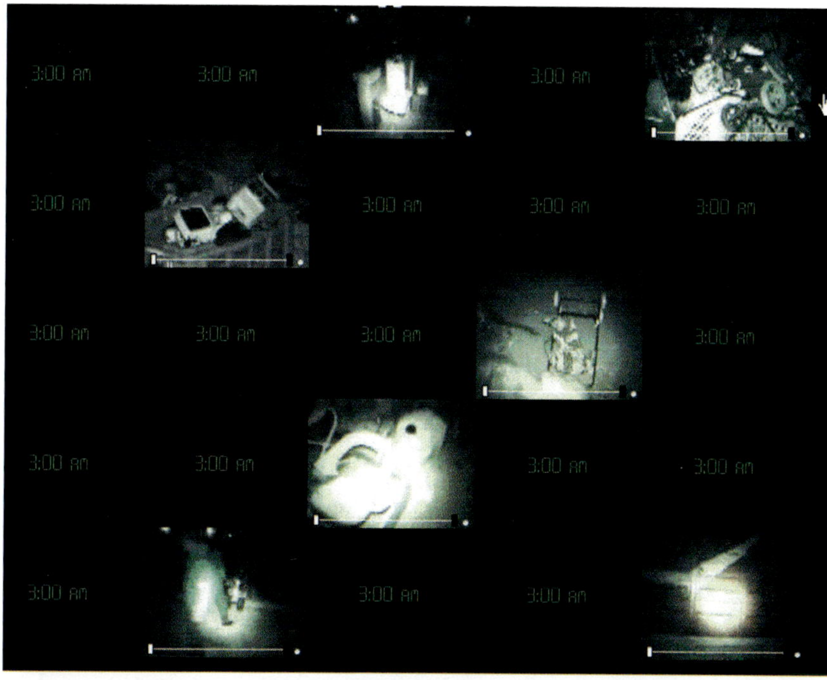

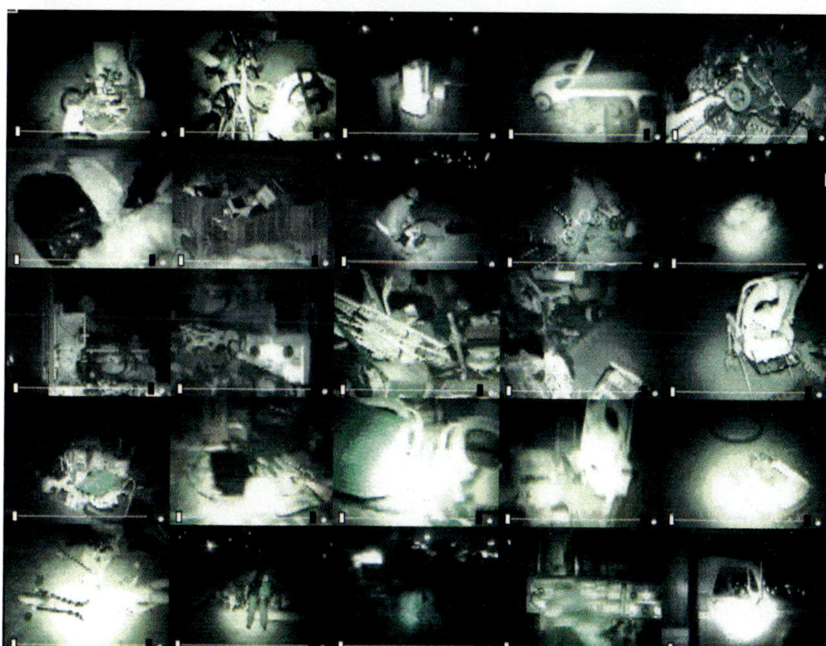

1.3–4. Arcángel Constantini, *unosunosyunosceros* [someonesandsomezeros].

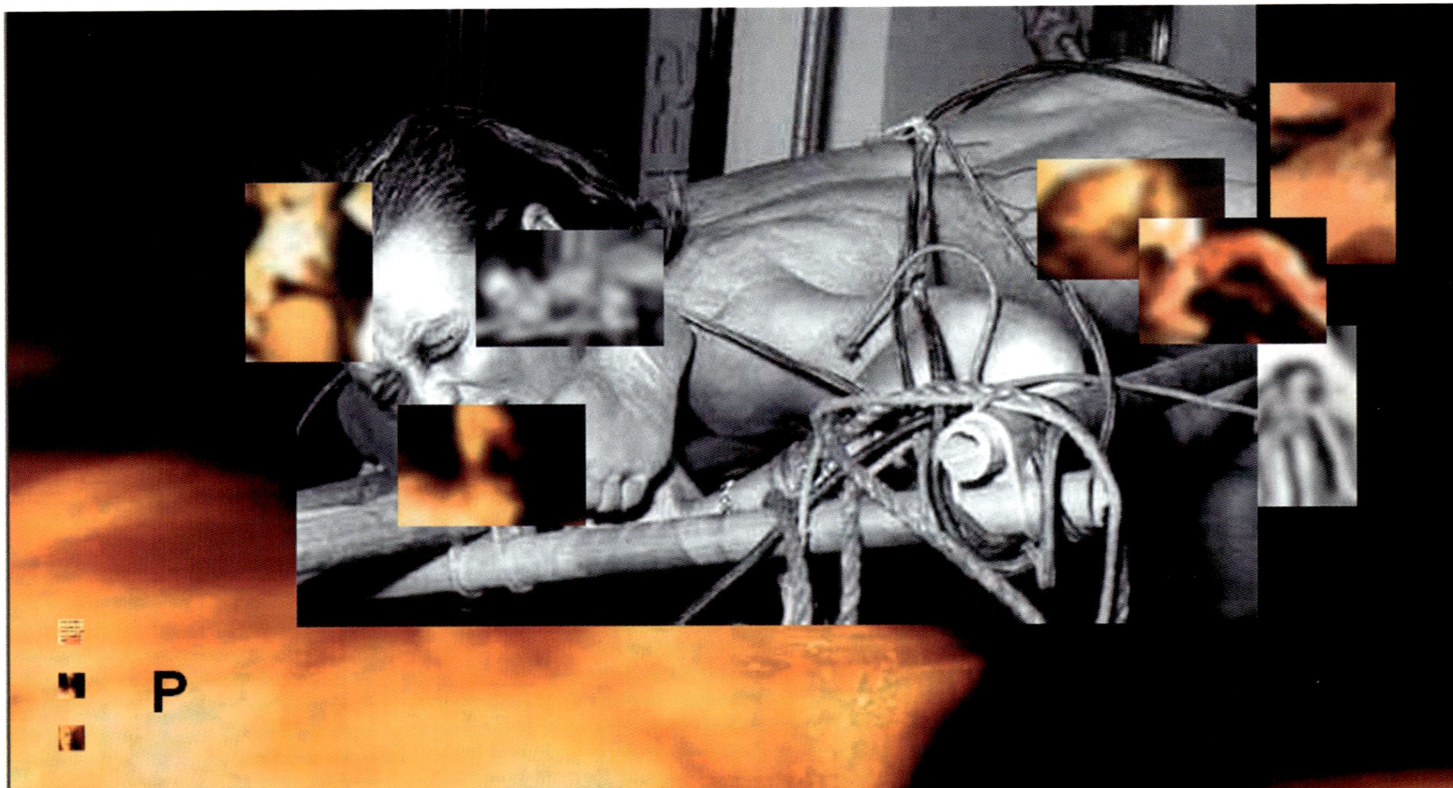

3.1. Corpos Informáticos, 'Quecorpo' [What Body]: A Static Arrangement of Nebulous Images.

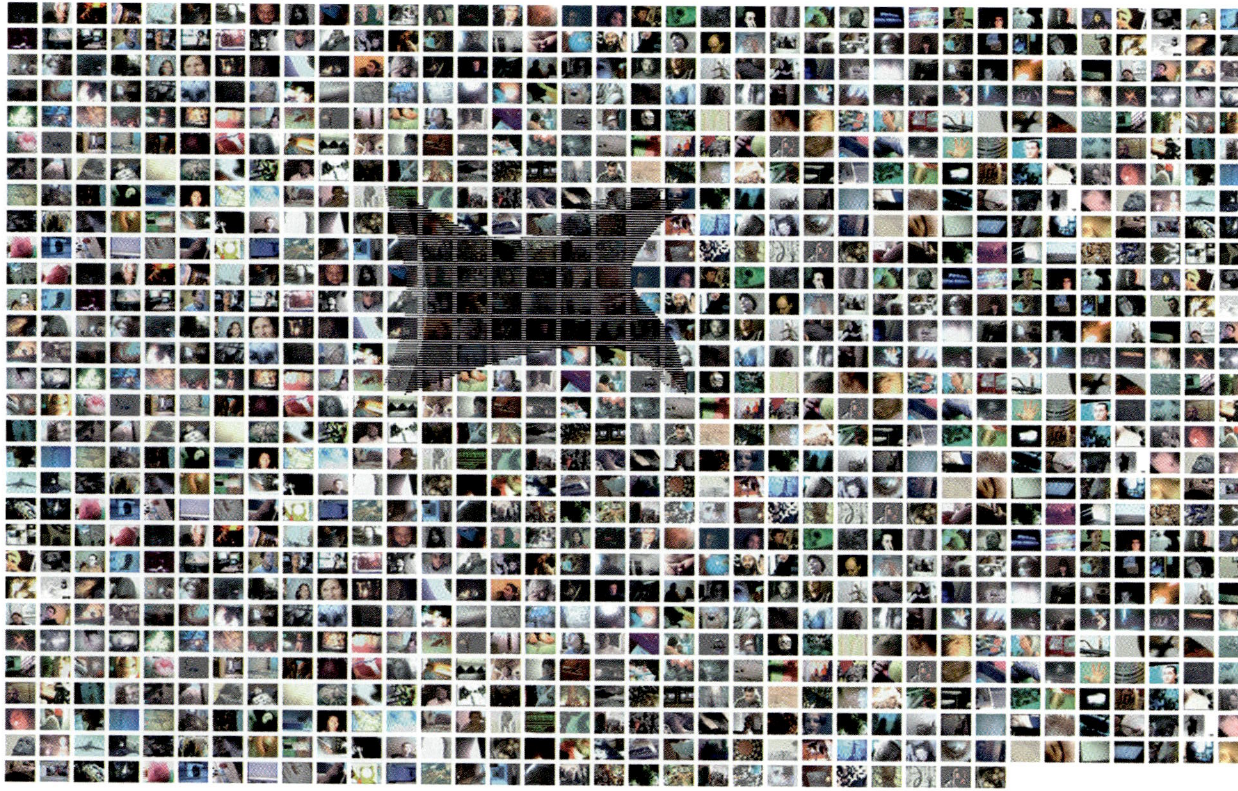

3.2. Corpos Informáticos, 'Telepresence': A Hypertextualised Collage.

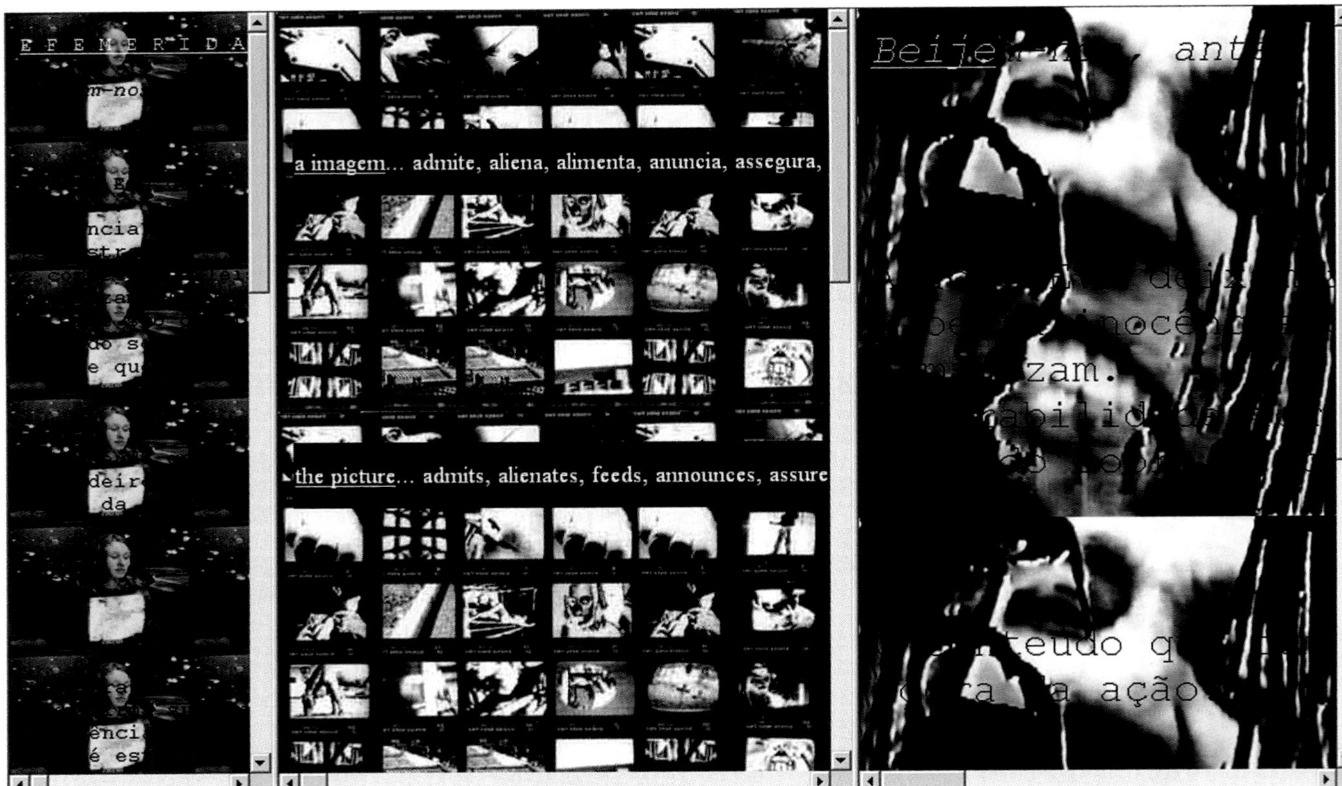

3.3. Corpos Informáticos, 'Dobras' [Folds]: The Dynamical Space of Webmension.

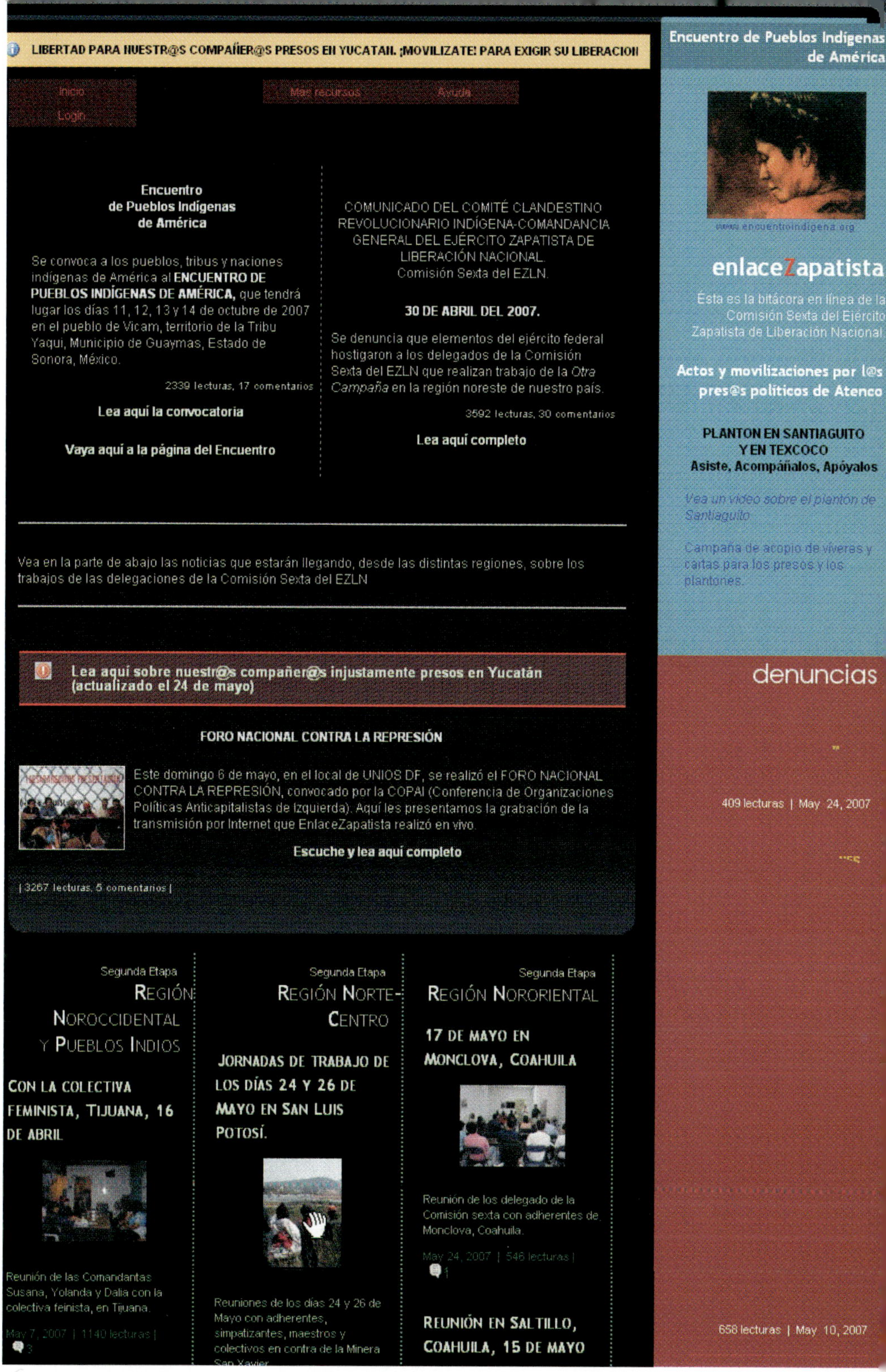

4.1. Homepage, *Enlace Zapatista* [Zapatista Link].

4.2. Homepage, *Asamblea Popular de los Pueblos de Oaxaca* [The Popular Assembly of Oaxacan Peoples].

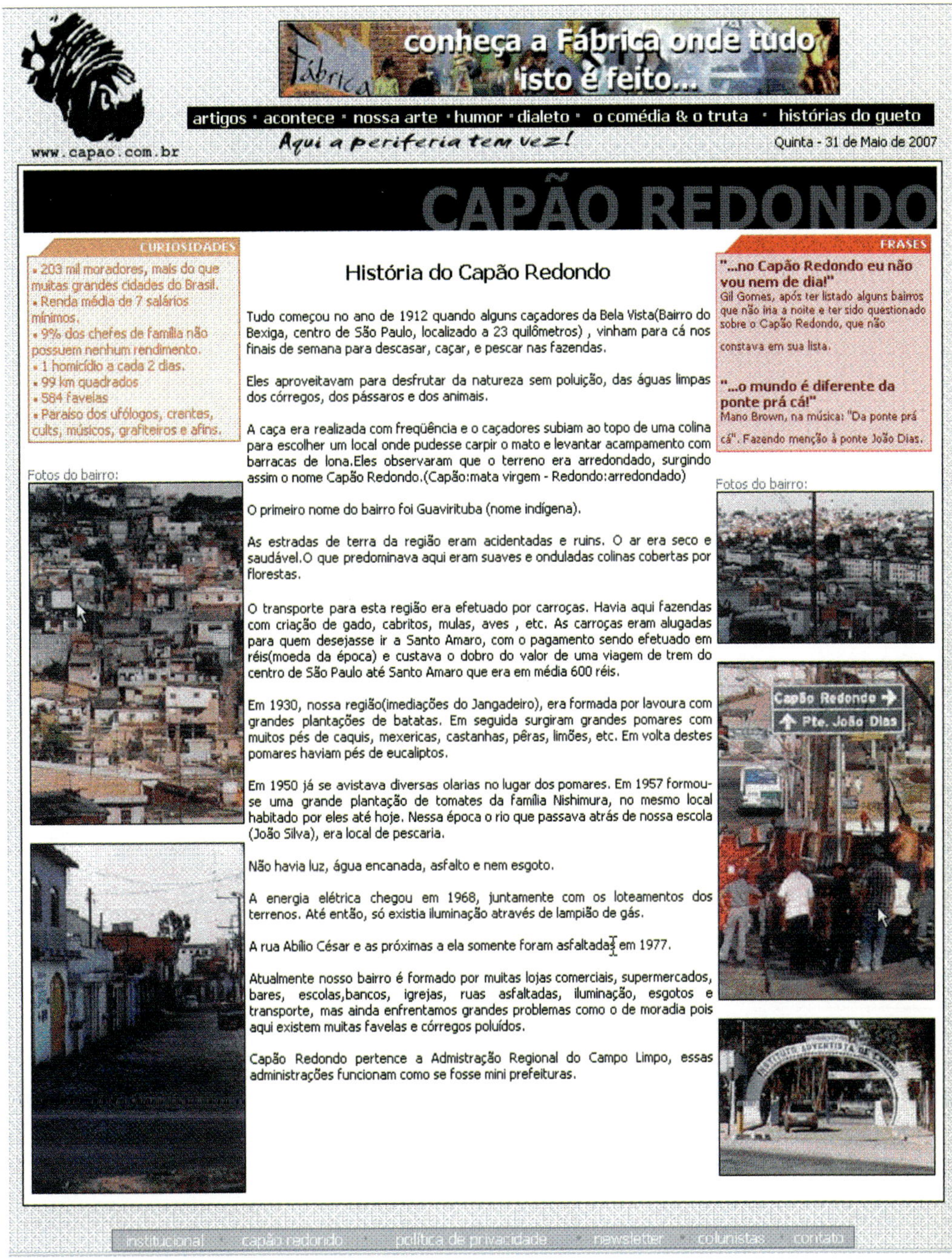

www.capao.com.br

conheça a Fábrica onde tudo isto é feito...

artigos · acontece · nossa arte · humor · dialeto · o comédia & o truta · histórias do gueto

Aqui a periferia tem vez!

Quinta - 31 de Maio de 2007

CAPÃO REDONDO

CURIOSIDADES

- 203 mil moradores, mais do que muitas grandes cidades do Brasil.
- Renda média de 7 salários mínimos.
- 9% dos chefes de família não possuem nenhum rendimento.
- 1 homicídio a cada 2 dias.
- 99 km quadrados
- 584 favelas
- Paraíso dos ufólogos, crentes, cults, músicos, grafiteiros e afins.

Fotos do bairro:

História do Capão Redondo

Tudo começou no ano de 1912 quando alguns caçadores da Bela Vista(Bairro do Bexiga, centro de São Paulo, localizado a 23 quilômetros) , vinham para cá nos finais de semana para descasar, caçar, e pescar nas fazendas.

Eles aproveitavam para desfrutar da natureza sem poluição, das águas limpas dos córregos, dos pássaros e dos animais.

A caça era realizada com freqüência e o caçadores subiam ao topo de uma colina para escolher um local onde pudesse carpir o mato e levantar acampamento com barracas de lona.Eles observaram que o terreno era arredondado, surgindo assim o nome Capão Redondo.(Capão:mata virgem - Redondo:arredondado)

O primeiro nome do bairro foi Guavirituba (nome indígena).

As estradas de terra da região eram acidentadas e ruins. O ar era seco e saudável.O que predominava aqui eram suaves e onduladas colinas cobertas por florestas.

O transporte para esta região era efetuado por carroças. Havia aqui fazendas com criação de gado, cabritos, mulas, aves , etc. As carroças eram alugadas para quem desejasse ir a Santo Amaro, com o pagamento sendo efetuado em réis(moeda da época) e custava o dobro do valor de uma viagem de trem do centro de São Paulo até Santo Amaro que era em média 600 réis.

Em 1930, nossa região(imediações do Jangadeiro), era formada por lavoura com grandes plantações de batatas. Em seguida surgiram grandes pomares com muitos pés de caquis, mexericas, castanhas, pêras, limões, etc. Em volta destes pomares haviam pés de eucaliptos.

Em 1950 já se avistava diversas olarias no lugar dos pomares. Em 1957 formou-se uma grande plantação de tomates da família Nishimura, no mesmo local habitado por eles até hoje. Nessa época o rio que passava atrás de nossa escola (João Silva), era local de pescaria.

Não havia luz, água encanada, asfalto e nem esgoto.

A energia elétrica chegou em 1968, juntamente com os loteamentos dos terrenos. Até então, só existia iluminação através de lampião de gás.

A rua Abílio César e as próximas a ela somente foram asfaltadas em 1977.

Atualmente nosso bairro é formado por muitas lojas comerciais, supermercados, bares, escolas,bancos, igrejas, ruas asfaltadas, iluminação, esgotos e transporte, mas ainda enfrentamos grandes problemas como o de moradia pois aqui existem muitas favelas e córregos poluídos.

Capão Redondo pertence a Admistração Regional do Campo Limpo, essas administrações funcionam como se fosse mini prefeituras.

FRASES

"...no Capão Redondo eu não vou nem de dia!"
Gil Gomes, após ter listado alguns bairros que não iria a noite e ter sido questionado sobre o Capão Redondo, que não constava em sua lista.

"...o mundo é diferente da ponte prá cá!"
Mano Brown, na música: "Da ponte prá cá". Fazendo menção à ponte João Dias.

Fotos do bairro:

Capão Redondo →
↑ Pte. João Dias

institucional · capão redondo · política de privacidade · newsletter · colunistas · contato

6.1. Homepage of *www.capao.com.br*. Photographs: Bruno Jureidini.

Letralia Tierra de Letras

Letralia | Itinerario
Editorial Letralia | Aula Letralia
Ciudad Letralia | TransLetralia
Contacto | Foro literario

La revista de los escritores hispanoamericanos en Internet

¿Qué es Letralia? | Archivo | Cómo publicar | Concursos | Eventos | Servicios | Herramientas | Favoritos | Página de inicio

Año XII • Nº 164
11º aniversario
21 de mayo de 2007
Cagua, Venezuela

Buscar

EDITORIAL
Salud
Jorge Gómez Jiménez

MATERIAL ESPECIAL
Especial 11º aniversario: La Tierra de Letras saluda a la Tierra de Letras

INFORMACIÓN
Breves
Noticias

ARTÍCULOS Y REPORTAJES
La lección de Andrés Bello
Manuel Cabesa
Por los caminos del Homosapiens
Manuel Zapata Olivella
Entre paréntesis, amor, de Rolando Gabrielli. Del poeta nació el amor, que creció y se hizo poema
Fedor García Luna
Los descendientes de Babel
Daniel Navarro
Crítica a la biología pura
Miguel A. Schmucke P.

ENTREVISTAS
Evelio Rosero Diago: Desde la paz preguntan por nosotros
John Jairo Junieles
Leonardo Maicán, un narrador apasionado por la historia: "El escritor es un cronista de su época"
Rafael Ortega
Efraim Medina Reyes: "Mi mayor fracaso es no tener un hijo"
Juan Ensuncho Bárcena

SALA DE ENSAYO
Retorno al problema del anonimato
Musa Ammar Majad
Papel de Estraza siglo XX: la poesía de Zoila M. Cuevas Paralizábal
Juan Carlos Hernández Cuevas
Una transformación inconclusa
Giovanni González Arango

LETRAS
Poemas
Leonardo Hernández Cala
El olor de las nubes
Sergio Llorens
Poemas
Jenny Levine Goldner
Destiempo (Nuestra casa era un nido, donde las aves solían no encontrarse)
Piera Pallavicini
Manhattan en la caverna
Dinapiera Di Donato
Tres relatos
Roger Ferrer Ventosa
Seico de versos hipotéticos
Adriana Lamela
El Valle de Virginia
María Elvira González

Letralia: once años

Letralia Tierra de Letras 11 años

El 20 de mayo de 1996 circuló la primera edición de *Letralia, Tierra de Letras*, que fue recibida en los buzones electrónicos de doce suscriptores primigenios. Hoy, a once años de camino, con miles de lectores en todo el mundo y reconocida como una de las publicaciones líderes en su género, *Letralia* se saluda a sí misma: un grupo de escritores, llegados a la Tierra de Letras en diversos momentos de su historia, comparten con nuestros lectores cómo ha sido su experiencia letraliana.
Material especial:
La Tierra de Letras saluda a la Tierra de Letras

Última hora
La enfermedad, de Alberto Barrera Tyszka, obtiene premio de la Editorial Popular de Pekín

La novela *La enfermedad*, del escritor venezolano Alberto Barrera Tyszka, acaba de obtener el premio que la Editorial Popular de Literatura de Pekín otorga a las mejores novelas en español, tal como lo confirmó este miércoles 22 de mayo el reconocido hispanista chino Zhao Deming. La novela de Barrera Tyszka comparte el premio con *Pasiones griegas*, del escritor chileno Roberto Ampuero. Ambas novelas serán publicadas en chino a finales de este año.
Noticias

Editorial Letralia publica ensayo sobre la literatura y la prevención del sida

En el III Encuentro Colombo-Venezolano de Escritores, celebrado en la ciudad venezolana de La Grita (Táchira) en noviembre de 1995, el sexólogo Cruz Yayes Barco presentó este trabajo en el que proclama la necesidad de que los escritores, como voces privilegiadas de la sociedad, participen activamente en la modificación del discurso sexual, dotándolo de franqueza y madurez, como una vía de primer orden para prevenir la epidemia del sida. Este 23 de mayo, cuando en Venezuela se celebra el Día Nacional para la Prevención del Sida, **Editorial Letralia** lo publica en forma de libro digital, de acceso gratuito en el Web y como archivo .pdf, con la intención de contribuir a la formación de una conciencia en torno a este problema de dimensiones mundiales.
Noticias

Falleció la escritora venezolana Elizabeth Schön

Letralia en tu buzón
Tu e-mail
Suscríbete
¿Quieres ser notificado cada vez que aparezca una nueva actualización de *Letralia*?
Otras listas de correo de Letralia.com

Prueba las nuevas herramientas de Letralia
Dos nuevas herramientas para los habitantes de la Tierra de Letras: nuestro buscador para el navegador Mozilla Firefox y nuestra barra de herramientas para Microsoft Internet Explorer y Mozilla Firefox.
Servicios

Libros digitales
31 cuentos de amor rosados y no tanto
Carmen Rosa Barrere
La escritora argentina Carmen Rosa Barrere interpreta los 31 preceptos del Tratado del amor cortesano, *el libro que Andreas Capellanus escribió en 1184 bajo encargo de la Condesa María de Troya, y los convierte en igual número de relatos que – inundados de picardía, pasión y ternura a partes iguales, e ilustrados con obras maestras de la pintura– abordan el tema eterno del amor desde una gran variedad de perspectivas.*
Colección Narrativa
Editorial Letralia

Firmas exclusivas en la metrópolis de las letras
Fuera de campo
Andrés Pérez Domínguez
Ciudad Letralia

Traducciones en la encrucijada de las lenguas
Anne Rice: Lestat el vampiro (extracto)
Traducción del inglés al español: Nicole Lafourcade
TransLetralia

Salud
Nuestro especial de aniversario, "La Tierra de Letras saluda a la Tierra de Letras", está compuesto por el testimonio de varios viajeros que, tras vagar por los inconmensurables océanos de Internet, echaron anclas en *Letralia* y se sentaron con nosotros alrededor del fuego.
Jorge Gómez Jiménez.
Editorial

7.1. Homepage of Venezuelan literary e-mag, *Letralia*.

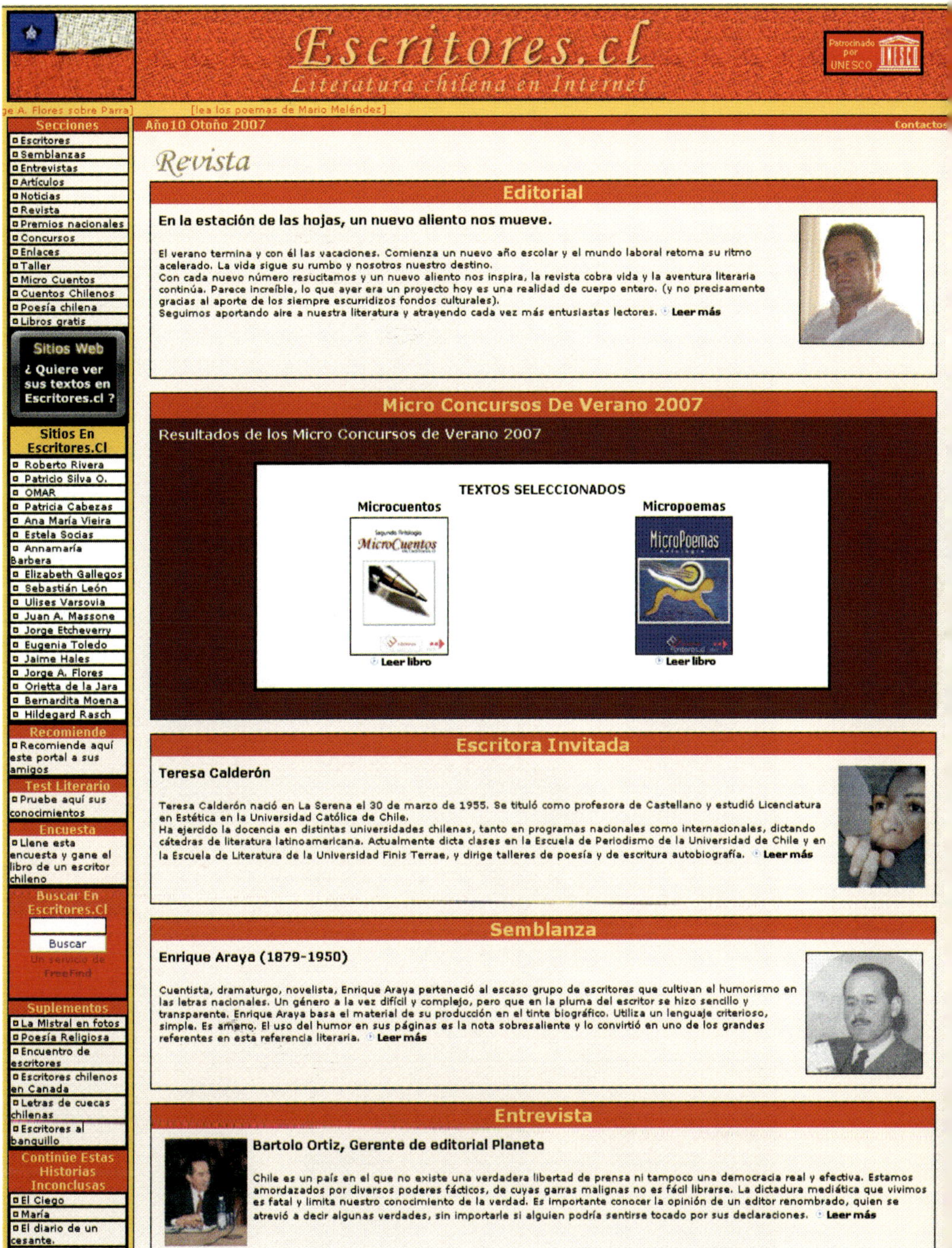

7.2. Homepage of Chilean literary e-mag, *Escritores.cl*.

8.1. Fran Ilich, *net. work*. Ilich is wearing the Zapatista-style balaclava; hypermedia writer Blas Valdez is on the far right of the image.

13.1. Navigation map, *Tierra de extracción* [Land of Extraction], artwork by Andreas Meier, novel written and directed by Doménico Chiappe.

February 27, 2006

oJo aLeGrE ** *

Filed under: General — noemi @ 7:00 pm

Útil y divertido es para mí sacar el ojo de su cuenca. Si necesito ver qué pasa en la estancia de al lado, lo ruedo discreta por el piso. Puedo leer mientras veo una película o conversar con Juana y observar a Chana. Si quiero saber más sobre una persona, ruedo el ojo por el piso hasta que alcanzo a mirar la suela de su zapato y ver su estado. Incluso logro dormitar, echando un ojo al gato y otro al garabato. A veces me lo quito para dormir y descanso mucho mejor. Lo remojo en té de manzanilla para conservarlo fresco y puro. Me da terror que me quieran mandar el mal de ojo, en serio. Pero lo que ahora mismo me tiene preocupada, es que está adquiriendo una especie de miopía, presbicia y astigmatismo, todo al mismo tiempo, y el otro ojo, que está mucho más sano, no consigo sacarlo de la cuenca. ¿Qué voy a hacer?

14.1. Noemí Guzik Glantz, 'oJo aLeGrE' [Happy Eye], 27 February 2006.

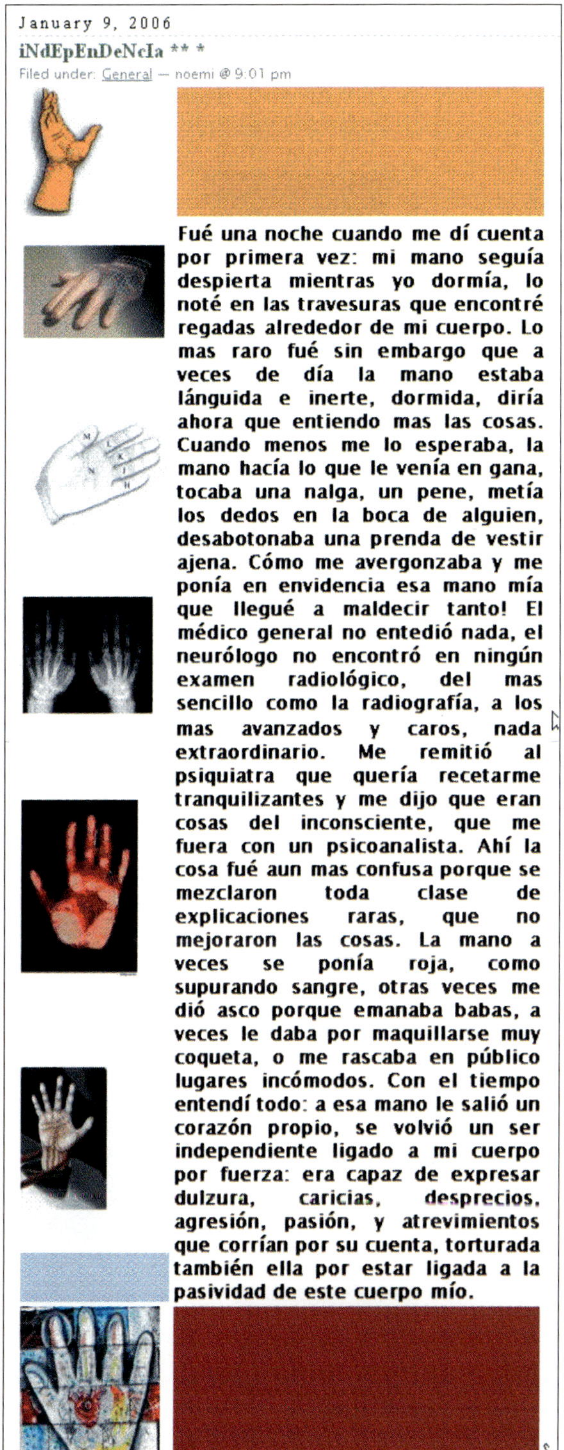

January 9, 2006

iNdEpEnDeNcIa ** *

Filed under: General — noemi @ 9:01 pm

Fué una noche cuando me dí cuenta por primera vez: mi mano seguía despierta mientras yo dormía, lo noté en las travesuras que encontré regadas alrededor de mi cuerpo. Lo mas raro fué sin embargo que a veces de día la mano estaba lánguida e inerte, dormida, diría ahora que entiendo mas las cosas. Cuando menos me lo esperaba, la mano hacía lo que le venía en gana, tocaba una nalga, un pene, metía los dedos en la boca de alguien, desabotonaba una prenda de vestir ajena. Cómo me avergonzaba y me ponía en envidencia esa mano mía que llegué a maldecir tanto! El médico general no entedió nada, el neurólogo no encontró en ningún examen radiológico, del mas sencillo como la radiografía, a los mas avanzados y caros, nada extraordinario. Me remitió al psiquiatra que quería recetarme tranquilizantes y me dijo que eran cosas del inconsciente, que me fuera con un psicoanalista. Ahí la cosa fué aun mas confusa porque se mezclaron toda clase de explicaciones raras, que no mejoraron las cosas. La mano a veces se ponía roja, como supurando sangre, otras veces me dió asco porque emanaba babas, a veces le daba por maquillarse muy coqueta, o me rascaba en público lugares incómodos. Con el tiempo entendí todo: a esa mano le salió un corazón propio, se volvió un ser independiente ligado a mi cuerpo por fuerza: era capaz de expresar dulzura, caricias, desprecios, agresión, pasión, y atrevimientos que corrían por su cuenta, torturada también ella por estar ligada a la pasividad de este cuerpo mío.

14.2. Noemí Guzik Glantz, 'iNdEpEnDeNcIa' [Independence], 9 January 2006.

14.3. Noemí Guzik Glantz, 'aCto nEcEsariO' [A Necessary Act], 28 January 2006.

with multimedia components, and a process of ongoing peer review and open-ended writing which is continually subject to refinement. These publications remain, however, the territory of the academic and a distinction should be drawn between e-journals which are overtly scholarly in approach and e-magazines, which may not necessarily be edited by academics and tend to function more broadly as online focal points for writers and literature enthusiasts. While these two types of publications frequently overlap – indeed the Internet may be working to blur the boundaries between traditional publishing formats – the role of e-magazines in facilitating clusters of interest is what merits attention here.

Whilst early thinkers, as Sorin Matei notes, posited the virtual community as a countercultural challenge to the tendency of modern society towards 'uniformity, regimentation, and massification' (Matei 2005), this perspective has been questioned by critics such as Steven Jones, who conjectures that the Internet may be 'another in a line of modern technologies that undermine traditional notions of civil society that require unity and shun multiplicity while giving impressions that they in fact re-create such a society' (S. Jones 1997: 25). While the Latin American literary e-magazines studied here aim to promote diversity and provide opportunities for authors to share their work and reach a wide audience – a goal undoubtedly precluded by former reliance on traditional print channels – the extent to which diversity is indeed prevalent in these spaces varies. This chapter will consider whether these magazines follow the countercultural ideals expressed by early commentators of virtual communities or whether they ultimately reinforce national canons, privileging the familiar and, importantly, failing to reach the diverse audience they seek. A key element of critical cyberculture studies – the so-called 'third generation' of scholarship which moves beyond simple description of popular cyberculture, virtual communities, and online identities – is the analysis of 'social, cultural, political and economic considerations which encourage, make possible, and/or thwart individual and group access to [online] interactions' (Silver 2000: 10). In heralding the brave new world of information available to all, the first and second wave of cyberculture studies have, according to Silver and others, neglected to consider the widening gap between the information rich and the information poor. Despite Latin America's recent boom in Internet connectivity, vast swathes of society across the region remain unaffected by the digital age and are at risk of being left behind altogether (Molloy 2000). Significantly, the majority of Internet users across Latin America tend to be urban, male, white, upper class, and proficient in English (Gómez 2000). While it is beyond the scope of this chapter to analyse the audiences of each e-magazine in question, the reality that only certain sectors of Latin American society and only certain countries across the region have access to online material, should be borne in mind when considering these publications.

ii. *El hablador*: The Traditional Literary Review

El hablador [The Speaker] was established in 2003 by a group of Peruvian postgraduate students and as such is the youngest online literary magazine under consideration here. Nevertheless, its professional design and diverse content have resulted in its becoming a significant player in the world of Spanish-language e-publications, with the majority of its readership being based in Peru. The exploration of literary aesthetics that the magazine purports to undertake places some emphasis on 'a desire to imagine other ways of creating literature'; as such *El hablador* aims to make a conscious effort to the explore the very medium it has chosen to employ.[2] The editorial's observation that 'the complex exchanges between traditional spaces and the new media explosion, despite having created considerable distortions, must, of necessity, be read from a critical perspective' aspires to a balanced and critical approach to the new medium. In a country such as Peru, the editors say, which suffers from a general lack of interest in reading and lack of channels for book dissemination, the magazine is particularly keen to explore the relationship between digital and print publication, and the opportunities afforded by the former.

El hablador is published three times a year and follows a straightforward format. Under the subheadings of 'Debate' and 'Estudios' [Studies], readers will find theoretical and critical articles on primarily Peruvian literature and culture, with later issues broadening in scope to engage with literature from other Latin American countries. Indeed, by taking its name from a novel by one of Peru's greatest writers,

2 The quotation here taken from the *El hablador* website is my own translation from the original Spanish. All further quotations from the three literary websites in question are also my own translations.

Mario Vargas Llosa's *El hablador* (1987), the magazine inscribes itself within a national literary tradition. Carlos Jáuregui theorises that (Jáuregui 2000: 364):

> the survival of cultural geography, [...] national space, and a new kind of Latin Americanism are all being reconstituted in the online digital world, just as these very concepts (nation, Latin America and Hispanicity) are perceived to be in crisis within a globalised world whose icon is precisely the Internet.

By emphasising its Peruvian foundations and focus, *El hablador* supports this theory and in so doing problematises the assumption that virtual communities are not 'geopolitical' but based on common interests (Jáuregui 2000: 364). However, its opening of scope demonstrates a move away from national identity to focus on the Spanish language itself, regardless of locality.

The magazine's format – critical studies, interviews, and original prose and poetry – has remained unchanged since its inception. The simple format renders site navigation easy and makes for an accessible literary review with a broad, intellectual appeal. While the contents remain concise, usually with two or three contributions to each section, the articles tend to be well developed and scholarly in nature with the focus being high literature and political issues in Latin American culture. *El hablador* seeks to 'make clear its own view of the reality of literature in Peru in order to shift away from a purely academic perspective and a focus on stereotypical literature', and seeks to address a balance of canonical and 'alternative' literature.[3] In a country relatively lacking in history of literary discourse such as Peru, this e-magazine takes on the enormous task of attempting to sustain and generate interest in its national literary greats, while simultaneously looking beyond traditional, better-known texts and reflecting on the nature of literary criticism itself. Thus, alongside articles concerning Mario Vargas Llosa, Alfredo Bryce Echenique and popular young writers such as Jaime Bayly, readers find studies on, for example, book piracy in Peru and literary criticism in the national press. As such, the magazine pitches itself within national canons with some tentative steps beyond.

[3] Personal email correspondence with Mario Granda.

The editorial from the first issue invites readers to engage in a dialogue concerning 'themes of mutual interest' which reads as an appeal to foment a community around common threads. Indeed, the site runs an email discussion group which to some extent facilitates the path for participation in the magazine. Furthermore, a links section points readers to other Spanish-language literary websites of interest and thus demonstrates *El hablador*'s position within the wider context of the online literary publications that are mutually supportive rather than competitive. However, despite the magazine's overarching concern with debating the importance and value of literature, opportunities afforded by new technology have yet to be fully harnessed by the editors of *El hablador*. The site remains an object of static text with no opportunity for interactivity (the email discussion group is hosted by Yahoo and cannot be viewed from the main site). This fact is acknowledged by Mario Granda, one of *El hablador*'s editors: while the magazine hopes to attract 'critical' readers – 'those who read the magazine and write comments to us about it' –, Granda notes that this does not occur a great deal since the magazine 'lacks spaces that permit interaction with readers'.[4]

Carlos Jáuregui notes that a number of online literary publications 'search for a textual authority by inscribing themselves within the genealogy of printed books and magazines. [...] E-publications' mimetic design, however, is not always nostalgic for the printed world, but a simulation of the materiality and structure of a book' (Jáuregui 2000: 362). Similarly, while not specifically imitating handwritten manuscripts as is the wont of some online publications (*Proyecto Sherezade* is the example cited by Jáuregui), *El hablador* does emulate the structure of a print magazine: articles span several 'pages'; navigation is enabled by a drop-down list of contents, or by the initial opening contents page of each issue. Hypertextual links are all but absent in the essays, which precludes the sense of contextual connectivity afforded by the web. While the magazine often features articles debating digital versus print publishing, it does not fully exploit its own status as a digital artefact and harness the opportunities for linking across texts and broadening references that electronic publishing offers. As such, a sense of online community between the users and across related websites is undermined here.

4 Personal email correspondence with Mario Granda.

Clearly, the question of resources is at stake, and it could indeed be argued that simplification will ensure a greater readership. Jáuregui notes that the general trend of Spanish-language literary magazines is for simplification, avoiding 'technical and graphical complexity and the use of frames and erratic links in its presentation' (Jáuregui 2000: 361). In Peru, as in many other countries across the region, there is still no Internet connection by monthly contract and the high costs of installing the Internet at home mean that the majority of users only go online in public booths. Thus, in order to maximise their time online, rather than contribute to the site by sending comments, for example, readers will simply download the magazine's texts. *El hablador*'s remit is to disseminate literary criticism, to generate interest in Peruvian and Latin American culture, and to function as a space for unpublished writers to disseminate their work. It would be churlish to criticise its laudable attempts to achieve this, and certainly its years online to date have demonstrated editorial commitment and a sustainable model. However, to make a serious impact on and to push the boundaries of the world of electronic publishing, *El hablador* would ideally employ some of the strategies central to some of the most successful literary websites: that of actively generating the sense of virtual community by allowing that community to take some responsibility for the website content. While *El hablador* seeks to encourage participation and debate, the magazine's average reader has little opportunity to contribute. The community created by the readership, while undoubtedly alive – daily page views average close to 100, 60% of which are from Peru – is mostly invisible and silent. *El hablador* remains, albeit in a sophisticated way, an object 'in itself' rather than an instrument at the service of information dissemination. Thus *El hablador*, still in its relative infancy, represents the first stage in the development of e-magazines: that of a primary focus on textual criticism.

iii. *Letralia*: Creating Literary 'Place' in Cyberspace

The year 1996 saw the birth of what is now one of the undisputed giants of literary websites in Latin America. Produced and edited in Venezuela by the writer, Jorge Gómez Jiménez, *Letralia: tierra de letras* can claim the title of one of the longest-running literary e-magazines in Latin America and represents a very different approach to *El hablador*. The current substantial, well-designed and user-friendly

Letralia website (see fig. 7.1) belies a rather troubled past: the basic practical difficulties of turning the original idea of a Venezuelan cultural magazine into reality; the trials of unreliable Internet connections and servers; and the challenges of reaching a wide readership, all on an almost nonexistent budget (Gómez Jiménez 2004). Yet *Letralia* has overcome obstacles to become a real success story in terms of longevity, sustained readership and site development: what began as a newsletter distributed by email has become one of the most significant portals to Latin American literature online[5] – and far exceeds the scope of a literary magazine. Updated online twice a month, *Letralia* now distributes four related but distinct electronic bulletins and has diversified from the simple format of articles of literary criticism and review: it now publishes complete books online and maintains diverse but related websites discussing literature in translation and providing training to would-be writers. *Letralia* receives over 5000 hits a day, and its contributors number over 1070.[6] With such a large network of users, it could be argued that *Letralia*'s success is due in part to its fostering of a virtual community.

To some extent, *Letralia* follows the format of *El hablador* with each issue presenting new critical articles and reports, book reviews, and publishing original short stories and poems. Each issue also offers related news items and announcements of events and publications. The magazine's scope is broad and encompasses literature from throughout Latin America.[7] Articles, which tend to be succinct and accessible, cover a wide range of literary issues: indeed, *Letralia* has come to

5 In 2006, *Letralia* was a finalist in the Culture category of the annual Stockholm Challenge Award, a global networking programme for ICT entrepreneurs. Its mission is to 'demonstrate how information technology can improve living conditions and increase economic growth in all parts of the world' (Stockholm Challenge Award).

6 Information supplied by Jorge Gómez Jiménez via email. It should be noted the number of hits does not denote the number of users and as such is perhaps not the ideal way of measuring a site's popularity. A hit is scored when a webpage is accessed, but a single user may access the same webpage several times in one session thus generating multiple hits.

7 *Letralia*'s original focus was literature solely from Venezuela. By the time of the third issue, *Letralia* was invited to move to the RedIRIS (Red Académica y de Investigación de España) servers, thus facilitating greater distribution and stability. The one condition of this migration was that the magazine should broaden its appeal and not limit itself to Venezuelan literature. As such, *Letralia* grew to cover literature from all of Latin America (Gómez Jiménez 2004).

represent an extremely valuable means of discovering new work from the region. Like *El hablador, Letralia* focuses on national literary greats but also does its utmost to promote the work of new writers.

One of *Letralia*'s salient features is the repeated use of territorial metaphors. The magazine's subtitle, for example, is 'Tierra de letras' [Land of Letters] and references to land and territory – in other words, space, the physical structure of community as opposed to place, the socio-cultural properties (Porter 2004) – permeate Gómez Jiménez's writings about his magazine. Notions of geographically bound communities are embedded within thinking about virtual communities with some pundits arguing that the latter's development is kindled by nostalgia for the former (Rheingold 1993; Wellman and Gulia 1999). Indeed, the fact that the term 'cyberspace' has currency at all signifies reliance on physical metaphors when describing something intangible. Cyberspace has been defined as 'incontrovertibly social spaces in which people still meet face-to-face, but under new definitions of "meet" and "face"' (Stone 1991: 85). It is the geographical lack that *Letralia* could be seen to attempt to fill by means of its territorial metaphors, and this in turn has resulted in the establishment of a strong virtual community.

The *Letralia* enterprise is founded upon the belief that 'we literature lovers share common territories' and that 'these territories make up the Land of Letters, whose ideal villages are without borders and whose roads have neither taxes nor restrictions' (Gómez Jiménez 2004). Gómez Jiménez is referring here to the economic and political barriers facing writers in Venezuela – and indeed throughout Latin America – in terms of publishing their work and reaching a readership of any size, and that the online environment offers an alternative 'land' of opportunity. He also invokes a sense of claiming land, creating a space for 'homeless' writers to inhabit and share. Furthermore, the name *Letralia* is a play on 'Italia', deriving from *eit* (life) and *alere* (to feed), meaning the region which nurtures life. Correspondingly, *Letralia* means the region or land which nurtures literature (Gómez Jiménez 2004). This metaphor permeates later developments of the site, notably *Ciudad Letralia*, an offshoot website where authors are invited to write on particular themes or 'avenues', usually of an international focus. *Ciudad Letralia* is, in other words, the intersection where roads from different terrains meet. The description of *Ciudad Letralia* provided on the website is especially illuminating ('¿Qué es Ciudad Letralia?'):

> In the particular Letralian geography, Letralia City is rather like the capital of the Land of Letters, and its avenues are named by authors brought to you exclusively by us. In this space we publish texts by a wide range of specially invited Spanish-speaking writers in order to give you, the reader, new routes to follow, and to diversify the unique Letralian demographic. Each avenue represents a way of viewing and moreover a way of *writing*, our lives. Together, these avenues constitute the ideal city where the inhabitants of the Land of Letters are free to roam.

Land, territory, city, roads, and avenues: the metaphors abound. What is more, readers and contributors to the magazine are repeatedly referred to as 'Letralians': such rhetoric delineates *Letralia* in terms of both space and place, inhabited by citizens. It directly appeals to the so-called nostalgia for lost physical communities and consequently confirms its legitimacy as a 'real' community. It is, therefore, by means of discourse that this virtual community is forged.

Where *Letralia* also succeeds in the fostering of virtual community is in its inclusive nature and tone. The site's language is familiar and personal; the emphasis throughout is on the *people* involved. All contributors are listed by name, accompanied by a brief biography and email address, thus enabling readers to contact writers personally. Readers are directly addressed: repetition of both the formal and informal Spanish forms of 'you' – *usted* and *tú* – is apparent in the website's contents, with feedback and comments invited throughout. Such language not only emphasises the human element to the site – important in the digital age where face-to-face contact may be undermined – but generates a sense of belonging. Inviting readers to contribute to a site fosters a sense of ownership and sustains the site itself, as Ridings and Gefen have noted (2004). In their discussion of online reciprocity and attachment felt in virtual communities, Wellman and Gulia argue that many Internet users do indeed offer support to each other within particular groups and that those with strong attachments to the group or organisation in question are more likely to help others within it. *Letralia* subscribes to this notion, realising that the participation of its users is key to the sustenance of the site.

Letralia has developed specific channels to facilitate participation. As Gómez Jiménez says, 'not only do we have the impression that we work in the centre of a substantial community, but it is our very objective to stimulate the cohesion of that community, at least within the margins of our technical limitations'.[8] To this end, *Letralia* features an online discussion forum; provides guidance on the art of writing itself; and distributes a bulletin entitled 'Escritores de Letralia' [Letralia Writers] to all accepted contributors, which provides information on publishing initiatives, events, paid work for writers and editors, and other material of interest. In keeping with its strapline, 'La revista de escritores hispanoamericanos en Internet' [The Internet Magazine of Latin American Writers], *Letralia* is a magazine about, by, and for Latin American writers, working to blur boundaries between reader and writer. *Letralia* aspires to give all readers the opportunity to be writers themselves in keeping with the egalitarian ideals of the Internet: online, readers become 'writers' by selecting the order in which the electronic text is read (Fajardo 1999; Wakeford 2004: 36) and this is concretised by the user-participation model of *Letralia* and others.

According to Wellman and Gulia, what differentiates virtual communities from 'real-life' communities is the basis upon which individuals develop intimate relationships: 'people on the Net have a greater tendency to develop feelings of closeness on the basis of shared interests rather than on the basis of shared social characteristics such as gender and socioeconomic status' (1999: 171). While this suggests the potential of the virtual community to encourage diversity, the important point here is that virtual communities should not be compared to 'real' communities for they are entirely different entities. Moreover, the emphasis on shared interests is highlighted by Gómez Jiménez:

> Letralians from all over the world are able to contact each other in order to work together and this, of course, improves the literary experience of everyone who participates. A community with these characteristics, obviously united by language and literature, offers its members diverse alternatives to reduce the natural difficulties facing those who would like to see their work in print.[9]

8 Personal email correspondence with Jorge Gómez Jiménez.
9 Personal email correspondence with Jorge Gómez Jiménez.

The shared interests of reading and writing bind this group into a cohesive whole with the title 'Letralians', and this particular adhesive factor is regularly reinforced by *Letralia*'s very personable editor.

In keeping with the sense of *Letralia* being very much a people-based endeavour, the personality of Gómez Jiménez is prevalent throughout the site. He draws readers into the site with his affable editorial columns, which narrate the history and development of *Letralia* and current issues in the literary world. Links are provided throughout the site to Gómez Jiménez's own website and blog, and readers are invited to contact the editor direct via his personal email address. He has become the leader, narrator, and facilitator of this community and is justifiably proud of his achievement, as reflected in much of the site's rhetoric which highlights its status as one of the most robust literary portals on the web. His inclusive tone infuses the site with 'sufficient human feeling', as stipulated by Rheingold, necessary for the sustenance of an online community. Inspired by the editor's pride, users can feel that they are participating in a success story, an against-the-odds battle to make Latin American literature accessible to all.

In terms of its place within a wider community of literary websites, *Letralia*'s 'Itinerario' [Itinerary] – an extensive directory of weblinks – has proved a shrewd endeavour and serves a dual purpose. Firstly, by listing a vast number of related websites together with descriptive comments, it functions as an important portal to Latin American literature online. Secondly, by linking to all these websites – and for the most part the links are reciprocated – *Letralia* not only improves its Google ranking but positions itself as central within the growing network of Latin American literary websites, generating more visits from diverse routes, and establishing itself as *the* authority to Latin American literature online.

Thus, *Letralia* subscribes to the type of community outlined by Gauntlett – that which springs up around websites themselves, generating community through content and rhetoric rather than tools such as blogs and instant messaging. The fact remains, however, that *Letralia*'s audience is still the privileged few, with statistics revealing that the majority of visits come from Spain, Venezuela, the US, Mexico, and Argentina, with the rest of Latin America very under-represented. *Letralia* undoubtedly reaches a relatively large audience but – and this is not the fault of the magazine – access is still not as widespread as hoped. Nonetheless, longevity and creativity have resulted in *Letralia* moving beyond a static cultural artefact to become something more dynamic: an informal literature network and portal, a 'home' for Latin American literature online.

iv. *Escritores.cl*: The Online Literary Club

For Ernesto Langer Moreno, the editor of the Chilean literary website, *Escritores.cl,* the notion of a virtual literary community is central to his work. Langer is convinced that the Internet has created unprecedented opportunities for writers, not only as an economic means of publication and wide dissemination, but also for its role as facilitator of communities: 'the Internet allows the literary community to open up, bringing together interested parties and forming a great 'revitalising' network. Never before in history has a writer been able to communicate with so many like-minded people, comment on texts and share information about the issues that concern us' (Dante 1999). Furthermore, Langer evokes the organic processes of ongoing textual commentary and consequent rewriting enabled by the Internet, in that texts may be published, comments are invited, and writers can adapt their work in reaction to the comments: 'thanks to the Internet writers can compare, share and promote their work in an unprecedented way' (Dante 1999). *Escritores.cl* is constructed around these principles and of the three websites under consideration here, is perhaps the one that moves furthest away from the 'magazine' format to become an interactive forum for Chilean writers.

Langer brought to the project technical expertise gained from working for a major Chilean Internet service provider. His aim was to create a dedicated space for Chilean literature on the web and to assist those writers unable to maintain their own websites, usually for financial reasons. Established in 1998 and now deemed to be the major literary website in Chile (Dante 1999), *Escritores.cl* enjoys sponsorship from UNESCO and in 2005 received on average between 1500 and 2000 hits per day, a figure almost double that of 2004 ('Estadísticas de uso'). Like *Letralia,* its success is due in part to the very people-orientated nature of the site, but *Escritores.cl* takes this further. It moves away from a primary focus on literary criticism and lives up to its name by making the writers themselves the foundations for the site.

The structure of *Escritores.cl* differs greatly from *Letralia* and *El hablador*: the front page lists a summary of the 'revista' [magazine], with an editorial column, 'semblanzas' [features on individual writers], and topical articles about, for example, good writing style (see fig. 7.2). However, the notion of the site as a 'magazine' is undermined by the left-hand navigation panel that breaks the 'revista' up into its component parts. Here, users may browse across sections from previous issues, which are listed in the following order: Escritores [writers], Semblanzas [short biographies], Entrevistas [interviews], Artículos [articles], Noticias [news], Revista [magazine]. Clicking on 'Revista' here takes the user back to the homepage. While this navigation is rather confused, what can be noted is the privileging of the writers over and above other features; the 'magazine' becomes subsidiary to the main aim of the site, to promote Chilean writers and their work. Such emphasis on writers is reiterated by *Escritores.cl* acting as a host for the personal websites of a collection of Chilean authors, wherein biographies, bibliographies, and a selection of works may be made available.

In a similar way to *Letralia*, the figure of the editor looms large over *Escritores.cl*: an editorial column is included by Langer in each new issue, while his blog and personal website are both accessible from the homepage. The blog in particular is used by Langer to champion the cause of writers in Chile struggling to publish. This blog does not, however, correspond to now common understandings of this format, and remains a static page of text.

The articles published on *Escritores.cl* tend to be pithy and accessible; less textual criticism and more commentary on literature in general in Chile. Articles presenting, for example, overviews of literary criticism in Chile, the disappearance of Chilean literary magazines, literary prizes, and new work by major writers such as Isabel Allende can be found here. As such, many of these articles read more as opinion pieces than literary analysis but then, the site has never claimed to serve the same function as *El hablador*, for example. What the contents do reinforce is a strong sense of nationhood, in keeping with Jáuregui's speculations. Langer states that he wishes the site to be an open forum, and he will consider for publication any work that is sent to him (Dante 1999). That said, the themes of the articles remain within canonical areas and male writers dominate the site's 'semblanzas'. Consequently, whether *Escritores.cl* genuinely fulfils its open access goal is questionable. This issue is redressed somewhat in the 'Club Literario', a genuine attempt to forge an online community of writers. Individuals are invited to subscribe to and participate in this group, for free, in order to share texts and commentaries. This takes place in the form of an email group; while photographs and biographies of members are published online, the interactions between the members remain private to the group. Although rather crude in its presentation in that member emails and home addresses are published online, the Club nonetheless represents one of the few attempts in Latin America to foment a virtual literary community based on shared interests and mutual support. Langer describes the Club thus: 'this is a literary club made up of "people" who have to get used to and adapt to a digital form of communication in order to be integrated into and share with the group. Some manage to do this while others simply disappear.'[10] By placing 'people' in inverted commas Langer draws attention to the virtual nature of this group but this is not to deny its validity. Wellman and Gulia have shown that 'the Net successfully maintains strong, supportive community ties', countering the arguments of some pundits who claim that virtual communities are not truly communities (Wellman and Gulia 1999: 181). Virtual communities differ in nature from so-called 'real' communities but this is not to say that they are pale imitations of 'real life' (Wellman and Gulia 1999: 181). Interesting also is Langer's observation that becoming accustomed to communication in electronic form is a prerequisite for participation in the group; the fact that some members persist and others disappear is illustrative of the continuing relative lack of ICT proficiency and access in Latin America. While the goals of the Club Literario are laudable, membership remains open only to those with the necessary IT skills; to the privileged few with access to computers and education in this regard.

Nonetheless, this bringing together online of Spanish-speaking writers has resulted in the publication of two anthologies of short stories and poetry by the club's members. The presentation of the second edition inscribes itself very much in the discourse of virtual community: 'the thing these writers have in common is their serious interest in literature and their participation in the great literary community that makes up [*Escritores.cl*]' ('Voces online'). With contributors based

10 Personal email correspondence with Ernesto Langer.

all around the world, the anthology manifests the view of virtual community summarised by Wellman and Gulia: 'cyberlinks between people become social links between groups that otherwise would be socially and physically dispersed' (Wellman and Gulia 1999: 183).

Arguably, one of the most successful features of *Escritores.cl*, and that which differentiates it from other Latin American literary publications, is its discussion forum and ongoing process of textual commentary. For the most part serious and discursive, the forum addresses such themes as whether literary criticism exists in Chile; what, if anything, constitutes feminine writing; and the advantages and disadvantages of the relationship between the Internet and literature. The forum has over 170 members – with some more active than others – and has become a platform for sharing advice and providing support, in keeping with Wellman and Gulia's findings that 'even when on-line groups are not designated to be supportive, they often are. As social beings, those who use the Net seek not only information but also companionship, social support and a sense of belonging' (Wellman and Gulia 1999: 173). This is particularly played out in a forum thread started on 29 October 2005 which asked for advice on establishing a writers' group. The thread received thirty-one replies and developed into an impassioned discussion on why people write. Similarly, the site's poetry forum invites comments on individual poems submitted by forum or Club Literario members. While *Escritores.cl* has a dedicated page inviting book reviews from users, the forum is a far more dynamic space where comments range from the eulogistic to the contemptuous. Debate is also frequently sparked among the forum posters themselves. This forum represents a tentative initial step into more interactive user participation in *Escritores.cl*, encouraging readers to be critics, publishing their comments, and generating a greater sense of site ownership among users themselves. Sociologists have found that when it is available, the 'chat' functionality of a website tends to be the most used by visitors to that site (Wellman and Gulia 1999: 173). Langer has, therefore, been wise to incorporate such forums into *Escritores.cl*, simultaneously generating new, fresh content, creating a community of communicating users and systematically increasing the number of site visits. *Escritores.cl* therefore represents an interesting development: a 'visible' and vocal community producing tangible objects, taking full advantage of technology to further and strengthen the group ties.

Conclusion

The virtual community is but one category within which e-magazines may be analysed but the desire to bring like-minded people together in a productive way pervades all three websites considered here and so merits examination. *El hablador* represents what may be considered a first stage in the development of the literary e-magazine, focusing primarily on textual criticism with a format reminiscent of print design. A sense of community is encouraged but yet to be made fully 'visible'. *Letralia* emphasises its status as a literary 'space' in which readers and writers may wander and commune, whereas *Escritores.cl* is very much an online literary club based upon mutual support and knowledge sharing. And while *Escritores.cl* may be the most advanced in its use of forums, none of the sites really exploit to the full those Internet tools designed to facilitate online communities such as blogs, chatrooms, or instant messaging. Their communities are forged very much on common interests and compelling content, often submitted by users themselves; all three aim to ensure, with varying degrees of success, that their respective publications are more than simply a static textual object. Taking into account the longevity and high number of page visits received by sites such as *Letralia* and *Escritores.cl*, we might conclude that the success of literary websites is directly related to the sense of community on which they are founded; in other words, online success is determined by the extent to which e-magazines embrace opportunities afforded by new media. While originally inscribing themselves within a print magazine tradition, these e-publications ultimately move beyond these parameters to become something else entirely, something more reminiscent of an Internet portal. In other words, they work with the technology to create new avenues of communication. While some work remains to be done in terms of reaching the desired broad audience, and opening doors for greater experimentation with literature in digital format, Latin American literary e-magazines offer unprecedented creative platforms for communities of writers and readers in the region and beyond.

Aguirre Romero, Joaquín María 1997a. 'Literatura en Internet. Qué encontramos en la WWW?', *Espéculo*, 6 (8 September), http://www.ucm.es/info/especulo/numero6/lite_www.htm, last accessed 10 June 2007.

—— 1997b. 'La incidencia de las Redes de comunicación en el Sistema literario', *Espéculo*, 7 (November 1997 – February 1998), http://www.ucm.es/info/especulo/numero7/sistemal.htm, last accessed 10 June 2007.

—— 1999. 'Cultura y redes de comunicación: las revistas electrónicas', *Espéculo*, 11 (March–June), http://www.ucm.es/info/especulo/numero11/rev_elec.html, last accessed 20 June 2007.

Burnett, Gary, Katherine M. Chudoba, Michael H. Dickey, and Michelle M. Kazmer 2003. 'Inscription and Interpretation of Text: a Cultural Hermeneutic Examination of Virtual Community', *Information Research*, 9:1, http://informationr.net/ir/9–1/paper162.html, last accessed 20 June 2007.

Cooper, Wesley 2002. 'Information Technology and Internet Culture', *The Journal of Virtual Environments*, 6:1, http://www.brandeis.edu/pubs/jove/HTML/V6/iculture.html, last accessed 20 June 2007.

Dante, Waldemar 1999. 'Entrevista: Ernesto Langer Moreno', *Escritores.cl*, http://www.escritores.cl, last accessed 20 June 2007.

Escritores.cl. http://www.escritores.cl, last accessed 20 June 2007.

'Estadísticas de uso para escritores.cl' 2005. *Escritores.cl*, http://www.escritores.cl/varios/estadisticas.htm, last accessed 20 June 2007.

Everett, Margaret 1998. 'Latin America On-line: The Internet, Development and Democratization', *Human Organization*, 57, 385–402.

Fajardo, Carlos 1999. 'Hacía una estética de la cibercultura', *Espéculo*, 10 (22 January), http://www.ucm.es/info/especulo/numero10/est_cibe.html, last accessed 20 June 2007.

Fernback, Jan, and Brad Thompson 1995. 'Virtual Communities: Abort, Retry, Failure?' http://www.well.com/~hlr/texts/VCcivil.html, last accessed 10 June 2007.

Gauntlett, David 2004. 'Web Studies: What's New?', in David Gauntlett and Ross Horsley, eds., *Web.studies: Rewiring Media Studies for the Digital Age*, 2nd edn. (London: Arnold), pp. 3–23.

Gómez, Ricardo 2000. 'The Hall of Mirrors: The Internet in Latin America', *Current History*, 99 (634), 72–77.

Gómez Jiménez, Jorge 2004. 'Cosmogonía de la Tierra de Letras', *Letralia*, 24 May. http://www.letralia.com/109/articulo01.htm, last accessed 20 June 2007.

El hablador, http://www.elhablador.com/, last accessed 20 June 2007.

Hagel, John, and Arthur G. Armstrong 1997. *Net Gain: Expanding Markets through Virtual Communities*. (Boston, MA: Harvard Business School Press).

Holdom, Shoshannah 2005. 'E-Journal Proliferation in Emerging Economies: The Case of Latin America', *Literary and Linguistic Computing*, 20:3, 361–65.

Jáuregui, Carlos 2000. 'Writing Communities on the Internet: Textual Authority and Territorialization', in Debra A. Castillo and Edmundo Paz-

Soldán, eds., *Latin American Literature and Mass Media* (New York: Garland), pp. 358–74.
Jones, Steven G., ed. 1997. *Virtual Culture: Identity and Communication in Cybersociety* (London: SAGE).
Jones, Quentin 1997. 'Virtual-Communities, Virtual Settlements and Cyber-Archaeology: A Theoretical Outline', *Journal of Computer-Mediated Communication*, 3:3, http://jcmc.indiana.edu/vol3/issue3/jones.html, last accessed 20 June 2007.
Kollock, Peter, and Marc Smith 1996. 'Managing the Virtual Commons: Cooperation and Conflict in Computer Communities', in Susan Herring, ed., *Computer-Mediated Communication*. (Amsterdam: John Benjamins), pp. 109–28.
— eds. 1999. *Communities in Cyberspace* (London: Routledge).
Letralia: tierra de letras, http://www.letralia.com, last accessed 20 June 2007.
Matei, Sorin 2005. 'From Counterculture to Cyberculture: Virtual Community Discourse and the Dilemma of Modernity', *Journal of Computer-Mediated Communication*, 10:3, http://jcmc.indiana.edu/vol10/issue3/matei.html, last accessed 10 June 2007.
Mitra, Ananda 1997. 'Virtual Commonality: Looking for India on the Internet', in Steven G. Jones, ed., *Virtual Culture: Identity and Communication in Cybersociety* (London: SAGE), pp. 55–79.
Molloy, Molly 2000. 'Background on the Development of the Internet in Latin America', http://lib.nmsu.edu/subject/bord/laguia/netdev.html, last accessed 20 June 2007.
Muñoz, Nefer 1999. 'Communications Lat Am: Internet Grows by Leaps and Bounds' (Interpress Service), http://lib.nmsu.edu/subject/bord/laguia/munoz.txt, last accessed 20 June 2007.
Porter, Constance Elise 2004. 'A Typology of Virtual Communities: a Multi-Disciplinary Foundation for Future Research', *Journal of Computer-Mediated Communication*, 10:1, http://jcmc.indiana.edu/vol10/issue1/porter.html, last accessed 20 June 2007.
Porter, David, ed. 1996. *Internet Culture* (New York: Routledge).
Proyecto Sherezade. http://home.cc.umanitoba.ca/~fernand4, last accessed 20 June 2007.
'¿Qué es Ciudad Letralia?', *Ciudad Letralia: la metrópolis de las letras*. http://www.letralia.com/ciudad/quees.htm, last accessed 20 June 2007.
Rheingold, Howard 1993. *The Virtual Community: Homesteading on the Electronic Frontier* (Reading, MA: Addison-Wesley).
Ridings, Catherine M., and David Gefen 2004. 'Virtual Community Attraction: Why People Hang Out Online', *Journal of Computer-Mediated Communication*, 10:1, http://jcmc.indiana.edu/vol10/issue1/ridings_gefen.html, last accessed 20 June 2007.
Silver, David 2000. 'Looking Backwards, Looking Forward: Cyberculture Studies 1990–2000', in David Gauntlett, ed., *Web.studies: Rewiring Media Studies for the Digital Age* (Oxford: Oxford University Press), pp. 19–30.
Silvio, José F. 1995. 'Potential Users and Virtual Communities in the Academic World', http://funredes.org/ftp/misc/SOCI-WW-E–95-JSINET.

DOC, last accessed 3 May 2006.

—— 1996. 'Virtual Communities and Information Resources in Latin America', http://funredes.org/ftp/misc/SOCI-AL-E–96-JSINET.DOC, last accessed 3 May 2006.

Smith, Anna DuVal 1999. 'Problems of Conflict Management in Virtual Communities', in Marc A. Smith and Peter Kollock, eds., *Communities in Cyberspace* (London: Routledge), pp. 134–63.

Sreenivasan, Sreenath 1997. 'New Neighborhood, No Money Down', *The New York Times*, March 17, Section D, p. 5.

Stinson, Douglass 1998. 'Internet Fever', *Latin Trade*, 6:8, 61–64.

Stockholm Challenge Award. http://www.stockholmchallenge.se, last accessed 20 June 2007.

Stone, Allucquere Rosanne 1991. 'Will the Real Body Please Stand Up?: Boundary Stories about Virtual Cultures', in Michael Benedikt, ed., *Cyberspace: First Steps* (Cambridge, MA: MIT Press), pp. 81–118.

'Voces Online', *Escritores.cl*. http://www.escritores.cl/varios/antologia2/, last accessed 20 June 2007.

Wakeford, Nina 2004. 'Developing Methodological Frameworks for Studying the World Wide Web', in David Gauntlett and Ross Horsley, eds., *Web. studies: Rewiring Media Studies for the Digital Age*, 2nd edn. (London: Arnold), pp. 34–50.

Watson, Nessim 1997. 'Why We Argue about Virtual Community: A Case Study of the Phish.Net Fan Community', in Steven G. Jones, ed., *Virtual Culture: Identity and Communication in Cybersociety*. (London: SAGE), pp. 102–32.

Wellman, Barry, and Milena Gulia 1999. 'Net Surfers Don't Ride Alone: Virtual Communities as Communities', in Marc A. Smith and Peter Kollock, eds., *Communities in Cyberspace* (London: Routledge), pp. 167–94.

8

Negotiating a (Border Literary) Community Online *en la línea*

Paul Fallon

> 'What can we do to stop being boring?'
> [...]
> 'Start a media revolution!'
> [...]
> 'But ... what is a media revolution?'
> 'Well, I don't know.'
>
> Ilich 2004a

i. A Media Revolution?: Text and Hi-tech

This dialogue, which appeared from 2004 to 2005 in Fran Ilich's Net-film *Being Boring,* originally available through his website, *delete.tv* contains several elements that I see as characterising Northern Mexican border authors' online work. In the film, two young women, without their television for a week, try to avoid 'being boring'. After the exchange cited above, they take their first 'revolutionary' action by hitting an 'enter' button. The young women, like the border authors, ponder how to make their time meaningful, reflect on the power of new media, and attempt to negotiate using that power. Their conversation also signals the perplexing newness of electronic media and the strong desires involved; the concept sounds appealing, but they are not entirely sure what it is nor what to do. Finally, the fact that this film no longer exists online, due to files degrading on QuickTime, signals the ephemerality within which the new media border artists operate.

I have argued elsewhere that the narratives of better-known border writers such as Gabriel Trujillo Muñoz, Rosina Conde, Luis Humberto Crosthwaite, and Rosario Sanmiguel generate distinctive temporal representations that reflect struggles over values (Fallon 2004). Even as these authors began to establish themselves and contribute to the development of literary communities along the border, they consistently expressed concerns regarding the *temporalities* of the literary field itself as they felt the rise of new media threatened their work. That is, the authors showed a consistent preoccupation, both within their texts and as part of their activity in the field – their expression in newspapers and conferences, their activity as editors, and so forth – with the length of time it takes to write, be published, and gain a readership in an area with little established literary infrastructure, wide exposure to US mass media and increasing governmental support for audiovisual rather than print media. In other words, not only were the authors worried about establishing their own position in the literary field, they also concerned themselves with establishing the existence of a literary field in itself. Furthermore, these more established authors saw other media as a competitive threat to the temporalities of literature proper.

However, many of the emerging writers along the border who started to gain prominence in the 1990s, such as Dolores Dorantes, Carlos Gutiérrez Vidal, Fran Ilich, Rafa Saavedra, and Heriberto Yépez, view literary and multimedia expressions as complementary. These younger authors' activities enable possible links with limited, temporary communities that represent both shifts and continuities in reading culture. An increased ephemerality characterises their work on a variety of levels. Their writing often takes up as subject matter the style-conscious, shifting quotidian experiences of youth, often recounting only brief, fragmented episodes. Rather than waiting to appear in traditional books or magazines, the authors have sped up distribution of their work through photocopies, fanzines, and the Internet. They also signal an altered, possibly more fleeting relationship between writers and readers in their Internet work, due to the emphasis on the present moment in blogs and to the increased control they see readers as having. Furthermore, with the possibility afforded by instant distribution over the Internet, these authors write not only to create enduring texts for a stable community of readers, but also, frequently, to invoke the real-time of current events: the texts form part of larger cultural happenings, they record real-time chats, and they publicise cultural and political goings on. Finally, as the film *Being Boring* illustrates, the electronic media themselves do not guarantee lasting products, as texts written only a matter of days, weeks, or years before may no longer exist in cyberspace now.

In this chapter, therefore, I signal how these newer artists react to and develop the changing temporalities afforded by the new media. At the same time, I will also note a tension between their thinking through online possibilities and the practices they put into effect. This temporal focus offers an alternative to existing tendencies in critical treatments of border writing and/or cyberspace. Studies by D. Emily Hicks (1992) and José David Saldívar (1997), for example, emphasise the new possibilities for subjectivity that border writing offers due to its deterritorialising mobility, although they do not discuss specifically Mexican border authors. Frequently metaphoric, this 'spatial' perspective regarding borders often ignores temporal concerns that the authors themselves express and the constraints within which the writers operate. Furthermore, such an emphasis on mobility overlooks the writers' own efforts to locate themselves and their literary practice by calling for institutional support and consciously associating themselves with a specific region. Cyberspace criticism by authors such as Steven G. Jones (1997) and Gabriela Coronado and Bob Hodge (2004) also shares the strong celebratory tone and spatial focus of this tendency in border criticism. I offer my discussion here to help assess concretely the negotiation of temporalities in cyberspace writing on the border.

While an interest in, and the relative availability of, technology along the border inspired northern border writers who began writing in the 1980s, the emerging authors not only write about technology but also (in)fuse their texts with it. Many began their work with collective fanzines, taking advantage of the low cost of copying and putting out limited numbers of ephemeral copies of their work (Zavala 1995–1996: 26–32). Likc thc fanzine concept itself, the writing of the younger authors often incorporates an interest in music with an attempt at self-expression. Tijuanenses Ilich, Ejival and Saavedra, as well as Mexicali resident Gutiérrez Vidal all associate themselves strongly with musical movements such as rave and electronica. Saavedra describes his work thus: 'Since I'm also a DJ of electronica, I take "samples" from different sources and mix them in my writing.

I play with the rhythm, with music, just like a DJ does. I scratch, make loops' (de Sainz 2001: 1). These authors do not think simply in terms of the literary; rather than specialise in literature, they study communications in college, author multiple websites, and measure their success through other media as well.

The protagonist of Ilich's first novel, *Metro-pop*, for example, sets his sights on the movies, hoping to be accepted into the Manhattan film school (Ilich 1997: 135–36). Ilich himself investigated such options, wrote scripts for Discovery Channel, and worked in the Multimedia Centre of the Centro Nacional para las Artes [National Centre for the Arts] in Mexico City. As editor of the Centre's online magazine, *Undo*, he affirmed the value of different media: 'we think of new media as a space of expression, as a habitable space that responds to quantum physics in a more lively way than Lawrence Durrell and the *Alexandria Quartet* can' (Ilich 2002a). Though the older generation of border writers see literary and multimedia expression as competing options, many of this emerging group negotiate the different media as mixable elements suitable for sampling, remixing, or even plagiarising.

This flexibility that these authors perceive regarding the media with which they work relates closely to a sense of temporality distinct from that of the older writers. As Humberto Félix Berumen notes, like the *Onda* writers of the 1960s, these authors mark their age and focus by incorporating youthful colloquial speech to narrate contemporary young people's everyday experiences that take place over short periods of time (Berumen 2001: 73–74). Unlike the *Onda* writers, though, they write during and of 'cybernetic times' as critic Ignacio Trejo Fuentes affirms of Ilich (cited in Berumen 2001: 74). One group, calling itself Contra-Cultura (menor) [(minor) Counter Culture], regularly contributed to the local cultural supplement in Tijuana, submitting a variety of pieces, including one short manifesto that underlined its desire to break with earlier generations. In it, the members of the group declare that past movements are failures: 'the 1960s revolution, feminism, the civil rights movements, psychedelia, and all that didn't work' (Contra-Cultura (menor) 1993: 11). They revel in an emphatically youthful impudence: 'Viva techno-pacifist anarchy! [...] that's what you detest most about us. Right, adults?' (1993: 11). Though they refuse to be trailblazers, they affirm their desire to have a voice: 'we are not thinking about influencing other people, everyone decides for him/herself', 'we think the only way out

[...] is freedom of expression' (1993: 11). Tellingly, they criticise what they see as a constant preoccupation that existing artists had over funding: 'We don't believe that the artists' main complaint should be about the lack of money or exhibition space, but we're sure that it's the first thing for [...] the people who want to become famous' (1993: 11). Thus, these writers rhetorically turn away from the temporalities of traditional publishing that so concerned the writers who had preceded them. That is, they declare their independence from any need to appeal and wait for external, institutional support to have their work appear.

Instead, these younger writers see other options in the quicker turnaround of the photocopier, graffiti, and the Internet. Their own fanzines supplement the venues of exposure offered by the more established authors' publishing work. Contra-Cultura (menor)'s own *Cinemátik* distributed between 1000 and 2000 copies, bettering the usual local book production numbers. As Gabriel Trujillo Muñoz notes, the younger authors' writing 'has come to light more in independent, marginal publications than with an institutional stamp' (Trujillo Muñoz 1997: 112). Online distribution offers another, more affordable venue; once Saavedra's first book sold out, the publisher, La Espina Dorsal, made the entire text available online for some time. Carlos Gutiérrez Vidal produced a virtual novel, *Platero y tú* [Platero and You] although it is now only available in traditional book form (Gutiérrez Vidal 2003: 73–107). Taking up such options from the outset of their careers, these younger artists did not share earlier authors' consistent preoccupation with the time spent producing or consuming literary work. Rather, given the relative ease of publishing, the possibilities of Internet exposure, and the more established base from which to operate locally, as Saavedra's first collection of short stories announces, they write instead of 'leisure and hate' (Saavedra 1996).

ii. Post(ing) Literature; or, How Long for the 'We' of Weblog?

Despite the negativity that 'hate' connotes and their own lack of faith in achieving significant long-term changes in the systems enveloping them, these young authors also look to larger, if ephemeral, communities. The groups they reach out to come together not through traditional literary representations, but rather through a combination of media. In an Internet piece, Saavedra describes a very limited form of communion he associates with his musical interests (cited in Villalobos 2000: 16):

> In the club radiant you are, radiant I am, radiant are we. Logic doesn't exist, time seems infinite to us, emotion is an honest smile that gives away the very moment in which WE transform into/on E, the collective I [...] Upon noting the hedonistic feeling [...], a fortunate pan proves that nothing is the same as it was. Then somebody decides to get a close-up of our happy face as if they knew that we'll never leave here, that we don't want to leave here.

Rather than overtly political advocacy, the text registers – and possibly enacts – a successful tactical escape from everyday pressures and restrictions. The dancers enter the discotheque and make it theirs, if only temporarily.[1] Heriberto Yépez, in an online essay on weblog literature, posits this writing as an alternative means of coming together, 'part of a possible attack on the mercantile character of writing (above all writing directed against the book). Writing on the Net (without *getting paid* and without a resulting *physical object*) would seem to be an anti-capitalist act' (Yépez 2003a). A blog represents a reading community that he hopes 'will appear and disappear from the screen whenever the author or the reader so decides' (Yépez 2003a). For his part, Ilich has presented projects such as 'Borderhack' (Ilich 2000) and 'Modem Drama' (2002b) in activist fashion. The first brought a variety of groups together through the Internet to work against national divisions: '*Hactivists,* internet artists, cyberculture devotees, electronic musicians and punk rockers are ready to erase the border in Tijuana-San Diego even if only for a few days' (Ilich 2001: 6). Ilich presents the Net-film 'Modem Drama' to high school and university classes in order to inspire debate and problem solving, since the audience votes on and discusses optional viewing segments (Ilich 2002b). Most recently Ilich has organised the online conference *net.work: información, producción cultural y políticas en la red* [information, cultural production and politics on the web] (Ilich 2006a) in similar

1 Saavedra's investment in the idea of such radiance comes through, too, in the title of the new Tijuana arts magazine he edits, *Radiante*, available online (Saavedra 2005).

fashion to his 'Borderhack' project (see fig. 8.1 for an image of the participants, including Ilich wearing a Zapatista-style balaclava and hypermedia writer Blas Valdez on the far right of the image). No generation of passive conformists, these authors produce texts – and events – that imagine larger social collectives contesting the status quo. More so perhaps than the more established border writers, the younger authors enact borderline tactics as they invoke communities that depend on ephemeral convergences with little idea of a proper place of their own.[2]

The advent of blogging along the northern Mexican border further altered the communities invoked. On the one hand, these blogs still affirm regional identifications, as can be seen in the Tijuana Bloguita Front (TJBF), a web of interconnected sites written by Tijuanenses which Saavedra organised, and in *Blogqueblog*, which collected blog metacommentary. Saavedra, Yépez, and other northern border writers such as Dorantes and Caballero have contributed prodigiously with postings. Similarly, Ciudad Juárez blogger Zerk begins his list of links with others from his hometown, 'the City of Crime' (Montecristo 2003), again affirming the importance of locality.

However, beyond simple regional affiliation, many writers highlight other positive characteristics offered by the blog: several, for instance have made reference to the democratising nature of the form. Saavedra describes it as 'a return to the "Do it Yourself" punker' (Saavedra 2002) and Yépez notes 'you don't have to be Anybody to open one' (Yépez 2003c). These comments draw attention to the increased opportunity for participation in the writing process that the blog offers, and the fact that it offers a venue to writers who would not normally have had access to conventional print publications. In addition to this, the blogs have also afforded a new, quick way of organising, and

2 By describing the negotiations the border authors use to connect with a reading community as 'borderline tactics', I adapt Michel de Certeau's distinction between tactics, which are temporal practices not associated with a proper place, and strategies, which are practices that arise from a separate spatial or institutional localisation (Certeau 1984). These two terms mark the opposite poles of a spectrum of activities along which different cultural agents may move, such that with increasing authority, activity becomes less tactical and more strategic. The border writers' texts and actions that I discuss here are neither the strategies of established actors in a clearly marked domain nor the tactics of powerless agents, but rather they represent borderline tactics that help shape a developing field of cultural production.

of creating communities online. Calls and advertisements for cultural events abound, and the bloggers have rapidly co-ordinated protests to denounce, for example, the arrests of two fellow border artists and distributed chain emails objecting to a 'pro-life' doctor's appointment to head a US national drugs committee (Dorantes 2004a). And finally, blogs have also afforded these writers greater involvement in political concerns, as can be seen by the fact that Yépez established a blog dedicated to the Zapatista movement (Yépez 2003b), and Ilich hosts a support website for the Zapatistas' 2006 'Otra Campaña' [Other Campaign] (Ilich 2006b). Thus this online work offers writers connections far beyond those arising from the national programme to promote cultural expression in the region, El Programa Cultural de las Fronteras [The Border Cultural Programme].

Limits to these positive traits exist, of course. As Lisa Nakamura notes, '*lack of access* to the Internet [...] continues to cut particular bodies *out* of various histories in the making' (Nakamura 2002: xii, emphasis in original). Though access concerns go largely unmentioned by the border bloggers, dominant power relations do not simply disappear on the Net. Though women make up an increasing blogging presence – they constitute half the contributors to TJBF – one male, echoing the ruse of Sor Filotea, wrote a diatribe against an independent publishing project run by women (*Un blog propio*). Traditional ideas of geopolitical hierarchies maintain some sway, too. For a time, Yépez dialogued with three Mexico City writers on their blog, *Nowhere Blog Front*, that proposed, in part, that the idea of place did not influence aesthetic judgments. Ironically, after debating several points, one of the bloggers affirmed that 'we'll leave you with your Tijuanense security, Yépez; there you'll be famous, even in Helsinki; here, you're just one of many' (*Nowhere*).

Assumptions about race and technology also continue. When Carlos Gutiérrez Vidal proposed a plagiarising aesthetic, he argued it 'would be the most intelligent form of saying to other Mexicans that we are not Chicanos and to other Californians that we are not Indians with shawls' (Gutiérrez Vidal 1999). Beyond the defensive exclusionary positioning (as not-Chicano and not-Indian), his affirmation refers to conceptions commonly held in Mexico that associate indigenous peoples with artisan handicrafts and separates them from high technology (Coronado and Hodge 2004: 90–96). In Mexico, such separations loom large: in 2003, only 250 cities had Internet connections and the highest Internet penetration, in the Mexico City area, reached only 14 per cent (Serrano Santoyo and Martínez Martínez 2003: 147; 156). Moreover, questions of control also arise even for those with access. Though Ilich has had his own blog and has 'traditional' stories posted online, in his view, more successful electronic narrative 'would have to go far beyond publishing through services like blogger that maintain those writing completely isolated from the code in which they write' (personal communication).[3] He points out here the limited creative horizons and the fairly rigid formatting that result from bloggers not involving themselves in the codes structuring the online presentation of their writing. Ilich also cautiously notes that because of issues of access and digital literacy, 'the internet holds new promises that are not completely fulfilled' (Ilich 2004b).

Despite such unfulfilled promises, several authors have forged ahead with their own sites and have tried to lay the groundwork for continuing online writing as a practice. They continue to maintain their links to their local community and affirm historical ties between their online presentations and the work of a variety of established authors, such as Alfonso Reyes, Félix Guattari, and Juan Ramón Jiménez. They declare their affection for writing: 'I can't deny that I love to blog. I prefer blogging to looking after my dog' says Dorantes, in a tongue-in-cheek fashion (Dorantes 2004b). Perhaps more practically, others have made efforts to make financially profitable – or at least self-supporting – sites such as Gutiérrez Vidal's online publishing house Crunch!, Ilich's server *possibleworlds.com*, and the alternative art spaces Lui Velazquez and *Bulbo.tv*. Meanwhile Yépez defends not only blogs, but the establishing of a blogging 'scene' as a tactical move to gain a foothold. While he does not see the need for 'scenes' in the US due to greater publication opportunities, for him, '[his] blog has been key to attacking the literary politics of Mexico' since there 'blogs have helped to [over]throw borders on how age, prior status, etc., affect literary "role playing"' (Yépez 2003d). His ultimate objective for his blogs and writing, though, lies beyond simple recognition: 'Post-literature is the goal. Writing not as a fancy field of culture, but as an element that participes [sic] in the reshaping of culture' (Yépez 2003c).

[3] For a more detailed discussion of the sorts of restrictions at which Ilich hints here, see Galloway 2004.

The emphasis on the present moment associated with the practice of blogging that forms the basis of its appeal seemingly also holds the seeds for its destruction. With limited press options in Mexico, instant publication on the Net offers an attractive possibility. Further, according to Yépez, the author–reader relationship changes radically: by visiting a blog, 'the reader of Web literature is the one who controls the quantity, durability and placement of the text' (Yépez 2003a). Meanwhile, in its democratising role in blogs, 'writing will no longer have as its purpose the building of Authors, but just the spreading of writing', taking away the author's special status (Yépez 2003c). Furthermore, the physical appearance of the blog page emphasises the present since the first page is the last thing written. Thus, for Yépez, 'the past gets left behind' (Yépez 2003a), and what remains is 'the now of consumption, the now of linear emphasis on the present' (*Blogqueblog*). While this immediacy enables writing as political action in distributing messages and protests, it also threatens to subsume blogs to the logic of consumption. Thus, after some three months on the metablog, *Blogqueblog*, another blogger states: 'At first it seemed fun to me, suddenly I felt it a fashion, if you don't have a blog you're *out* [...]. For now, I'm bidding blogging farewell for a while [...]. We'll see you next year, if this still exists!' (*Blogqueblog*). No more postings followed on that site. Even more recently, after many defences of the practice, Yépez has announced that 'if you're a blogger and the only reason that others know about you is because of your blog, you're a loser. Get to writing books, asshole, or songs or scripts' (Yépez 2006). He goes on to pronounce that 'El blog is almost dead' (Yépez 2006).

Addressing the effects of a just such a forward-focused, (post-) modernist thinking associated with new media, Alan Liu calls for an injection of history in the arts and a response to 'the death of literature' (Liu 2004: 1–9). Similarly, in Latin American contexts, Carlos Alonso, Idelber Avelar, and Brett Levinson link literary discourse with a shift in nation-state associations that they argue needs to be thought through, specifically, by mourning (Alonso 1998: 165, 175–76; Avelar 1999: 20–21; Levinson 2001: 30; 188–91). For example, Avelar rejects currently dominant literary forms such as pop postmodernism, populist identity narratives, and *testimonios*, which all avoid mourning and 'confronting the epochal crisis of storytelling and the decline in the transmissibility of experience' (Avelar 1999: 20). He emphasises 'literature's recent defeats' and insists 'on the reflection on the conditions of possibility of literature's very untimeliness in the current marketplace' (Avelar 1999: 230–31). In a similar vein, Brett Levinson addresses the end of literature while simultaneously privileging the literary as a 'domain charged with the articulation of the convergence, boundary or end of things, even for the end of literature' (Levinson 2001: 30). All four also reject an identity politics as a resolution to this situation (Liu 1990: 92–96; Alonso 1998: 176; Avelar 1999: 20; Levinson 2001: 25). Each addresses the apparent drop in the status of literature since the Boom yet affirms the value of literary discourse in the face of a consumerist culture increasingly dominated by mass media.

In expressing their concerns regarding the viability of literary discourse, the border authors and their texts enact a negotiation towards which Liu, Alonso, Avelar, and Levinson gesture. However, while the critics argue against using identity politics as a way of recuperating the literary, these border writers seem to do just that, as they focus frequently on new temporalities in the region and on their role in representing (them to) a larger community. Their particular positions play a significant role in their taking up a practice that would seemingly conflict with the critics' arguments. Specifically, the border authors experience and express this shift in the status of literature within a local context that lacks a strongly established literary infrastructure, while the critics discuss it in an international arena, with respect to established literary discourse. The cultural agents on the border attempt to position themselves within a (set of) regionally identified literary field(s) even as they must negotiate a 'time' for literary activity online. I view their efforts as making claims to authority during a legitimation crisis over the 'temporalities' of literature itself. According to Carol J. Greenhouse, expressions of temporality provide the ground for possible characterisations of agency, as reckonings of time mark what counts as changes, activities, and people legitimately worth noting. Because of this, 'legitimation crises are occasions to articulate, and perhaps invent, a view of agency in terms of which aspirants or incumbents can claim effective rulership' (Greenhouse 1996: 14). Saavedra's seemingly open, yet supposedly irrelevant, rhetorical question about the reasons for the Tijuana Blog Front underlines this motivation. He facetiously asks whether they are 'an attempt to legitimise something so seemingly volatile and intranscendent as these blogs? Or simply one more demonstration of the success of networking online [...]. It's all the same' (*Blogqueblog*).

Both options hint at the validity and meaningfulness of their Internet activity: either the blogging collective attempts to legitimise blogs, only seemingly volatile and intranscendent, or they demonstrate the success of online communication connections. The insistent emphasis in such metablogs on justifying the time spent on Internet expression and on establishing its connection to literature reflects an effort to register the activities involved and to have those activities valued by a larger group in hopes of subsequent support. I see these border authors' texts and actions, like the critical work of others – including my own here –, as working through a larger discourse on the changing relations between literature, intellectuals, and the state, as global capitalism, mass media, and popular cultural values contribute to those shifts.

However, even as these writers develop and promote the potential of their expression, many traditional literary practices still characterise their work. I argue that, though their work participates in a media (r)evolution, the literary training and preferences of many of the young authors factor strongly in the frequently 'standard' form of their Internet work. Arturo Escobar, in his study on the anthropology of cyberculture, signals that specific groups of actors' understanding and implementations of technical entities and practices could 'explain why particular technologies are adopted and not others' (Escobar 1994: 212). Thus, whereas those trained in film work or in computer programming might use more visually or technically oriented presentations, the bloggers have let textual tendencies dominate. As Ilich's description of successful electronic narrative hints above, consistent exploration into the new presentations and expressions performable using machine codes on the Internet has yet to occur. Instead, many fall into old habits of repeating the bookish blog form. Even those who seemed to have experimented most with cyber-possibilities, like Ilich, Gutiérrez Vidal, and Omar Pimienta, for their part, also show the continued role of the traditional cultural powers. They all receive governmental and university support; Ilich now works in Mexico City, and Pimienta will be going to University of California in San Diego in 2007. While the new media afford new opportunities, old habits still have strong effects.

In conclusion, the continued and growing literary practices of writers like Dorantes, Ilich, Gutiérrez Vidal, Saavedra, Pimienta, and Yépez signal that literature, far from being dead, remains a force to be reckoned with online on the border. Yet these younger authors' relative lack of concern regarding traditional literary infrastructure, their ease in turning to new electronic media, and their rapid rise to favourable positions using those media to reach an audience indicate that they perceive a different role for literature that will evolve in dialogue with the new forms and create new rhythms. The situation merits a continued and more detailed analysis to allow for a broader perspective on the different border narratives as the terms of that negotiation change. Among many other possibilities, the ephemerality involved in the new media works and the increasing availability of video online may quickly diminish the influence of established literary practices. It remains to be seen what forms such expression will take and who will be reading, as literature on the borderline adapts, and is adapted, to literature online. Whether or not Yépez's and the critics' view of post-literature has come about, he and other writers along the border have begun to establish that literature is, has been and will continue to be posted.

References

Alonso, Carlos 1998. *The Burden of Modernity: The Rhetoric of Cultural Discourse in Spanish America* (New York: Oxford University Press).

Avelar, Idelber 1999. *The Untimely Present: Postdictatorial Latin American Fiction and the Task of Mourning* (Durham, NC: Duke University Press).

Berumen, Humberto Félix 2001. *Narradores bajacalifornianos del siglo XX* (Mexicali: Instituto de Cultura de Baja California).

Un Blog propio. http://www.unblogpropio.blogspot.com, last accessed 22 June 2007.

Blogqueblog. http://www.tjbf.blogspot.com, last accessed 22 June 2007.

Certeau, Michel de 1984. *The Practice of Everyday Life*, trans. Steven Rendall (Berkeley, CA: University of California Press).

Contra-Cultura (menor) 1993. 'Breve Manifiesto de Contra-Cultura (menor)' *Contraseña* 56, 12 September, 11.

Coronado, Gabriela, and Bob Hodge 2004. *El hipertexto multicultural en México posmoderno: Paradojas e incertidumbres* (Mexico City: Centro de Investigaciones y Estudios Superiores en Antropología Social).

Dorantes, Dolores 2004a. *Tabla sin asidero*, 22 February. http://dorantes.blogspot.com/2004_02_22_dorantes_archive.html, last accessed 22 June 2007.

—— 2004b. *Tabla sin asidero*, 2 May, http://dorantes.blogspot.com/2004_05_02_dorantes_archive.html, last accessed 22 June 2007.

Escobar, Arturo 1994. 'Welcome to Cyberia: Notes on the Anthropology of Cyberculture', *Current Anthropology*, 35:3, 211–31.

Fallon, Paul 2004. 'Borderline Tactics: Time, Subjectivity, Nation and State in Contemporary Narrative Practices along the Northern Mexican Border'. Doctoral thesis, University of Kansas.

Galloway, Alexander R. 2004. *Protocol: How Control Exists after Decentralization* (Cambridge, MA: MIT Press).

Greenhouse, Carol J. 1996. *A Moment's Notice: Time Politics across Cultures* (Ithaca, NY: Cornell University Press).

Gutiérrez Vidal, Carlos Adolfo 1999. 'Plagiar la infancia', http://www.angelfire.com/tx/AVTEXTFEST/ensayo/cagv99.html, last accessed 28 November 2003.

—— 2003. 'Golden Showers (Platero y tú)', in Gutiérrez Vidal and Carlos Adolfo, *Berlin 77 y otros relatos* (Mexicali: Fondo Editorial de Baja California), pp. 73–107.

Hicks, D. Emily 1992. *Border Writing: The Multidimensional Text* (Minneapolis, MN: University of Minnesota Press).

Ilich, Fran 1997. *Metro-pop* (Mexico City: Consejo Nacional para la Cultura y las Artes, Ediciones SM).

—— 2000. 'Borderhack', http://www.delete.tv/borderhack/eng/index.html, last accessed 22 June 2007.

—— 2001. '¡Borrar la frontera!' *TijuanaMetro*, October, 6.

—— 2002a. 'Contextualizando la crítica textual en algo más que sólo texto: ideas y el espacio de un cpu' *Undo*, http://jmvelazco.cnart.mx/undo/columna/ilich2.html, last accessed 22 June 2007.

—— 2002b. 'Modem Drama', *BIG Torino 2002-bigguest.net – riflessioni*, http://www.bigtorino.net/bigguest/riflessioni/txt08.php, last accessed 27 November 2003.

—— 2004a. *Being Boring*. http://delete.tv/being_boring, last accessed 22 June 2007.

—— 2004b. *Remezclando la realidad con los narrative media (medios narrativos)*, http://www.zonezero.com/magazine/articles/remixing/remixingsp.html, last accessed 20 April 2006.

—— 2006a. *net.work: producción cultural, información y políticas de las redes*, conference, 8–10 December, Mexico City, proceedings at http://sabotage.tv/imgs/net.work_final.jpg, last accessed 28 January 2007.

—— 2006b. *La otra campaña en WWW*, http://laotrainformacion.org, last accessed 22 June 2007.

Jones, Steven G., ed. 1997. *Virtual Culture: Identity and Communication in Cybersociety* (London: SAGE).

Levinson, Brett 2001. *The Ends of Literature: The Latin American 'Boom' in the Neoliberal Marketplace* (Stanford, CA: Stanford University Press).

Liu, Alan 1990. 'Local Transcendence: Cultural Criticism, Postmodernism, and the Romanticism of Detail', *Representations*, 32, 75–113.

—— 2004. *The Laws of Cool: Knowledge Work and the Culture of Information* (Chicago, IL: University of Chicago Press).

Montecristo, Zerk 2003. *Introducción a la locura*, http://lapaginadezerk.blogspot.com, last accessed 22 June 2007.

Nakamura, Lisa 2002. *Cybertypes: Race, Ethnicity, and Identity on the Internet* (New York: Routledge).

Nowhere Blog Front 2003. http://www.nbf.blogspot.com, last accessed 26 December 2004.
Saavedra, Rafa 1996. *Esto no es una salida: postcards de ocio y odio* (Tijuana: La Espina Dorsal).
—— 2002. 'Crossfader: the first chapter'. *Crossfader*, http://crossfader.blogspot.com/2002_12_29_crossfader_archive.html, last accessed 22 June 2007.
—— 2005. *Radiante Press*, http://radiantepress.blogspot.com/2005_11_01_radiantepress_archive.html, last accessed 22 June 2007.
Sainz, Pablo de 2001. 'Rafa Saavedra – Writing Is Like Making Tacos!' *La Prensa San Diego* 9 November, http://www.laprensa-sandiego.org/archive/november09/RAFA.HTM, last accessed 11 November 2003.
Saldívar, José David 1997. *Border Matters: Remapping American Cultural Studies* (Berkeley, CA: University of California Press).
Serrano Santoyo, Arturo, and Evelio Martínez Martínez 2003. *La brecha digital: Mitos y realidades* (Mexicali: Universidad Autónoma de Baja California).
Trujillo Muñoz, Gabriel 1997. *Literatura bajacaliforniana siglo XX.* (Mexicali: Editorial Larva).
Villalobos, José Pablo 2000. 'Generation (Me)X: Transbordering Culture in Rafa Saavedra's *Buten Smileys*', paper presented in a special session dedicated to 'Crossing Borders–Crossing Lines/Cruzar Líneas–Cruzar fronteras: Revisiting Literary Representations of Bandidos, Pachicos and Other Fronterizos', Modern Language Association Convention, Washington, DC, 27–30 December.
Yépez, Heriberto 2003a. 'Literatura weblog', *Literaturas.com*, http://www.literaturas.com/heribertoyepezweblogfebrero2003.htm, last accessed 11 November 2003.
—— 2003b. *Plan la Realidad-Tijuana*, http://www.planrealiti.blogspot.com, last accessed 23 November 2004.
—— 2003c. *The Tijuana Bible of Poetics!*, http://thetijuanabibleofpoetics.blogspot.com/2003_01_01_thetijuanabibleofpoetics_archive.html, last accessed 22 June 2007.
—— 2003d. *The Tijuana Bible of Poetics!*, http://thetijuanabibleofpoetics.blogspot.com/2003_02_01_thetijuanabibleofpoetics_archive.html, last accessed 22 June 2007.
—— 2006. *e.n.s.a.m.b.l.e*, http://www.hyepez.blogspot.com, last accessed 22 June 2007.
Zavala, Haydé 1995–1996. 'Los jóvenes por escrito: una lectura de las publicaciones alternativas en Tijuana', *Cultura Norte* 37, 26–32.

II

Cyberliterature: Avatars and Aficionados

9

Posthumanism in the Work of Jorge Luis Borges

Stefan Herbrechter and Ivan Callus

> This is no longer the earth on which man lives.
>
> Heidegger 1993: 106

There is no doubt that Jorge Luis Borges is a major literary precursor of contemporary interactive and multimedia works. It is almost commonplace to see tales such as 'Funes el memorioso' [Funes the Memorious], 'La biblioteca de Babel' [The Library of Babel], or 'El jardín de senderos que se bifurcan' [The Garden of the Forking Paths] as prefigurations of cyberliterature. Borges' web presence is vast – from sites dedicated to 'Webmaster Borges', which claim that 'the greatest influence on the Argentine writer was a phenomenon invented after his death [namely: the Internet]' (Wolk 1999), to the all-encompassing site of the 'Jorge Luis Borges Center for Studies and Documentation' hosted by the University of Iowa.

This chapter aims to demonstrate the depth and importance of Borges' legacy not only to cyberliterature but to discussions of the entire contemporary 'posthuman' paradigm. Even though Borges rarely speaks in any direct way of technology and of the cybercultural futures which it makes possible, his speculative fictions and other prose writings provide glimpses of posthuman conditions that are more fully portrayed by writers such as William Gibson and Philip K. Dick or in films such as *The Matrix* (Wachowski 1999) and *Minority Report* (Spielberg 2002). His work thereby can stake a claim to a foundational presence within contemporary debates on the future of the archive, memory and consciousness, on the machinic and the digital prosthetisation of the human, and on the pervasiveness of communications systems and their reshaping of the very notion of the literary. Much of this has to do with the way in which many of Borges' writings are readable as unsurpassable experiments in how to make thinkable the impossible and the unrepresentable. The current obsession with the posthuman, as that which reconfigures the actual and the possible once technology re-engineers human potential, institutes a new physics and redefines inscription itself, is therefore everywhere present in Borges. For is it not the posthuman order which would make it possible to inhabit infinite libraries and archives, perceive plenitude in a pinprick, remember all experience, and return to roads not taken?

i. Critical Posthumanism

Posthumanism can be understood in at least two ways. Firstly, as the contemporary critical and theoretical discourse that rethinks what it means to be human by re-engaging with and radicalising a long history of critiques of humanism – of which the anti-humanist, poststructuralist, and postmodern movements of the last third of the twentieth century were maybe only the most advanced and coherent examples. This critique has always focused on conceptual flaws within humanist ideals, like the liberal individual self, realism and representation, essentialism and truth, autonomy and universalism. The renewed urgency for such a posthumanist critique of humanism arises out of extensive technological developments both at nano- and cosmic level which promise to change beyond recognition and maybe even challenge humanity in its survival. We refer to the discourse that privileges critical continuity in the face of these changes as 'critical posthumanism' (Herbrechter and Callus 2003, 2004a, 2004b). It understands the 'post' in 'posthuman', in analogy with Lyotard's notion of the postmodern, as the return of the repressed 'non-human' in various forms. Just as the modern is 'always already' marked by its particular anticipated *and* repressed postmodern, humanism is haunted by the non-human – the supernatural, animal, lesser-than-human, object – that it continues to exclude. Therefore in order to evaluate critically the current changes that are driven by technology and more or less effectively contained by politics, it is necessary to bear in mind the critical tradition that has been shadowing the rise of the humanist paradigm to its current point of apparent self-surpassing. We differentiate this critical posthumanism from the second meaning that posthumanism has acquired and which refers to a much less critical and more celebratory desire which more or less wholeheartedly embraces the so-called opportunities which leaving the humanist paradigm behind seems to promise. While we entirely recognise the importance of current technological change we also feel that a long-term critical view of a humanism that always adapts to and incorporates its repressed posthumanisms will serve as a good vaccine against rampant contemporary technophilia and technological determinism. In the context of these parameters our project is to seek past, present and future allies for a critical posthumanism. These allies can be found in those thinkers and writers that have been working at the edges and margins of 'Western metaphysics', and we claim Borges as one such ally – not only as a precursor of certain contemporary trends that contribute to a posthumanist climate, but far more importantly, as a critical commentator of our present. We therefore juxtapose Borges with some of his posthumanist commentators – N. Katherine Hayles in particular – for the sake of unsettling causality, teleology, and finality. Borges, we claim, is an exponent of what might be called 'posthumanism without technology', which brings to the fore the precariousness of the human; the human not so much threatened by 'his' technology but by 'its' very humanity, imagination, and existence. What Borges might contribute to critical posthumanism is a memory of the posthuman long before the invention of any cyborg-, nano- or biotechnology.

ii. Precursivity and Critical Anticipation

Borges is a prime example of a 'literary philosopher' (Gracia *et al.* 2002), which places Borges' work within the vicinity of the fantastic, the mythological and the postmodern on the one hand, and science fiction and the posthuman on the other. It is therefore no wonder that he should often be cited strategically at the beginning of posthuman thought experiments, whether critical, fictional or philosophical. In a sense, and quite ironically, Borges himself encourages the idea of his prefiguring the posthuman. It is the very logic of precursivity – for example to contemporary forms of posthumanism – that is problematised in Borges' writing. The topos that one man is all men, that one human is both the archetype, essence, and the 'end' of all humanity is ubiquitous in Borges' fictional and critical essays. For 'the writer' this means that the logic of engendering works backwards rather than merely causatively forwards. This is most clearly expressed in 'Kafka y sus precursores' [Kafka and His Precursors], where Borges concludes by saying that 'every writer *creates* his own precursors. His work modifies our conception of the past, as it will modify the future. In this correlation the identity or plurality of the men involved is unimportant' (Borges 1970: 236).

Within this vision of 'posthuman' humanity, Borges makes several crucial appearances in Katherine Hayles' groundbreaking volume *How We Became Posthuman* (1999). Firstly, in the opening pages, he is named as one of a number of precursors to the cybernetic notion of reflexivity, as Hayles comments that 'Las ruinas circulares' [The Circular Ruins] illustrates 'the system generating a reality [that] is shown to be part of the reality it makes' (Hayles 1999: 8). However, it is possible to go beyond a mere analogy between Borges' fiction as precursor to 'modern-day' reality, because his 'dreamed' reality could easily be extended into the very posthuman condition Hayles is attempting to embrace critically in her strategic intervention. It would be difficult to ignore in Borges' story the parodic anticipation of some of the more naïve creationist scenarios circulated in posthumanist or transhumanist circles. It may come as no surprise that Borges' 'stranger', willing to bring about a posthuman 'dreamexistence', is a professor dreaming up a multitude of silent students in what could only be the interdisciplinary '(post)humanities of the future' (Borges 1970: 73):

> the man was lecturing to them on anatomy, cosmography, magic; the countenances listened with eagerness and strove to respond with understanding, as if they divined the importance of the examination which would redeem one of them from his state of vain appearance and interpolate him onto the world of reality.

The dreamer-demiurge's narcissistic choice of one single student fails, and subsequently he reverts to dreaming merely a proto-Deleuzian 'body-without-organs': 'the penumbra of a human body as yet without face or sex' (Borges 1970: 75). In order to bring this altogether non-technological 'artificial intelligence', this 'Adam of dreams', to life, the Frankensteinian dreamer invokes the 'monstrosity' (not the electricity) of the gods.

There is something eerily cyborgian about the dreamed phantom in 'Las ruinas circulares' and something eminently posthuman in the insight that the dreamer in the end realises that he himself is merely the phantom of another dreamt reality, or, in analogy, that humans have 'always already' been cyborgs, contaminated with their own posthumanity. What Borges thus 'prefigures' is not only the phantasm of the posthuman but also its very impossibility, which justifies including his writings within a tradition of critical posthumanism.

Monsters, according to Zamora, are part of Borges' 'lifelong exploration of the status of the real, and more particularly, his exploration of the relations of philosophical idealism and literary form' (Zamora 2002: 48). This monstrous 'zoología fantástica' plays an important part in the gradual 'dehumanisation' of the individual human as part of Borges' 'intellectual teratology' (Zamora 2002: 56). Zamora claims that for Borges monstrosity 'is a state of being that he defines as the unnatural combination of natural parts, the possible permutations of which, he tells us, "border on the infinite"' (Zamora 2002: 58). In the way Borges' monsters challenge 'the Western binarism between nature and culture' and 'inhabit at once the realm of nature and artifice' as a 'man-made species', they clearly prefigure Donna Haraway's cyborg, who 'has no origin story [...] The cyborg skips the step of original unity, of identification with nature in the Western sense. This is its illegitimate promise that might lead to subversion of its teleology as star wars' (Haraway 2004: 9).

Not only could Borges be seen as one of the precursors of contemporary cyberculture, but also Borges' writing could be understood as a kind of 'cyborg writing' as such, which problematises the idea of a self-conscious writing self in charge of the meaning it produces but rather thinks of itself as 'a kind of disassembled and reassembled, postmodern collective and personal self' (Haraway 2004: 23). What Donna Haraway's feminist recuperation of the cyborg in its technological and less technological forms and Borges' writings have in common is the suspicion of the (liberal, Western) self. Both see the breaking away from a strong idea of personality or selfhood as a liberation; and both see this liberation realised in 'textuality' and thus privilege an ontological view of writing (Haraway 2004: 33):

> Cyborg writing must not be about the Fall, the imagination of a once-upon-a-time wholeness before language, before writing,

> before Man. Cyborg writing is about the power to survive, not on the basis of original innocence, but on the basis of seizing the tools to mark the world that marked them as other.

Borges' attitudes towards the self, impersonality and immortality are widely known and span his entire writings.

While Haraway is of course mainly concerned with 'liberal technologies' and their 'phallogocentric origin stories' to arrive at something like cyborg (or posthuman) writing, Borges' critique of identity and origin as a basis for humanist metaphysics obviously takes a longer-term historical and rather 'old-fashioned' spiritual view, thus bypassing modern technologies altogether. However, if 'writing is pre-eminently the technology of cyborgs, etched surfaces of the late twentieth century' (Haraway 2004: 34), then, anachronously, Borges will have been among the cyborgian writers of that late twentieth century (and beyond). The challenge of the 'troubling dualisms' in Western tradition – 'self/other, mind/body, culture/nature, [...] reality/appearance, whole/part, agent/resource, maker/made, active/passive, right/wrong, truth/illusion, total/partial, God/man' (Haraway 2004: 34) – is thus not confined to 'high-tech culture' but finds its untechnological anticipation in Borges.

iii. Memories of the Posthuman

Hayles makes further use of Borges in her criticism of Foucault's abstract theoretical notion of 'the body', to which she prefers a processual idea like 'embodiment'. The same criticism is then levelled at 'theory' in general which, according to Hayles, 'by its nature seeks to articulate general patterns and overall trends rather than individual instantiations' (Hayles 1999: 197). Here she strategically uses Borges' 'Funes el memorioso' to create an analogy between theory and Funes' 'number scheme': 'If embodiment could be articulated separate from the body – an impossibility for several reasons, not least because articulation systematizes and normalizes experiences in the act of naming them – it would be like Funes's numbers, a froth of discrete utterances registering the continuous and infinite play of difference' (Hayles 1999: 197). It is worth recalling that the narrator of Borges' story ironically reports that one Pedro Leandro Ipuche 'has written that Funes was a precursor of the supermen, "a vernacular and rustic

Zarathustra"' (Borges 1970: 87). Funes, in many respects, could be seen as an 'embodiment' of the Nietzschean Übermensch but also as posthuman in the sense that the narrator describes the infallibility of his memory – a perfect recording device that one might provocatively name 'cyborg memory', but without technology. It is all the more surprising that Hayles does not exploit Borges' story any further, beyond a rather tangential number analogy, because Funes actually stresses the embodied nature of his posthuman memory (Borges 1970: 92). It is precisely the embodiment of what seems to be the entirety of mankind's memories that makes Funes experience his memory as a 'garbage heap'. The key passage of the story, the turning point where the narrator bursts into commentary mode, again relates not only to Borges' precursivity to posthuman ideas but also their critique. In fact, the narrator seems almost surprised by the belatedness of technology for the posthuman (Borges 1970: 92). What follows is an explanation of the radical inhumanity of Funes' 'computational' memory: 'the truth is that we live out our lives putting off all that can be put off; perhaps we all know deep down that we are immortal and that sooner or later all men will do and know all things' (Borges 1970: 92). However, the real challenge for posthuman memory lies not so much in the embodied recording or inscription process or with the informational computation, but with the aspect of psychical repression necessary to separate actual experience from imagination, remembrance and invention (Borges 1970: 93). Funes' vertiginous world of perfect memory, the narrator reminds us, is incapable of accounting for 'ideas, of a general, Platonic sort' (Borges 1970: 93), and invites one to imagine a posthuman as 'the solitary and lucid spectator of a multiform, instantaneous and almost intolerably precise world' (Borges 1970: 94). Again, this seems to be a case where a seminal work on posthumanism, mentioning Borges in a seemingly self-contained way, will have to admit that the thinkability of the posthuman relies heavily on pretechnological conditions entirely outside its remit.

iv. [Cyber]culture and [Hyper]textuality?

The same pattern, of Borges being an acknowledged but ultimately downplayed precursor to posthumanism, continues in Hayles' *My Mother Was a Computer* (2005). One of Hayles' main arguments here is that the digital code is radically different from linguistic code, or that machines speak an entirely different language than humans, which therefore poses the urgent problem of 'translation'. Chapter 4, 'Translating Media', begins by referring to Borges' 'Pierre Menard, autor del Quijote' [Pierre Menard, Author of the *Quixote*] to discuss the 'transformation of a print document into an electronic text as a form of translation' (Hayles 2005: 89). What Hayles calls Borges' 'mock-serious fantasy', the idea of rewriting Cervantes' *Don Quixote* word for word but in a contemporary cultural context, is taken as a precursive analogy of 'more mundane operations carried out every day around the globe' (Hayles 2005: 89). Borges' premonition of this hypertextuality, in this and other stories, raises the same question: namely, whether an electronic version of a work would still be the same work, or indeed, whether hypertextuality is merely another form of textuality or something qualitatively, or even ontologically, entirely different.[1]

Hayles duly admits that Borges' 'idea of translation' – as interpreted by Efraín Kristal in *Invisible Work* (2002) – is a proto-deconstructive approach that sees translation as at once the general condition of textuality (the impossibility of an original, including Borges' logic of precursivity) and the text as a (Deleuzian) 'assemblage' and 'rhizomatic network' (Hayles 2005: 114–15). In line with her previous strategy, Hayles praises Borges for his foresight but then quickly moves on: 'that Borges arrived at this view while working exclusively in print should caution us not to overstate the fluidity of electronic texts compared to print [...] It remains the case, however, that the resources of print are *different* than the resources of electronic textuality, and that each medium interacts with and influences the others' (Hayles 2005: 115).

However, sticking with Borges' 'Pierre Menard' would inevitably lead to another encounter with the posthuman without technology. As the narrator clearly states, Menard was doing something radically different from rewriting the same story in another medium, namely reinventing the original (Borges 1970: 65–66). It is not a question of recreating the same, a perfect 'simulacrum', or of 'becoming Cervantes' (Borges 1970: 66); the challenge is to reproduce a singularity, one

1 Hayles in fact also discusses 'La biblioteca de Babel' in this passage, and speculates about the feasibility of something like a 'digital book' (Hayles 2005: 96).

might say, or a perfect 'contingency' (Borges 1970: 67), or, indeed, an absolute identity, without repetition.

Menard's venture seems to involve the oxymoronic creation of an identical singularity under radically different conditions, or the creation of a perfect repetition while accepting radical contextuality. It is true that this idea could be used as an illustration of the Derridean understanding of the im/possibility of translation: translation as that which is impossible but at the same time most necessary or desirable. In this sense, it is no paradox to say that 'Cervantes's text and Menard's are verbally identical, but the second is almost infinitely richer. (More ambiguous, his detractors will say, but ambiguity is richness)' (Borges 1970: 69). This seems to capture precisely the impossibility *cum* desirability of 'perfect' machine translation: the resistance of and to ambiguity. Instead, Borges' view seems much more radically posthuman than mere technological intermediality. The question whether textuality can be translated from print into electronic format, from the lettered to the digital, involves the idea of a 'palimpsest' of singularities which nevertheless cohere and form a unified experience within a 'subject'. Independently of technoculture, and in a 'deconstructive' vein, Borges' Menard thus found a posthuman 'technique' that bypasses the modern logic of originality and the technology of translation: 'Menard (perhaps without wanting to) has enriched, by means of a new technique, the halting and rudimentary art of reading: this new technique is that of the deliberate anachronism and the erroneous attribution' (Borges 1970: 71).

Rather than seeing Borges' texts as merely a proponent of hypertext *avant la lettre*, what makes Borges a critical posthumanist is that he anticipates not only the potential but also the limitations of the digital. While Borges does conceive of a cyborg textuality, this cyborg textuality is very different from what usually ranks as cyberliterature. While, in 'El jardín de senderos que se bifurcan' for example, he 'discovered the essence of bifurcation theory thirty years before chaos scientists mathematically formalized it' (Weissert 1994: 223), and while he 'does not hesitate to postulate that an infinite number of alternative events coexist, as in so many multiple universes or so many infinite sets' (Thiher 2005: 239), Borges' fiction nevertheless merely insinuates 'the possibilities of self-generative readings' which produce 'a multiply-interpretative and highly self-conscious reader' (Stoicheff 1991: 93). If Borges' 'metafiction sensitizes the reader to transcoding rather than to certainty', it is rather to the literary legacy than to 'fiction as yet unwritten' that it urges the reader to turn (Stoicheff 1991: 94). The implication of this is that it may be rather problematic to see Borges as a straightforward precursor of cyberliterature with its promise of liberated, self-generated textuality and reader interactivity, and with boundless rhizomatic narrative networks and interconnectivity at a formal, textual level. Borges' 'promise' rather occurs at a discursive, conceptual level. While his stories depict conceptual complexity *ad infinitum*, formally, their narratives show almost classical restraint. If Borges' scenarios were to be implemented within the new (digital) media and cyberliterature, then this could not merely happen at a conceptual but mainly at a formal level, which until now has rarely been the case, and it is not at all clear whether digital technology is in fact a good 'translator' or mediator of textual information. Instead of convergence between Borges and cyberliterature there might in fact be contradiction. This is why, when we speak of Borges as an ally for a posthumanism without technology, it is also in order to do justice to an imaginary that resists technological determinism, and which resists its own technologisation, digitalisation, and translation into (mere) 'fantasy information structures' (Murray, in Wardrip-Fruin and Montfort 2003: 3).

v. Science 'as' Fiction, or Technognosis

Returning to Hayles, her most sustained engagement with Borges had already occurred in *The Cosmic Web* (1984), where she relates the mathematical 'field concept' to literature on the basis of the two ideas of interconnectivity and self-referentiality. Comparing Borges' with Nabokov's responses to the field concept, she argues that Borges is attracted to the field concept, 'because its discontinuities reveal that everything, including itself, is no more than a game' (Hayles 1984: 138). In line with her strategy of showing an inspirational link between science and literature, Hayles dwells on Borges' discussion of Cantor's set theory and how this 'led directly to the discovery of paradoxes of self-referentiality', 'indefinite expansion' and the possibility for creating 'new kinds of Strange Loops' in his writings (Hayles 1984: 142–43). For Hayles, Borges uses these paradoxes to exploit rather than to suppress any inconsistencies, 'because he hopes to use them to reveal the essential fictionality of the model. His intent is thus subversive'

(Hayles 1984: 143). She refers to Borges' strategy in a combination of Baudrillardian ('seduction') and Deleuzian ('fold') terms.

It is fascinating to see that in this early text on Borges, Hayles does in fact credit him and his stories with the (subversive) power to create a kind of dialogic imagination between literature and science, fiction and reality. Her readings of 'El Aleph' [The Aleph] and 'Tlön, Uqbar, Orbis Tertius' are at once powerful, detailed and persuasive. However, it can already be seen that, by focusing on Borges' 'literary strategy' in his 'metaphorical appropriation' of scientific models, the flow of the argument will inevitably return to science: 'where Borges' fiction differs from scientific models of the field concept, however, is in using the concept to suggest that everything, including reality, is a fiction' (Hayles 1984: 151). Hayles ends by challenging Borges' 'Nueva refutación del tiempo' [A New Refutation of Time] (Borges 2001: 317–32) on the grounds that Borges remains unable to free himself from the very 'Newtonian' notion of time he tried to escape. By imposing a circular structure on the infinite series, according to Hayles, he has to admit the limitations of his own artistic project (Hayles 1984: 166). However, Borges' stories, and 'El Aleph' in particular, might be more powerful in their self-referentiality than they seem. Although there is a circular structure that seems to try to recapture the runaway infinite series, it nevertheless never manages to do so without a 'twist' – a Heideggerian '*Verwindung*', or a 'Strange Loop' rather in the manner of a Möbius strip, which, precisely, does not turn into a simple 'cybernetic' feedback structure. Hence the ineffability of the Aleph as explained by the narrator – the simultaneity that like Hayles' intermediality, in a sense, does not translate into a successive medium like language – might just be another realist lure (Borges 1971: 26).

The 'unimaginable universe', the total vision of the whole and all its parts at once, this piece of ultimate nanotechnology without technology, is undialectisable for the human mind, just like Cantor's *Mengenlehre* [theory of assemblages] mentioned in the 'Postscript' which insists on distinguishing between the nature and the name of the Aleph (Borges 1971: 29). Instead of resolving the final paradox between the fictionality or reality of the Aleph, Borges' story instead adds to the confusion: the narrator questions the truthfulness of the Aleph whose reality has given rise to the rival's fiction (Borges 1971: 29–30).

Let us repeat that our argument is not that Hayles' use of literature to elucidate scientific metaphors is wrong or that a link between scientific ideas and literary strategies does not exist, or should not be made; rather, in line with the idea of a critical posthumanism, one must ask whether the very link is not 'contaminated' by unacknowledged humanist assumptions. It might be argued that at the heart of the desire to resolve the difference between literature and science is an irreducibly humanist model in which both literature and science are ultimately seen as serving an end to human understanding or human self-legitimation – an anthropomorphism difficult, and maybe impossible, to avoid as long as literature and science (co-)exist. It should be remembered that in this context a writer like Borges may be legitimately called posthumanist in the sense that his choice of genre to a certain extent seems to unhinge both the fictionality of 'literature' and the factuality of 'science'. As Deborah Knight, in her critique of 'humanist ethical criticism', asks: 'what sense will [humanistic ethical criticism] be able to make out of the mock-essay, that fabulous Borgesian genre, that completely subverts both the expectations of realist literary fiction and any straightforward application of the idea that as readers we are in communication with an author (however implied) who is merely communicating things to us known as fact?' (in Gracia *et al.* 2002: 23–24). To see Borges as a kind of 'science fiction writer' could therefore be justified as long as one takes the phrase literally (science 'as' fiction and vice versa). Science fiction is one of the most important fictional genres that underpins the cultural dynamic and the cultural imaginary of posthumanism. It is also one of the main genres that engages with the representation of contemporary cultural and social change. Even though Borges is certainly not a straightforward political writer, at a deeper, metaphysical level his texts do of course engage with the notion of utopian and dystopian visions of change in cultural values, namely through the articulation of spirituality, eternity and the fantastic.

What might make Borges an ally for critical posthumanism – as an engagement with scenarios of the inhuman, past, present or future – is that the profound existential anxiety that exists side by side with Borges' irony and nihilism is precisely not resolved in some return to humanist morality. It might be gesturing towards a posthumanist ethics instead, which seems to be what Coetzee insinuates in relation to Borges' Gnosticism (Coetzee 2002: 173):

> Borges's Gnosticism – his sense that the ultimate God is

> beyond good and evil, and infinitely remote from creation – is deeply felt. But the sense of dread that informs his work is metaphysical rather than religious in nature: at its base are vertiginous glimpses of the collapse of all structures of meaning, including language itself, flashing intimations that the very self that speaks has no real existence. In the fiction that responds to this dread, the ethical and the aesthetic are tightly wound together.

It is striking how absent technology is from such a vast logistical challenge as posed by 'La biblioteca de Babel' – which others call the universe, as the narrator remarks. Nothing is said about the workings of the latrines, in each of the infinite number of hexagonal galleries; no details are given about the functioning of the ventilation of the infinite number of 'vast air shafts'; and the reference to the 'powering' of the Library, especially its electrical wiring and lighting, remains mysterious: 'light is provided by some spherical fruit which bear the name of lamps' (Borges 1970: 78).

Thus could 'posthumanism without technology' be merely some kind of 'technognosis', or a simple repression of technological materiality by an irrational insistence on radical spirituality? Is it simply a negation of the techno-logical that can be found in so many writers of the first half of the twentieth century? Is it merely a Heidegger-like attempt to invalidate technology's specificity by re-ontologising it and binding it to the metaphysical *longue durée* of humanity?[2] Or is Borges' envisaged posthuman condition merely another techno-apocalyptic scenario in the vein of *The Terminator* (Cameron 1984) where an inanimate machine-world 'survives' humanity (compare Borges 1970: 85)? Is posthuman for Borges merely synonymous with posthumous? Maybe. But we would like to believe there is another, more serious and critical aspect to Borges' irony and nihilism.

Borges' special value for critical posthumanism lies in the fact that his writings, in a sense, constitute an archive of the future even before

2 The (re)mythologisation of technology coincides with certain 'techno-gnostic' aspects in more celebratory contemporary posthumanisms. In particular, some of the posthuman desires expressed by so-called 'transhumanists' could be described as gnosticism's reinvention through technology, very similar to Heidegger's notion of technology as a kind of 'techno-gnosis', from which 'only a God can save us' (compare Heidegger 1993: 105–107).

it arrived. He was, for example, famously unimpressed by the idea of 'artificial intelligence' and a machinic future set to replace humanity, arguing that 'it would be risky to await revelation from the all-knowing machine' (Borges 2001: 155). However, in a typical turnaround move, Borges assigns the machine with a future for poetry, or the aesthetic imaginary. In fact, the idea of the machine as poetic – as the automatic other within the self – makes the poet 'himself' machinic (Sarlo 1993: 59–61).

In summary, studying the links between Borges and emerging cyberculture and its theorisation can provide important and broader statements on the relations between literature and the post-human(ist). The discourse and the imagination Borges brings to bear do not only prefigure what the posthuman order might achieve, they also anticipate its own critique. Even without technology, Borges' ingenious imaginary arrives at the posthuman before it, as the very memory of the uncreated and perhaps uncreatable order which technology might just set about fashioning in the more or less posthuman future.

References

Aizenberg, Edna, ed. 1990. *Borges and His Successors: The Borgesian Impact on Literature and the Arts* (Columbia, MO: University of Missouri Press).

Baudrillard, Jean 1994. *Simulacra and Simulation*, trans. Sheila Glaser (Ann Arbor, MI: University of Michigan Press).

Borges, Jorge Luis 1970. *Labyrinths: Selected Stories and Other Writings*, ed. Donald A. Yates and James E. Irby, trans. Donald A. Yates, James E. Irby, *et al.* (London: Penguin).

— 1971. *The Aleph and Other Stories 1933–1969*, ed. and trans. Norman Thomas di Giovanni (London: Jonathan Cape).

— 2001. *The Total Library: Non-Fiction 1922–1986*, ed. and trans. Eliot Weinberger (London: Penguin).

Coetzee, J.M. 2002. *Stranger Shores: Essays 1986–1999* (London: Vintage).

Gracia, Jorge J.E., Carolyn Korsmeyer, and Rodolphe Gasché, eds. 2002. *Literary Philosophers: Borges, Calvino, Eco* (New York: Routledge).

Graham, Elaine L. 2002. *Representations of the Post/Human: Monsters, Aliens and Others in Popular Culture* (Manchester: Manchester University Press).

Haraway, Donna 2004. 'A Manifesto for Cyborgs: Science, Technology, and Socialist Feminism in the 1980s', in *The Haraway Reader* (London: Routledge), pp. 7–45.

Hayles, N. Katherine 1984. *The Cosmic Web: Scientific Field Models and Literary Strategies in the Twentieth Century* (Ithaca, NY: Cornell University Press).

— 1999. *How We Became Posthuman: Virtual Bodies in Cybernetics, Literature, and Informatics* (Chicago, IL: University of Chicago Press).

—— 2005. *My Mother Was a Computer: Digital Subjects and Literary Texts* (Chicago, IL: University of Chicago Press).
——, ed. 1991. *Chaos and Order: Complex Dynamics in Literature and Science* (Chicago, IL: University of Chicago Press).
——, ed. 2004. *Nanoculture: Implications of the New Technoscience* (Bristol: Intellect).
Heidegger, Martin 1993. '"Only a God Can Save Us": *Der Spiegel*'s Interview with Martin Heidegger', in *The Heidegger Controversy*, ed. Richard Wollin (Cambridge: MIT Press), pp. 91–116.
Herbrechter, Stefan, and Ivan Callus 2003. 'What's Wrong with Posthumanism?' *Rhizomes* 7, special issue dedicated to 'Theory's Others', http://www.rhizomes.net, last accessed 22 June 2007.
—— 2004a. 'The Latecoming of the Posthuman, Or, Why "We" Do the Apocalypse Differently, "Now"', *Reconstruction*, 4:3, http://www.reconstruction.ws/043/callus.htm, last accessed 22 June 2007.
——, eds. 2004b. *Discipline and Practice: The (Ir)resistibility of Theory* (Lewisburg, PA: Bucknell University Press).
The Jorge Luis Borges Center for Studies and Documentation. http://www.uiowa.edu/borges/borges.htm, last accessed 22 June 2007.
Kristal, Efraín 2002. *Invisible Work: Borges and Translation* (Nashville, TN: Vanderbilt University Press).
The Matrix 1999. Directed by Andy and Larry Wachowski (USA: Warner Bros. Pictures), 35mm/colour, 131 mins.
Minority Report 2002. Directed by Steven Spielberg (USA: DreamWorks SKG), 35mm/colour, 139 mins.
Ryan, Marie-Laure, ed. 1999. *Cyberspace Textuality: Computer Technology and Literary Theory* (Bloomington, IN: Indiana University Press).
Sarlo, Beatriz 1993. *Jorge Luis Borges: A Writer on the Edge*, ed. John King (London: Verso).
Stoicheff, Peter 1991. 'The Chaos of Metafiction', in *Chaos and Order: Complex Dynamics in Literature and Science*, ed. N. Katherine Hayles (Chicago, IL: University of Chicago Press), pp. 85–99.
The Terminator 1984. Directed by James Cameron (USA: Pacific Western), 35mm/colour, 103 mins.
Thiher, Allen 2005. *Fiction Refracts Science: Modernist Writers from Proust to Borges* (Columbia, MO: University of Missouri Press).
Wardrip-Fruin, Noah, and Nick Montfort, eds. 2003. *The New Media Reader* (Cambridge, MA: MIT Press).
Weissert, Thomas P. 1991. 'Representation and Bifurcation: Borges' Garden of Chaos Dynamics', in *Chaos and Order: Complex Dynamics in Literature and Science*, ed. N. Katherine Hayles (Chicago, IL: University of Chicago Press), pp. 223–43.
Wolk, Douglas 1999. 'Webmaster Borges', http://www.salon.com/books/feature/1999/12/06/borges/print.html, last accessed 22 June 2007.
Zamora, Lois Parkinson 2002. 'Borges' Monsters: Unnatural Wholes and the Transformation of Genre', in *Literary Philosophers: Borges, Calvino, Eco*, ed. Jorge J. E. Gracia, Carolyn Korsmeyer, and Rudolphe Gasché (London: Routledge), pp. 47–84.

10

Julio Cortázar's *Rayuela* and the Challenges of Cyberliterature

Rob Rix

i. *Rayuela*, the Book

In 1963 the novel *Rayuela* [Hopscotch], by Julio Cortázar, was published in Argentina, two years before Ted Nelson coined the word 'hypertext' (Labbé 1996). The rapidly gained cult status and reputation of *Rayuela* owed much to its physical appearance and entity as a big black brick of a book, which when opened immediately cast off its guise as a novel and announced itself as a labyrinth of texts whose reading order could, if the reader chose, be ordained by a numerical chart. This was presented with the following gloss: 'this book is many books, but above all it is two books' (Cortázar 1970: 'Table of Instructions').[1] One could be read from chapter 1 to chapter 55, the other following the chart. Reading this was like being given the keys to Aladdin's cave, and given choices that could lead to endless treasures, or to abominable trapdoors. The reader could choose to go straight to chapter 73, and read that 'yes, but ...' which is both affirmation and caveat, certainty and doubt, existential dilemma: 'yes, but who will cure us of the muffled fire, the colourless fire that runs along the Rue de la Huchette at nightfall' (Cortázar 1970: 438). When the reader jumped to chapter 1, as indicated at the end of this text – chapter 73 – buried in the depths of the volume, the quest was on: 'Would I find La Maga?' (Cortázar 1970: 15). The narrative had, as it were,

1 All translations from *Rayuela* are by the author of this chapter; the published translation is Julio Cortázar, *Hopscotch* (New York: Pantheon Books, 1987), trans. by Gregory Rabassa.

begun *in medias res*, with a specific question posed in the middle of a more diffuse question, a question regarding a character in the context of an ambience, a location, and an invention which can be creative or self-destructive, as chapter 73 elucidates. From the very beginning, *Rayuela* is a novel that deconstructs itself in the reading.

The narrative is evasive, aleatory, improvised, collaged, and interspersed with the 'disposable chapters'. This is the sense in which *Rayuela* is a hypertext, an embryonic cybernovel which both anticipates and lays down challenges for today's manifestations of cyberliterature. Cortázar's instinct as a writer, his method and purpose, are imbued with the energy and discipline of improvisation, eclecticism, the scepticism of the anti-novel, and the absurdity of the comic novel. Inviting the reader to participate as accomplice in the creation of the fiction, he anticipated the potential offered to readers of cyberliterature in a not-too-distant future. Cortázar invited a different kind of reader identification, not based on empathy with 'characters' or seduction by description, evocation, and dramatisation, but rather on a problematic and intermittent engagement with what he termed the 'figures' that his writing traced and proposed, and which the reader's own preoccupations, experiences, imaginings, and desires would inform. These 'figures' in a sense foreshadow the multiplicity of fictional constructions that readers' choices produce in the itineraries followed through hyperfictions. This break with traditional readership was facilitated through the links, breaks, interstices, bridges, absences, abysses, webs, strings, and mishaps which coincide in the odd odyssey of Oliveira and which invite the reader to intervene, to get involved, in order to make sense of it. Of course, Cortázar did not conceive of renouncing the authorial voice altogether and leaving the reader to do all the work – even *62: modelo para armar* [62: A Model Kit] (Cortázar 1968) is much more than raw materials and notes for assembly, waiting for the reader to choose, arrange, direct, and deploy with complete autonomy. But if skipping up and down the hopscotch presents its challenges, thrills, and spills, the careful mounting of the armature of *62: modelo para armar* often feels like a hopeless endeavour as it continually defies the reader's attempts to keep it assembled or make it function in any articulate way, as is the case, it may be said, with some cyberliterature today.

Returning to *Rayuela*, this novel is structurally a rather primitive hypertext, with one-way links between the quasi-narrative 'story' of the two sides of Oliveira's trajectory (Paris and Buenos Aires, 'that side' and 'this side') and the miscellaneous extra chapters ('from other sides'). However, the question of structure is merely a point of departure. Cortázar gave no sign that he was aware of or interested in the developments in computer technology that were leading to the hypertext phenomenon, but he was acutely conscious of wanting to involve the reader in the creation of a novel in a new, albeit rather undefined, way. The real impact of this 'recommended' but ultimately optional reading of the text is the way that it interferes with and interjects any possible conventional narrative, reminding us always that this is literature, writing, to be thought about and mulled over, but not to be considered escapism. 'Much of its structural power is derived from the tension between Cortázar's devices and our expectations of a novel' suggest Christopher Keep, Tim McLaughlin, and Robin Parmar in their website dedicated to '*Hopscotch* as a Hyperbook' (Keep *et al.* 2000). The quotations, aphorisms, jazz lyrics, reflections, additional dialogues, poems, theorisations, ephemera, documentary items, and other 'noises off' interrupt the telling of Oliveira and La Maga's adventures in Paris, and later of the *ménage à trois* of Oliveira, Talita, and Traveler in Buenos Aires, hauling the reader out of identification with characters and circumstances to give food for reflection, time out for distancing, stimulus for re-engagement with what is in some ways an existentialist/absurdist narrative. Rather than filtering out this sort of detritus to leave an impression of smooth narrative control and authority, the writer leaves it all in for the reader to pick through, enjoy, apply, discard, or remember, freely. In the longer version, which includes the 'disposable' chapters, there is no one ending, as the reader is left swinging between chapters 131 and 58, between the manic appeal for revenge on the dog, and the apparently tranquillised nirvana that constitute Oliveira's final alternatives in paranoia, insanity and/or self-destruction. Yet all good searches come to an end when, as at this impasse, one puts the book down or, nowadays, 'disconnects' from the Internet, and as with any finished sojourn in cyberspace, the end of the novel returns the reader to the *hic et nunc*, the clear light of day or the dark depth of night that lies outside the screen, outside the pages which it makes no sense to turn any more, even though the text being read appears to be only part way through the volume. The only home page is the table of instructions at the start, that chart of numbers with its half-ironic commentary on the multiple nature of the book and the range of readers' choices available.

The many possible reader choices in relation to *Rayuela* could be seen to prefigure choices when reading fiction on the Internet. All read as they see fit, and while some readers habitually skip the 'descriptive bits' to get on with the drama, others keep stopping to think, to re-read, to dig away beneath the surface, or to protest, discard, throw down in contempt. Yet Cortázar was never solely concerned with the aesthetics of creativity, but always promoted an ethics of writing. In the 1950 essay 'Situación de la novela' [Situation of the Novel] he defines the two traditional roles of the novel: the one, hedonistic, as entertainment, diversion, escapism, and the other as opposition to certain realities which are exposed, or as the proposition of realities that should be (in Cortázar 1994: 215–41). This is a notion of the novel as an agent of change in relation to the reader, in that the reader who actively engages in the fictional project – Cortázar's 'reader accomplice' – will be transformed in some way in terms of his/her perceptions and understanding of reality, and therefore in his/her responses to that reality. The fictional literary theorist, Morelli, expounds his project in chapter 97: 'the real and only character that interests me is the reader, to the extent that something of what I write should help to change, shift, surprise and alienate him' (Cortázar 1970: 497–98).

More than forty years on from *Rayuela*, the notion of a new type of reader is still current. This notion has been heavily accented by the emergence of a new 'space' for literature which brings with it the dynamic possibilities of hypertext and hypermedia documents, in a range of formats from e-magazines to personal websites and blogs. Instances of these new possibilities can be glimpsed in some of the most interesting and experimental hypertext and hypermedia fictions by cultural producers across the continent that derive their inspiration from Cortázar's seminal novel, although not all live up to the challenges posed by *Rayuela*. Nevertheless they may all be read 'through a Cortazarian lens', and, as my conclusion will show, Cortázar's 'reader accomplice' can be fruitfully considered alongside the new types of reader that hypertext creates.

ii. *Rayuela* Online and Hypertext Theory

Rayuela is now available online in digital form, on a site named after the projected 'machine' for reading the novel, the 'Rayuel-o-matic' which Cortázar glossed rather ironically in his volume of miscellanea

La vuelta al día en ochenta mundos [Around the Day in Eighty Worlds] (1967).[2] However iconic this presentation of the novel might be, it does not in any sense enhance the experience of reading the work, which depends for its innovative effects on the very fact that it is in book form. Other works by the same author might well have benefited from the possibilities offered by web publishing, as Cortázar broke out of conventional formats such as the novel, the short story, and the essay. *Historias de cronopios y de famas* [Cronopios and Famas] (1962) and *Un tal Lucas* [A Certain Lucas] (1979) would have admirably suited the organisational and progressional possibilities offered by weblogs, as would his last major project, written in collaboration with Carol Dunlop, *Los autonautas de la cosmopista* [Motornauts on the Cosmoway] (Dunlop and Cortázar 1983). His texts accompanying photographs or artwork, such as *Alto el Perú* [High Peru] (1984, with Manja Offerhaus), *Silvalandia* [Silvaland] (1975, with Julio Silva), or *Prosa del observatorio* [Prose from the Observatory] (1972), would have found enhanced and cheaper forms of dissemination online, whilst his espousal of a comic adventure format in *Fantomas contra los vampiros multinacionales* [Fantomas against the Multinational Vampires] (1975) would also have suited the aesthetic of cyberspace.

Amongst the many and varied definitions of cyberliterature, what is of interest for comparison or contrast with Cortázar's work is hypertextual and hypermedia literature posted or sited on the Internet, with or without reader/viewer contributions or participation in the 'writing'. Many claims have been made in a relatively short time for the revolutionary possibilities of writing on the Internet: adjectives such as 'interactive', 'collaborative', or 'non-linear', are regularly cited to distinguish these forms of literature from print-based writing (see for example Auerbach 1995, Barrera Linares 2005, Lamarca 2006, Leibrandt 2003, De Moraes 2004). One thing is certain, however, and that is the reader's – or user's – freedom to re-arrange, re-combine, and even abandon any specific text at any time 'with a clear conscience', as Cortázar put it in his instructions for reading *Rayuela*. Of course, reading in printed form does not in any way preclude such operations; it is simply that these are perceived as 'natural' and even 'priority' actions for the online reader, whose mouse is ever at the ready to click on choices and alternatives, whether within or outside

2 See *Proyecto Rayuel-o-matic Digital Universal*.

of the domain currently visited. Spanish theorist and practitioner of hyperfiction, Antonio Rodríguez de las Heras, sees this feature as a problem to be resolved in the design of projects, which must try to ensure a 'confinement' of text in order to counteract the tendency for text to leak or to haemorrhage (Chartier and Rodríguez de las Heras 2001: 34):

> we jump from one web-page to another without having finished reading, there's an impulse in pointing with the cursor to active words which announce links to other pages before finishing the text on screen, the temptation of curiosity to see the new, to reach the next screen more than to read what each screen contains.

It is worth underlining, therefore, that the looseness or instability of cyberliterature is an inbuilt feature of the medium, not an authorial choice.

Technical issues thus loom large in the practice of cyberliterature, as the structure and dynamics of a hypertext or hypermedia document determine to some extent their 'readability', yet the organisation of text, links, and nodes does not in the end make a work of cyberliterature successful. William Dickey notes that hypertexts 'admit and encourage several concerns of contemporary art': these include multiplicity of perspective, rejection of a single rhetorical authority and of linear causative organisations, admission of aleatory organisations and relationships as more accurate representations of experience, and an effective illusion of the simultaneity of experience (Dickey 1994: 144). These elements represent the potential of a medium which is still relatively new, but they are neither guaranteed to be present in any given project of writing on the web, nor do they in themselves guarantee any measure of interest or readability for the 'readers' who engage with such writing.

Theorists insist on the role of the writer(s) or creator(s) of web literature as merely the initiators of a process in which reading and writing the 'text' are intricately conjoined or meshed, and in which the very stability, durability, unity, order, and sequentiality of a given text are no longer guaranteed. For the web is a medium of ephemerality, fluidity, dynamism and diversity in which narrative momentum, for example, is difficult if not impossible to sustain (see, for instance, Barrera Linares 2005). However, as Susana Pajares Tosca has noted, 'hyperfiction writers seem to consider disorientation as a positive value' (Pajares Tosca 1999), apparently confirming Cortázar's projection of narrative dislocation as an alternative to the narrative tricks or resources normally used to hold the reader's attention. Pajares Tosca also argues that hypermedia is probably more suited to poetry and poetic prose than to narrative proper: 'hyperfiction therefore seems to be a new form between poetic prose and poetry. It combines relatively long and complex texts with poetic structures and figures' (Pajares Tosca 1999).

This analysis fits perfectly with the prose of *Rayuela*, in which the only significant narrative drive comes from the initial question 'Would I find La Maga?', while the remainder of the novel is full of tableaux, interludes, pataphysical encounters, meditations, and other poetic explorations and 'figures'. The 'disposable' divagations in *Rayuela* lead the reader to imagine or expect that these add-on texts may somehow hold the key, or clues, to the meaning of the narrative text as such. Each diversion from the 'story' promises some kind of revelation or disclosure, as, at the same time that one text closes, another is opened. This technique appears to pre-empt what Harpold has noted regarding the effect of traversing the links in a hypertext narrative, thus: 'hypertextual (dis)closure evokes anxiety because it leads you to exactly what you were looking for, but not what you thought you wanted. And it is possible to continue reading only so long as you never quite find it' (Harpold 1994: 210).

Susana Pajares Tosca distinguishes between two types of reader involvement, one in 'constructive hyper-fictions' involving multiple authorship, and the other in 'explorative hyper-fictions' which 'allow the reader to take decisions about the reading trajectory, choosing which links to establish at any given moment' (Pajares Tosca 1997). In this second type, despite this freedom of choice between links, everything within the work is already written, so that the reader does not contribute new writing, but merely makes choices within what is on offer. In either case, what makes the reader want to continue to select and/or contribute to a hyperfiction may respond to an almost infinite range of factors, or at least as many different factors as there may be readers. Harpold's paradoxical statement quoted above does however capture one essential aspect of hyperfiction which distinguishes it from much 'traditional' novel-writing: the absence, indeed the impossibility, and necessarily the undesirability of narrative closure.

While disorientation may therefore be, at least in principle, a positive feature of hyperfiction, not all theorists see it as such; for example Yankelovich, Meyrowitz, and Van Dam (1991: 58) include it as a negative feature along with eyestrain, thus echoing one of Tristram Shandy's ironical concerns for his readers' eyes (Sterne 1967: 286). Harpold hints at similar risks in his comment on Michael Joyce's foundational hyperfiction *Afternoon, a Story* (1990): 'you could spend a long time deciphering the looping traces of this misremembered history' (Harpold 1994: 190). However, these considerations of reading comfort and/or frustration in relation to on-screen works have mainly technical implications for hyperfiction creators, such as the desirability of keeping discreet chunks of text – or 'lexia' – relatively short, or the desirability of allowing readers to keep a record of their trajectory so that it can be abandoned and resumed at a later date – unless the author's intention is to encourage every re-reading to be different. As readers become more familiar with and accustomed to online and on-screen reading many of the frustrations associated with hypertext use may diminish, such as the sense of being 'lost in hyperspace', of having chosen 'the wrong path' through a fiction, or of not being able to make sense of the puzzle whose pieces are dispersed and not always easy to re-discover once encountered and discarded or moved away from.

In attempting to assess the success, or the significance of a given hyperfiction, it is worth remembering that prescriptions regarding the extent to which such works should offer readers structural overviews, facilities for tracking and/or recording their own progress, or other supporting frameworks should not seriously be entertained; similarly, prescribed dosages of narrative coherence or cohesion must also be disregarded. Hyperfiction authors are as free as any other novelists to thrust the willing reader into an apparent chaos, and run the risk of alienating their audience, just as they are free to lead by the hand with an excessive zeal and concern, thus infantilising those who attempt to engage with the work. The notion that there must be a happy medium, or balance between disorientation and excessive support also seems to be dubious, if not irrelevant. Sarah Auerbach has noted the curious frequency with which 'its authors try to preserve elements of linear fiction, such as plot and characters' and claims that 'the key is to sufficiently stimulate the reader's interest in the subject [via such traditional devices] so as to counterbalance the enmeshed, non-argumental nature of hypertext. It is not enough to offer choices for the mere pleasure of choosing' (Auerbach 1995). This comment challenges the facile view that hypertext fiction engages the reader simply by offering choices of itinerary through texts, while the previous comment reminds us that conventional literary devices for engaging the reader will not necessarily function in the same way in the Internet environment.

iii. Latin American Hypertexts, through a Cortazarian Lens

Searching the web for examples of Latin American hyperfiction has both illustrated some of the preceding questions and also thrown up a number of other issues perhaps best dealt with through examples. What follows is neither so much an attempt to evaluate these projects, nor to compare them with Cortázar's work, but rather a commentary which tries to elucidate some of the realities of current Latin American hypertext through the application of what might be termed a Cortazarian lens or literary gaze.

In addition to websites which function to pay homage to Cortázar in one way or another, such as *Isabelle, el libro* [Isabelle, The Book] (Piñero 2006), created by Jennifer Piñero, who styles herself 'La Maga', there are other sites which more properly engage with the new fictional possibilities proposed by Cortázar. One such example is Colombian author Jaime Alejandro Rodríguez Ruiz's *Gabriella infinita* [Infinite Gabrielle] (2005), a multimedia puzzle novel, centred on the quest of Gabriella Ángel for her disappeared lover and teacher, Federico. The reader explores clues through mouse-controlled links to books, papers, sound files, and videos in three areas denominated 'ruinas', 'mudanza', and 'revelaciones' [ruins, removal, and revelations] many of which take us to nostalgic reminiscences of a youthful revolutionary age – the 1960s –, a range of secondary characters including a series of transgressive women and a schizophrenic patient named 'Guerrero' [Warrior], newspaper cuttings, rather in the style of Cortázar's *Libro de Manuel* [A Manual for Manuel] of 1973, and the frustrated meetings of a group in some ways reminiscent of the 'Serpent Club' from *Rayuela*. The reader gradually pieces together a mystery out of these elements, some of which lack narrative or dramatic force, consisting of rather long scrolls of text – such as the 'stories' of women – or of recited text – the 'audio-cassettes' – which are flatly non-dramatic monologues. Other sound files include repetitive non-diegetic musical sound, and while the work employs many features of the multimedia potential of cyberliterature, and belongs in Pajares Tosca's 'explorative' category, it does not necessarily address or solve issues of narrative impetus and reader engagement which have been identified earlier in this chapter as key questions for cyberliterary creation. This may be a result of the work starting life as a 'conventional' novel before being transformed into a hypertext and later a hypermedia novel.

La huella de Cosmos [The Trace of Cosmos] (2005) meanwhile, is a collective novel directed by the Peruvian-born Venezuelan writer Doménico Chiappe who contributes a chapter to this volume in which he explains some of the creative processes involved in crafting such a project. Designed and written by a team of collaborators working to fairly strict parameters, the work consists of short text scenes that are the fragments of a puzzle which readers decipher as they navigate the work. Technically well organised, with an accent on concision, it has a comic-strip science fiction aesthetic with explicit acknowledgements to, among others, *Blade Runner*, Isaac Asimov, the rock opera *Tommy* by The Who, and Fritz Lang's *Metropolis*, and it is self-consciously aware of the virtual nature of its digital medium, introducing as its eponymous protagonist Cosmos, a digital vampire who, as a fictional creation, 'invades' the real world of the text. It progresses to a kind of cyber-gangster denouement, but leaves all the contributors to give their own gloss on the outcome, their own varying interpretations of the different possible endings. For the collaborators as readers/writers, this is a 'constructive' hyperfiction in Pajares Tosca's terminology, although for readers not involved in the writing team it is 'explorative', allowing intervention only through e-mail messages logged in a space which is not part of the narrative proper, but rather a site for appreciation and interpretation.

Finally, an interesting new development is the publication in traditional print form of Ecuadorean Leonardo Valencia's *El libro flotante de Caytran Dölphin* [Caytran Dölphin's Floating Book] (2006). This enigmatic work, in which the eponymous mystery writer has disappeared after publishing his only book – the fragmentary and apparently lost *Estuario* –, is set in a Guayaquil flooded by a tsunami. Nothing is sure or secure in a novel which insists on the floating nature of words and texts, and which has a complementary website where readers – or non-readers – can contribute to the apocryphal *Estuario* with original texts or with changed versions of the fragments included in Valencia's novel, thus collaborating in the collective development of a fictional world which is always expanding. In the website version, Mexican Eugenio Tisselli joins Valencia in 'authoring' the work, and together they propose an exciting and original project, consciously moving the novel from book form to web-based format (and possibly back again in the future). This venture has enormous potential to be a free and fully collaborative fiction-writing initiative, offering a genuine open door to the kind of 'reader accomplice' advocated by Cortázar. Still in its early stages at the time of writing (August 2006), it remains to be seen whether Valencia's floating book website will attract the attention and collaboration it seeks, to become a successful and significant landmark (or watermark!) in Latin American cyberfiction.

While these comments on two fairly sophisticated and complex hyper-novels and an innovative fiction website may seem somewhat perfunctory, this is not to question their validity or value as literary experiments on the web. The extent to which they subvert narrative conventions in their textual components, and thus confront the challenges posed by Cortázar in terms of the role of the reader as accomplice, varies in each case. Cortázar's vision of the new reader was partly a reaction against what he saw as the manipulative aesthetics of nineteenth-century realism and naturalism, partly an avant-garde development from modernism towards a radical ethics of writing fiction which he only fleetingly achieved in his novels, but which is a driving force in much of his shorter fiction and miscellaneous writings. The elusive energy which ensures narrative engagement in stories from 'Las babas del diablo' [Blow-up] or 'El perseguidor' [The Pursuer] in *Las armas secretas* [The End of the Game and Other Stories] (1959) through to 'Diario para un cuento' [Diary for a Story] from *Deshoras* [Unreasonable Hours] (1982), the poetic flights of *Prosa del observatorio* (1972) and the quirky curiosities to be found in *La vuelta al día en ochenta mundos* and *Último Round* [Final Exam] (1984), all testify to his transcendence of the conventional novelistic enterprise and his awareness that in a not-too-distant future the 'book' as we know it was to burst from its binding and discover new freedoms and possibilities, in which the reader would play a more active and immediate role in the very act of literary creation. The Internet undoubtedly promises such a mutation in our understanding and use of fiction, and there is evidence that experiments are emerging to engage new kinds of readers in the elaboration of new fictional spaces, not least in the Spanish-speaking world.

References

Auerbach, Sarah 1995. 'Ficción hipertextual: una teoría literaria', *Hipertulia*, http://www.ucm.es/info/especulo/hipertul/auerbach.html, last accessed 27 June 2007.

Barrera Linares, Luis. 2005. 'La literatura en Internet: ¿Una vuelta a los orígenes?', *Ficción breve venezolana*, http://www.ficcionbreve.org, last accessed 27 June 2007.

Bush, Vannevar 1945. 'As We May Think', The Atlantic Monthly, July, 101–108.

Cavale, Cristina 1998. *Perra virtual* (Barcelona: Seix Barral).

Chartier, Roger, and Antonio Rodríguez de las Heras 2001. 'Cibercultura: El futuro del libro y el libro del futuro, Una conversación entre Roger chartier y Antonio rodríguez de las heras' [sic], *Litterae: cuadernos sobre cultura escrita*, 1, 11–40.

Chiappe, Doménico 2005. *La huella de Cosmos*, http://www.e-novelacolectiva_com.htm, last accessed 21 April 2006.

Cortázar, Julio 1959. *Las armas secretas* (Buenos Aires: Sudamericana).

—— 1962. *Historias de cronopios y de famas* (Buenos Aires: Ediciones Minotauro).

—— 1967. *La vuelta al día en ochenta mundos* (Mexico: Siglo Veintiuno). Also available online at http://www.literatura.org/Cortazar/Vuelta_al_dia/LV_maquina.html, last accessed 27 June 2007.

—— 1968. *62: modelo para armar* (Buenos Aires: Editorial Sudamericana).

—— 1970. *Rayuela* (Buenos Aires: Editorial Sudamericana). First published 1963.

—— 1972. *Prosa del observatorio* (Barcelona: Lumen).

—— 1973. *Libro de Manuel* (Buenos Aires: Editorial Sudamericana).

—— 1975. *Fantomas contra los vampiros multinacionales* (Mexico: Libros de Excélsior).

—— 1979. *Un tal Lucas* (Madrid: Editorial Alfaguara).

—— 1982. *Deshoras* (Madrid: Editorial Alfaguara).

—— 1984. *Último Round* (Mexico: Siglo XXI).

—— 1987. *Hopscotch*, trans. Gregory Rabassa (New York: Pantheon Books).

—— 1994. *Obra crítica II* (Madrid: Alfaguara).

——, and Manja Offerhaus 1984. *Alto el Perú* (Mexico: Editorial Nueva Imagen).

Cortázar, Julio, and Julio Silva 1975. *Silvalandia* (Mexico: Editorial Cultural GDA).

De Moraes, Dênis 2004. 'Palabras en red: las mutaciones de la literatura en Internet', *Revista Contratiempo*, http://www.revistacontratiempo.com.ar/moraes.htm, last accessed 27 June 2007.

Dickey, William 1994. 'Poem Descending a Staircase: Hypertext and the Simultaneity of Experience', in Paul Delaney and George P. Landow, eds., *Hypermedia and Literary Studies* (Cambridge, MA: MIT Press), pp. 143–52.

Dunlop, Carol, and Julio Cortázar 1983. *Los autonautas de la cosmopista* (Barcelona: Muchnik Editores).

Harpold, Terence 1994. 'Conclusions', in George P. Landow, ed., *Hyper/Text/Theory* (Baltimore, MD: The Johns Hopkins University Press), pp. 189–222.

Keep, Christopher, Tim McLaughlin, and Robin Parmar. 2000 'The Electronic Labyrinth'. http://www.iath.virginia.edu/elab/elab.html Accessed 18 April 2005

Labbé, Carlos 1996. 'Ni Herbert Quain ni el rey de Theuth: notas en torno a la (inminente) literatura hipertextual', *Letras en Línea*, http://www.letrasenlinea.cl/hiper/hiper-herbert-teuth.htm, last accessed 22 June 2007.

Lamarca Lapuente, María Jesús 2006. 'Hipertexto, el nuevo concepto de documento en la cultura de la imagen', http://www.hipertexto.info/documentos/literat.htm, last accessed 27 June 2007.

Leibrandt, Isabella 2003. 'Hipercultura e hiperficción: una cuestión terminológica', *Espéculo*, 25, http://www.ucm.es/info/especulo/numero.html, last accessed 20 March 2006.

Letralia: tierra de letras, http://www.letralia.com, last accessed 27 June 2007.

Pajares Tosca, Susana 1999. 'La cualidad lírica de los enlaces'. *Hipertulia*, http://www.ucm.es/info/especulo/hipertul/link.htm, last accessed 27 June 2007.

Pajares Toska [sic], Susana 1997. 'Las posibilidades de la narrativa hipertextual', *Espéculo*, 6, http://www.ucm.es/OTROS/especulo/numero6/s_pajare.htm, last accessed 27 June 2007.

Piñero, Jennifer 2006. *Isabelle, el libro*, http://www.literabinto.com, last accessed 23 March 2006.

Proyecto Rayuel-o-matic Digital Universal, http://español.geocities.com/rayuel_o_matic/indice_proyecto.html, last accessed 23 April 2006.

Rodríguez Ruiz, Jaime Alejandro 2005. *Gabriella infinita*, http://www.javeriana.edu.co/gabriella_infinita/proyecto/hipertexto.htm, last accessed 16 June 2006.

Sterne, Laurence 1967. *The Life and Opinions of Tristram Shandy* (Harmondsworth: Penguin). Originally published in instalments 1759–1767.

Valencia, Leonardo 2006. *El libro flotante de Caytran Dölphin* (Madrid: Editorial funambulista). Also available at http://www.libroflotante.net, last accessed 27 June 2007.

Yankelovich, Nicole, Norman Meyrowitz, and Andries van Dam 1991. 'Reading and Writing the Electronic Book', in Paul Delaney and George P. Landow, eds., *Hypermedia and Literary Studies* (Cambridge, MA: MIT Press), pp. 53–79.

11

Contemporary Brazilian Fiction: Between Screens and Printed Pages

Ana Cláudia Viegas

Introduction: Benjamin, Simmel, Lévy

The intersection of literature and information technology prompts a number of theoretical questions. These are not necessarily new, but they take on new dimensions as the Internet reshapes the cycle of production, transmission, and consumption of the written word. Such questions include the changing roles of reader and author made possible by the advent of hypertext and the practice of the collective creation of texts, as well as debates about the notions of author and work, in the light of the intensification of techniques such as collage, montage, appropriation, and re-creation as processes of artistic creation, and the ongoing erosion of the 'aura' of the work of art (Benjamin 1970b). They also include delicate matters such as the ascription of authorship and subsequent questions of copyright – an area where legislation clearly needs revising and updating in accordance with this new mode of transmission of a literary text; and the redefinition of the criteria by which we ascribe value to the literary text, in view of its transmission in the midst of a multiplicity of other types of texts, images and sounds.

Any reflection upon the social changes brought about by new media must entail analysing the new forms of interaction that are enabled between media and society. In other words, we should move from the analysis of the media as such to an analysis of social mediations (Martín-Barbero 1993). Walter Benjamin, in his classic 1935–1936 text about 'technical reproducibility', points to the historicity both of aesthetic values and of human perception, indicating that new media signify changes in the body, consciousness and human actions, and not just new forms of expression (Benjamin 1970b). And now, at the turn of the twenty-first century, according to Pierre Lévy, 'we are experiencing one of those rare moments in which, triggered by a new technological configuration, that is to say a new way of relating to the cosmos, a new kind of humanity is invented' (Lévy 1990: 18).[1] In this chapter I explore how that 'new kind of humanity' is reflected in contemporary Brazilian literature, and, in particular, the impact that technological innovations such as hypertext and remote-control television consoles have had on the form and content of literature in print form.

In recent years the joining of the patterns of production, transmission, and reception of literature with other areas of the media and the appropriation of the expressive forms of those media by literary texts, have introduced new challenges for traditional book culture, today hybridised with non-literary genres and audiovisual communications media. Furthermore, the spread of these new media, especially television from the 1950s onwards and then, at the end of the 1970s, computers, has brought about significant transformations in forms of representation and knowledge. Nowadays, a new, dynamic conception of reading confuses the functions of reader and author, to the extent that the former, in the role of navigator, edits the text that s/he reads, participating in the structuring of the hypertext and in the creation of new links. The notion of authorial identity seen as an integrated subjectivity responsible for the imparting of sense to the text is also questioned in hypertextual reading/writing, in which the condition of the unique text – the property of a single author – gives way to a text in constant transformation through the participation of multiple authorial voices.

Network connections also allow the Internet user to navigate by way of various sites and links, making the reading of the screen a sliding between surfaces, accompanied by the fragmentary montage of new texts, in a process similar to the act of 'zapping' between the images of different TV channels. This process is concerned with cognitive and communicative experiences which can be considered in

1 Translation by Mike O'Brien.

the light of Georg Simmel's and Walter Benjamin's comments on the experience of modernity: Simmel characterises modern, metropolitan 'man' as 'blasé', and Benjamin defines the impact of modernity on human subjects as the 'experience of shock'.

The psychological basis for the modern, metropolitan type of individuality consists, according to Simmel, in the intensification of nervous stimuli, resulting from the sudden and uninterrupted alternation between exterior and interior stimuli. These contrasting, rapid, concentrated stimuli in constant change lead to a 'blasé' attitude, the essence of which consists in the blunting of a person's ability to discriminate: 'the meaning and differing values of things, and thereby the things themselves, are experienced as insubstantial. They appear to the blasé person in an evenly flat and gray tone; no one object deserves preference over any other' (Simmel 1950: 414). When analysing the topic of the crowd in Baudelaire, Benjamin describes 'the disintegration of the aura in the experience of shock' (Benjamin 1970a: 196). The destruction of the aura of the work of art explains the new perception and sensitivity of the masses rather than art itself. It also explains our increasing sense of the proximity of the most distant and sacred things, made possible through technological innovations. When Benjamin chooses the cinema as the privileged setting of the distracted and divided attention, a symptom of the profound transformations of the structures of perception, it is not a question of technological optimism or of a belief in progress, but of a mode of thinking about the transformations of experience that makes him pioneering.

The inability to differentiate and the change in perception characterised by a 'short attention span' encouraged by the mass media, such as cinema and television, may be considered useful tools for an analysis of the method of hypertextual reading. Text on a computer screen can be characterised as an edition, a single montage, through which a supply of potential information is produced for a particular reader. Pierre Lévy distinguishes the pairs real/possible and actual/virtual, in such a way that the virtual is not opposed to the real, but to the actual (Lévy 2001: 29). The possible is defined as being like the real, only non-existent or latent. As it is already completely constituted, when it materialises it does not imply creation. Actualisation of the virtual, on the contrary, constitutes the invention of a solution required by a complex set of problems. It is not concerned with the occurrence of a predefined state or choice from amongst a predetermined set of options, but of the production of new qualities, the invention of a new form starting from a dynamic configuration of forces and purposes. Thus the digital images on our screens are not virtual in themselves, but possible images. The dialectic actual/virtual only occurs during the interaction between computer systems and human subjectivities, 'once the indeterminateness of meaning and the propensity of the text to signify come into play, a tension that actualization, or interpretation, will resolve during the act of reading' (Lévy 1998: 53).

Thus the act of reading is defined as an actualisation of the meanings of a text, and the hypertext as a virtualisation of the processes of reading. The arrangement of even a traditional written text into paragraphs, chapters, summaries, indices, notes, and cross-references contributes to its expression over and above a traditional linear reading, turning the act of reading into a process of selection, schematisation, and construction of an intertextual network. The structure of hypertext in a network formed by nodes and links between these nodes is not restricted to the digital medium. Concepts like those of intertextuality and dialogism already assume the text to be a web of multiple textualities just as the reading of an encyclopedia is evidently of a hypertextual order. What is new in the digital hypertext is the speed of transfer from one node to another and the association, in the same medium, of texts, sounds and images in movement. But what of the increased hypertextual awareness and aesthetics employed in contemporary Brazilian literature in print form?

i. Literature in Print Form and New Technologies

The Brazilian literary texts produced in the 1890s and in the first decades of the twentieth century have already been studied with regard to their interaction with modern inventions: the tram, the aeroplane, the motorcar, the photograph, the telephone, the gramophone, the cinema and, especially, the typewriter. Forsaking fragile and fluctuating pre-, post-, and neo-classifications, Flora Süssekind has explored the most characteristic feature of Brazilian fiction of that period: 'the dialogue between literary form and technologically produced images, sound recordings, mechanical movements, new printing processes' (Süssekind 1987: 18). After starting with the representation of these industrial artefacts in the literature of the period, Süssekind goes on to analyse how contact with these innovations ceased to be a mere object of description or discussion and went on to shape the technique of certain authors.

But how does this interaction between literature and technology reveal itself in the print literature of the closing decades of the twentieth century? If the typewriter was the image privileged by Süssekind as a means of reflecting on that dialogue at the beginning of the twentieth century, what are the marks left by the computer on the writing of the latest generation? The so-called 'new technologies', both digital and virtual, make up the contemporary scene, sharing in everyday life as well as in the actual imaginary. If these new media typify new modes of thinking, feeling, and perceiving, how might their presence be noted in contemporary texts?

Just as it was for the authors who rose to fame in the era preceding the Semana de Arte Moderna [Modern Art Week] of 1922, this dialogue is produced in different ways: virtual technologies are both objects of representation as well as influences on the rhetorical strategies used in the writing itself. In the first instance, we have urban landscapes full of screens, digital images, cellular phones, computers, and a whole host of technological paraphernalia used by the characters and narrators of contemporary fictions. As for the marks left on the literary work, we can cite the increased fragmentation, the highly visual nature of the writing, the use of multimedia narrative forms, and the appearance of 'microrrelatos' [almost aphoristically short stories].

Examples of the rhetorical strategies used by the generation of writers who have exchanged the typewriter for the computer, can be found in the works of Luiz Ruffato such as *Eles eram muitos cavalos* [There Were Many Horses] (2001), *Mamma, son tanto felice* [Mother, I Am So Happy] (2005a) and *O mundo inimigo* [The Hostile World] (2005b). The story of *Eles eram muitos cavalos* describes everyday life in São Paulo in seventy sections which, although numbered and titled, offer no sense of continuity, no plot as a connecting theme, and only the 'effervescent montage' of overlapping and juxtaposed close-ups.[2] It is a mosaic of different kinds of text – captions, weather forecasts, classified ads, prayers, letters, menus, astrological advice, expressions of condolence, book lists, automated replies, even two pages covered with a black rectangular shape – arranged with different layouts, letter

2 García Canclini defines the contemporary city 'as a videoclip, an effervescent montage of discontinuous images' (García Canclini 2001: 84).

formats, and typographic signs. The textual diversity of web pages is thus expressed on the printed page.

Ruffato's reader can begin at any point and follow any direction. The reading experience is multilinear rather than linear. It is both hesitant and indefinite. Just as in the new virtual spaces themselves, 'rather than following tracks and migrations within a fixed domain, we leap from network to network, from one system of proximity to the next' (Lévy 1998: 31). This labyrinthine, multilinear reading also leads us down different intertextual paths. Thus Oswald de Andrade's *Memórias sentimentais de João Miramar* [The Romantic Memoirs of João Miramar] of 1924 and Cecília Meireles' *Romanceiro da inconfidência* [Ballad of the Minas Revolt] of 1953 are both virtually present in Ruffato's proto-hypertext and capable of being actualised by individual readers.

For example, the title, reiterated by the epigraph – 'There were many horses / but no-one now knows their names / their pedigree, their origin ...' – and by the dedication – 'For Cecília' –, leads us to Meireles. When evoking the era of the exploitation of gold in the Minas Gerais region in the eighteenth century, and the historic fact of the *Inconfidência Mineira* – a popular movement in Minas Gerais rejecting excessive taxation and the abuse of power on the part of the Portuguese crown – Meireles' text highlights the hard lives and deaths of so many 'nobodies'; people who do not figure in the histories of the deeds of great men. Similarly, in Ruffato's text, the characters of this urban chaos do not have names, nor does the reader know where they come from or where they are going to – we only capture fragments of scenes in the dizzying rhythm of the narrative.

It is also impossible not to notice echoes of De Andrade in Ruffato's text. The numbered and titled fragments the of *Memórias sentimentais de João Miramar*, in which various textual genres are mixed and graphic material is emphasised, are virtually present in Ruffato's proto-hypertext, and can thus be actualised by the reader. However, the cinematographic cuts and the telegraphic writing of Oswald de Andrade are sped up in Ruffato's text to the point of almost totally obliterating the fragile narrative of the character who is lost amongst these disconnected memories.

In fact, the rhythm of Ruffato's text echoes the speeding up of urban life from the beginning of the industrialisation of São Paulo – the subject of De Andrade's work – to the present day. Cinematic montage, as defined by Sergei Eisenstein (1986: 14–18), gives way to a kind of zapping, to images that appear and disappear as if by the command of a remote control and which leave the viewer/reader in a 'blasé' state, unable to discriminate due to an excess of information. Nevertheless, arguably the author retains control over this process and thus the simulation of zapping is a literary effect that assimilates a typical feature of televisual aesthetics, but also supplements it, alternating ridicule, tenderness, violence, naivety, hope, and deception.

Ruffato's two other books – *Mamma, son tanto felice* and *O mundo inimigo* – are part of a project for a series of five volumes entitled *Inferno provisório* [Provisional Hell]. Both narrate the destruction of rural life in the face of modernisation through fragmented but interrelated texts that can be read separately or together. The characters – poor Italian immigrant farmers – suffer the social and emotional consequences of Brazilian industrialisation from the 1950s onwards. The stories from each of the volumes re-introduce and interweave characters and situations, thereby creating an effect of intersecting planes in the reading and construction of meaning. Past and present are mixed in fragments of memory thus creating a 'badly structured quasi-novel' (Nina 2005: 6). Typographical changes signal the different tempos and voices present in the texts to the reader.

In the second volume, in which several people begin to migrate to the big cities, there is a noticeable acceleration in the rhythm of the language, just as in *Eles eram muito cavalos*. This coincides with the increase in speed and intensity of stimuli characteristic of the formation of metropolises. In the later books of the series we can imagine the continuation of that process. A note at the end of each volume states that readers may recognise some passages, since a number of stories come from the author's other books but have been 'rearranged'. Thus creation is governed by repetition and revealed through the weakening of what is viewed as authentic and original in the age of technical reproducibility. We can thus observe in Ruffato's books an aspect of the relationship between cyberculture and Brazilian fiction published after 1990: he makes conscious use of many of the rhetorical strategies of digital media and thus his page effectively becomes a screen.

Conclusion

Taking Ruffato's books as examples, we can see how Brazilian fiction is changing in the face of technological innovation. Even printed texts use hypertextual ways of writing and, as a consequence, require new readings. There are, of course, other writers who choose to write fully fledged hypertexts online, and further research is necessary on these works to consider the extent to which they actualise the technological innovations foreshadowed by Ruffato's print texts.[3] Nevertheless, what is clear is that this kind of digital hypertext fiction is reshaping the cycle of production, transmission, and consumption of literature. It also offers a way of exploring the 'new kind of humanity' and new aesthetic possibilities that emerge in the new medium.

Translated by Mike O'Brien

References

Benjamin, Walter 1970a. 'On Some Motifs in Baudelaire', in Walter Benjamin, *Illuminations*, ed. Hannah Arendt, trans. Harry Zohn (London: Jonathan Cape), pp. 157–202.

— 1970b. 'The Work of Art in the Age of Mechanical Reproduction', in Walter Benjamin, *Illuminations*, ed. Hannah Arendt, trans. Harry Zohn (London: Jonathan Cape), pp. 219–53. Originally written 1935–1936.

De Andrade, Oswald 2001. *Memórias sentimentais de João Miramar*, 14th edn. (São Paulo: Globo). Originally published 1924.

Eisenstein, Sergei 1986. 'Word and Image', in Sergei Eisenstein, *The Film Sense*, ed. and trans. Jay Leyda (London: Faber & Faber), pp. 13–59.

García Canclini, Néstor 2001. *Consumers and Citizens: Globalization and Multicultural Conflicts*, trans. George Yúdice (Minneapolis: University of Minnesota Press).

Lévy, Pierre 1990. *Les Technologies de l'intelligence: L'avenir de la pensée à l'ère informatique* (Paris: La Découverte).

— 1998. *Becoming Virtual: Reality in the Digital Age*, trans. Robert Bononno (New York: Plenum).

— 2001. *Cyberculture*, trans. Robert Bononno (Minneapolis: University of Minnesota Press).

Martín-Barbero, Jesús 1993. *Communications, Culture and Hegemony: From the*

[3] Whilst beyond the scope of this chapter, Brazilian hypertext novels which could warrant further study include Daniel Pellizzari's *Quatro gargantas cortadas* [Four Cut Throats] (1997), or Marco Palácios' *A dama de espadas* [The Queen of Spades] (1998).

Media to Mediations, trans. E. Fox (London: SAGE Publications).
Meireles, Cecília 1983. *Romanceiro da inconfidência: crônica trovada da cidade de Sam Sebastiam* (Rio de Janeiro: Nova Fronteira).
Nina, Cláudia 2005. 'As fronteiras existenciais de Ruffato', *Jornal do Brasil*, 'Idéias' section, 9 April, p. 6.
Pellizzari, Daniel 1997. *Quatro gargantas cortadas*, http://www.geocities.com/SoHo/Studios/1875/indice.html, last accessed 27 June 2007.
Palácios, Marcos 1998. *A dama de espadas*, http://www.facom.ufba.br/dama/index.html, last accessed 24 November 2006.
Ruffato, Luiz 2001. *Eles eram muitos cavalos* (São Paulo: Boitempo).
—— 2005a. *Mamma, son tanto felice* (Rio de Janeiro: Record).
—— 2005b. *O mundo inimigo* (Rio de Janeiro: Record).
Simmel, Georg 1978. *The Philosophy of Money* (London: Routledge and Kegan Paul).
—— 1950. 'The Metropolis and Mental Life', in *The Sociology of Georg Simmel*, trans. Kurt Wolff (Glencoe, IL: Free Press), pp. 409–24.
Süssekind, Flora 1987. *Cinematógrafo de letras: Literatura, técnica e modernização no Brasil* (São Paulo: Companhia das Letras).

12

Creative Processes in Hypermedia Literature: Single Purpose, Multiple Authors

Doménico Chiappe

i. Hypermedia Narratives

With the arrival of digital formats changes have occurred in the process of literary creation. In the traditional book, whatever the narrative voice or voices used in the text, the point of view corresponded solely to the author who worked alone, concerned only with his or her text. This is no longer the case. A hypermedia work will not usually have a single author, given the complexity of its conception. The creation of a multimedia narrative requires the involvement of a number of disciplines and therefore the intervention of numerous authors. The contrasting points of view of the artists involved, who interpret the story and transmit their perceptions, all converge in the work to be exhibited and this poses a challenge for these multiple authors. Writers of multimedia works – part of the artistic vanguard which I term 'hypermedism' – must explore innovative creative formats and, at the same time, achieve high quality content. Hypermedia works must display more than formal innovation, giving a literary depth to the works offered to readers.

In an authentic multimedia project the authors share the credit, as each one contributes a narrative plane from the artistic elements which, in the work's totality, are in balance and have equal importance. Alongside writers, plastic artists, musicians, and photographers there is the programmer who interprets the ways in which different arts are related to each other within the hypermedia narrative. The programmer in that sense contributes the collective vision by organising what could be really quite chaotic. To use a theatrical comparison, the programmer fulfils the director's role, and the designer of the multimedia work fulfils that of set designer. Another contributor who should be included in the authorial credits is the person who conceptualises the work and the way it can be navigated; the person who ensures that aleatory navigation of the work does not lead to a loss of coherence. This may be the programmer, the designer, or the 'author' of the work.

And finally, there is also an executive function which the authors must fulfil or delegate, and which consists of analysing, approving, and correcting the results of each stage of the work and communicating all the information pertaining to the project, so that the necessary debates can take place at the probable points of conflict and relevant decisions can be made as the project progresses. The person attending to this task must also evaluate the results of the assemblage of the work as a whole, carry out tests to make sure it works, supervise publication on the Internet or in other formats and serve as co-ordinator and link between the different kinds of authors.

During the process of creation, this multidisciplinary team can choose to make a closed work, in which the potential is there for readers to discover and follow different reading itineraries, but without allowing changes to the artistic message or purpose. In this case, the creative act should not be an example of unstructured, chaotic group work with no-one holding the reins, nor a trivial pursuit destined to use the medium as a showcase for digital pyrotechnics. Indeed, the artistic purpose will be lost if it is left entirely to chance, unless of course the purpose is precisely to leave a work adrift.

In these closed works, where readers are allowed to mould pre-existing material (Murray 1998: 152–53), they may create and interpret, without leaving any direct trace of this on the work of art itself, by virtue of elements which induce passive interaction, modifying the readers' perceptions and the itinerary through which the work is followed. Understanding the re-creation of discourse – the artistic proposition of hypermedism – will have more to do with 'free associations' as conceived of by Freud and Jung than with any unidirectional imposition established by the author. The last word will thus be left to the reader; the author will abstain from providing a conclusion and will try instead to make the reader think of one for him/herself. Nevertheless, the set of elements provided by the author and his/her team may continue to express a clear intention and message. This is one of the challenges which face the writer of this new rhetoric.

This position is opposed to that maintained by those who claim one of the advantages of the new format is its ability to leave the last word to the reader, thus transcending the closed text of the print medium. This would be an alternative option which the multidisciplinary authorial team could choose: to allow infinite continuation so that the readers construct the work, making it apocryphal and never definitive. Hypermedia authors must confront this dilemma: are they ready to abandon their unfinished works and let readers supplant them, thus renouncing their role as an artist in order to be innovative?

The novel *Tierra de extracción* [Land of Extraction], of which I am the co-author together with Andreas Meier, is an example of a closed hypermedia work, created by two main authors and various collaborators who joined in the elaboration of parts of the complex mesh which makes up the work. Why a novel? Because the work interweaves a number of plot-lines and because each one of these plots has a different protagonist. Also, because the multimedia novel seeks polyphony not just through the fictional characters, each of whom brings his/her own cosmogony, but also through the creators who intervene in the artistic process. Thus the narrative levels are multiplied. Music, plastic arts, literature, and photography all tell the story, each with its own point of view, each contributing a different vision. The work is polyphonic, therefore, not just because there are different characters with different consciousnesses, but because at the meta-narrative level, there are also creators with different consciousnesses.

With a single artistic purpose and a (loosely) unified narrative thread in mind, we traced several plans of the work to be carried out: one for the literary side of things, another for the music, another for the plastic arts, and another for the *mise-en-scène* (the programming and design). Each conforms to a series of rules which govern the multimedia package. The novel should have a rhizomatic structure of interlinking chapters, in the manner of Gilles Deleuze and Félix Guattari's *A Thousand Plateaus* (1980). I call these kinds of chapter 'balls of mercury', as they are like the metallic blobs which spill from a broken thermometer. They can join up with each other again or remain dispersed, without losing their rounded form. The chapters are written in a brief, concise form. They each tell a micro-story in themselves, but at the same time they are fragments of a larger narrative framework which becomes apparent through the reading. Another key aspect of the structure of the hypermedia novel is the puzzle to be figured out. This is a way of challenging readers to reconstruct a coherent story and, at the same time, of generating such tension and intrigue that they feel compelled to explore the work in its totality.

In *Tierra de extracción* we decided that the written word would represent the first level of rhetoric, the gateway that would allow readers to relate to the other forms of narrative in the novel. Music is another narrative level, in which song lyrics offer a first-person point of view and cover an aspect which is reserved only for song: the innermost thoughts of the chapter's protagonist – their subconscious. There is one song for each protagonist and there are compositions that are divided into two, three or four parts, each one with different arrangements, according to the chapter in which they appear. The words and music were composed by the novel's author, but each song was given to a different musician (Ojo Fatuo, Jorge Ramírez, Slam Ballet, Culto Oculto, Daniel Armand). They read the chapters and worked on the musical arrangements that they thought were appropriate. Then they recorded them with their own perspective, thus adding another layer of polyphony.

A different method was used with images. The narrative material was handed to the plastic artists and the photographers (Ramón León, Manuel Gallardo, Humberto Mayol, Edgar Galíndez, Pedro Ruiz). With complete freedom, the painters expressed in their works the aspects that most impressed them. The photographers searched among their work for images that they considered to be linked, in some way, to the texts and music. There are photographs from different countries and situations that complement others which are more directly relevant to the narrative and which are the result of extensive research in two important Venezuelan photographic and press archives (Shell-CIC-UCAB and *El Universal*).

The individual screens which make up the novel were configured, one at a time, with combinations of these materials. And just as in a theatrical play, an artistic vision was needed for the *mise-en-scène*, the staging and the direction of the work: Andreas Meier took on this role and each one of the chapters constitutes a small work of Net-art. As far as the design was concerned, we tried not to impress the user with vacuous technological wizardry, but rather to achieve a simple interface, in order to avoid having to include instructions. The work does not abuse its readers with technical excesses, which is quite common when hypermedia authors attempt to exploit the maximum potential of a piece of software. That would mean giving in to digital pyrotechnics, which would be empty and trivial. What you would have on screen would be an endless and exclusively ornamental circus. The difficult art of writing a story shows how it should be done: if any element of the plot is unnecessary for the denouement, it should be eliminated. A writer should present readers with a labyrinth which is set out in such a way that those who explore it patiently do not become lost.

ii. Collective Novels

For some years now the creation of 'collective novels' in which readers may add lines or chapters to the narrative has proliferated on the Internet. The publisher Anaya experimented with the idea for two consecutive years. For the first book, *No tiene título* [Untitled], written between 25 May and 10 June 2001, the editor, Emilio Pascual, imposed the genre of the thriller, with twelve characters whose names and occupations were given. On this first occasion, the publisher decided that users/readers would be able to see where a new collaborator had participated in the development of the work, which, in the end, consisted of eleven chapters. However, when it is read, contradictions between the various participants are discovered. In this case, the literary pleasure was to be found more in the sensation of creating than in that of reading. Thus the participants – but not the readers – found some compensation for the poor outcome. The following year, more strict rules for participating were imposed. The publisher's second attempt was entitled *La sorpresa de Olivares* [Olivares' Surprise]. The project, written between 31 May and 16 June 2002 and directed by Joaquín Ordoqui, was co-written by fourteen participants and, furthermore, included a team of readers who wrote the final paragraphs 'with the intention of tying up loose ends and closing sub-plots' (Ordoqui 2002). Neither of these two novels dealt with hypermedia materials, as they concentrated on the collective creation of written texts via virtual participation.[1]

Earlier in the twentieth century, the Surrealist movement had already experimented with the collective creation of works of art through techniques such as the game 'exquisite corpse' in which players would take turns to write – or draw – on a sheet of paper, folding over their contribution before passing the sheet on to the next person.[2] In this type of sequential composition there was no understanding between authors, incoherence had primacy, and there were no aesthetic considerations – this was what the Surrealists sought. A modern version of an 'exquisite corpse' has been proposed by the magazine *Soho* and published as *Erotic Novel* (n.d.).

For this project the editors invited pre-selected authors to contribute texts. However after five chapters, it became obvious that there were disadvantages to having each author write one link. The different styles and plots composed a book of stories rather than a 'novel'. What one author proposed, another undid in the following text. This does not mean that individual authorship is necessary to guarantee quality: there must be agreement about the creative purpose, and a co-ordinator should guarantee the achievement of the artistic objectives. Such co-ordination should promote discussion among members and take decisions where there are disagreements. In a literary sense, this will allow the contributions of readers – whether expert or novice – to be edited, encouraged, or merged, so that they can be added to the work without diminishing its aesthetic value. Put simply, in order to avoid the complete incoherence of Surrealist 'exquisite corpses', collective literary works on the web need co-ordination.

If it is true that 'interactivity reaches its full meaning of active participation in the creative process' (Ryan 2004: 98), it is only in a collective creative project that, from the start, seeks a commingling of ideas and discourses, that such interactivity can be maximised.

1 In this kind of project the community that participates is defined by its common language – in this case, Spanish – and any Spanish speaker is allowed to participate. Thus geographical frontiers are dissolved thanks to virtuality. Although these two projects were launched in Spain, the participants – as I discovered when I directed the collective work *La huella de Cosmos* – came from Latin America as well as Spain.

2 See André Breton's *Le Cadavre exquis: Son exaltation* of 1948, in English translation in Waldberg 1965: 93–95.

The participants must commit themselves to the artistic purpose, and debate it in parallel discussion spaces, for the work itself is not the appropriate place to exchange opinions. These parallel forums allow for the private space which all artists need yet also oblige them to work with other authors on the same subject in a co-ordinated way. The participants, therefore, find themselves in a non-simultaneous debate in the present, which enriches the composition and facilitates the meeting of minds.

In the collective novel *La huella de Cosmos* [The Trace of Cosmos] which I directed between June and December 2005, we differentiated between the space dedicated to the novelistic work written for the reader, and the zone in which participants discussed and offered their ideas. In the discussion forum every proposal was offered up for debate. And it was from this zone that the hypermedia texts which would be published as chapters of the said novel emerged. In this project, the free participation of all the interested parties was combined with the existence of a director who could suggest the development of certain plot-lines and who edited the definitive texts, seeking to give them a unified style and coherence, and without straying from the outlines drawn up by the users of the forum.

In the forum of *La huella de Cosmos* a tight bond formed between participants who established both alliances and enmities – reading the product of bitter arguments and even of one or two flirtations might yield the plot of another potential novel in which the characters write a book together ... But this sense of collective authorship was complicated by the fact that the majority of the members of this literary community opted to sign with nicknames – first names without last names, initials or pseudonyms – thus fighting shy of assuming the responsibility of 'authorship'. Furthermore, how many of these writers were not more virtual than real? That is, how many pseudonyms could hide the same person, making their interactions in the forum an actual fiction? How many were playing a role rather than acting as they would in person?

The frontier established by traditional authorship is dissolved and redirected, in cases such as the writing of this collective novel, towards metafiction. For, who can assure the readers that I, as director of *La huella de Cosmos*, have not been all or many of the participants in the forum? Or perhaps I, Doménico Chiappe, do not exist and my name is the signature of a collective or a company ... When I proposed this experiment to the sponsors I wanted to avoid the literary anarchy of 'exquisite corpses', be they Surrealist or hypermedia in nature, and, instead, imitate, in the forum, the functioning of an individual brain when creating: inspiration, ordering, creation, evaluation, selection and editing. The forum would reveal everything that went into the composition of a definitive work and would be available separately. Thus, readers of the definitive work would not have to be caught up in the creative process unless they wanted to be.

Detecting the strategy chosen by each participant in the forum is not possible. The majority chose not to allow any subsequent contact. But we can speculate that a single participant may have taken on one character in the story and developed it exclusively. Or assumed different personalities, under different nicknames, to set up a game which would be impossible in traditional publishing, but which could be an advantage for the collective literary work, despite the use of anonymity.

iii. Recycling and the Reader as Literary DJ

Hypermedia is nourished by original creations produced specifically for the medium, but also by the recycling of works not suitable for hypermedia in themselves, but which can be transformed with a bit of imagination. Not only original texts and artwork are used. Everything and anything can be used to tell a story, but the organisation of such materials within a literary framework is crucial. This editorial re-ordering of elements is another form of authorship, and readers can participate in this editorial work too.

We can imagine the reader of the future as a modern DJ. Not the classic disc-jockey who chose records and broadcast them without a pause, but one who now alters recorded commercial music, composing his or her own songs in so doing. The use of programmes for altering sounds allows DJs to compose and perform music without any knowledge of musical theory or any command of instruments. Supported by computer programmes, the literary DJ will assimilate the contents of hypermedia works and redeploy them, taking intertextuality, graphic interface and musical mix to extremes. In so doing, this literary DJ will 'write' his or her own book. This can be considered an art form as long as it is an authentic expression with a creative purpose. Not all readers will make their own mixes, just as not all contemporary music fans will become DJs. Only a minority with initiative and the necessary talent will do so.

In art the ideas and ingenuity of predecessors who have fed evolutionary processes have always been re-used. In previous eras works belonged to tradition and no-one claimed authorship. The ancient bards transmitted stories from generation to generation through song but, in contrast to the bards, in the future works will be re-used as if they were recyclable materials, and not even the basic structures will be kept. Readers will create their own works and the pleasure sought in art will be that of self-expression, no longer that of interpretation. The intimacy of artistic enjoyment will be exteriorised and exhibited.

In hypermedia, individual works – those of literary DJs – will be derived from those produced by groups of artists and from old compositions distorted by the new author which may then be mixed with other elements. Ultimately the original 'texts' may or may not be identifiable, in the same way as in contemporary musical 'sampling' where the tempo, tone and rhythm of an existing composition are changed so as to make the music, style and voices unrecognisable. 'Authors' will not need to have any knowledge of literary, musical, artistic, or photographic techniques, because all they will need to express themselves will be the ability to use computer software.[3]

We are not facing the disappearance of the author as a consequence of potential changes in publishing markets. We are facing a redefinition of authorship. There will be a new concept of authorship because there will also be a new concept of readership – one that will multiply authors. Just as the Internet has ushered in a new era of reading, it has done the same with writing. There has probably never been so much written and in such varied ways as now: emails, diaries and blogs, personal and corporate websites, communications media with infinite publishing capacity, news commentaries, attempts to write literature, ramblings and rantings, and – why not? – traditional quality literature published by virtual publishers and communities. The role of the new reader had already been glimpsed by Italo Calvino in *If on*

[3] See Paul Fallon's account of Rafa Saavedra's work in chapter 8 of this volume for an 'actual' example of a literary DJ. The suggestion in this chapter, however, relates to the 'virtual' potential of literary DJ-ing, to use Pierre Lévy's terminology (Lévy 1998).

a *Winter's Night a Traveller* [1979] when he spoke of a woman 'who is always reading another book besides the one before her eyes, a book that does not yet exist, but which, since she wants it, cannot fail to exist' (Calvino 1982: 61). Readers can now construct the book which before they could only imagine when their minds wandered from the pages which lay before them.

When programming languages are finally taught in school in the same way as mathematics, the majority of readers will be able to take on a fully active role and develop the maximum expression of interactivity: that of creator. This reader of the future, who constructs an almost completely different work out of the work in hand, is very different from 'creators' such as Jorge Luis Borges' 'Pierre Menard, autor del Quijote' [Pierre Menard, Author of the *Quixote*]. Menard is described as '[not wanting] to compose another *Quixote* – which is easy – but the *Quixote itself*' (Borges 2000: 65). It goes without saying that Menard never envisaged a mechanical transcription of the original; he did not propose to copy it. His admirable ambition was to produce pages which coincided – word for word and line for line – with those of Miguel de Cervantes. But Borges' was a parody of literary creation rather than a vision of the future and readers in years to come will not be like this reader-copyist, since without any concern for issues of copyright, they will mould the huge diversity of material at their disposal to remake works to their own taste.

The mysterious processes which produce good art can occur in these derivative works of hypermedia just as much as they can in 'original' works of art. How can a work evoke the same feelings from one end of the earth to another, from one century to another, and have, at the same time, as many individual interpretations as there are readers? How can its quality overcome, in the end, the workings of the market which captures direct and indirect audiences? How can we enjoy a text without needing to understand the personal complexities of the author? The work of art is like a magical potion whose effects vary according to who drinks it; a potion which, in a few cases, will survive its circumstances and its epoch to continue to cast its spell on those who imbibe it. Hypermedia novels, collective works, and the recycled mixes of literary DJs, all have the potential to cast their spell – or their net – over an increasingly diverse reading public.

Translated by Rob Rix

References

Borges, Jorge Luis 2000. 'Pierre Menard, Author of the *Quixote*', trans. James E. Irby, in *Labyrinths*, ed. Donald A. Yates and James E. Irby, preface by André Maurois (Harmondsworth: Penguin), pp. 62–71.

Calvino, Italo 1982. *If on a Winter's Night a Traveller*, trans. William Weaver (London: Picador).

Chiappe, Doménico, dir. 2005–. *La huella de Cosmos*. http://www.e-novela-colectiva.com, last accessed 20 April 2006.

—, Andreas Meier, *et al*. 2002. *Tierra de extracción*. A newer, but still incomplete, version is now available at http://www.newmedios.com/tierra, last accessed 27 June 2007.

Lévy, Pierre 1998. *Becoming Virtual: Reality in the Digital Age*, trans. Robert Bononno (New York: Plenum).

Murray, Janet H. 1998. *Hamlet on the Holodeck: The Future of Narrative in Cyberspace* (Cambridge, MA: MIT Press).

Ordoqui, Joaquín 2002. *La Sorpresa de Olivares*, http://www.anaya.es/cgi-bin/novela_colectiva/novela_interactiva.pl?ruta=blanco#, last accessed 27 June 2007.

Pascual, Emilio, dir. 2001. *No tiene título*, http://www.anaya.es/cgi-bin/novela_colectiva/novela_interactiva.pl?ruta=blanco#, last accessed 27 June 2007.

Quiroz, F., *et al*. 'Novela erótica', *Revista Soho*. http://soho2.terra.com.co/soho/articuloView.jsp?id=3195, last accessed 29 July 2005.

Ryan, Marie-Laure 1999. *Cyberspace Textuality: Computer Technology and Literary Theory* (Bloomington, IN: Indiana University Press).

Waldberg, Patrick 1965. *Surrealism* (London: Thames & Hudson).

13

Hypertext in Context: Space and Time in the Hypertext and Hypermedia Fictions of Blas Valdez and Doménico Chiappe

Thea Pitman

> And what is happening is that, rather than looking for its niche in the Enlightenment idea of culture, the audiovisual experience redefines culture in terms of the way we relate to reality; in other words, in terms of the transformations which it produces in our perception of space and time.
>
> (Martín-Barbero 2000: 61)

In the article cited above Jesús Martín-Barbero explores some of the key issues thrown up by the development of audiovisual, and, increasingly, digital culture as it pertains to Latin America. In particular he focuses on the question of space, exploring the relationship between cultural products and their 'embeddedness' in a given space such as the nation; and on that of time, examining how changes in the conceptualisation of time in new media may accommodate a distinctively Latin American perspective on history and narrative. What this chapter proposes to do is to test some of Martín-Barbero's arguments by applying them to two seminal works of Latin American hypertext fiction.[1] As a by-product

[1] In this study, I will use the term hypertext to encompass both hypertext and hypermedia forms unless otherwise stated. Ensslin defines three different types of hypertextual literature: hypertext proper (composed of small lexia linked in a variety of different ways and requiring an element of reader interactivity during reading), hypermedia (which expands the principles of hypertext to cover

of this investigation, it intends to elucidate the ways in which such works may be seen to relate to and participate in the development of the canon of Latin American literature, placing particular emphasis on areas where hypertextual elements combine with and enhance Latin American cultural features. By way of a conclusion, this chapter will consider whether hypertext endangers Latin American culture by force-feeding 'globalised' cultural products to audiences in the region, leaving them adrift in global time and space, or whether it can perhaps offer a local, emancipatory, resistant solution to the more nefarious effects of globalisation on Latin American culture.

i. Pain and Petroleum

Mexican/American author Blas Valdez (b. Guadalajara, 1972)[2] has been hailed as one of the pioneers of hypertextual narrative in Mexico (Chimal 2002: 79) and in Latin America in general (Chiappe 2003a).[3] His proclivity for hypertextual narrative manifested itself even in his early pre-Internet works – the short stories of *Restos de corazón* [Remains of the Heart] (1998) are extremely brief, ludic narratives which are open-ended in structure, requiring reader participation in order to construct possible meanings. Valdez himself also claims that all his work is essentially hypertextual – 'hypertext to me feels like home, it feels natural' –, relating the experience of reading and writing hypertext fiction to his personal experience of a variety of neurological disorders (Valdez 2006).

After a BA in Multimedia Communication in the United States in 2000, Valdez started to write and program full-blown hypertextual works with hypermedia elements, commencing with *Dolor y viceversa* [Pain and its Opposite] (2001/2002), a series of twelve short stories, accessible via a traditional index, which between them contain the traces of an ill-fated thirteenth story not indicated in the index. The

different media); and cybertext where 'text becomes a programmed "machine", taking control of the reading process' (2007). I have yet to find evidence of 'cybertextual' work being produced by Latin American authors.

2 Valdez's father is Mexican; his mother a United States citizen. He grew up in both Mexico and the USA and is identifiable as a fully fledged citizen of either nation-state, or, perhaps, of both and neither simultaneously.

3 For a picture of Valdez in the company of Mexican hactivist Fran Ilich and others, see fig. 8.1.

first drafts of the stories that make up *Dolor* were written (on paper) in the late 1990s. They were subsequently transferred to the editing software program Macromedia Director by the author himself, together with artwork by Valdez and others – photos, video clips, graphics, and music –, and first presented in public at the 'State of the Arts' festival held at UCLA in 2002. The work was subsequently exhibited in its full hypermedia version at the Mexartfest in Kyoto and Artmedia festival at the Universidad Maimónides in Buenos Aires. Today only the hypertextual version can be accessed online.[4]

The leitmotif of the collection, as the title indicates, is 'pain and its opposite'; or rather, they are all fatefully doomed love stories, written in a very unsentimental style. A description of one of the more malevolent characters in the story '0+' [Zero Positive] may serve here as a guide to the tone of the collection: the rapist and murderer Bruno is described as behaving 'with impressive indifference' and when he reads a document containing key information – the blood test results of the woman he has just raped which demonstrate that she is zero positive – he reads it 'as one would read a shopping list, with minimal emotion'.[5] The collection as a whole is reminiscent of Raymond Carver's short stories of the 1970s and 1980s, Bret Easton Ellis's *American Psycho* (1991) and some of the more disturbing recent work of Chuck Palahniuk, although none of these authors are direct sources of inspiration on the author.

Peruvian/Venezuelan author Doménico Chiappe (b. Lima, 1970) and his hypermedia novel *Tierra de extracción* [Land of Extraction] (2002) need little introduction to readers of this anthology (see chapter 12 in this volume). The initial inspiration for *Tierra de extracción* stems from Chiappe's studies in oceanography in the early 1990s during which time he performed fieldwork in and around Lake Maracaibo in Venezuela. The first drafts of some of the plot lines that make up *Tierra de extracción* were written (on paper) after Chiappe had abandoned oceanography and was starting to make a living as a writer in Caracas in the mid 1990s. Nevertheless, he quickly realised that the

4 My comments on his work in this chapter are largely directed towards the hypertext version. Much of the information concerning the author's background and sources of inspiration in this paragraph and elsewhere in the chapter stems from personal conversations and correspondence with the author. The same is true of similar material concerning Chiappe.

5 All translations are my own unless otherwise acknowledged.

complexity of what he wanted to achieve did not fit traditional print formats because of the 'web'-like structure of the story and because of his need to spill over into other media such as music. As a result of this, Chiappe started to explore the pragmatics of transferring his work to a digital medium and of finding a team of people to help him with the complexity of the task, most significantly Andreas Meier, the technical director of the work as it is today. Although the beginning of the composition of the novel technically dates from 1996, its first version in Macromedia Director was exhibited in conjunction with the symposium on 'El desafío de la escritura multimedia' [The Challenges of Multimedia Communication] hosted by the Universidad Católica Andrés Bello in Caracas in May 2000 and distributed as a CD-Rom by the Venezuelan publishing house Comala. Nevertheless, Chiappe and Meier continued to work on the project and a second, much improved, version was exhibited at the Museo de Arte Contemporáneo in Caracas in 2002. Since then the work has continued to evolve and Version 3.0 was made freely available online in 2007.[6] Chiappe's work has met with critical acclaim both in Venezuela, Spain, and elsewhere in the Hispanic world, both in traditional print media as well as in online journals such as *Letralia* (see, for example, 'Escritura multimedia').

The novel itself is comprised of sixty-three small chapters which may be made up of one or more lexias and some of which have little by way of a traditional textual component and instead exploit the full potential of the 'new architectures of language' available in hypermedia (Martín-Barbero 2000: 69; see the introduction to this volume). Ultimately, although one still feels a strong tendency to ascribe primacy to the textual dimension of the 'novel', the other modes/media used – music, art, photography, newspaper cuttings – can stand apart from the text, telling their own story in their own way and they are executed in a sophisticated and thought-provoking manner which adds to, rather than distracts from, the textual dimension.

The chapters are all accessible via a navigation map which is arranged along four main axes (see fig. 13.1).[7] The way of moving

6 For the purposes of this chapter, the second version of *Tierra – Tierra de extracción, versión 2.0* – has been used, as supplied to me by the author at the time of writing (July 2006).

7 In version 3.0 three of the chapters are only accessible during certain readings rather than directly from the navigation map, and one further 'invisible' chapter is even harder to find, thus heightening the ludic nature of

from chapter to chapter which suggests itself is to read one's way up the axes: clicks on the left or right-hand side of the screen within individual chapters generally confirm this ordering. Such a method offers some sense of sequential development along the five main plot lines which comprise the novel. Nevertheless, clicks at the top or bottom of the screen within individual chapters move the reader from one axis to another in a more graphically erratic but thematically cogent manner – this is a way of following the fates of individual characters as they appear in different plot-lines.[8]

ii. Embeddedness and Multiple Temporalities

Jesús Martín-Barbero's main concern about new media is that in the audiovisually and digitally mediated world culture suffers increasing 'disembedding' which he posits as a loss: 'for when it is disembedded from its national space culture loses its organic links with its territory, and with language, which is the very fabric of the work of the intellectual' (Martín-Barbero 2000: 62). While I do not want to endorse Martín-Barbero's hankering here for such a stable, traditional, anchored relationship between culture and national or even regional space, I do want to explore some of the implications of this statement, and suggest that hypertext can offer a space where literature, Latin American or other, can be just as embedded or disembedded as it has been since at least the early twentieth century and where it can make a deliberate effort to convey its position on this matter to its audience. It is not just a case of the medium and its mediations being essentially disembedded because of the ease with which materials can be circulated around the globe – in this argument the form and content of hypertext works can overcome such technical 'disadvantages'.

Typical assumptions about hypertext by conservative cultural critics tend to assume that the minority language – in this case Spanish – will be overpowered in cyberspace by the language of cultural imperialism and the lingua franca of the Internet – English (see cultural debates

the novel (personal email correspondence with the author, 30 August 2006).

8 The narrative itself concerns the interrelated lives and loves of a whole host of characters. Of these the most developed are all men. Female characters display much less psychological depth and are prone to being essentialised through recurrent emphasis on their sexuality. Although beyond the scope of this chapter, this is a problematic issue worthy of further attention.

outlined by Kim 2003: 181–84, and Ensslin 2007). Typically such critics assume that authors will either prefer to write in English or simplify their mother tongue for easier translation into, or correspondence with, English. Indeed, in the case of Spanish-speakers, the fear is that they may opt to write in a kind of 'Spanglish' or even 'ciberespanglish'.[9] This is the argument for the 'disembedding of language' in cyberliterature, yet this is manifestly not true of cyberliterary production by Latin American authors. To date I have found no evidence of authors preferring to publish in English, and a brief perusal of Valdez's and Chiappe's work reveals that both writers use the ideolects that they preferred prior to moving to the digital medium: Valdez has always written a very pared down, terse, and ironic kind of prose with short sentences and little regional vocabulary, 'suitable for translation into English' (cf. arguments of cyber-sceptics outlined in Kim 2003: 182); Chiappe's style is much more allusive and effusive, though no less effective, inflected by regionalisms particular to the Caribbean coast of South America. Even the title of *Tierra de extracción* does not offer itself up for easy translation.[10]

With respect to the representation of historico-geographically and socio-culturally identifiable places – of 'territory' in Martín-Barbero's terms – Valdez's work is patently less 'embedded' in Latin American culture than Chiappe's. Many of the stories are nominally set in the wealthier neighbourhoods of Mexico City – Polanco, Pedregal, Chapultepec –, and the protagonists are by and large (upper-)middle-class young adults from the capital. The plot-lines also map closely onto the co-ordinates of life for this sector of society in the post-apocalyptic metropolis as relayed in urban myths: AIDS and casual sexual encounters, random violence and premeditated terror, new drugs and illicit raves. Nevertheless, there is no obvious way in which any direct comment on contemporary Mexican or Latin American society can be read into these stories. The protagonists are part of a globalised community, meeting up by chance or by fate as much in

9 See, for example, the concerns expressed by Castro Roig (2001).

10 *Tierra de extracción* refers to the place where petrol is extracted from the earth, but also to one's place of origin. Chiappe plays further with the meaning of the title: not only can something be extracted from the land – petrol or people – but the land also extracts something from the people, trapping them, sapping their ability to leave. Further webs of semantic associations link these meanings of the title to other of the recurrent themes and images in the text.

New York as in Mexico City. In Deleuzian terminology, their territory is the 'smooth space' of the 'lines of flight' that link Mexico City to other points on the globe: it is characterised by constant transformation and movement, and by pervasive parallelism and contingency.[11] Indeed, many of the stories feature a character named Mariana, an air-hostess, and the account of the blowing-up of a plane in which she is flying is reiterated in several of the stories – Mariana dies different deaths in both 'Iluso' [Dreamer] and 'Für Elise', and there are references to her / the plane in which she dies in 'Debut y despedida' [Beginning and End] and 'Violanchelo' [Cello / Raping Chelo]. Furthermore, Valdez consistently refuses to contextualise: for example, he does not give a sense of causality to the actions of the bungling suicide bomber on Flight 1301 from Mexico City to New York in 'Iluso' by encasing the event in a sociopolitical context.

The more clearly embedded nature of Chiappe's novel is evident in the recurrent references to Venezuelan topography and history. Furthermore, the novel engages with a substantial cross-section of Latin American cultural and social phenomena, from exploitation at the hands of multinationals to the many faces of social deprivation, and from prodigious natural habitats to the massive impact of *telenovelas* (regionally produced television soap operas). This is a novel that is about Venezuela, the nation-state, and its insertion into the global economy via the petroleum industry: 'this is Venezuela, a land of extraction, murmured one of the workers' ('Lluvia' [Rain]). This kind of approach is of course what is familiar to many readers of Latin American fiction. Nevertheless, Valdez's more deterritorialised approach is not unknown in Latin American fiction, the most famous exponent of this being, of course, Jorge Luis Borges.

Evidence of differing degrees of cultural 'embedding' and confirmation of the validity of the different approaches of Valdez and Chiappe with

[11] In their attempt to break free from the constraints of traditional (print) culture, Deleuze and Guattari in *A Thousand Plateaus: Capitalism and Schizophrenia* (1980), envisioned a new culture based on performativity rather than the word (logos), and premised on becoming rather than essence, on nomadism rather than fixity, on loose associations (rhizomatic in nature) rather than hierarchies, and on 'smooth spaces' and 'lines of flight' rather than the 'striated spaces' of traditional culture, where 'striated space' is characterised by 'routine, specification, sequence, and causality' (see Moulthrop 1994: 302–303 for this useful summary of their arguments).

respect to the canon of Latin American literature is also apparent in their use of intertextuality. Arguably, both works are extremely well embedded in Latin American literature, even if Valdez's intertexts also speak of his more disembedded approach to Latin America in general.

Valdez openly acknowledges as sources of inspiration for his work the Argentine writers Julio Cortázar and Ernesto Sábato, both of whom pertain to the more disembedded current in (avant-garde) Latin American literature. Both writers also stand as key precursors in a Latin American proclivity for digital fiction and for hypertextuality: Sábato was one of the first Latin American writers to start experimenting with transferring his literary endeavours to the digital medium (Ahumada 2000: 26) and Cortázar's *Rayuela* [Hopscotch] (1963) has been signalled by hypertext theorists across the globe as one of the most seminal proto-hypertexts in world literature, along with the writings of fellow Argentine writer Jorge Luis Borges (for Borges and Cortázar, see chapters 9 and 10 in this collection).[12]

Indeed, Valdez consciously set out to write a 'cyber-*Rayuela*'[13] and, although his stories are hardly reminiscent of Cortázar's novel in their brevity or in their unsentimental aesthetic – in the latter case they are more clearly reminiscent of Sábato's work[14] – their webbed structure as a collection and their narrative relocations do seem to allude to the world of *Rayuela*. Furthermore, and perhaps most importantly, *Rayuela* is an inspiration to Valdez in terms of his approach to the new medium itself. His work most closely resembles Cortázar's in the way in which it challenges the limits of the medium in which it is written: where *Rayuela* pushed at the boundaries of the print novel thus paving the way for hypertext fiction as we now know it, *Dolor y viceversa* does not just follow *Rayuela*'s lead, but instead it seeks to push at the boundaries of hypertext fiction. Or rather, if hypertext fiction is characterised by its lack of closure, its multi-linearity and its interactivity, then Valdez imposes some rather strict boundaries on

12 Strictly speaking, Borges' 'El jardín de senderos que se bifurcan' [The Garden of Forking Paths] and 'Examen de la obra de Herbert Quain' [An Examination of the Work of Herbert Quain] (1942) function as metatextual prophesies of the multiple temporalities that hypertext would make available rather than as proto-hypertexts in themselves (Boulter 1991: 138–38).

13 Personal email correspondence with the author, 13 December 1999.

14 Indeed, there are clear echoes of *El túnel* [The Tunnel] (1948) in 'Nelly sin pulso' [Dead Nelly] and 'Autoretrato #16' [Self-portrait Number 16].

his work. For example, Valdez uses hypertextual links as a way of offering the reader *illusory* escape routes which inexorably lead back to, and compound the pain of, the conclusion already apparent in the first lexia. In many of the stories, he has disenabled the back-button function to force the reader to follow the story to its bleak conclusion rather than search for happier endings. Indeed, in this respect, these stories may be seen to be anti-hypertexts and Valdez's strategies echo those observed by Robert Coover who warns that, in a backlash against the 'vast networks and principles of randomness and expansive story lines' that constitute hypertext, writers will inevitably feel the need 'to struggle against them, just as one now struggles against the linear constraints of the printed book' (Coover quoted in Moulthrop 1995). As a result, however, Valdez's (anti-)hypertexts also remain strongly hierarchical in structure and logocentric in essence.

Furthermore, where subject matter related to cyberpunk and to cyberculture in general is frequent in hypertext works in an Anglophone context, thus backing up form with content, despite the unsentimental aesthetic, the subjects of these stories are emphatically not members of the cyberpunk generation as it pertains to Mexico. Indeed, many are evident technophobes – see, for example, Alex, the 'novice terrorist' who cannot deactivate the time-bomb in 'Iluso', and who is described as 'he who so often criticised technology'. What all this means is that Valdez is very aware of the traits and the traps of hypertext, but rather than retreat into print culture, he tries to trap hypertext itself by denying it some of its most recognisable characteristics. As Moulthrop has argued, 'Resisting hypertext is by no means a simple matter', but, following Mouthrop's arguments a bit further, Valdez's focus on 'breakdowns', physical, psychological and social, taken alongside the strategies mentioned above, suggest that this is our best hope of finding a resistant form of hypertext as well as a challenge to the social order (Moulthrop 1995). Valdez's is thus a conceptually avant-garde project despite the shortcomings mentioned earlier.

In Chiappe's case, the intertexts constitute some of the more clearly embedded examples of twentieth-century Latin American fiction: the work of Juan Rulfo, Mario Vargas Llosa, Horacio Quiroga, Salvador Garmendia and Alfredo Armas Alfonso,[15] and most obviously of all,

[15] The latter two authors pertain to the social realist/regionalist current in Venezuelan literature.

Gabriel García Márquez. Although Chiappe refutes any sense that his work might be derivative of magical realism, ascribing many of the similarities – prodigious natural phenomena and similar historical paradigms – to the proximity of García Márquez's Colombia to the region of Venezuela featured in *Tierra de extracción*, there is clearly more to it than this. *Tierra* narrates the development of a settlement – Menegrande, located on the shores of Lake Maracaibo – and its development over a period of nearly 'one hundred years' – from 1914, the date of the opening of the first petroleum extraction plant in Venezuela in the environs of Menegrande, to the present day – in a way which can only remind the reader of the even less literal 'hundred years' of *Cien años de soledad* [One Hundred Years of Solitude] (1967). The prophetic and baroque overtones also coincide, as do the themes of travel and prodigious sexuality; of encounters, cultural or sexual, and the resulting heterogeneity and coexistence of radically different worlds that is Latin America. But what is significant is not so much the echoes of García Márquez as the fact that Chiappe has successfully transferred the Marquesian world to the digital medium and exploited the extra facets of the new medium to good effect in so doing, in particular its ability to handle complex temporalities.[16]

These complex temporalities can be fruitfully considered through Martín-Barbero's comments on the treatment of time in audiovisual and digital media: 'the perception of time within which the audiovisual sensorium is inserted and/or inaugurated is characterized by the experience of simultaneity, the snapshot and flow' (Martín-Barbero 2000: 62). While this can lead to the mass media's 'cult of the present', to 'a weakening of the past' and 'an absence of future' (Martín-Barbero 2000: 63), he goes on to assert that the move towards time being conceived as constant 'flow' is (Martín-Barbero 2000: 64):

> the most authentic metaphor for the end of 'grand narratives', both religio-political and aesthetic. [...] For by proposing the equivalence of all discourses – news, drama, science, pornography or financial data – and the interpenetrability of all

16 Chiappe also acknowledges Cortázar and Borges as key influences in terms of the more structural aspects of his work – the presence of doubles, parallelisms, forking paths, *mise-en-abîme* structures, and so on (personal email correspondence with the author, 26 July 2006).

genres, we are left with the exaltation of what is changeable and diffuse, of the absence of closure, and of temporal indeterminacy as the key to the production of aesthetic pleasure.

All of this – equivalence of discourses, absence of closure, temporal indeterminacy – constitutes an accurate description of some of the most recognisable features of hypertext. Furthermore, with particular relevance to hypertext fiction in a Latin American context, Martín-Barbero emphasises the importance of hypertext's refusal of linear historiography: in the introduction to this anthology, with particular reference to (hypertext) fiction on the Internet, he singles out its ability to allow Latin Americans freedom from rigid, totalising, linear, historical narratives by allowing different time-planes to co-exist (see also Martín-Barbero 2000: 70–71). He does admit that this is not the unique preserve of *online* hypertext fiction, citing *Rayuela* as a key example of the co-existence of multiple temporalities in Latin American literature, but hypertext intensifies this particularly Latin American approach to time and to history on a massive scale.

Thus in Valdez's work we can find examples of present-day Mexico City co-existing with the pre-Columbian and early Conquest periods: there is an echo of Julio Cortázar's fantastic short story of 1956, 'La noche boca arriba' [Night Face Up] (included in *Final del juego* [The End of the Game]), in Valdez's 'Tlahueliloc' where a rave in the Museo Nacional de Antropología cleverly merges with a bloody battle between pre-Columbian tribes with the police doubling as conquistadors. Other stories such as 'Iluso' move abruptly backwards and forwards in time thus destroying a sense of causality or development and also insinuating that all these times – past, present, and future – already co-exist. There are also cases of impossible temporalities where, for example, a lover is discovered to have died before the birth of the main protagonist ('Hasta que la muerte nos separe' [Until Death Do Us Part]).

In Chiappe's case, historically the action of the novel spans the whole of the twentieth century. Nevertheless, the narrative frequently suppresses references to historical time – temporal links between different chapters are rarely clear –, and, together with the prophetic tone of many passages and direct references to myths and to cyclical temporalities, it suggests a reading where Menegrande and its environs constitute a timewarp and a trap. This is also accentuated by the emphasis on cyclical journey patterns and labyrinthine paths which suffuse the narrative.

Of course, these complex temporalities are a key feature in much Latin American fiction since the Boom – as explored above, the work of Cortázar and García Márquez are the obvious references here – but the facility that hypertext has to represent such temporalities is a feature than can and should be used to emphasise this aspect in order to 'appropriate' the new medium.

iii. Globalisation, Emancipation and Resistance?

Nevertheless, to return to Martín-Barbero's comments about the dangers of 'cultural disembedding', we should be aware that the focus of his attention is not really intertextuality or the representation of space and time in any given cultural product so much as how consumers of cultural products may be disorientated by the apparent proximity and hence importance of global culture via the screens of new technology and the corresponding distance or waning in importance of their local culture (Martín-Barbero 2000: 61).

There are two counterarguments to this stance. In the first case, following the arguments of Alberto Chimal, we might suggest that, no matter how superficially globalised the subject matter, both Valdez and Chiappe's works offer 'different points of view [with respect to globalisation] from those of the First World' (Chimal 2002: 80; see also the introduction to this volume). Chiappe's work deals with the impact of one form of globalisation in Venezuela – the petroleum industry managed by multinationals such as General Asphalt and Royal Dutch-Shell. However, this is globalisation as seen, and as countered/resisted, from a Venezuelan perspective. Chiappe makes a concerted effort to explore how the petroleum industry has affected Venezuelan society, considering such issues as the growth of prostitution around the settlements where petrol extraction plants are located,[17] the poisoning of water supplies, and the corruption of society. As the narrator of *Tierra de extracción* comments ('Fácil' [Easy]):

[17] This is made apparent through the use of hemerographic supporting materials, rather than through the narrative of libertinous activities that take place in the Grand House discotheque in Menegrande.

> This Land of Extraction doesn't only offer the riches of its soil to those who would plunder them; it also allows its people to be attacked. [Black] gold is extracted, but so too are people's lives; along with the petroleum go people's values; with the stolen cars, people's morals; with biodiversity, their ability to love; with wads of money, their ability to reason.

Furthermore, he also represents petroleum in a localised context – 'el mene' is the indigenous name given to crude oil in the region – and in fact the incantatory repetition of the topography of the region – place names as well as the presence of substantial reserves of fossil fuels in the subsoil – results in the land taking on the role of lead protagonist.[18] 'El mene' even stands as a symbol of the novel's construction: both literally, in its underground movements between 'vases communicants' and its sporadic bubbling up to the surface, and metaphorically, in the web of semantic associations that Chiappe weaves around it, it is essentially rhizomatic, and the rhizome constitutes one of the most common structures of hypertext narratives (Moulthrop 1994).

In Valdez's case, the work clearly does participate in a more globalised world, and perhaps some of the value of the work of a writer such as Valdez lies in his ability to create characters who are citizens of the world, not bound to an exclusively Mexican or Latin American *Weltanschauung* and not remotely interested in commenting on or relating to Latin American identity. Like Valdez himself they are not Mexican, not North American, not Chicana/o, not Latina/o – they do not need labels of this type whatsoever. The national/regional and sociocultural framework for identity so prevalent in Latin American studies has dissolved and this should be applauded not lamented. Nevertheless, if we so desire, this may still be recuperated, in Chimal's terms, as a 'Latin American' version of 'global culture': it might be argued that, at some level, the sheer bleakness and unflinching nature of Valdez's outlook and his anti-hypertextual, resistant approach coincide with a 'Latin American', politicised response to the First World's more utopian dreams of the possibilities of the new medium.

A second counterargument to Martín-Barbero's concerns would have it that, as the French hypertext theorist Jean Clément argues (Clément 2000),

[18] Chiappe himself confirms this reading of the novel (c.2003b).

> What characterises hypertext is the pre-eminence of the local over the global. It is true that most hypertextual systems offer a global vision of their structure, but this vision is not accessible through the text itself, but rather it belongs [...] to the level of paratext. For readers, a hypertextual work will always be that bit that they have read; that is to say, that part of the whole that they have extracted during their passage through the work, the partial actualisation of a virtual hypertext that they will never know in its totality.

Thus, even if the content of individual lexias does not refer to something local for the reader, the dynamic between the local and the global in the synecdochic structure of hypertext should keep such important dynamics alive in the hearts and minds of consumers of such cultural products. Indeed, Martín-Barbero concedes that digital culture does have an emancipatory role, precisely because of this facility to negotiate between the local and the global (Martín-Barbero 2000: 70):

> Faced with the fraudulent utopia of the 'information society' – fraudulent because it claims to be neutral – art offers the last territory for technological experimentation which is emancipatory in spirit. [...] I am referring to its ability to communicate, to make the modern communicate with the traditional, the personal with the other, the global with the local.

This 'emancipatory' negotiation between the local and the global is precisely what we have seen at work in the characters of Valdez's short stories and in Chiappe's localised narrative of globalisation in Venezuela.

Furthermore, some postcolonialist critics champion hypertext as emancipatory precisely because many of the key characteristics of hypertext are simultaneously those that best represent postcolonial experience. As the Hawaiian scholar Jaishree K. Odin argues, both hypertextual and postcolonial aesthetics require the switching 'from the linear, univocal, closed, authoritative aesthetic [...] to that of [a] non-linear, multivocal, open, non-hierarchical aesthetic' (Odin n.d.). She goes on to contend that the aesthetic of hypertext 'is most suited for representing postcolonial cultural experience because it embodies our changed conception of language, space, and time' (Odin n.d.).[19] Although, as noted in the introduction to the current volume, such arguments may be overly optimistic, hypertext might still thus be championed by some as an ideal medium through which Latin American writers should continue to explore their attitudes to space and time, globalisation and resistance. One might even suggest that it is a medium that postcolonial subjects can and should strategically 'counter-colonise' both in order to get their voices heard, and because it can translate their experience of the world so effectively.

Nevertheless, other critics of hypertext still advise caution with respect to such emancipatory, postcolonialist claims. For Stuart Moulthrop, one of the pre-eminent critics and practitioners of hypertext in an Anglophone context, hypertext is still predominantly logocentric and conservative, not a guarantee of freedom from established orders, social or linguistic. Exploring how the concepts of Deleuze and Guattari elaborated in *A Thousand Plateaus: Capitalism and Schizophrenia* (1980) might map onto hypertext, he argues that at first hypertext would appear to offer 'a laboratory or site of origin for a smoothly structured, nomadic alternative to the discursive space of late capitalism' (Moulthrop 1994: 304) and that this suggests that perhaps experiments in hypertext fiction might be able to propose radical (re)visions of culture and society as we know it. Ultimately, however he concedes, as Deleuze and Guattari do, that 'technonarcissistic' experiments might look radical, but ultimately may turn out to be very conservative (Moulthrop 1994: 309). He thus queries hypertext's ability to function as a site of resistance, just as he above queries whether it is possible for writers to resist the pull of hypertext.

What we have seen in the work of Valdez and Chiappe offers food for thought in the light of the above. In the eyes of Martín-Barbero, Chiappe's sophisticated 'new architectures of language' may well be deemed emancipatory, particularly when taken in the context of his ability to address issues of globalisation from a Latin American perspective in so doing. In those of Moulthrop, Valdez's attempted resistance of hypertext might be seen to be the closest one can get to

[19] Further debate concerning the intersection of postcolonialism and hypertext, including citation of Odin's work, may be found in Landow (2006: 346–58), as well as in the introduction to this volume.

a radical (re)vision of (implicitly Latin American) culture and society. Whatever the case, the work of both writers is proof that sophisticated and potentially radical hypertext/hypermedia works are being produced by Latin American authors and that such work provides a complex site of negotiation between the global and the local.

References

Ahumada, Yoyiana 2000. 'En busca del libro del futuro', *Primicia*, 10 October, pp. 26–28.

Boulter, Jay David 1991. *Writing Space: The Computer, Hypertext, and the History of Writing* (Hillsdale, NJ: Lawrence Erlbaum Associates).

Castro Roig, Xosé 2001. 'El *ciberespanglish*, el español comercial y el español neutro en la red', *Panace@*, 2:5, 36–41.

Chiappe, Doménico 2003a. 'De la poesía virtual a la novela multimedia: otras formas de narrar', *Letralia*, 8:98, 18 August, http://www.letralia.com/98/ensayo01.htm, last accessed 27 June 2007.

—— c.2003b. 'El libro sin hojas', *Telos: cuadernos de comunicación, tecnología y sociedad*, http://www.campusred.net/intercampus/rod12.htm, last accessed 27 June 2007.

—— *Escritores venezolanos de hoy: Doménico Chiappe*. http://www.trama.org.ve/chiappe Accessed 8 December 2006.

——, Andreas Meier, *et al.* 2002. *Tierra de extracción*, version 2.0 (Macromedia Director), most of the work is now also available at http://www.newmedios.com/tierra, last accessed 27 June 2007.

Chimal, Alberto 2002. 'Subir, desde abajo: el cuento mexicano en internet', *Tierra Adentro*, 117/118, 76–82.

Clément, Jean. 2000. 'Del texto al hipertexto: hacia una epistemología del discurso hipertextual'. Translated from the French by Susana Pajares Tosca, http://www.ucm.es/info/especulo/hipertul/clement.htm, last accessed 27 June 2007.

Deleuze, Gilles, and Félix Guattari 1988. *A Thousand Plateaus: Capitalism and Schizophrenia*, trans. Brian Massumi (London: Athlone).

Ensslin, Astrid, 2007. *Canonising Hypertext: Explorations and Constructions* (London: Continuum).

'Escritura multimedia' 2000. *Letralia: Tierra de letras*, 5:92, 17 July, http://www.letralia.com/92/litin092.htm, last accessed 27 June 2007.

Kim, Aeju 2003. 'The Geography of Cyberliterature in Korea', in Rachel C. Lee and Sau-ling Cynthia Wong, eds., *AsianAmerica.Net: Ethnicity, Nationalism, and Cyberspace* (New York: Routledge), pp. 177–92.

Landow, George P. 2006. *Hypertext 3.0: Critical Theory and New Media in an Era of Globalization* (Baltimore, MD: The Johns Hopkins University Press).

Martín-Barbero, Jesús 2000. 'Art/Communication/Technicity at Century's End', trans. Hugh O'Donnell, in Anny Brooksbank Jones and Ronaldo Munck, eds., *Cultural Politics in Latin America* (Basingstoke: Macmillan), pp. 56–73.

Moulthrop, Stuart 1994. 'Rhizome and Resistance: Hypertext and the Dreams of a New Culture', in George P. Landow, ed., *Hyper/Text/Theory* (Baltimore, MD: The Johns Hopkins University Press), pp. 299–319.
— 1995. 'Traveling in the Breakdown Lane: A Principle of Resistance for Hypertext', *Mosaic*, 28:4, 55–77, http://iat.ubalt.edu/moulthrop/essays/breakdown.html, last accessed 27 June 2007.
Odin, Jaishree K. n.d. 'The Performative and Processual: A Study of Hypertext/Postcolonial Aesthetic', http://www.postcolonialweb.org/poldiscourse/odin/odin1.html, last accessed 27 June 2007.
Valdez, Blas 2006. 'Hypertext Disorder', virtual presentation given at the 10th Annual Symposium on Contemporary Narrative, dedicated to 'Latin American Cyberliterature and Cyberculture / La ciberliteratura y cibercultura latinoamericanas', University of Leeds, 29 March.
—, *et al.* 2001 – private link; 2002 – full public access online. *Dolor y viceversa*, hypertext version (Macromedia Director), http://www.blasvaldez.com/dolor, last accessed 27 June 2007.

14

Virtual Bodies in Cyberspace: Guzik Glantz's Weblog

Claire Taylor

Within the rapid growth of the use of the Internet as a form of expression in Latin America, the weblog, more commonly known by its shorthand 'blog', has taken a particularly strong hold in several Latin American countries. Worldwide, the number of weblogs was estimated at over 100 million in 2005 (Duncan 2005) although given the explosion of the weblog format, this number will no doubt already be out of date. The site *bitacoras.com*, a portal for blogs in Spanish, currently links to 148,566 Hispanic blogs (accessed 2 March 2006), with some 598 blogs in Mexico City alone. Other, smaller sites list blogs on a country-by-country basis, with the Mexican site, *Blogsméxico*, currently listing some 4599 at the present date of writing.

Reasons for the popularity of the blog format are many, some of which have been enumerated by Heriberto Yépez in his 'Literatura weblog'. As Yépez notes, the popularity of this form of expression is partly due to the ease of opening and publishing a weblog, but also, crucially, is due to the ability to evade some of the problems associated with print publishing: 'The weblog can serve as a refuge and as a stimulus for amateur or emerging authors whose probability of publishing (and, therefore, of the production of certain texts due to their length, ideology, themes or language) would be non-existent or smaller in print publishing and institutional spaces' (Yépez 2003). Indeed, in a Latin American context, where the middle class is small, and many have little or no disposable income to buy print material, the weblog can be a way to reach audiences that would not normally buy copies of printed books. Granted, access to the Internet is still patchy, and in many ways may reinforce existing socio-economic disparities (see chapter 7 in this volume), but nevertheless the number of Internet users in Latin America, currently standing at some 79,033,597 clearly offers a wide potential readership.[1] Moreover, as Sánchez Badillo notes, weblogs evade the censorship of print media since the apparatuses of control common to print media (editors, proofreaders, newspaper proprietors, and so forth) are lacking (Sánchez Badillo n.d.), thus offering a more liberated space for self-expression.

The weblog format in itself is a recent phenomenon, making its first appearances in the late 1990s, and becoming more widely available with the 1999 launch of Pyra's free weblogging software (Mead 2002; Turnbull 2002). Since the format is still in its infancy, theorisations about this new form of expression are still in the making. While theorists have focused to date on the transformations the weblog entails with regard to print narrative,[2] relatively little has been said about the relationship that the weblog has to the notion of the embodied author behind its creation. The problematic issue of embodiment in cyberspace is, I would argue, encapsulated by the neologism 'weblog', a term which reveals its contradictory status. Clearly the second part of the term, the log or *bitácora* recalls the epistolary nature of the journal or diary; as Matheson has noted, 'a weblog can be characterized as an online diary, a page of small entries chronologically organized down from the latest entry' (Matheson 2004: 448). This epistolary nature invokes a subject and a body behind the writing, making reference, through its accompanying promise of autobiographical revelations, to the notion of access to an embodied subject. At the same time, the diary has also frequently been noted as a self-reflexive genre, concerned with *creating* this access to an embodied subject as effect (Raoul 1989; Hassam 1992; and Bunkers and Huff 1996). In this way the diary purports to convey the 'real' person behind the writing, and relies on the notion of the embodied subject, yet is shot through by tension due to its self-reflexive status.

If these are the implications of the second part of the neologism, the first part of the neologism pulls in an opposing direction. For it reminds us that this is an artefact of the *web*, of the cybernetic realm

1 Estimated figure as of December 2005 taken from Miniwatts Marketing Group 2006.

2 See for instance Shayne Bowman and Chris Willis on how news blogs transform traditional journalism into 'participatory journalism', and use a 'publish, then filter' model (Bowman and Willis 2003: 21).

of disembodied users and notoriously fabricated identities. As Deborah Lupton has noted, 'a central utopian discourse around computer technology is the potential offered by computers for humans to escape the body. [...] The dream of cyberculture is to leave the "meat" behind and to become distilled in a clean, pure, uncontaminated relationship with the human body' (Lupton 2000: 479). The cyberrealm, therefore, has always been envisioned as a disembodied one, and theorists of cyberspace have noted the significance of disembodiment in online exchanges (Clarke 1995: 124). Yet, as Lupton's term carefully reminds us, the discarding of the body can only ever be *utopian*; as Anne Balsamo and others have noted, while 'fictional accounts of cyberspace play out the fantasy of casting off the body as an obsolete piece of meat', this can only ever exist as a fantasy, and in fact cyberfictions 'do not eradicate body-based systems of differentiation and domination' (Balsamo 1996: 128). The body in cyberspace, thus, is not quite the free-floating escape from the flesh that cyberpunk theory might have promised.

There will, therefore, be contradictions and tensions involved in the weblog format due to its very makeup: it attempts an uneasy synthesis of the *log*, pulling in one direction towards bodily presence, yet undercut by textuality; and simultaneously the *web*, pulling towards virtualisation but undercut by inevitable corporeality. Thus the invocation of self-presence or bodily integrity in the weblog, due to the paradoxes inherent in its very format, will be problematic.

One particularly interesting response to these inherent contradictions of the weblog is the excellent literary-graphic weblog by Mexican Noemí Guzik Glantz, which engages with the tensions underlying this format, and which, in so doing, provides for the emergence of a postcolonial consciousness in the blog. The frequency with which other blogs and sites link to Guzik Glantz's blog is evidence of is popularity; moreover, her blog in itself has a strong following, with regular postings to her daily updates, averaging between twenty to thirty replies each day. Born in 1955 in Mexico City, Guzik Glantz studied psychology at the Universidad Iberoamericana, where she also undertook her doctorate. She trained in psychotherapy and has worked as a psychotherapist for twenty-three years, as well as lecturing at various universities, including her current post at the Universidad de las Américas in Mexico City. Her weblog, which she started writing January 2005, was initially text-based, but has become increasingly multimedia, and currently combines short narrative with images – sometimes photographs, sometimes graphics, and sometimes paintings. The growth in the multimedia format in her blog is due in part to the growing ease in searching for and downloading images from the web; as Guzik Glantz herself has noted, she uses Google Image Search to find the images to accompany her postings.[3] In this way, her weblog recalls Yépez's assertion that the weblog has become 'writing for the visual era' (Yépez 2003), as her narrative switches effortlessly from text to image.

Issues of corporeality and subjectivity are explored in the interplay between text and image in Guzik Glantz's work, as she frequently examines the status of the body in cyberspace and in the contemporary world. Her narratives repeatedly portray the body as distorted, disjointed, and in pieces.[4] One such example of this exploration of corporeal forms comes in a recent entry in her weblog entitled 'oJo aLeGrE' [Happy Eye] of 27 February 2006 (see fig. 14.1), which takes the form of a short, fantastical narrative accompanied by a single image:

> It's very useful and entertaining for me to take my eye out of its socket. If I need to see what's happening in the next room, I roll it discreetly along the floor. I can read whilst I watch a film, or chat with Juana and look at Chana. If I want to know more about a person, I roll the eye along the floor until I manage to look at the soles of their feet and see their social status.
>
> I even manage to have a snooze, keeping one eye on the cat and the other on my writing. Sometimes I take it out to sleep and I rest much better. I dunk it in camomile tea to keep it fresh and pure. I'm truly scared that someone might put the evil eye on me. But what really has me worried at the moment, is that it's becoming kind of short-sighted, long-sighted, and astigmatic, all at the same time, and I can't get my

3 Personal correspondence with the author, 14 March 2006.

4 In addition to the postings discussed in this chapter, there many other instances of the body coming under scrutiny in Guzik Glantz's weblog – too many to discuss in detail within the confines of this chapter. Other postings on this topic worth of attention include: 'aSomBrO mOmeNtáNeo' of 1 January 2006, 'eXcEsoS' of 9 July 2005; and 'cArGaMeNto' of 30 June 2005.

other eye, which is much more healthy, out of its socket. What am I going to do?

The tale recounted in this entry about the narrator removing an eye and being able to undertake several tasks at once – reading whilst watching a film, for instance – is a subtle parody of our modern world's call for multi-tasking abilities. As with many of Guzik Glantz's entries, this narrative taps into contemporary consciousness, and gives back to us, in ironic form, the absurdities of modern living.

Yet at the same time the taking apart of the body and the independence of this organ are also symptomatic of the dismemberment of the body in the cyberrealm. The body, literally, loses its integrity in this tale; the cyberbody of the 'blogosphere' comes apart. Thus the removal of the eye in Guzik Glantz's tale both resonates with and yet challenges the notion of 'leaving behind the meat' as envisioned by cyberpunk writers. The organ – the 'meat' – is removed, but crucially never actually left behind, as it continues functioning and retains a strong physical presence throughout. Thus this narrative engages with the tensions and contradictions of cyber-expression as delineated by Balsamo, Lupton and others; as Guzik Glantz reveals, although corporeal expression may be altered by its incursion into the cyberrealm, the body still inheres.

Moreover, in addition to the text itself, Guzik Glantz's graphics function to underline the transformations of the body in the cyberrealm: we are presented not with a photograph of a human eye to accompany her tale, but a graphic of a mechanistic eye.[5] The eye of Guzik Glantz's image appears more a cog than an organ, suggesting the conjunction of human and machine – arguably a visual metaphor for cyberspace, in which human interaction is enabled through technological means. If Shawn Wilbur has argued that the computer as Internet terminal is a sort of 'vision machine', in that 'it involves the user, primarily through vision, in forms of telepresence which may mimic any or all of the senses' (Wilbur 2000: 48), then Guzik Glantz's image provides us with quite literally a vision *machine*: a mechanical eye.

Indeed, this theme of the fragmented or distorted body runs

5 Guzik Glantz has commented that her purpose in selecting this particular image of the eye was that it represents, 'the eye [and] the socket at the same time' (personal correspondence with the author, 14 March 2006).

throughout much of Guzik Glantz's weblog production. An earlier entry of 9 January 2006 entitled 'iNdEpEnDeNcIa' [Independence] seems almost a companion piece to the posting about the eye. This time, the narrative describes the growing independence of one of the narrator's hands (see fig. 14.2):

> It was at night when I realised for the first time: my hand stayed awake whilst I slept, I noticed from the mess spread around my body. However, the strangest thing was that in the daytime my hand was listless and sluggish – asleep, I would say, now that I understand better what's going on. When I least expected it, my hand would do whatever took its fancy, it would touch someone's buttock, or penis, put its fingers into someone's mouth, or unbutton someone else's clothes. How ashamed of it I was and how it made a fool of me, that hand that I ended up cursing so much! My GP didn't understand anything, the neurologist couldn't find anything unusual in any of the radiological tests, from the simplest such as an X-ray, to the most advanced and expensive. He referred me to a psychiatrist who wanted to prescribe me tranquillisers and told me it was all to do with my unconscious, and that I should see a psychoanalyst. Then it got even more complicated because all sorts of strange explanations were thrown in together, which didn't help matters. My hand sometimes became red, like it was bleeding, at other times it disgusted me because it drooled, sometimes it decided to be flirtatious and put on make-up, or it scratched me in inconvenient places in public. As time went by I understood it all: this hand had developed its own heart, it had become an independent being tied to my body by force: it was capable of expressing tenderness, caresses, scorn, aggression, passion, and boldness of its own accord, it too was tortured by having to be tied down to the passivity of my body.

This rather tongue-in-cheek narrative which describes how the hand gains an independent life and causes the narrator many problems with its inappropriate conduct, can easily be read as an allegory of the interface between the body and cyberspace. That is, the independence of the hand represents the hand which clicks the mouse as it enters and then navigates through cyberspace. The hand gains its own cyber-identity, as, through clicking, it visits other worlds that the body of the narrator does not. In this way, the hand has an entire life that the body of the narrator does not have, even to the extent of experiencing emotions – the tenderness, caresses, scorn, aggression, passion, and boldness that the narrative lists. This is endorsed by the images that illustrate the tale which depict the hand in various guises, ranging from the hypertechnological digital imaging of the hand to the low-tech wax cast. Despite the range of different images of the hand, they all coincide in their depiction of the hand not as part of a bodily whole, but severed or free-floating. In some ways recalling the famous scene of Luis Buñuel's *Un Chien andalou* [An Andalusian Dog] (1929) with its severed hand – a connection reinforced by the references to psychoanalysis in the text narrative – the images chosen by Guzik Glantz create a sense of bodily disunity, and portray the hand attempting to transcend its relationship to the body, gaining independence in the cyberrealm.

However, this allegory reaches its strongest point as the narrative ends, and the tables are turned. Here, at the narrative's close, the narrator has come to realise that the hand feels tied down, and is just as resentful of the body as the narrator was of the hand's misdeeds. Again, this vision fruitfully intersects with the notion of cyberspace; of the meat which the floating cyber-identity is desperate to leave behind, but to which it remains tethered. It is, of necessity, tied to the physical body which enables its entrance into the cyberrealm; that is, only by virtue of the physical body eating, sleeping, maintaining itself, can the cyber-identity ever exist.

While the two postings discussed above deal with real parts of the body which gain unusual attributes, other entries concentrate on artificial parts of the body. One such example of this is the posting of 28 January 2006, entitled 'aCto nEcEsariO' [A Necessary Act] (see fig. 14.3):

> Today I had to get rid of and free myself, I strew the world
> with some superfluous things:
> the beautiful red shoes ended up on the train track
> my favourite toy plane on a park bench
> the amber keyring on a ledge
> the lipstick in the women's toilets so that someone could
> use it

> and the tooth with your chip encrusted in it, in a dark
> corner lost amongst gloomy streets

Here, the brief tale tells us of the female narrator disposing of unnecessary items, which start with the relatively harmless 'beautiful red shoes', but end with the more threatening 'tooth with your chip encrusted in it'. This latter item signals the invasion of the body by technology, as the body part itself is replaced by a glass simulacrum. Moreover, the fact that this simulacrum is occupied by a chip has connotations of surveillance, and of the intrusion of electronic monitoring devices into the space of the body. The 'your' of this phrase is deliberately ambiguous, leaving the reader unsure as to whether it may represent the second person of amorous verse – and so perhaps functioning as an allegory for the inhabitation of the self by a lover, with the chip functioning as a memory chip – or, more sinisterly, the second person of a nameless, faceless, surveillance, an Orwellian thought police whose scrutiny is no longer conducted through an exterior telescreen (Orwell 1949), but interiorised. This brief story thus ends chillingly with the encroachment of technology into personal space. Disturbingly, it reveals that the interface between the body and technology has resulted in the quite the opposite of leaving the meat behind as promised by the utopian narratives of cyberpunk; instead, the meat is invaded by the technological.

These various narratives of corporeal transformations taking place at the interface between the body and technology take on further significance in a text-only narrative of 10 February 2006. Entitled 'Le oTorGarOn el eMplEo' [They Gave Her the Job], this tale begins as a seemingly mundane description of a job offer, but, as the narrative progresses, the requirements of the job encroach ever more upon the body:

> They confirmed that they'd give her the job, without many requirements. Of course, those glasses with burgundy frames would have to be replaced by contact lenses. And those nails, yes, they were pretty, but nail varnish is necessary, because everybody paints their nails these days.
>
> Her skin, well it was very smooth, but a bit of make-up would make it wonderful, and her hair, well, there was a lot to be done there: you couldn't have a mop like that in a high-

> class office like this! (Of course, those weren't the exact words).
>
> Everything else was fine, although high-heeled shoes make your legs more shapely and give a certain distinction and elegance to a woman. Speaking of clothes, tailored cashmere suits look beautiful on dynamic, contemporary women.
>
> And that's all, although, if possible, jewellery shouldn't be so tacky, instead something discreet made from good material would be excellent. Better not to wear long ear-rings because that gives an unfortunately tarty impression.
>
> And, thinking about it, some pads to increase the size of the breasts would be perfect for this company, because it gives a feeling of prosperity and of being well fed, don't you think?
>
> And the rather rounded stomach gives the impression of an excess of carbohydrates and even wind; a corset to squeeze and hold it all in is recommendable.
>
> But in general there aren't any major requirements, let's say that this young lady is now employed to answer the phone to clients' complaints for the Bank in the Call Centre that will start running next week.[6]

This short narrative resonates with other of Guzik Glantz's postings in its focus on the body and its presentation, but, tellingly, as the story reveals, the reorganisation of the body is not restricted to the cyberrealm. Here, the reorganisation of the body takes place in our hypermodern, late capitalist world, through a series of artificial incursions into the body, as the body is required to submit to cultural and business norms.

Moreover, this narrative invites a postcolonial reading in the context of Mexico's relationship to its more powerful neighbour to the north. It is significant that Guzik Glantz chooses to locate her tale in a call centre, a phenomenon of late capitalist society whose nomenclature, an Anglicism borrowed from the vocabulary of US business practice, suggests international flows of capital. The call centre could thus arguably be seen as the virtualisation of the workplace. That is, the jobs that take place in this 'real' environment, in which the call centre can be thousands of miles away from its clients and its products, inhabit

6 Filed under: General – noemi @ 6.29p.m.

virtual spaces, and function through virtual networks, in the same way that cyberspace does. Call centre workers, by the very nature of the call centre, are physically distant from the users of the service they provide – and may frequently be located in another country, where wages are lower and labour less regulated. In a specifically Mexican context, it is worth noting the recent growth of call centres across the border from the US in Mexico, servicing a US customer base by means of employing a cheaper Mexican workforce.[7] Tellingly, literature on the subject touts the advantages of 'eager and talented young people willing to work for rock-bottom wages for years to come' (Hersch 2002), and notes this as one of the reasons for US companies to move their call centres to countries such as Mexico.[8] Such a scenario clearly suggests the exploitative conditions of such virtual jobs. Thus, Guzik Glantz's narrative suggests, we may already be virtualised, even when we are not blogging; the virtualisation of the workplace and the artificialisation of the body have already taken place in the 'real', as much as the cyber, world.

Yet, having said that, Guzik Glantz's story is hardly celebratory of the potential of such virtual jobs; whilst her narrative makes clear reference to these new working conditions, she suggests that the virtualisation of the workplace in the call centre format enacts oppressive rules on women and their conduct. Such virtual working conditions are deeply embedded in postcolonial relations of inequality, and exemplify Mexico's troubled relationship to the neo-colonial power of the US. One fruitful way of reading this is through Chela Sandoval's notion of cyborg skills of the oppressed, which provides a critique of the conditions of marginalised groups functioning in/for First World nations. Guzik Glantz's tale, with its accretion of commands and its progressive encroachment into the personal space of the woman employee, provides an ironic reflection on conditions of employment suffered by many Mexicans working *in* their own country, yet working *for* a boss to the north. If services for First World nations are with ever greater frequency being outsourced to call centres in developing nations such as Mexico, these

7 See John W. McCurry who notes that Mexico has a growing call centre sector, mostly in the border towns of Tijuana and Reynosa, as well as Mexico City (McCurry 2003: 1).

8 It is also significant that Hersch notes that countries such as Mexico are 'deregulating their telecommunications sectors' in order to make themselves more attractive to call centres (Hersch 2002).

services could be an example, we may argue, of the 'techno-human conditions' under which the oppressed are obliged work, according to Sandoval (Sandoval 1999: 248). Yet Guzik Glantz's tale, with its ironic hyperbole, could perhaps function as an instance of the 'cyborg skills required for survival' under these conditions (Sandoval 1999); that is, Guzik Glantz's narrative does not stand outside the discourses of late capitalist techno-jobs, but clearly critiques these conditions in her hyberbolic narration. Thus her narrative could function as a type of 'cyborg consciousness' as Sandoval has put it: 'The technologies which together comprise the methodology of the oppressed generate the forms of agency and consciousness that can create effective forms of resistance under postmodern cultural conditions, and can be thought of as constituting a "cyborg", if you like, or at least a "cyber" form of resistance' (Sandoval 1999: 249). Sandoval's argument links cyborg skills with a postcolonial consciousness, and provides a fitting description for Mexico's relationship to the neo-colonial power of the US in the twenty-first century. The cyborg skills which arise are a product of this relationship, but also, crucially, space for survival. Thus, Guzik Glantz's weblog narratives could offer this cyber form of resistance; clearly implicated in our hypertechnological world both in content and format, yet offering ironic critiques of the workings of the modern world.

In this way, Guzik Glantz's weblog raises important questions about the status of bodies in the cyberrealm and in our late capitalist world, and insistently – even obsessively – reminds the reader of the inherent contradictions and tensions involved in personal expression in cyberspace. Her tales link these tensions to flows of global capital and to the conditions of the oppressed, and the fragmented bodies and subjects which inhabit her blog are arguably the product of such conditions. The fragmented body, and indeed virtualisation itself, are, Guzik Glantz suggests, not only the product of the cyberrealm, but also of our contemporary society. Thus the weblog format in which corporeal presence and disembodiment are in constant tension, provides the ideal site in which to explore these issues. If the weblog format is based on contradictions that still remain to be resolved, then Guzik Glantz's weblog, exploiting and exploring such contradictions, offers, along the way, a tentative Mexican cyborg consciousness.

References

Balsamo, Anne 1996. *Technologies of the Gendered Body: Reading Cyborg Women* (Durham, NC: Duke University Press).

Bitácoras.com: El portal de los weblogs en español. http://www.bitacoras.com, last accessed 27 June 2007.

Blogsméxico: Directorio de Bitácoras Mexicanas, http://www.blogsmexico.com, last accessed 27 June 2007.

Bowman, Shayne, and Chris Willis 2003. *We Media: How Audiences Are Shaping the Future of News and Information* (Reston, VA: American Press Institute), http://www.hypergene.net/wemedia/download/we_media.pdf, last accessed 27 June 2007.

Bunkers, Suzanne L., and Cynthia Anne Huff, eds. 1996. *Inscribing the Daily: Critical Essays on Women's Diaries* (Amherst, MA: University of Massachusetts Press).

Un Chien andalou 1929. Directed and produced by Luis Buñuel (France: Buñuel), 35mm/black and white, 16 mins.

Clark, Nigel 1995. 'Rear-View Mirrorshades: The Recursive Generation of the Cyberbody', in Mike Featherstone and Roger Burrows, eds., *Cyberspace/ Cyberbodies/Cyberpunk: Cultures of Technological Embodiment* (London: SAGE Publications), pp. 113–33.

Duncan 2005. 'The *Blog Herald* Blog Count October 2005: Over 100 Million Blogs Created', *The Blog Herald,* 10 October, http://www.blogherald.com/2005/10/10/the-blog-herald-blog-count-october–2005, last accessed 27 June 2007.

Guzik Glantz, Noemí. *Noemí Guzik Glantz.* http://noemi.guzikglantz.com, last accessed 27 June 2007.

Hassam, Andrew 1992. *Writing and Reality: A Study of Modern British Diary Fiction* (Westport, CT: Greenwood).

Hersch, Warren S. 2002. 'Sun, Sea, Surf and Call Centers: Jamaica, Mexico, Puerto Rico and Panama Are Doing Much to Woo Call Centers', *Call Center Magazine,* 9 April, http://www.callcentermagazine.com/article/CCM20020823S0013, last accessed 27 June 2007.

Lupton, Deborah 2000. 'The Embodied Computer/User', in David Bell and Barbara M. Kennedy, eds., *The Cybercultures Reader* (London: Routledge), pp. 477–88.

McCurry, John W. 2003. 'Calling on Canada: North American Call Center Trends Show a Clear Signal from Up North', *Site Selection Magazine,* March. http://www.telvista.com/articles/site_selection_blakewolf.pdf, last accessed 27 June 2007.

Matheson, Donald 2004. 'Weblogs and the Epistemology of the News: Some Trends in Online Journalism', *New Media & Society,* 6, 443–68.

Mead, Rebecca 2002. 'You've Got Blog: How to Put Your Business, Your Boyfriend, and Your Life Online', in *We've Got Blog: How Weblogs Are Changing Our Culture* (Cambridge, MA: Perseus), pp. 47–56.

Miniwatts Marketing Group 2006. 'Internet Usage Statistics for the Americas', *Internet World Stats,* http://www.internetworldstats.com/stats2.htm, last

accessed 27 June 2007.
Orwell, George 1949. *Nineteen Eighty-Four: A Novel* (London: Secker & Warburg).
Raoul, Valerie 1989. 'Women and Diaries: Gender and Genre', *Mosaic* 22:3, 56–65.
Sánchez Badillo, Jorge n.d. 'Los *weblogs* en la sociedad de la información', http://www.aweblog.org/docs/weblogs_soc_info.pdf, last accessed 27 June 2007.
Sandoval, Chela 1999. 'New Sciences: Cyborg Feminism and the Methodology of the Oppressed', in Jenny Wolmark, ed., *Cybersexualities: A Reader on Feminist Theory, Cyborgs and Cyberspace* (Edinburgh: Edinburgh University Press), pp. 247–63.
Turnbull, Giles 2002. 'The State of the Blog Part 1: Blogger Past', in *We've Got Blog: How Weblogs Are Changing Our Culture* (Cambridge MA: Perseus), pp. 78–85.
Wilbur, Shawn P. 2000. 'An Archaeology of Cyberspaces: Virtuality, Community, Identity', in David Bell and Barbara M. Kennedy, eds., *The Cybercultures Reader* (London: Routledge), pp. 45–55.
Yépez, Heriberto 2003. 'Literatura weblog', *Literaturas.com: Revista Literaria Independiente*, February. http://www.literaturas.com/heribertoyepezweblog-febrero2003.htm, last accessed 27 June 2007.

A Cyberliterary Afterword: Of Blogs and Other Matters[1]

Edmundo Paz Soldán

Some weeks ago, one of the most important websites dealing with topics related to literature written in Spanish, *Moleskine literario* [Literary Moleskin], undertook a survey to elect the most influential literary critic of contemporary Peruvian literature. Gustavo Faverón was elected the winner. What was interesting about this was that, even if Faverón has published essays and articles in prestigious academic journals and has been the editor of an important cultural review in Peru, his influence is due, above all to *Puente aéreo*, the blog that he has been writing for a couple of years now. As Iván Thays, responsible for *Moleskine*, has commented: 'I doubt there's anyone, of any point of view, who is interested in discussing literary or cultural topics in Peru who doesn't read *Puente aéreo*' (Thays 2006).

This is a sign that times are changing: only a short time ago, it would have been unthinkable that a Latin American literary critic could have gained legitimacy through the web. But now this is becoming increasingly possible. And not only that: having a presence on the web is becoming, bit by bit, a key way to disseminate critical discourse and to contribute to literary and cultural debates. For example, the Brazilian Idelber Avelar, one of the most respected critics, has a very popular blog indeed. And writers themselves are not lagging behind: Iván Thays is one of the most respected writers of new Peruvian narrative. The list of authors who have blogs includes Alberto Fuguet, Santiago Roncagliolo, Jorge Volpi (although only intermittently), and the author of these lines.

1 This piece is based on an article originally published under the title 'De blogs y literatura', in *La Tercera* (Chile), 2 July 2005.

What has happened is something very natural: in Latin American literature there has always existed a tradition of strong relationships with new technologies and the mass media. Considering only the twentieth century, we can find in many novels, chronicles, essays, and poems an attempt to establish a dialogue – frequently stimulating, although at other times tense – between literature and new technologies. There is also a continuous desire to reflect on the changing role of literature in a mediatised environment in which cinema, photography, computers, and the Internet occupy ever more central places. And this is reflected in this volume: the essays collected in this book reveal the diversity and richness of what the editors term Latin American cyberculture and cyberliterature. Within this are included canonical authors such as Jorge Luis Borges and Adolfo Bioy Casares (see chapters 2 and 9 in this volume), but also new border writers from the North of Mexico (see chapter 8). Similarly, this book also discusses the new technological formats that writers use to distribute their texts, sell their books, and engage in dialogue with their readership, as well as considering issues of editorship of Peruvian, Venezuelan, and Chilean literary e-mags (see chapter 7).

The fertile dialogue that can be found in this book is a welcome counterpart to the initial apparition of an apocalyptic discourse in the literary world about new media and technology. More than 100 years ago, the arrival of cinema in Latin America was received by the Modernists with a mixture of enthusiasm and anxiety. The Mexican Amado Nervo was among those who believed that this augured the end of an era, and who, in a chronicle written in 1898, wrote that the new technologies of the time would produce a striking result: 'there will be no more books; the phonograph will keep in its dark urn the old extinguished voices; cinema will reproduce prestigious lives' (Nervo, cited in Duffey 1996: 13).

But new media and new technologies do not necessarily mean the disappearance of other media and other technologies. What they enact is, instead, a reconfiguration of the media environment and of the technological landscape that surrounds us. It is not the case, as in the song by the Buggles, that video will kill the radio star, but it can indeed marginalise that star – the star will become irrelevant if s/he does not adapt to the new rules of the game and become 'mediatised'. A dialogue is also created – sometimes divergent but never lacking in important literary results – between the different media. Writers such as William Faulkner and James Joyce – the owner of the first cinema in Dublin – incorporated into their writing narrative techniques derived from cinema; poets such as Guillaume Apollinaire and Octavio Paz experimented with the typography of typewriters and the influence of radio. And, conversely, cinema can learn from literature: the precision of film noir dialogue was discovered by scriptwriters in Ernest Hemingway's short stories. Amongst authors of more recent generations, Manuel Puig and Alberto Fuguet have concentrated on the identificatory processes of the individual with the diverse media and technologies that surround him/her.

The arrival of the Internet has meant a reinvention of our mediatic environment. Despite what the ominous forecasters of culture tell us, the electronic book has not yet consolidated itself; its sales have failed even with such commercial writers as Stephen King. It is true that it is a question of time until the electronic book is perfected and there appears a model capable of making us abandon paperbacks and hardbacks – indeed, the new Sony Reader shows a great advance with regard to previous models. Nevertheless, for the present, traditional support for the book is stronger than ever.

Literary culture is, slowly but surely, finding its own space on the Net. On the one hand, there are the more 'traditional' websites dedicated to a particular writer where you can find an archive of incidental texts, photos, works of criticism, and other miscellaneous items – in *ClubCultura.com* you can access twenty sites dedicated to writers, including ones on Roberto Bolaño and Juan Rulfo. There are also sites where you can download novels and short stories, above all the classics. For example, one night, when I was due to give a class on Latin American nineteenth-century literature, I found I had left my copy of Esteban Echevarría's 'El matadero' back in my office. A swift search on the Internet meant I could solve the problem quickly, and also, incidentally, discover a website called *El Aleph*, 'where the books are free', and which prides itself on having nearly 3000 titles in Spanish for downloading.

On the other hand, the Internet has already influenced the creation of several literary texts. In the Anglophone world, various novels have already been published in email or chat format; in Spanish, at this moment in time I am only aware of one: *La ansiedad* (2004) by the Argentine author Daniel Link. In order for these contemporary versions of the epistolary novel to gain literary prestige we need someone to write a work of the same quality of Choderlos de Laclos's *Dangerous Liaisons* (1782) in chat and/or email. There have also appeared novels which deal with the impact of the Internet on daily life, such as *Ático* (2004) by the Spanish writer Gabi Martínez, which is based around virtual games. But literature does not only reflect the evolution of the Net: to a certain extent, it also prefigured it before it ever became a reality. Texts such as Borges' 'The Garden of the Forking Paths' of 1941 – that perfect short story about proliferating universes and infinite bifurcations – are proof of this, or, similarly, within the genre of science fiction, the novel *Neuromancer*, by William Gibson.

But the literary star of the day is the blog. The blog is a travel log in the cyberspace, a textual practice which combines elements of the diary, the notebook, literary criticism, the opinion column, the short story, the epigram, and whatever other literary genres we might care to add. The blog is currently threatening to supplant the novel as the great genre in which everything can find its place. Thanks to the appearance of a new technological format we are witnessing, in 'real time', the birth of a new literary genre. In Latin America the chronicle has been, since the end of the nineteenth century, one of the privileged genres of our modernity, capable of giving us many of our classic texts – I am thinking here of the North American chronicles of José Martí, and of the chronicles of Manuel Gutiérrez Nájera. And nowadays the tradition still produces great exponents such as Carlos Monsiváis and Pedro Lemebel who publish in newspapers and books. But perhaps the true contemporary form of the chronicle is being written on the Internet by the authors of blogs.

There are blogs of all types: those which are purely text-based, or those which play with audiovisual formats, and so forth. There are the 'star' blogs such as, in the case of Spain, that of Javier Arce – *El hombre que comía diccionarios* [The Man Who Ate Dictionaries] – and who maintains his personal diary in various languages, with quotations taken not only from dictionaries, but also from writers as diverse as Lucretius and Jack Kerouac. Or there is Spanish writer Arcadi Espada's blog, which is so prestigious that it is soon to be awarded the prize of … being published in traditional print format. Then there are blogs written by critics such as Faverón, or by writers such as Iván Thays – with links to newspaper supplements, notes about what Thays is currently reading, and local debates. There is also Mexican writer Cristina Rivera Garza's blog, which is written in the tone of a diary giving intimate confessions. Or Chilean writer Sergio Gómez's blog (available from *ClubCultura.com*), which is something between a travel journal and a personal chronicle. And, of course, there are the blogs by talented young writers who have just published their first novel, such as that by Peruvian writer Luis Hernán Castañeda, or those by unpublished writers such as the Bolivian Miguel Esquirol.

These authors are quickly discovering that they do not need books to reach a wide readership. Esquirol's modest blog, for instance, has around 150 readers daily: many more than some writers of my generation. It is clear that libraries and bookshops alone will no longer suffice in the search for good (and bad) literature. This volume of collected essays, in its analysis of new literary forms taking place online, and new relationships between text and reader, makes an important contribution to this debate, and may well help to define the emerging canon of Latin American writers in cyberspace.

Translated by Claire Taylor

References

El Aleph. http://www.elaleph.com, last accessed 27 June 2007.

Arce, Javier. *El hombre que comía diccionarios*, http://www.elhombrequecomiaddiccionarios.com, last accessed 27 June 2007.

Avelar, Idelber. *O biscoito fino e a massa*, http://www.idelberavelar.com, last accessed 27 June 2007.

Borges, Jorge Luis 1962. 'The Garden of Forking Paths', in *Fictions*, trans. Anthony Kerrigan (London: Calder & Boyars). Originally published 1941.

Castañeda, Luis Hernán. *El diario de Antoine Doinel: apuntes de un escritor francés que jamás escribió sobre Francia*, http://luishernancastaneda.blogspot.com, last accessed 27 June 2007.

ClubCultura.com: El portal cultural de la FNAC. http://www.clubcultura.com, last accessed 27 June 2007.

Duffey, J. Patrick 1996. *De la pantalla al texto: La influencia del cine en la narrativa mexicana del siglo XX* (Mexico City: UNAM).

Espada, Arcadi. *El blog de Arcadi Espada*, http://www.arcadi.espasa.com, last accessed 27 June 2007.

Esquirol, Miguel. *El forastero*, http://elforastero.blogalia.com, last accessed 27 June 2007.

Faverón, Gustavo. *Puente aéreo*, http://www.puenteareo1.blogspot.com, last accessed 27 June 2007.

Fuguet, Alberto. *Alberto Fuguet: escritor/lector*, http://albertofuguet.blogspot.com, last accessed 27 June 2007.

Gibson, William 1984. *Neuromancer* (London: Gollancz).

Gómez, Sergio. *Diario de Sergio Gómez,* http://www.clubcultura.com/diariode/3/sergiogomez.html, last accessed 27 June 2007.

Laclos, Pierre-Ambroise-François Choderlos de 1987. *Dangerous Liaisons,* trans. by Richard Aldington (London: Routledge). Originally published 1782.

Link, Daniel 2004. *La ansiedad* (Buenos Aires: El Cuenco de Plata).

Martínez, Gabi 2004. *Ático* (Barcelona: Destino).

Paz Soldán, Edmundo. *El diario de Edmundo Paz Soldán,* http://www.clubcultura.com/diariode/21/edmundopazsoldan.html, last accessed 27 June 2007.

Rivera Garza, Cristina. http://www.cristinariveragarza.blogspot.com, last accessed 27 June 2007.

Roncagliolo, Santiago. *Santiago Roncagliolo: Blog/Barcelona,* http://blogs.elboomeran.com/roncagliolo/el_blog_de_santiago_roncagliolo/index.html, last accessed 27 June 2007.

Thays, Iván. *Moleskine literario: notas literarias en un cuaderno moleskine,* http://www.notasmoleskine.blogspot.com, last accessed 27 June 2007.

—— 2006. 'Encuesta: Gustavo Faverón', 24 November, http://www.notasmoleskine.blogspot.com, last accessed 27 June 2007.

Volpi, Jorge. *Jorge Volpi,* http://www.elboomeran.com/pagina_volpi.php, last accessed 27 June 2007.

Conclusion: Latin American Identity and Cyberspace

Claire Taylor and Thea Pitman

The various contributions to this volume have all dealt with cultural products by Latin American practitioners that engage with notions of cyberspace in a variety of forms, whether through their actual existence as online works, or through interaction with the key tropes of cyberculture or hypertexts. As can be seen from these chapters, approaches to cyberspace and the new practices it offers are varied, and are frequently inflected not only by their interactions with other, more established, cultural forms, but also by regional differences. Thus the strategic use in a São Paulo suburb of globalised Internet technologies (websites), and of cultural forms pre-existing the Net (rap music) to produce a localised expression of place has parallels with, and yet is distinct from, Gómez-Peña's cyber-performance art, for example, which elaborates and plays with border identities. Similarly, the practices of Latin American literary e-mags, for instance, which rely on some pre-existing norms of print culture, and yet create tentative cybercommunities through renegotiations of local and global space, share some concerns with the 'social netwar' of the Zapatistas and other NGOs, and yet have clearly different political and cultural aims. Thus each of the practitioners examined in this volume has engaged with cyberspace in different, although interconnected ways: rather than there being *a* Latin American cyberculture, it is instead a question of differing practices which make use, often strategically, of globalised technologies for temporary negotiations and representations.

Such *strategic* uses of technology must entail a thinking through of the common conceptualisations of online practice in itself. A brief survey of the metaphors used in English to describe Net activity, including terminology such as 'surfing', the 'Information Superhighway', or 'blogs', foregrounds issues of travel as the primary conceptualisation of the activity of the Internet user, as do equivalent terms used in Spanish and Portuguese – 'navegar', 'la supercarretera de información' / 'la estrada super da informação', 'bitácoras', or 'cibernauta'/'internauta'. Arguably, these travel metaphors can be linked to the notion of the tourist gaze (see, for example, Nakamura 2002: 40), and even, as some have claimed, to an implied (neo)colonial perspective. David Trend, for example, points out that: 'it takes little imagination to recognize the parallels between the unexplored territory of the cyberworld and the 'new world' imagined by the colonizers of the modern era. This view of the internet as primordial battleground can be seen as an extension of historical patterns of Enlightenment advance' (Trend 2001: 296).

Clearly, therefore, there are neo-colonialist assumptions underlying many of the value-laden terms that are used to describe online activity, just as there are in the metaphors and tropes of travel and travel writing (see, for example, Pratt 1992). Indeed, this has been confirmed by Timothy Allen Jackson who argues that cyberspace 'embodies the last territorial frontier for empire-building', and that the new media may 'contribute to the construction of enclaves of the technologically plugged-in surrounded by the plugged out' (Jackson 2001: 349). These metaphors, in particular Jackson's provocative use of the 'last frontier', and Trend's reference to the 'new world', all suggest connotations of empire-building which have problematic implications for Latin American cyberculture.

Indeed, we might note that while the metaphors used in English reflect more closely a modern tourist and leisure gaze, the equivalents in Spanish are more clearly colonialist ones; the use of 'navegar' in place of 'surfing', for instance, recalls the Iberian empires in the Americas which were built precisely on the act of navigating the seas to conquer 'new' lands. Similarly, the blog neologism has been most frequently translated as 'bitácora' in Spanish – a term which cannot help but recall the founding *Cuadernos de bitácora* of Columbus. Thus the term used to refer to the one of the most popular forms of Internet expression amongst Latin Americans, inevitably evokes the founding moments of 'discovery' of the continent, a process which involved a Eurocentric naming, identifying, and labelling of the Americas as other.

For this reason, the various studies within this volume must be read in the light of this problematic terminology, in which there lies an inevitable tension between the expression of Latin American identities, and the neo-colonialist metaphors which pervade Net discourse. Nevertheless, it may not be a question of Latin American practitioners simply taking up, uncritically, this imperialistic baggage: we may ask whether it could be a case of, to paraphrase Ashcroft *et al.*'s famous formulation, Latin America writing – or blogging – back to the metropolis (Ashcroft, Griffiths, and Tiffin 1989). Clearly, the question remains as to whether the assumption of these terms such as *navegar* or *bitácoras* can be strategic; whether it might represent a form of reclaiming the ground for Latin Americans, and of refusing to offer cyberculture or blogs for the imperial gaze. Although these terms have not always been engaged with in a self-conscious way by Latin American practitioners online, there is nevertheless a growing awareness of the need to interrogate these terms.

Indeed, it is notable that in recent years some practitioners and theorists have attempted to promote new Internet terminology that resists such neo-imperialist drives. Cyberfeminists, for instance, have suggested the term 'netweaving' as one which avoids the problematic connotations of much web terminology; as Sohail Inayatullah and Ivana Milojevic define it, 'net-weaving would be done in a context of community or friendly groups and not in a context of alienated individuals' (Inayatullah and Milojevic 1999: 84). In a Latin American context specifically, Arturo Escobar's discussion of networks highlights the presence of 'women networkers or netweavers', who, according to Escobar, are engaged in formulations of 'new political actors' and are the source of 'promising cultural practices and possibilities' (Escobar 1999: 32). Such notions of netweaving, which resonate with much recent thinking about offline forms of alternative networks (see, for instance, Jara Holliday 2001), suggest new spaces and forms of solidarity which can be crafted through creative uses of technology. Meanwhile Harry Cleaver, in his article on the networks of co-operation that Indian and peasant groups are developing in Mexico, indicates the rejection of the term 'net' as one 'evok[ing] being caught', and notes that participants prefer the term 'hammock' (Cleaver 1994). Whilst the term 'hamaca' has yet to be taken up with any regularity by Latin American cyber practitioners, Cleaver's observations do point to an increasing self-consciousness in the use of Internet terminology in the region, and suggest the potential for the revitalising of Internet activity from a Latin American perspective.

The varied terminology used to describe Net activity, thus, has an ambivalent relationship to Latin America: whilst many of the standard terms used to describe online interaction have neo-colonialist assumptions, efforts to create alternative terms may pave the way for new understandings of the potential of cyberspace. Future work on Latin American cyberculture needs to address more fully these intersections between cyberculture, postcolonial theory, and Latin American identities. In a Latin American context, negotiations with postcolonial theory are ongoing, and considerable debate has been generated as to the applicability or otherwise of the term 'postcolonial' to the region (see Taylor 2007). These questions must also be thought through the new opportunities offered by the new media, which, as several researchers have noted, complicate standard notions of the centre and the periphery, and generate debate as to their potential for expressing – or alternatively, suppressing – subaltern identities. Arguably, the most interesting and radical use of the Internet in a Latin American context will occur if the new media enables new identities and forms of expression, and allows for the expression of postcolonial consciousnesses. The new forms of cultural agency which may be enabled by the Internet are, perhaps, most likely to come in the form of NGOs, and in emerging forms of cybercommunities and netweaving constructed online. Cyberspace and cyberculture, still in their infancy, may offer strategic opportunities for Latin American practitioners to express new and resistant forms of identities online in the future.

References

Ashcroft, Bill, Gareth Griffiths, and Helen Tiffin 1989. *The Empire Writes Back: Theory and Practice in Post-colonial Literatures* (London: Routledge).

Cleaver, Harry 1994. 'The Chiapas Uprising and the Future of Class Struggle in the New World Order'. First published in Italian in *RIFF-RAFF: Attraverso la produzione sociale*, March, pp. 133–45. http://www.eco.utexas.edu/facstaff/Cleaver/chiapasuprising.html, last accessed 27 June 2007.

Escobar, Arturo 1999. 'Gender, Place and Networks: A Political Ecology of Cyberculture', in Wendy Harcourt, ed., *Women@Internet: Creating New Cultures in Cyberspace* (London: Zed Books), pp. 31–54.

Inayatullah, Sohail, and Ivana Milojevic 1999. 'Exclusion and Communication in the Information Era: From Silences to Global Conversations', in Wendy Harcourt, ed., *Women@Internet: Creating New Cultures in Cyberspace* (London: Zed Books), pp. 76–87.

Jackson, Timothy Allen 2001. 'Towards a New Media Aesthetic', in David Trend, ed., *Reading Digital Culture* (Oxford: Blackwell Publishing), pp. 347–53.

Jara Holliday, Oscar 2001. 'El trabajo en red: tejer complicidades y fortalezas', http://www.preval.org/documentos/2061.doc, last accessed 27 June 2007.

Nakamura, Lisa 2002. *Cybertypes: Race, Ethnicity, and Identity on the Internet* (New York: Routledge).

Pratt, Mary Louise 1992. *Imperial Eyes: Travel Writing and Transculturation* (London: Routledge).

Taylor, Claire, 2007. 'Latin America' in John McLeod, ed., *The Routledge Companion to Postcolonial Studies* (London: Routledge), pp. 120–28.

Trend, David 2001. 'Reading Digital Culture', in David Trend, ed., *Reading Digital Culture* (Oxford: Blackwell Publishing), pp. 295–96.

Suggested Further Reading

i. General Works of Criticism/Theory on Cyberculture and Cyberliterature

Atton, Chris 2004. *An Alternative Internet: Radical Media, Politics and Creativity* (Edinburgh: Edinburgh University Press).

Balsamo, Anne 1996. *Technologies of the Gendered Body: Reading Cyborg Women* (Durham, NC: Duke University Press).

Bell, David 2001. *An Introduction to Cybercultures* (London: Routledge).

Bell, David and Barbara Kennedy, eds. 2000. *The Cybercultures Reader* (London: Routledge).

Benedikt, Michael, ed. 1991. *Cyberspace: First Steps* (Cambridge, MA: MIT Press).

Boulter, Jay David 1991. *Writing Space: The Computer, Hypertext, and the History of Writing* (Hillsdale, NJ: Lawrence Erlbaum Associates).

Castells, Manuel 1989. *The Informational City: Information Technology, Economic Restructuring and the Urban-Regional Process* (Oxford: Blackwell Publishing).

—— 1996–1998. *The Information Age: Economy, Society and Culture,* 3 vols (Oxford: Blackwell Publishing).

CLCWeb: Comparative Literature and Culture: A WWWeb Journal. http://clcweb-jouranl.lib.purdue.edu.

Cyborg Citizen. http://www.routledge_ny.com/ref/cyborgcitizen/cycitpgs/kunst.html.

Delaney, Paul, and George P. Landow, eds. 1994. *Hypermedia and Literary Studies* (Cambridge, MA: MIT Press).

Ebo, Bosah, ed. 2001. *Cyberimperialism?: Global Relations in the New Electronic Frontier* (Westport, CT: Praeger).

Ensslin, Astrid 2007. *Canonising Hypertext: Explorations and Constructions* (London: Continuum).

Featherstone, Mike, and Roger Burrows, eds. 1995. *Cyberspace/Cyberbodies/Cyberpunk: Cultures of Technological Embodiment* (London: SAGE Publications).

Flanagan, Mary, and Austin Booth, eds. 2002. *Reload: Rethinking Women + Cyberculture* (Cambridge, MA: MIT Press).

Gauntlett, David, and Ross Horsley, eds. 2004. *Web.studies: Rewiring Media Studies for the Digital Age,* 2nd edn. (London: Arnold).

Greenberg, Mark L., and Lance Schachterle, eds. 2002. *Literature and Technology* (London: Associated University Press).
Haraway, Donna. 1991. *Simians, Cyborgs, and Women: The Reinvention of Nature* (London: Free Association Books).
—— 1997. *Modest_Witness@Second_Millennium.FemaleMan©_Meets_OncoMouse?: Feminism and Technoscience* (New York: Routledge).
Harcourt, Wendy, ed. 1999. *Women@Internet: Creating New Cultures in Cyberspace* (London: Zed Books).
Hayles, N. Katherine 1999. *How We Became Posthuman: Virtual Bodies in Cybernetics, Literature, and Informatics* (Chicago, IL: University of Chicago Press).
—— 2005. *My Mother Was a Computer: Digital Subjects and Literary Texts* (Chicago, IL: University of Chicago Press).
——, ed. 1991. *Chaos and Order: Complex Dynamics in Literature and Science* (Chicago, IL: University of Chicago Press).
Herring, Susan, ed. 1996. *Computer-Mediated Communication* (Amsterdam: John Benjamins).
Internet World Stats: Usage and Population Statistics, http://www.internet-worldstats.com/index.html, last accessed 27 June 2007.
Jones, Steven G., ed. 1997. *Virtual Culture: Identity and Communication in Cybersociety* (London: SAGE Publications).
Journal of Computer-Mediated Communication. http://jcmc.indiana.edu, last accessed 27 June 2007.
Journal of Virtual Environments. http://www.brandeis.edu/pubs/jove/HTML.
Landow, George P. 2006. *Hypertext 3.0: Critical Theory and New Media in an Era of Globalization* (Baltimore, MD: The Johns Hopkins University Press).
Landow, George P., ed. 1994. *Hyper/Text/Theory* (Baltimore, MD: The Johns Hopkins University Press).
Lee, Rachel C., and Sau-ling Cynthia Wong, eds. 2003. *AsianAmerica.Net: Ethnicity, Nationalism, and Cyberspace* (New York: Routledge).
Lévy, Pierre 1998. *Becoming Virtual: Reality in the Digital Age,* trans. Robert Bononno (New York: Plenum).
—— 2001. *Cyberculture,* trans. by Robert Bononno (Minneapolis, MN: University of Minnesota Press).
Loader, Brian D., ed. 1998. *Cyberspace Divide: Equality, Agency and Policy in the Information Society* (London: Routledge).
Lovejoy, Margot 2004. *Digital Currents: Art in the Electronic Age* (London: Routledge).
Murray, Janet H. 1998. *Hamlet on the Holodeck: The Future of Narrative in Cyberspace* (Cambridge, MA: MIT Press).
Nakamura, Lisa 2002. *Cybertypes: Race, Ethnicity, and Identity on the Internet* (New York: Routledge).
Pickover, Thomas 1999. *Surfing through Hyperspace* (Oxford: Oxford University Press).
Porter, David, ed. 1996. *Internet Culture* (New York: Routledge).
Rabinowitz, Lauren, and Abraham Geil, eds. 2004. *Memory Bytes: History, Technology and Digital Culture.* (Durham, NC: Duke University Press).

Rheingold, Howard 2000. *The Virtual Community: Homesteading on the Electronic Frontier* (Cambridge, MA: The MIT Press). Revised edition.
Ryan, Marie-Laure 1999. *Cyberspace Textuality: Computer Technology and Literary Theory* (Bloomington, IN: Indiana University Press).
Smith, Marc A., and Peter Kollock, eds. 1999. *Communities in Cyberspace* (London: Routledge).
Tofts, Darren, ed. 2002. *Prefiguring Cyberculture: An Intellectual History* (Cambridge, MA: MIT Press).
Turkle, Sherry, 1995. *Life on the Screen: Identity in the Age of the Internet* (New York: Simon & Schuster).
Trend, David, ed. 2001. *Reading Digital Culture* (Oxford: Blackwell Publishing).
Van de Donk, Wim, *et al.*, eds. 2004. *Cyberprotest: New Media, Citizens and Social Movements* (London: Routledge).
Wardrip-Fruin, Noah, and Nick Montfort, eds. 2003. *The New Media Reader* (Cambridge, MA: MIT Press).
Weimann, Gabriel 2006. *Terror on the Internet: The New Arena, the New Challenges* (Washington, DC: United States Institute of Peace Press).
We've Got Blog: How Weblogs Are Changing Our Culture (Cambridge, MA: Perseus, 2002).
Wolmark, Jenny, ed. 1999. *Cybersexualities: A Reader on Feminist Theory, Cyborgs and Cyberspace* (Edinburgh: Edinburgh University Press).

ii. Works of Criticism/Theory on Latin American Cyberculture and Cyberliterature

Arquilla, John, and David Ronfeldt 1993. 'Cyberwar is Coming!', *Comparative Strategy*, 12:2, 141–65, reprinted in John Arquilla and David Ronfeldt, eds., *In Athena's Camp: Preparing for Conflict in the Information Age* (Santa Monica, CA: RAND, 1997), pp. 23–60.
Belejack, Barbara 1997. 'Cyberculture Comes to the Americas', *NACLA Report on the Americas*, November/December, http://hartford-hwp.com/archives/40/071.html, last accessed 27 June 2007.
Bob, Clifford 2005. *The Marketing of Rebellion: Insurgents, Media, and International Activism* (Cambridge: Cambridge University Press).
Bonilla, Marcello, and Gilles Cliche, eds. 2004. *Internet and Society in Latin America and the Caribbean* (Penang, Malaysia: Southbound; Ottawa, Canada: International Development Research Center). Available from the IDRC at: http://www.idrc.ca/en/ev–45776–201–1-DO_TOPIC.html, last accessed 27 June 2007.
Carrión Carranza, Carmen, ed. 1998. *Nuevas tecnologías para las humanidades* (Mexico City: Universidad Nacional Autónoma de México).
Castillo, Debra A., and Edmundo Paz-Soldán, eds. 2000. *Latin American Literature and Mass Media* (New York: Garland).
Cleaver, Harry 1998. 'The Zapatistas and the Electronic Fabric of Struggle', in John Holloway and Eloína Peláez, eds., *Zapatista!: Reinventing Revolution in Mexico* (London: Pluto Press), pp. 81–103.

Coronado, Gabriela, and Bob Hodge 2004. *El hipertexto multicultural en México posmoderno: Paradojas e incertidumbres* (Mexico City: Centro de Investigaciones y Estudios Superiores en Antropología Social/Porrúa).
Corrales, Javier 2002. 'Lessons from Latin America', in Leslie David Simon, *et al.*, *Democracy and the Internet: Allies or Adversaries?* (Washington, DC: Woodrow Wilson Center Press), pp. 30–66.
Dos Santos, Alckmar Luiz, ed. 2003. *Leituras de Nós: Ciberespaço e literatura* (São Paolo: Instituto Cultural Itaú).
Escobar, Arturo 1994. 'Welcome to Cyberia: Notes on the Anthropology of Cyberculture', *Current Anthropology*, 35:3, 211–31.
Everett, Margaret 1998. 'Latin America On-Line: The Internet, Development and Democratization', *Human Organization*, 57, 385–402.
Ferrer, Aldo 1999. *De Cristóbal Colón a internet: América Latina y la globalización* (Mexico City: Fondo de Cultura Económica).
Finquelievich, Susana, ed. 2000. *Ciudadanos, a la Red: Los vínculos sociales en el ciberespacio* (Buenos Aires: Ediciones CICCUS, la CRUJIA).
Gómez, Ricardo 2000. 'The Hall of Mirrors: The Internet in Latin America', *Current History*, 99:634. Available from the International Development Research Centre, http://archive.idrc.ca/pan/pubhall_e.htm, last accessed 27 June 2007.
Gómez-Peña, Guillermo 2001. 'The Virtual Barrio', in David Trend, ed., *Reading Digital Culture* (Oxford: Blackwell Publishing), pp. 281–86.
—— 2005. *Ethno-Techno: Writings on Performance, Activism, and Pedagogy* (New York: Routledge).
Hahn, Saul c.2000. 'Case Studies on Development of the Internet in Latin America and the Caribbean', http://isoc.org/inet2000/cdproceedings/8d/8d_5.htm, last accessed 27 June 2007.
Hoeg, Jerry 2000. *Science, Technology and Latin American Narrative in the Twentieth Century and Beyond* (Cranbury, NC: Associated University Presses).
Holdom, Shoshannah 2005. 'E-Journal Proliferation in Emerging Economies: The Case of Latin America', *Literary and Linguistic Computing*, 20:3, 361–65.
Martín-Barbero, Jesús 1993. *Communications, Culture and Hegemony: From the Media to Mediations*, trans. E. Fox (London: SAGE Publications).
—— 2000. 'Art/Communication/Technicity at Century's End', trans. Hugh O'Donnell, in Anny Brooksbank Jones and Ronaldo Munck, eds., *Cultural Politics in Latin America* (Basingstoke: Macmillan), pp. 56–73.
Molloy, Molly 2000. 'Background on the Development of the Internet in Latin America', http://lib.nmsu.edu/subject/bord/laguia/netdev.html, last accessed 27 June 2007.
O'Donnell, Susan, and Guillermo Delgado 1995. 'Using the Internet to Strengthen the Indigenous Nations of the Americas', *Journal of Media Development*, 42:3, 36–38.
Pajares Tosca, Susana 2004. *Literatura digital: el paradigma hipertextual* (Cáceres: Universidad de Extremadura).
Preston, Shelley 1994. 'Electronic Global Networking and the NGO Movement: The 1992 Rio Summit and Beyond', *Swords and Ploughshares: A Chronicle of International Affairs*, 3:2, http://www.globalpolicy.org/ngos/role/

policymk/internet/2000/131100.htm, last accessed 27 June 2007.
Romera Castillo, José, Francisco Gutiérrez Carbajo, and Mario García-Page, eds. 1996. *Literatura y multimedia, actas del VI seminario internacional del Instituto de Semiótica Literaria, Teatral y Nuevas Tecnologías de la UNED,* Cuenca, 1–4 July 1996 (Madrid: Visor Libros).

Ronfeldt, David, *et al.* 1998. *The Zapatista Social Netwar in Mexico* (Santa Monica, CA: RAND).

Rueda Ortiz, Rocío 2005. 'Apropriación social de las tecnologías de la información: ciberciudadanías emergentes', Foro: comunicación y ciudadanía, *América Latina en movimiento,* 28 November, http://www.movimientos.org/foro_comunicacion/show_text/php3?key=5930.

Sánchez-Mesa, Domingo, ed. 2004. *Literatura y cibercultura* (Madrid: Arco/Libros).

Schuler, Douglas and Peter Day, eds. 2004. *Shaping the Network Society: The New Role of Civil Society in Cyberspace* (Cambridge, MA: MIT Press).

Serrano Santoyo, Arturo, and Evelio Martínez Martínez 2003. *La brecha digital: Mitos y realidades* (Mexicali: Universidad Autónoma de Baja California).

Sommer, Doris, ed. 2006. *Cultural Agency in the Americas* (Durham, NC: Duke University Press).

Texto Digital, 1:1 (2004), proceedings of the symposium on 'Literatura e Informática' held at the the Universidade Estadual do Rio de Janeiro in 2003, http://www2.uerj.br/~textodigital.

Tamayo G., Eduardo 2005. 'Globalización, comunicación y movimientos sociales', Foro: comunicación y ciudadanía, *América Latina en movimiento,* 29 November, http://www.movimientos.org/foro_comunicacion/show_text.php3?key=5932, last accessed 27 June 2007.

Trejo Delarbre, Raúl 1999. 'La Internet en América Latina', in Néstor García Canclini and Carlos Juan Moneta, eds., *Las industrias culturales en la integración latinoamericana* (Mexico City: Grijalbo; Caracas: Sistema Económica Latinoamericano; UNESCO), pp. 311–56.

Trigo, Abril 2003. '*Cyber*nation (Or, *La Patria Cibernetica* (sic))', *Journal of Latin American Cultural Studies,* 12:1, 95–117.

Vouillamoz, Núria 2000. *Literatura e hipermedia: La irrupción de la literatura interactiva: precedentes y crítica* (Barcelona: Paidós).

Index